10 Smart
Things Gay
Men Can Do
to Find
Real
Love

10 Smart Things Gay Men Can Do to Find Real Love

JOE KORT, M.A., MSW

alyson books
new york

"Autobiography in Five Parts" copyright © 1993 by Portia Nelson from the book *There's a Hole in My Sidewalk*, Beyond Words Publishing, Hillsboro, OR. Reprinted here with permission of the publisher.

Manufactured in the United States of America.

This trade paperback original is published by Alyson Publications,
P.O. Box 1253, Old Chelsea Station, New York, 1001-1251.
Distribution in the United Kingdom by Turnaround Publisher Services Ltd., Unit 3 Olympia Trading Estate, Coburg Road, Wood Green,
London N22 6TZ England.

First edition: January 2006

07 08 09 a 10 9 8 7 6 5 4 3 2

ISBN 1-55583-898-7
ISBN-13 978-1-55583-898-0

Credits
Author Photograph by Glenn Triest
Cover Photograph by Uwe Krejci/Getty Images
.Interior and Cover Design by Matt Sams

Contents

Acknowledgments

To my partner, Mike Cramer. I will never be able to find the right words to express what you have meant to me and still mean to me and will always mean to me. From romantic love to real love you have totally changed my life and I am forever grateful to you.

To my best friend and sister, Lisa Kort-Jaisinghani, and her husband, Raj, and the family they are creating, which includes the lights of my life: Jacob, Zack, Noah, and Zoe. They are truly my guiding angels and add innocence and love to my life.

Deep gratitude is given to Brad Graber and his partner, Jeff Green, two of our closest friends and best men at our wedding. You helped strengthen our relationship. Thanks for supporting us and leading the way.

Thanks to Fran Brown, MA, whose contribution to my practice and the field of mental health adds a loving, humanistic element that people need in their lives. I am proud to be associated with you.

Thanks to all the lesbian couples I have seen who taught me so much about relational love.

I want to thank others who have supported my work over the years, including Sally Palaian, PH.D., Barb Shumard, MSW, Nancy Sparrow, MSW, John Hardwick, Mike Hill, Dave Abler, Lynn Grodzki, MSW, Jim Gerardi, Alan Semonian, and Rhonna Nelson, MSW.

I dedicate this book to Anne Schmidt, whose memory will on inside of me forever. She treated Mike and me as if we were her sons.

I was inspired to write this book from my involvement in the New Warrior Training Adventure of the ManKind Project (www.mkp.org).

For information on my workshops, therapy, trainings, supervision, and coaching services, go to www.joekort.com for regular updates and online newsletter.

Introduction:
Start Your Hero's Journey
and Let Your
Initiation Begin!

Lovers don't finally meet somewhere; they're in each other all along.
　　　　　—Rumi

"He used to make me feel so good! Now he brings me too much grief!"

"With all this conflict, how do I know if I'm with the right partner?"

"Before I get into a relationship, I'll need to get my own act together."

"Relationships shouldn't be so much work!"

"Maybe I'm not cut out for a LTR."

"I've got to love myself before I can love someone else."

"Gay relationships—particularly between men—never last."

I hear things like this from clients (even friends) all the time. But I usually can't agree. *By itself,* a relationship can help put your life in order. While you are in a relationship, loving yourself can come even more quickly. Your deepest healing and growth can occur in the context of a committed relationship. When someone says they cannot be in a relationship until they get their own act together, I find they are usually avoiding relationships with this thinking. They are making plans about what their relationships should look like and what the perfect partner should be like. I coach people to understand that the secret is not making plans for a relationship but instead to *be in one* and create the right relationship for you while you are in it. You get your act together by *being in a relationship,* not by being out of one.

Meanwhile, this book can help you understand why, in your relationships past and present, you've been making the same mistakes over and over. If single, you'll discover why you keep picking out Mr. Wrong or Mr. Right Now, instead of Mr. Right. In both dating and committed relationships, issues from childhood do emerge, and now you can become aware of them to stop them from interfering in getting real love.

What kind of feedback—even including the complaints and frustrations—do you hear from men you date, boyfriends, and partners? If you listen, inevitably you'll find something useful and helpful in whatever they say. What are your complaints and frustrations with your partners? Those complaints say a lot about you too, if you listen closely enough.

As that quote from Rumi points out, you and your partner are in each other all along. This book will show you how doing the work a good relationship requires will bring out the best as well as the worst of you and give you a deeper understanding of yourself. The fact is, relationships are a form of therapy. You'll meet partners who carry traits within you that you've denied or disowned, and will be drawn to those who express them freely. This returns wholeness to your psyche. So whatever you dislike and love in a partner are the same traits that lie inside you. Clichéd as that sounds, it's true.

Are you single? Before finding the right partner, you can do a great deal to make yourself even healthier, and even pick better partners through dating. While searching for the right partner, you can work on *becoming* Mr. Right, as well as picking him out. But you don't need to wait to become a better man to find that perfect guy: you'll become a better person—and partner—simply by being *in* a relationship.

Are you already in a relationship and want it to feel more comfortable and fulfilling? Then this book is for you and your partner too, because simply being in a relationship doesn't mean you stop working on yourself. In fact, being in relationship means you should continue working on yourself. Doing so can make a huge difference in making your relationship successfully enduring.

Ideally, it's best for both of you to work on yourselves together. But if your partner doesn't want to go to couples therapy or do much self-examination, that doesn't necessarily mean that there is no hope. Your partner simply may not be ready, or fear that doing work will bring up still more problems. This book will help you each look at how you contribute to your relationship problems—and yes, the nightmares, too. In fact, any relationship, whether just dating or being committed, often forces you to know yourself more than you'd like, because it raises issues that other simple friendships and therapy never do. Why this is will be addressed here as well. Any romantic relationship forces us to work more deeply on ourselves, making us stronger individuals.

Do you buy into the "happily ever after" myth that assures us that once we meet Mr. Right, all our problems will vanish in a twinkling? Wrong. Instead, that's when our real problems tend to begin—but ironically, that's a good sign, a positive indicator that you are with the right partner for you. In essence, you hire your partner to be your greatest teacher, and then go kicking and screaming into the classroom. Conflict in relationship with a partner almost always helps heal old issues you have not yet resolved. That is why you have picked this man. It is custom-made love!

Maintaining a good relationship *is* hard work. But is it ever worth it. *Real love* can't happen unless you're doing this hard work.

This book isn't a how-to manual. Instead, use it to find the Mr. Right within you, your potential partner, or the man you've currently chosen. If you're in a relationship, stop expecting your partner to make changes (not to say that your partner or boyfriend is completely off the hook). Take time out for a closer look at your own strengths and weaknesses first, and learn to soothe yourself in the face of what difficulties surface from dating and a committed relationship.

Doing this relational work will help you achieve your own emotional health, and you may even be surprised at the rewards that looking within yourself can bring.

The advice and insights herein are derived from the work of Dr. Harville Hendrix's Imago Relationship Therapy, Robert Bly, Terrence Real, John Lee, Joseph Campbell, and Carl Jung. The work of these men, and that of others I reference throughout, brought me to teach men how to love themselves *and* other men. Independently, each of these male gurus had something to offer for men working on themselves and their relationships. Together, these pioneers create a relational model for us gay men who are in romantic, affectional, spiritual, mental, psychological, and sexual relationships with other men. The work of these men will show you how to get real, mature love based on consciousness, intentionality, and maturity.

Harville Hendrix created Imago Relationship Therapy (IRT). This gender-neutral relationship therapy has been the most useful model and communication tool I've found in working with any couples—gay, lesbian, or straight. But it does not go far enough, particularly for gay male couples. Therefore, I bring in the folk tale of *Iron John*, as retold by Robert Bly, and will refer to it throughout this book.

Iron John is a parable about boys becoming men, about going from immature masculine to mature masculine. It shows us men how to access the masculinity deep within all of us, dramatizing the stages any boy must pass through to win his masculinity.

Any relationship calls for its partners to evolve from children to adults. Ours help us psychologically go from gay boys to gay men; they are an initiation into manhood. When you commit to a partner, that journey into manhood continues and deepens. But it's a long, hard one requiring consciousness, intentionality, and integrity from all three of you—you, your partner, and your relationship—if you want a lasting gay male relationship.

Terrence Real's work on patriarchy from his books *I Don't Want to Talk About It* and *How Can I Get Through to You?* reflects the harm that patriarchy has done to men through lack of receiving affection.[1] Given that we are socialized as men, this greatly influences our ability to give and receive real love in gay male relationships.

Are you a King, a Lover, a Warrior, or a Magician? Archetypal myths and their imagery will help put into perspective the type of man you are—and to what type of man you're drawn. And are you attracted to a King, Lover, Warrior, or Magician?

A book about gay male couples cannot be anything less than a book for men, inspired by the male clients whose stories I recount. Just because you are gay does *not* make you less of a man, even though there are plenty of messages out there contrary to this. In fact, coming out and being in a relationship with another male takes balls! It makes you even more of a man for your bravery in being out and visible as a man who loves men. So if you've read this far, pat yourself on the back and commend yourself for moving forward on your journey and intention to be a better man—both in and out of your relationships.

Coming out and finding Mr. Right is truly the kind of hero's journey that Joseph Campbell wrote about in *The Hero with a Thousand Faces*. While he was not speaking specifically about men—much less gay men—I am adapting his work to our experience. Each one of us heroes has had to take his own individual journey to find himself as a man, as gay, and as a gay man in relationship to others.

And once in a relationship, your adventure continues. This adventure involves quite a bit of work, and I'll spell out just what kind of work that is. I want to help you see dating and relationships as an adventure in which you evolve, and develop into someone you never could have dreamed of.

After *10 Smart Things Gay Men Can Do to Improve Their Lives* was published in 2003, hundreds of gay men from all over the world e-mailed, telephoned, and came to see me to say that what touched them most were my last three chapters on relationships. One man wrote that he wept while reading it, adding that he might still be together with his former partner if he had this information while they were together. Others spoke of their newfound hope of finding a partner and that my book provided them with a pathway. Yet some gay men accused me of being "too focused on relationships"—of claiming that the route to a quality life was in finding Mr. Right.

True, I'm very relationship-focused both in my personal life and professional practice, but by no means do I believe that you can't achieve a full life *without* Mr. Right. It can indeed be enough having friends and family around you; but I believe that healing and growth for the most part take place in the context of a committed relationship. That can mean a partner, close friend, family member, or someone with whom you've made a strong mutual commitment. With a romantic partner, healing and growth happen more quickly and intensely because dependency needs are greater, and the contact more frequent and intense than in most other adult relationships.

As a therapist I work with clients who suffer from depression or anxiety disorders, sexual abuse and sexual addiction disorders, chemical dependency, and general self-esteem issues, to name a few complaints. If my clients are in a relationship or enter into one at some point during therapy, I've noticed that many of them appear to have regressed, as if all the work we did was for naught—or else their individual work wouldn't translate into their relationships, their partners failing to understand the new person they've become. Studies show that when one partner enters treatment individually and the other doesn't, their relationship could be in trouble: having gained insight, the partner in therapy grows and becomes distant, and both are no longer on the same page.

I've learned that during and/or after individual work in therapy, clients benefit greatly from couples work. Even a few sessions will include the partner on the journey, to keep the relationship connected and even deepen it. That is why I offer workshops for couples. Even if someone comes to me to address an individual concern, I stress the importance of attending a couples workshop—thereby keeping his partner in the loop—to learn how to incorporate the insights into their relationship. I also encourage clients to keep their partners abreast of the work we're doing through regular discussions about what we're achieving in therapy.

Gay or straight, we men haven't been taught relational tools. Again, just because we are gay doesn't make us any less male; we were socialized as males just like our straight counterparts. By *relational* I mean the power of interacting, in a close and intimate way, with both another person and yourself. Genuine self-affirmation doesn't come easy, particularly for gay men, raised amid so much homophobia, homoprejudice, homonegativity, homo-ignorance, and heterosexism, having to play at being straight when we were really gay boys.

I make the assumption that we were gay from birth. At this time, no scientific findings reveal whether this is fact or fiction. While we have no trouble thinking of children as born straight, no one wants to think of a child as gay. Why not? Because when homo—ignorant people hear the word *gay*, they hear the word *sex* instead, and immediately begin to visualize sexual images—*adult* sexual images. Thinking of a child as gay therefore leads them to imagine—inappropriately, of course—the child engaged in adult sex. If we understand that straight people were once straight children, however, then we can understand that we gay men began as gay boys and teenagers, and our sexual and romantic orientation was no more or less about sex than is true of our straight counterparts.

Throughout this book I use *boyfriend* to refer to someone you're dating; I think of the term *boyfriends* as being Relationship Lite. I say partner to refer to someone with whom you've made a lifetime commitment. You can decide what works best for you. But for the sake of this book, I will use these terms accordingly.

This book will help support your hanging in there if you're single, arming you with the tools to know how to improve your relationship skills. If you are already partnered or dating a guy and having conflicts and trouble getting more serious with him, you'll find more encouragement to leave the relationship from most people than to stick it out. Our society sees relationships as disposable. If it isn't working, just go get another one—but you might be walking away from the relationship of your dreams and not even know it. With the exception of a boyfriend or partner who refuses to get help to stop domestic violence or addictions, most relationship concerns can be worked out *if you both want to work them out*.

In the following chapters, I've tried to cover the dilemmas I see most often in my practice. Single men in the early stages of dating or the first stage of love—romantic love—are not a high percentage of my clinical practice, since they rarely seek therapy. No matter how much pain someone's in, if he starts to date someone and fall in love, he either reduces the frequency in therapy or drops out. He gets bitten by the love bug, so to speak, and I'll discuss exactly what that love drug is. In entering a social or romantic relationship with gay men, you must leave heterosexuality behind and immerse yourselves in each other, just as we all were immersed in our religions, schooling, families, and neighborhoods. We must leave these familiar places and enter "Iron John's dark forest," where other gay men are.

Joseph Campbell writes about the Hero's Journey—how we feel a call for radical transformation and radical experience. He argues that this experience is not the romantic one portrayed in popular myths, movies and stories, but rather a scary one. Holding this book means you've taken your first step toward *the call*.[2]

The fable of Iron John has powerful meanings that lay the groundwork for what you are about to read. We will explore how your lost sense of belonging as a gay boy and a gay teen makes it harder and more challenging to find other gay men as partners and to date, given that you received no guidance from your parents or society. You had to go it alone. What gay rituals and initiations did we have to celebrate and embrace, if any? Which "gay myths" and stereotypes are positive and promote health, and which do not? Where are the elders who can teach you to establish healthy relationships and find real love?

Iron John

Once upon a time, a king sent a huntsman out into the forest to shoot him a deer, but the huntsman didn't return. Worried that some accident had befallen him, the king sent out twenty more huntsmen to search for the man, but they too didn't return. From then on, no one would venture into the forest.

After many years, an unknown huntsman, looking for an adventure, arrived at the castle and approached the king, offering to go into the dangerous forest. But the king would not consent, and said, "I fear you would never come out again."

"I will venture it at my own risk. I fear nothing," the adventurer replied, and with only his dog, betook himself *alone* into the forest. Soon the dog came to a deep pond, and could go no farther. Out of the water stretched a naked arm, seized the dog, and drew it under.

The adventurer went back to the village and fetched some of the people to bail water out the pond with buckets. When they did and could see to the bottom, there lay a Wild Man, whose reddish hair hung over his face, down to his knees. They bound him with cords and led him away to the castle, where there was great astonishment. The king had the Wild Man put in his courtyard in an iron cage, where people walked by and laughed and ridiculed him, and forbade the door to be opened on pain of death, giving the queen herself the key. And from then on, everyone could enter the forest safely.

The king's eight-year-old son was playing in the courtyard, and his golden ball—which he loved—fell into the cage.

"Will you give me my ball?" the boy asked the Wild Man.

"Not until you open the door for me," the Wild Man answered.

"No," said the boy, "my father, the king, has forbidden it."

The next day, when the king was out hunting, the boy went again and asked for his ball.

"Open my door," the Wild Man said.

"I cannot open the door," the boy said, "even if I wished, for I haven't the key."

"It lies under your mother's pillow; you can find it there," the Wild Man told him.

The boy wanted his golden ball back, so he went to his parents' bedroom, where his mother was sleeping. He approached her quietly, got the key from under her pillow, and raced back to the Wild Man's cage. Opening the door, the boy pinched his fingers, drawing blood. The Wild Man jumped out, gave the boy back his golden ball, and hurried away.

Afraid, the boy called after the Wild Man, "Don't go away, or I shall be beaten."

The Wild Man turned back, took him up onto his shoulder, and went with him hastily into the forest.

When the king came home and saw the empty cage, he asked the queen, "What happened?"

She knew nothing about it, and looked for the key, but it was gone. She called their son, but no one answered. The king sent people out to seek him, to no avail; but he could easily guess what had happened.

When the Wild Man reached the dark forest once more, he took the boy down from his shoulder, telling him, "You will never see your parents again. But I have compassion for you, for you have set me free, and I will keep you with me. If you do all I bid you, you shall fare well."

Thus chapter by chapter, you will first explore the lost gay boy you once were. The call to find yourself and come out therefore demands that you enter the dark forest alone, like the adventurer in *Iron John.*

We learn to be out of integrity with ourselves and others when we are not able to be out and open about being gay. This severely impacts our ability to be responsible and accountable, which is very difficult since you were taught not to be honest and forthright about who you are and the face you show to the world. Learning to be accountable and responsible and striving to be *in* integrity are necessary for a solid, authentic loving relationship. And you can do it— we all can, if we want to.

Finding real love demands that we go through that dark forest of relationships. Romantic love, the first stage of relationships, tries to show us the gold we have lost in our childhoods. Our buried treasures come out to play, and we find our inner gold easily through experiencing a new partner. In *Iron John,* Robert Bly interprets the golden ball as "that unity of personality we had as children—a kind of radiance, or wholeness, before we split into male and female, rich and poor, bad and good. The ball is golden, as the sun is, and round. Like the sun, it gives off a radiant energy from the inside...once the golden ball is gone, we spend the rest of our lives trying to get it back."[3] Relationships direct us to how to get it back, and this book will show you how.

During the Call of the Child, the next stage of relationships, the Wild Man reaches up and tries—sometimes successfully—to bring our partners down into the water, as we will see in chapter 3. Ultimately, during relationships, we recognize that we have a Wild Man who seeks his freedom. Relationships bring pain, conflict, and turmoil that cause many tears. In the story, the buckets of water stand for the quantity of tears we need to shed to find our caged Wild Man during our time in relationship.

As our relationships progress, we recognize the cage others have put us in by the way they've treated us. Like the caged Wild Man, we're laughed at and taunted by our peers and the heterosexist, homophobic society at large. Gay and straight alike, we're caged by the ways in which we had to adapt to the family and culture in which we were raised. Ultimately, we cage ourselves, and our Wild Man gets buried.

The power struggles of any relationship are attempts to get back what we lost long ago, symbolized by the golden ball. If we stay with him, the experience of having a partner will help you find the inner gold that you buried long ago as a child. It requires that you steal the key from under your mother's pillow, face your father's wrath and go against him, as you individuate into the man you are meant to become.

Wild Men are not aggressive. Bly distinguishes them from the Savage Man, who is hostile, insensitive, and full of rage. The Savage Man has repressed his nature, ignored his hurts, and in many ways is the antithesis of the Wild Man.[4]

Relationships help us come back into integrity with ourselves: they remind us of the gold we had as boys, and of the men we have become. If we pay attention, our relationships will also help us attain mature masculinity, bringing together our inner boy and Wild Man. There is wholeness, a positive transformation, a bringing together of men with men, the promise of real love. The expression "a man among men" becomes a love story.

As men, we gay males were wounded from the beginning, punished for being the "wrong kind of male." Whether you were a "sissy" or "butch," you knew unconsciously (and often, consciously) that the part of you attracted to other males wasn't acceptable. So your sense of masculinity was vandalized—and too often, gay men bring that trauma into adult love relationships.

No one prepared us for manhood. We have to prepare ourselves, but we can do it. In later chapters, We will explore male archetypes[5]

- The King: the part of you who can bless yourself and others, and has vision and boundaries;
- The Lover: the part of you that is emotional, sexual, and spiritual;
- The Magician: the part of you that sees options and guides you by using your intellect and your inner voice of reason.
- The Warrior: the part of you that does the footwork, enforces your boundaries, and ensures that your mental health work gets done.

All of these apply to your relationships. Which archetype is your strongest? Your weakest? And what about the men you choose—what archetypes are they?

To enter into an intimate relationship with another man, you must know what to expect. To get through the stages of love, you must find your authentic self, who's been caged up for most of your life. In relationships, you will find the key to your freedom to discover him. Together we will explore the shadows, the darker sides of love, and how they can sabotage any relationship if you don't understand them.

In a healthy relationship, unresolved issues with your mother and father inevitably will surface. We all "return to the scene of the crime" repeatedly, until it's solved. Relationships help us solve—and resolve—those crimes. Whether your childhood was healthy and easy or abusive and dysfunctional, the need to clear up those unresolved issues always remains. In the Iron John metaphor, we gay men must *steal* our self-determination and independence away from our mother—from under her pillow—and know what issues we have with her. The type of mother you have and how you perceive her dictates how you go about the theft.

And every man—gay or straight—must progress from boy to man with his father. What special issues do we gay men have with our fathers? And how do they impact your ability to enjoy real love? Understanding this is vital to being a man in your adult love relationships.

Communication is hard to achieve, particularly when conflict arises. How do you express yourself when you're angry with a partner, who you feel has gone from friend to enemy? How do you remove the parent projections off of him? I'll provide a helpful model for communicating more effectively, honestly, and safely with your partner—and others who are important in your life. Your mind works differently when you're being reactive, but you *can* get through even the most difficult fights. The communication styles outlined here will also help you with such difficult decisions as whether you and your partner choose to be monogamous. Chapter 6 will help you find out how to decide what is right for you.

How does sex play a part? Your Sexual Shadows can help you understand the type of man you are *really* looking for, both within yourself and in those you choose as a partner. What coded information is embedded in your sexual fantasies, sexual desires, and types of men you find attractive? Why are some men attracted to hairy bears, smooth twinks, punks, daddy or preppy types? What does this information say about you? Knowing this can only add to loving yourself and others more fully. The more you know yourself sexually and emotionally, the more you can fulfill yourself as a man—and a man in a relationship.

What if there's the complication of you and/or the other man being heterosexually married? How does a married gay man get back into integrity with himself, his wife, and, perhaps, his children? For the heterosexually married, specific dynamics play out: loss of heterosexual privileges, stages of coming out as a mixed orientation couple, and the extreme amount of guilt the heterosexually married gay man lives with before, during, and after coming out!

After you try all of this and do your best to work things out, what if it simply can't be done? Breaking up can feel like a death—a torturous time of feeling rejected and abandoned, isolated and unloved. How you get through it depends on the support you've built around you, and how safe you feel about what and how much you allow others to know. Here your inner Warrior is important to help march you through the hard emotions that will surface, particularly those of feeling like a failure.

And finally, after dating many guys, having been in or just witnessed other relationships, perhaps you've come to know that you're not interested in having one. Is that an acceptable decision? This is for *you* to decide. We live in a culture where couples are valued, but being single isn't. Are you not invited to parties because you are single? How do you react when others feel you *should* have a partner, and that something's wrong with you because you don't? Here lies the importance of friends and family and a strong sense of self. How can you hold on to your inner King's vision of being out of a relationship, and not cave in to what *others* want from you, while continuing to relate closely with friends and family?

Important, as well, is deciding whether you want to be in a short-term relationship or a long-term one. Real love is only for the long-term relationship crowd; but short term is fine—as long as you understand that real love will not await you there.

In my last book, we looked at the *gay* aspect of being a gay man. This book for gay relationships will examine the *man* part. Relationships offer us an initiation into many things, including, and especially, the kind of *man* you want to be.

Let your initiation begin!

References

1. Terrence Real, *I Don't Want to Talk About It: Overcoming the Secret Legacy of Male Depression* (New York: Scribner, 1997); idem, How Can I Get Through to You? Reconnecting Men and Women (New York: Scribner, 2002).
2. Joseph Campbell, *The Hero with a Thousand Faces* (Princeton, NJ: Princeton University Press, 1973).
3. Robert Bly, *Iron John: A Book About Men* (Vancouver, WA: Vintage Books, 1992).
4. Michael Flood, "Wildmen," XY: *Men, Sex, Politics*, vol. 1(4), Spring 1991, www.xyonline.net/Wildmen.shtml.
5. Robert Moore and Douglas Gillette, *King, Warrior, Magician and Lover: Rediscovering the Archetypes of the Mature Masculine* (New York: HarperCollins, 1990; reprint, San Francisco: HarperSanFrancisco, 1991).

Chapter 1
Live in Integrity and Be Accountable to Yourself and Your Partner

Boys everywhere have a need for rituals, marking their passage to manhood. If society does not provide them, they will inevitably invent their own.

—Joseph Campbell

How can we find real love for ourselves and other gay men—as well as be in gay male relationships as partners or friends—when, for our whole lives, we have been taught to hide from each other and run as far away as we can?

We gay little boys and teenagers are robbed of our sense of belonging. Over and over, we are told, "You don't belong here or with each other." Our early formative years are riddled with loneliness and isolation from the other gay boys and men who might otherwise support us in developing our gay identity. Heterosexual children and teenagers have the luxury of having heterosexual peers as well as adults—to model what being heterosexual is all about.

Robert Bly's *Iron John* expands upon the folk tale of the Wild Man in the dark forest, who is feared because he is not understood or humanized.[1] Our inner gay Wild Man is similarly feared and *de*humanized. In fact, society demonizes him; even the Catholic pope calls homosexuality evil. So our inner gay Wild Man hides out in the dark forests of rest areas, bathhouses, public restrooms, Internet chat rooms, and other places that aren't out in the open, but where any man can go. Later, even after coming out, our untamed Wild Man may take refuge in unsafe sex, the drug scene, and steroid use. He drags others down into the bottom of the pond, just as in the Iron John story.

To find real love for ourselves, we gay men have to confront the gay Wild Man and bring him out of the forest. This is what the process of coming out is really all about: coming out to oneself in order to integrate the gay little boy with the gay tamed Wild Man.

In order to find a partner and get to real love, you must let your Wild Man out of his cage. Until then, he is like the character in the story, taken from the bottom of the pond and caged in the village to be stared at and ridiculed. When your little gay boy finds him, finally brings him out, and goes off with him on his shoulders, this lets you begin to experience a sense of belonging and integration. Real love between partners and friends can help you achieve this final integration.

As a psychotherapist, I've always felt it extremely important to provide gay men with group therapy, workshops, retreats, and other community forums to help them achieve a healthy sense of belonging with one another. Gay men need permission to surround themselves with other gay men and establish friendships and relationships with them. Even so, they struggle to fit into the gay community, and even there they don't always enjoy a sense of belonging—as you'll soon see in several of the case histories herein. There are so many subcategories of gay life to choose from. Are you a bear or a circuit boy? An activist or a leatherman? A drag queen? A bar fly? A gay urban professional? A rural gay guy? Finding your gay niche can be hard—in an archetypal sense, you are on a hero's journey.

Joseph Campbell examines the archetype of the hero in *The Hero with a Thousand Faces*.[2] Campbell speaks of "the call," which typically occurs when you think you're happy and your life seems to be going fine. Then something suddenly happens to grab your attention and beckons you to approach. For many of us gay men, our first "call" is to come out and come back into integrity with ourselves and our gay identities. Then the call is to enter relationships—romantic and social. For you, the call is the realization that you are gay and now are presented with an opportunity to explore that—or not. Thereafter, deciding to find a partner and enter a relationship becomes another initiation—another coming out, if you will—into gay manhood.

This chapter focuses on how to become the man you need to be—a gay man among other gay men—so that you can find and keep the partner of your dreams. But before you find him, you'll need to do a lot of work on yourself as you go through the dating process—and then even more work once you find him.

Being gay, you need to enjoy a sense of community, to be a part of something. Feeling that you belong will give you self-esteem and confidence, as well as the safe psychological space to express yourself and learn the skills you'll need to meet and date other men. Whatever your relationship goal—long-term couple or even just casual dating—you'll need that gay community to support it.

Throughout your childhood, you were taught not to be honest with yourself, not to be congruent with the little gay male you really were. You were taught to present a false self and role-play at being heterosexual. As a result, like many gay men, you may find it particularly hard to be honest, accountable, and responsible with yourself and others. This will sabotage your relationships with everyone, particularly a partner. All relationships, including the one with yourself, require honesty, accountability, and responsibility. They demand that you have—and live in—integrity.

This chapter offers you a guide on how to make better decisions for yourself so that you can raise your Wild Man from the bottom of the pond. Achieving a sense of belonging is crucial to finding Mr. Right, so it's inevitable that you enter the dark forest and find your own personal Wild Man. Finding—and keeping—Mr. Right will require that *both* of your Wild Men come out and that together you carve a sense of belonging with each other that supports your relationship.

"When I told my parents I was gay, they said, 'Let's see how the Second Grade goes first, dear.'"

Carson Kressley's very funny joke on *Oprah* also speaks volumes of truth. Many of my gay clients tell me they can recall being "different" at an early age, but didn't know exactly why or what the difference was. Often, they'll say, "I just didn't feel that I fit in." Many of my clients (myself included) say that if only others had given their permission and blessing, we could have known why we were different from other boys—that just as heterosexual boys have crushes on girls, we had crushes on other boys. Perhaps we wanted to play with Barbie, not G.I. Joe. We knew who we were all along but simply had no word to identify what we were. Instead, that big part of who we are became demonized.

One friend of mine recalls a nun from his school expressing contempt while talking about homosexuality—a memory that has stayed with him ever since. He didn't consciously know he was *gay*, but ever since coming to understand who he is, that nun's face has haunted him.

This story illustrates the kind of unconscious awareness many gay boys and teens possess. Somewhere inside ourselves, we know we're gay, even if we don't know quite what to call it. We're constantly scanning to see whether things in our environment are safe or dangerous. Our unconscious minds are always taking notes, hypervigilant in our awareness of how others feel toward us.

We learn to operate in danger mode. When we don't feel safe, we cannot relax, play, mate, or even create and treat each other well. This makes it hard to go out and find relationships. We're taught to mistrust others, lest they betray us. If they discover our true identities, we'll lose everything: our families, friends, and pride. We'll constantly be humiliated for being the "sick perverts" we're taught we are. You've bought into this scenario from an early age, because children are vulnerable to these messages. Tell a child repeatedly that he's sick and wrong, and he'll believe it. Consequently, how can you ever find and keep Mr. Right, if your default is to protect yourself from betrayal by never trusting?

Before we can even begin to explore our one-to-one relationships with one another, romantic or otherwise, it's essential that we examine the terrain we're working in as a gay culture. Do we understand the playing field we're on? Ours is truly a hero's journey, against all odds. Our homophobic, heterosexist society doesn't want us to take it. Lacking the same training as that of our peers, we're on our own. We know we don't belong; we don't even know what it's like to belong. So we have to find out for ourselves, and we need to be brave to do so.

On our hero's journey toward our eventual goal of dating and relationships, we gay men must come out; some leave wives and girl-friends and families, some lose long-term friendships, and some realize certain things about their parents and others who raised and taught them about relationships. The playground of finding and being in long-term relationships (LTRs) is filled with treasures and land mines. The people we date and romance all hold up separate mirrors to us. You'll learn information about yourself that you weren't aware of until a boyfriend, partner, or even someone you're newly dating points it out. Any relationship requires that you be willing to examine the material that surfaces.

Initiation into Gay Manhood

In 2000, the University of Michigan offered the course "How to be Gay: Male Homosexuality and Initiation," taught by Professor David Halperin—the controversy surrounding which provides an excellent example of how gays and lesbians are not allowed to belong. In a Gannett News Service article, journalist Deb Price stated that the class "explores how gay men are introduced to the shared sensibility, culture and campy humor that help give them the comforting sense of belonging to a unique social group. As Professor Halperin explained in the university's course catalog, 'Just because you happen to be a gay man doesn't mean that you don't have to learn how to become one.'"[3]

Price relates how this class was accused of "recruiting" students into homosexuality. This "recruiting" concept is nothing more than an attempt to send gay men the message that they do not belong at University of Michigan or anywhere else. The prejudice we endure, individually and collectively, is the very thing that gets in the way of real love. An African-American woman on the local news expressed her dislike for this class, stating that "no one had to teach me how to be black." I remember thinking, How untrue. Her family and culture taught her from the day she was born. As gay men, we *do* need a class to be taught how to be gay, because we lack the family and cultural support to let us know what being gay is all about.

The Wild Man

In the story of Iron John, until he is found and released, the Wild Man is feared and despised as the opposite of civilized men. Untamed, he is forced to dwell at the bottom of the pond, where he takes down everyone who gets close to him. Your gay Wild Man retreats to the bottom of the pond because he's been told over and over that he doesn't belong. Believing he is safely locked away like the caged Wild Man brings a feeling of order to society—and to the gay man as well. But suppressing core parts of yourself and denying yourself access to important parts of your identity serve only to keep those aspects knocking on the door to come out—and often they emerge sideways. By sideways I mean doing and saying things to others unintentionally to hurt them or yourself and not being conscious about the damage you are doing. Suppressing important parts of yourself will cause you to damage your relationships with yourself and others—and worst of all, with your partners.

In actuality, every man—gay or straight—has a Wild Man inside, and we are all taught to suppress him. He takes different forms, depending on the individual. Our gay Wild Man has certain similarities and differences from his straight counterpart.

It's My Circuit Party, and I'll Die If I Want To

Watching gay men at circuit parties, shirts off, huddled together, moving to the beat of the music as if they were in a native American ritual dance, I sense the Wild Man out of his cage—as well as a profound sense of belonging. Often these circuit parties are all-nighters, lasting literally into the morning. These are our long-overdue slumber parties, which straight preteenagers enjoy as their rite of passage.

From the outside I see freedom, connectedness, and authenticity exuding from these men. And for many of the gay men, that is exactly what it is. Circuit parties, however, can also be the gay equivalent of the dark forest—filled with drugs, alcohol, and barebacking. To achieve a sense of belonging, this caged but still untamed Wild Man may drag you down through unsafe sex (causing STDs and HIV infection), overdosing on drugs or alcohol, and reckless living—which make you miss out on relationships, work, family and, inevitably, on life. Many guys who attend circuit parties fly from city to city, spending all of their time and money worshipping the DJs and enjoying pseudointimacy with one another. And missing from their lives is real love for themselves, their friends, and a partner.

Not that the circuit clubs and parties are evil; enjoying the DJs, the music, and your friends is a great way to have fun. Yet some gay men have turned their lives over to this lifestyle so that it interferes with any real, intimate relationships with friends and partners. Many men who come to see me in their forties and fifties, when the party is over, regret having put so much energy into something that gave them little in return. Like the Wild Man at the bottom of the pond, if this archetype is left isolated and unattended, he'll bring down others as well as himself.

Socialization and Belonging

Circuit parties offer many gay men a niche—a place to finally belong. This is what makes it so compelling to so many. Most pre-pubescent and adolescent boys achieve their sense of belonging through sports, horsing around with other guys, and talking about girls. At least tacitly, their fathers encourage them in these "masculine" pastimes. But even when a gay teenager succeeds in coming out, he nearly always lacks the kind of supportive peer group that his straight counterpart enjoys. His initiation into gay manhood comes later (if at all), inside bathhouses and gay bars. Later, sex parties and sex clubs become places where he can automatically fit in. To feel that they're one of the gang, some gay men even contract HIV on purpose—and are given the frivolous nickname of "bug chasers." (More about this in chapter 7, on your sexual shadow.) Or they begin using and abusing drugs to gain that sense of belonging.

To escape being teased or stigmatized as queer or a sissy, we gay boys were socialized to avoid contact with one another from very early on. We were taught to run from, rather than support and befriend, one another—forming a big obstacle to our sense of belonging and leaving an inner void that still needs to be filled. This inner void will get in the way of finding a partner and, ultimately, of feeling comfortable in *any* relationship—even friendships—with other gay men. So you now must go against the grain of the way you were influenced at an early age—or as psychologists say, imprinted.

Imprinting is a neurological phenomenon that occurs in birds and mammals in their first hours of life. I am reminded of the *I Love Lucy* episode titled "Lucy Raises Chickens," in which she tries to hide newly hatched chicks from Ricky. The chicks see her first, imprint on her as their mother, and follow her everywhere—a habit she uses to make them follow her to a safe hiding place. A newborn will typically bond to whatever animals it meets at birth, and begins to pattern its behavior after them. Often called bonding in humans, this usually refers to the relationship between newborns and their parents. How we're socialized in our early years, though, also imprints us and helps us develop our sense of belonging. In other words, it's not *only* our parents who imprint us, but our peers, teachers, and other older, more accomplished role models.

Jack, age forty-two, came to see me as a result of his second drunk-driving charge in five years and was ordered by the court to undergo therapy. He told me that for a while, he had been thinking about coming to see me to work on his issues at some point, but his pending legal charges forced the issue. "Now's as good of a time as any," he told me, "given this legal push."

Jack told me he had everything he ever wanted in terms of material goods. He was well traveled, had nice cars, lived in a large condo in an affluent area, made good money, and had fulfilled his dreams of having saved up enough for his retirement and anything else he wanted—except for a lasting, fulfilling relationship with a partner.

Jack said he enjoyed meeting gay men—particularly younger men, in their twenties—who liked to do crystal meth and go to circuit parties. Jack financed these guys' trips to circuit parties across the country and on gay cruises. He said it "bonded" him to these younger men and hoped that one of them might turn out to be his long-term partner. He didn't see himself as addicted to drugs or alcohol, but did admit that he abused them at times.

Jack knew that relationships with guys twenty years younger wouldn't pan out. Yet having come out in his early thirties and having missed out on the "gay scene," he longed to recapture the times that he'd missed in his younger years. He discovered the circuit club scene, met some people there, and began working out to shape his body, doing party drugs and steroids, and having a lot of sex. He traveled all over the country, saving most of his time and money for the next circuit party. Over time, he began to realize that the circuit scene, drug use, and attempts at relationships with men also frequenting the circuit scene were going nowhere. He strongly believed he could stop using crystal meth—that he controlled it, and it didn't control him.

But as he began trying to cut out crystal meth, Jack realized that he would lose all of his "friends" who still used it. Those twentysomething guys, he feared, would no longer want to buddy around with him if he wasn't doing crystal. And he was right. So he returned to using the drug and providing it so he could continue being friends with these guys and having sex with them. Crystal meth and sex was the common denominator in keeping their friendship.

Jack described the rush he got from doing crystal and the high of staying up all night having sex. He described feeling "alive, connected and a part of something," which he didn't feel otherwise. As his sessions with me progressed, and his unsuccessful attempts to cut down his drug use became increasingly apparent, he began to understand that his problems were bigger than he thought.

Crystal seems to provide a false sense of belonging to gay men; its pseudointimacy helps them feel connected, particularly when sex is involved. Obviously, this is not true attachment, and illustrates what the Wild Man at the bottom of the pond looks like. These guys, including my client, are taking each other down through these superficial attachments and a false sense of belonging. The drug use and sex may seem easy and pleasurable, but the severe damage done to mind and body will not lead to real self-esteem or love of others. Relationships demand emotions and hard work, neither of which is needed to do drugs and have sex.

In *Tweakers: How Crystal Meth Is Ravaging Gay America*, Frank

Sanello writes:

> The brain's natural reward system governs basic needs and drives like hunger, sex and thirst. When those needs are naturally satisfied, the brain rewards its owner with a small dose of pleasure-inducing neurochemicals such as dopamine. Crystal—tricky drug that it is—artificially rewards the user's brain by releasing torrents of dopamine and other neurotransmitters. Both the initial rush and the prolonged high from crystal occur from this sleight-of-hand stimulation of the brain.
>
> But this gusher of dopamine short-circuits the body's natural survival instincts. The brain's hunger, sleep and thirst centers shut down because of the increased amount of dopamine in the brain while an individual is using crystal.
>
> Crystal is dopamine's evil twin. Both drugs have a similar molecular structure. Dopamine affects the brain and spinal cord by interfering with the normal release of neurotransmitters, which are chemical substances used for communication between nerve cells. Dopamine is the main neurotransmitter methamphetamine acts on, and it's part of the brain's natural reward system. When you feel good about a job well done, derive gratification from family or social relationships, experience an overall feeling of contentment or believe that your life has meaning, dopamine is the neurochemical that creates these positive feelings.[4]

How sad that finding a sense of empowerment, community, and belonging—as well as embracing masculine energy—has to be fraught with out-of-control chemical use and risking one's life with overdoses, brain damage, and STDs, including HIV. What should bring those feelings of contentment is attachment to others. Dopamine and other chemicals in our body are ready for use once contact and connection are made *naturally*, as I'll explain later. True male bonding takes work—it involves real blood, sweat, and tears.

The experience of these tweakers involves none of that. These men think they're bonded, but they're not; they need to learn to love and bond naturally to each other.

Jack grew up as an only child. His father traveled quite a bit on business, leaving him alone with his mother, who was busy socializing with her own friends. Thus Jack was frequently left alone. With no siblings, friends, or parents around, he never learned what true intimacy felt like. Jack told me that when his father returned home from his travels, he felt like he competed with his mother for his father's attention.

I liked Jack as soon as he walked through my door. I think he could feel this, and that in itself was healing for him. In our work together, over time he was able to tolerate his feelings for me as another gay man with a genuine interest in him, unlike the attention he'd received from his family growing up. He began attaching to me, a gay man in his life, this time without drugs, alcohol, and sex being involved. He realized that in fact he was addicted to both crystal meth and alcohol, and joined gay Narcotics Anonymous and gay AA—which is another great place for achieving belonging and building relationships with other gays and lesbians.

Unlocking the Wild Man's Cage

Another way homophobes keep us caged is to label the effeminate gay man who cannot pass as a "fem" or a "queen." These homophobes can be straight or gay—and when gay, often they are even meaner to the caged Wild Man.

Merrill was a thirty-five-year-old graphics designer. When we first met in my waiting room, he was sitting with his legs crossed, holding a clutch purse. He was dressed in casual clothes with his shirt unbuttoned, exposing many gold necklaces on his chest. He also wore multiple bracelets and rings.

When he sat down in my office and started talking, he sounded extremely effeminate. At first I thought he was putting me on, presenting himself as stereotypically gay on purpose. I expected that at some point, he'd laugh and say, "Just kidding. I was just camping it up." But he didn't—this was my own internalized homophobia at work. As I soon discovered, Merrill's effeminate manner was utterly natural for him.

He had come to see me because the guy he was involved with was verbally abusing him, cheating on him, and using drugs. This wasn't the first time one of Merrill's boyfriends had treated him this way. Why did he keep meeting guys like this, over and over? When I asked him to tell me his history, he began by talking about Tom, his first boyfriend. If other people they knew were around, Tom made Merrill walk on the other side of the street so that they wouldn't be seen together. Tom said he didn't want to be harassed for hanging out with a "faggy" guy like Merrill.

Merrill would actually cross the street until whoever Tom had spotted was gone. Then Tom would snap his fingers, and Merrill would walk back across to rejoin him.

When Merrill was growing up, at home things were not much better. His father favored his other two brothers, both of whom were athletes and thrived in school, and took them on weekend trips. No one bothered to ask if Merrill wanted to come—he would wake up and find them gone.

Did that bother him? "No," he replied. "I wouldn't have wanted to go anyway." I didn't believe him. That exclusion had to be very hurtful, and his denial had to be a form of sour grapes.

If Merrill and his brothers fought, his parents would blame him. Over his protests, they would silence him and remove him from the other two sons. So even at home, he never really had a sense of belonging.

Merrill's innocence and naiveté, in addition to his effeminate behavior, seemed to be contributing factors in others' abusing him. In chapter 2, I'll explore how men in our society who are not exhibiting normative male behavior traits and thoughts are punished and abused, and how deeply that affects gay men.

Not surprisingly, research shows that effeminate and stereotypically gay males are more likely targets for abuse—even rape—from other men. Males struggling with their own homosexuality or homosexual impulses, or who have been sexually abused in childhood, are more likely to bully other men who appear to be gay" Unfortunately,

Merrill met up with men like this, and his naiveté helped bring even more abuse his way.

Though he spoke of being mistreated, still he gave others the benefit of the doubt—and gave them second, third, and even fourth chances. In his relationships, it was always others who rejected him and left, never the other way around. He said that when he felt desperately lonely, any attention was better than none.

I remarked on his high tolerance for insults, adding that if treated this way, most people would end a relationship. Did he have a history of being bullied? Yes, in middle school and high school, boys frequently called him "Mary" instead of "Merrill." In grade school, when he'd been a bit overweight, boys would taunt him for having boobs and squeeze his pectorals in a mocking way. After gym, they would corner him in the showers and hump him, pretending he was a girl. After school, they teased and spat at Merrill.

At home, he never told his parents what was happening, and even now had no explanation as to why he didn't. The reason, I suspected, was that he knew they weren't as interested in him as in his two siblings, and that they would blame *him* for provoking the abuse by acting so "badly." Moreover, what he endured at school is very shaming behavior for any young boy to undergo; admitting these feelings to others only exacerbates them.

Building Self-Esteem

To build a sense of one's own worth, each of us needs a feeling of belonging. This is the essential starting point from which you can add, remove, and modify where you came from originally and where you're headed—emotionally, mentally, and psychologically. And in psychosocial development, this is a crucial stage for every child to complete successfully. The foundation of a sense of belonging begins with the family you're born into, and continues with your socialization in school, on the playground, and in your house of worship—where you learn relational skills and how to get along with others.

Growing up, I recall my grandmother recounting her trip from Russia with other Jews to the United States. She spoke with pride of how she moved to a Jewish community in the Detroit area, where her Jewish friends called her by her Yiddish name. With tears in her eyes, she reminisced about her early life and her people, expressing a sense of belonging. She felt a shared solidarity with her kinfolk. Similarly, many neighborhoods enjoy a sense of community that makes residents take better care of their houses, schools, and stores. Students develop cliques to feel a closer connection to their peers and to offset the realization that their schools are often large and impersonal. College students identify with sports teams or various clubs and fraternities that allow them a sense of pride and belonging. Religion gives people a wider sense of belonging, a sense of purpose, and a feeling that the world isn't such a vast, cold place.

But during our childhoods, lesbians and gays such as Merrill don't enjoy this advantage. We don't usually achieve the comforts and psychological reassurance of belonging with other like-minded folk until adulthood, when we can develop our own social support groups. Born into heterosexual families, for the most part, we gays and lesbians are reluctant to declare ourselves and bond with each other—because we're warned not to, that doing so is "bad" and "wrong." We fear being bullied, ridiculed, rejected, humiliated or, worse, beaten and killed. This fear is legitimate; these things happen. Even when, as children and teenagers, we decide *not* to come out, our behavior and interests may "out" us, marking us to be singled out and ostracized like Merrill. Boys who are effeminate or inept at sports, girls who remain tomboys longer than seems acceptable, and others who don't conform with what's expected of their gender are often teased, humiliated, and excluded from groups where they could gain a sense of belonging.

Merrill had learned to handle everything on his own—alone— because his sense of belonging was nil. During college, he said, harassment from others stopped. But after graduating, he worked as a graphic artist in a marketing office where he was harassed constantly. On the men's room wall, employees would write things like "Merrill is a fag" or "Meet here at 8 P.M. to be sucked off by Merrill." On the wall appeared drawings of two men engaged in sex, with one of them labeled "Merrill." Anonymous notes appeared on his desk telling him what a "fag" he was. Women asked him where he bought his "purse." His bosses did nothing to stop the abuse, probably because Merrill never told a soul this was happening to him, or perhaps because the abuse expressed their own contempt for his effeminacy. Perhaps they even hoped he would quit. He'd developed a high tolerance for feeling like an outsider, since he'd put up with it his entire life, both at home and at school.

After some time in one-on-one therapy, I placed Merrill in a gay men's group, where he could meet healthy gay men who were striving for better lives and finally experience the sense of belonging that group therapy provides. But he was reluctant to enter group therapy; he wasn't sure how the others would treat him. I reassured him that if he didn't feel it was helping, he could stop coming. He did attend, but cautiously, keeping a tally of every meeting. Each check he wrote me bore the number of times he'd attended. In time, though, he found group to be a safe place where he was accepted for who he was. Privately, some group members expressed to me their discomfort with Merrill's effeminacy. I encouraged them to tell him themselves. This would let *them* explore their own patriarchal beliefs about how men should act and their own sexist belief that effeminate behavior is negative—which they could then identify as a problem of their own.

This was very difficult for group members to do, since they didn't want to hurt Merrill's feelings. But for group to be effective, members must be willing to tell one another things about their feelings and judgments that they otherwise wouldn't. If they don't speak up, there'll be no way of dealing with these issues, either for themselves or Merrill. Besides, Merrill needed to experience other men's judgments to give him a clearer sense of how he was perceived and deal more appropriately with these reactions. This sounds hard, and even though feelings do get hurt, in group they are always handled respectfully and dealt with in a safe way. Here, our main goals were to help men connect with Merrill, removing their obstacles such as internalized homophobia that would not let Merrill connect with them.

Merrill wouldn't be able to meet his Mr. Right without his understanding his past, which contributed to his being drawn to men who abused him. Imago Relationship Therapy, a model I use in working with couples and singles, states that we are imprinted at a young age and learn familiar love, and then grow into adults and are romantically drawn to the kinds of people who resemble our primary caretakers in both positive and negative ways.[5] Merrill was clearly doing this. Also, he needed to know how other gay men experienced him in order to understand what was working and what wasn't. Finally, he needed to repair his vandalized sense of belonging, which gay men's group therapy offered him the means of doing. As he dealt with these issues directly, he grew ready to meet Mr. Right.

Gay men, including myself, often think that their discomfort with men like Merrill or those who are in any way effeminate is internalized homophobia. But actually it's a form of sexism, misogyny, and gynophobia—completely different phenomena that contribute to the symptoms of internalized homophobia. I am convinced that at the root of homophobia, internalized and otherwise, is fear of, contempt for, and hatred of women that we are taught as children. Why else do so many straight people give a pass to lesbians? It is far less shameful for a woman to appear masculine than for a "fag" to act feminine. This has long been the case—they canonized Joan of Arc! Accordingly, even gay men, myself included, can be uncomfortable around very effeminate guys, whether they are gay or straight.

The Enemy Within: The Shame Factor

In the late 1960s, George Weinberg coined the term *homophobia*, meaning "the feeling(s) of fear, hatred, disgust about attraction or love for members of one's own sex," and the word first appeared in print in 1969. In his book *Society and the Healthy Homosexual*, he wrote about the prejudice that lesbians and gays are immoral, sick, sinful or somehow inferior to heterosexuals.[6] Such a view results in fear of associating in close proximity with lesbians and gays—physically, mentally, and emotionally—lest others perceive one as lesbian or gay. Fears of venturing beyond "accepted" gender role behavior can afflict gay men as well, though straight men are typically more homophobic.[7]

We can also internalize homophobia by projecting it onto our-selves. Not only self-destructive, this internalized shame is also destructive toward other gay men and interferes with your becoming and finding Mr. Right. In 1997, *The Advocate* published an article titled "The Enemy Within," in which Gabriel Rotello reported on a scientific study that measured the homosexuality of homophobes. Henry Adams, a professor of clinical psychology at the University of Georgia, "recruited 64 straight white male college students, rated their level of homophobia according to a standard psychological test, and divided the men into two groups: those who were homophobic and those who were not."[8] He hooked up the study subjects to plethysmographs, which measure arousal in the penis, and showed them three types of commercially available porn videos: heterosexu-al, lesbian, and gay male.

Adams's study found that the men who tested nonhomophobic were left cold by the gay porn videos, while those in the homopho-bic group were turned on—so much so that within four minutes, their plethysmographs showed averages of 60 percent to 80 percent of a full erection.

Rotello stated that the study had "troubling implications." Gay men were thrilled to learn this, since it proved that most homopho-bia is in fact a *phobia,* and that the homophobic men out there that are themselves gay. But Rotello states, "I suppose I should be happy that someone has finally proved that many of those parading fanat-ics, religious-minded prudes, and censorious busybodies are in the throes of repression and self-revulsion and are merely projecting onto me and those I love the thing they hate in themselves. In a way I am. But not *that* happy. Because...Adams's study also means...that many of the most maladjusted homophobes are really homosexual men....And that means that when we get dissed and discriminated against and bashed, we're often getting bashed by ourselves. That the men who hate us the most are *us*."

Returning to the Scene of the Crime

George, thirty-four, was a handsome guy, balding, with a medi-um athletic build. He came to me complaining of being socially withdrawn and isolated, particularly from the gay community. Being athletic, George could always socialize with heterosexual males working out at the gym, playing racquetball, and drinking with them at the straight bar. Among them, however, he always felt like a phony. While he appeared to be like them, all his life he knew inside that his sexual and romantic orientation was different. George worried that if he was discovered, he would be alienated. This secret, he felt, contributed to the depression he'd experienced throughout his life. Unlike Merrill, George showed no outward sign of being stereotypically gay. In fact, I wasn't sure until I asked him in our first session.

George wasn't able to articulate much of his feelings and inner self without a great deal of prompting from me. On weekends during the winter, George went to the straight bars. But he was alone during most of the week and would surf online and enter gay chat rooms. He spent hours at a time there, but never followed up to meet anyone. If any man wanted to hook up, George would make some excuse and log out. Still, he felt compelled to visit these chat rooms night after night, as the time he spent online steadily increased.

Scared and reluctant to attend gay social groups, George didn't have much of a social life, if at all. He worked, came home, and aside from going online, watched television unhappily with his dog. Straight bars and working out were his only channels to the outside world.

About his past, George said that love was "understood" in his home, but never expressed. There were no hugs or "I love yous"—he simply knew he was loved, and that others knew he loved them back. He didn't see this as a problem and in fact loudly protested to me, "Don't try and blame my parents." I offered the same reply I give all my clients: that it's not about blame, but accountability. But George would hear none of it.

He talked next about his school days, when he became close with four boys who were best friends. The five of them spent a lot of time together, and played baseball and basketball. One time in middle school, when George was fifteen, they engaged in mutual masturbation. He'd enjoyed it immensely—as any gay teen would. But the next day at school, these four outed him as gay, telling everyone that he had serviced them manually and orally. Since all four of them confirmed the story, it was four against one. Convinced that no one would believe him, George found himself the butt of ridicule at school. Now these same boys teased him, taunted him, and beat him up, along with the other students.

Now after school, he would come home and never leave the house. His stay-at-home mother questioned the change in his behavior, and he told her he had an argument with them and was no longer speaking to them. She did not probe any further. So with that trauma began his isolation, loneliness, and depression.

We began working with how George fixated on—and couldn't get past—that episode in his life. At first, this was all unconscious for him. He didn't realize he was recycling the same old issues that kept him isolated at home as an adolescent. I heard much evidence of *unintentional* parental neglect. Neglect need not be intentional, but often occurs when families are not demonstrative, depriving the children of affection. George didn't want to work on those family issues, however, but was instead able to examine how what had happened to him socially was playing out now. In other words, his socialization with other boys—an extremely important stage in his development—had been vandalized.

Psychologically, he was now operating from the same position as during his middle school years. Basically, he had no gay friends and mostly straight acquaintances—ultimately, no life. As I call it, he was *returning to the scene of the crime* again and again. He never solved the crime, because the answer lay in his socializing more, not avoiding it. He admitted to avoiding his neighbors and even retreating into his house if they came outside while he was there.

His way out involved being vulnerable and taking the risk of being hurt yet again. I reminded George that now he was an adult and not that scared, lonely little boy who had no defenses against what was happening to him.

As I do with so many gay clients, I recommended he enter a gay men's group for therapy and attend my workshops for gay men to help him achieve a sense of belonging in these venues. He joined both. The safeguards that therapy offers made it more comfortable for him to attend my offerings of workshops and retreats rather than venture out into the community by himself. Over time, he was able to ease into the gay community, joining the local gay community center, which offers many services, including some for gay youth. For him, this was tremendously healing, since he was able to give to other young gay men what he had been unable to get for himself.

Much of what keeps young gays and lesbians from establishing a sense of belonging is the heterosexism and homophobia that lies over us all like a wet blanket. It's traumatic to be gay in a hostile, heterosexist world. I explained some of this in *10 Smart Things Gay Men Can Do to Improve Their Lives,* but I want to expand on it here.

First They Came for Bert and Ernie . . .

To illustrate what is done to us as children, it's important to look at what happens—symbolically and metaphorically—to two-dimensional cartoon characters created *for* children. As the years go by, a growing number of cartoon characters have been forcibly outed. I am amazed that anyone would be concerned about the sexual and romantic orientation of any imaginary two-dimensional figure.

First, it was poor Bert and Ernie of *Sesame Street.* These two beloved American figures were minding their own business, taking baths together, singing silly songs together (probably Broadway tunes), sleeping next to each other in twin beds—with a picture of the two of them together over the headboard. Best buds they were! Bachelors at best. And then in 1990, the Reverend Joseph Chambers, a Pentecostal minister from Charlotte, North Carolina, decided that Bert and Ernie were a gay couple.

"They're two grown men sharing a house—and a bedroom!" bellowed Chambers, whose radio ministry is broadcast in four Southern states. "They share clothes. They eat and cook together. They vacation together and have effeminate characteristics. In one show Bert teaches Ernie how to sew. In another, they tend plants together. If this isn't meant to represent a homosexual union, I can't imagine what it's supposed to represent."

The Children's Television Workshop and *Sesame Street* both issued a statement defending the characters, saying that these two were in fact not a gay couple. Nevertheless, Bert and Ernie since have kept their distance from each other, onscreen. They are still friends, and my young nephews still say "Bert 'n' Ernie" in one breath. But the baths have stopped, and the pictures of them together are gone.

The message here is that viewing a couple who *might* or *could be* gay is bad and wrong for children. My father used to call the two men who lived next door to him "bachelors." We're raised to not notice any visible gay couples, and when we do, the adults around us assign them a different category.

Then in 1999, Reverend Jerry Falwell outed a Teletubby who was minding his own business and having fun with the other three Teletubbies. But he was purple (lavender!), carried his magic bag (a purse!), spoke in a high voice (effeminate!), and wore a triangle (symbol of gay pride!) on his head. The Itsy Bitsy Entertainment Company reassured everyone—including good old Jerry—that Tinky-Winky (whom they license as dolls and in other formats) is not gay.

While Tinky-Winky was being gay-bashed, I spoke to a nursing class on gay affirmative mental health. I was talking about good ole Tinky when a student nurse raised her hand and said that she worked on a children's ward, where all the Teletubbies were present *except* purple Tinky-Winky! This is a cruelly accurate metaphor for what happens to us gay boys. We are shown that no one wants us around—and particularly not around other children, even when we are children ourselves, as Tinky-Winky is.

Then came James Dobson, the founder of Focus on the Family, a right-wing Christian group—who singled out SpongeBob SquarePants, a cartoon character with his own half-hour cable show. Dobson has publically accused SpongeBob, or maybe his creators, with "promoting the gay agenda"—a claim once featured prominently on his Web site, along with the objection that SpongeBob's video, *We Are Family* calls for tolerance of all people and is to be shown in schools.

Actually, SpongeBob has been under suspicion for a while and is a gay icon for some. But his creators deny that he is gay and have also stated that those who think he is should "increase their medications." Too funny—and how clever—to suddenly put the whole argument in an adult perspective!

But female cartoon characters are never outed. The Organization for the Reparative Therapy of Homosexuality, religious organizations for the ex-gay movement, and NARTH (the National Association for Research and Therapy of Homosexuality) always target males. Again this arises from patriarchy and sexism, as I explained earlier and will explore further in the following chapter.

Peppermint Patty from the *Peanuts* comic strip, clearly a lesbian, is obviously in romantic love with Lucy, always following her around. She even has a friend Marcie—clearly a lesbian—who calls her "Sir"! And what about Velma from *Scooby-Doo?* Her hairstyle is very butch, and she always wears sensible clothes and shoes.

And what about the Powerpuff Girls? Those three flying tomboys can throw punches and save the day, one half hour at a time, better than any man in Townsville!

Why do those who oppose homosexuality make so little fuss about these lesbian cartoon characters, aside from a small uproar on the Internet? Because the vast majority of homophobic and antigay attacks are made by sexist patriarchal men—and some women, such as Women of America (WOA)—who require rigid gender roles. These men will allow women to stray, as long as it is for their benefit and pleasure. Straight men buy and rent DVDs of lesbian sex for their erotic entertainment. But these same good ole boys get disciplined for not conforming to strict gender roles. Their punishment is to be outed as gay—as if that is the worst insult a real man can endure.

Trauma

Trauma is an event in which a person experiences a strong charge of negative emotions, but can't express them. Though experts define psychological trauma in different ways, basically it's an individual's experience of one event or enduring conditions that make the person feel helpless, with no control over what is happening. Subjected to the full force of the event, he or she is rendered powerless. In her book, *Trauma and Recovery,* Judith Lewis Herman states that "traumatic events are extraordinary, not because they occur rarely, but rather because they overwhelm the ordinary human adaptations to life...they confront human beings with the extremities of helplessness and terror, and evoke the responses of catastrophe."[9]

This definition of trauma is fairly broad, according to Dr. Esther Giller, president and director of the Sidran Foundation. In her article "Passages to Prevention: Prevention Across Life's Spectrum," she writes that trauma "includes responses to powerful one-time incidents like accidents, natural disasters, crimes, surgeries, deaths, and other violent events. It also includes responses to chronic or repetitive experiences such as child abuse, neglect, combat, urban violence, concentration camps, battering relationships, and enduring deprivation. This definition intentionally does not allow *us* to determine whether a particular event is traumatic; that is up to each survivor. This definition provides a guideline for our understanding of a survivor's experience of the events and conditions of his/her life."[10]

Thus, any event or situation creates psychological trauma when it overwhelms an individual's ability to cope, leaving him or her with fears of physical harm, insanity, or death. The individual feels overwhelmed. Such circumstances commonly include abuse of power, betrayal of trust, entrapment, helplessness, pain, confusion, and/or loss. This certainly applied to George's situation as well as Merrill's.

As gay boys and adolescents, we experience chronic trauma by having to keep our homosexuality secret. We hear over and over— on the news, in churches or synagogues, in the media, in our schools, and perhaps in our own families—that being gay is wrong, sinful, and biblically forbidden. Hearing that nothing positive can come from being gay is traumatic for children. We know it is inside of us and we know it won't go away, try as we might. Our efforts are the direct result of these awful messages we are receiving. And yet very little is written about the negative effects of these messages on gay children.

When I entered sixth grade, I vividly recall my mother telling me I'd be going to gym and showering with other boys. I was excited about this and initially, I naïvely looked forward to seeing other boys naked. But soon I realized that I couldn't look too long for fear I'd be discovered and outed. Already the kids in school were on to me, particularly the bullies, for being different, wanting to spend time with girls, and not being good at sports. They had already labeled me the class fag; what would happen if, heaven forbid, I sprang an erection in the locker room?

So I went through gym class with blinders on, staring at walls, quickly getting undressed, showering, dressing, and leaving. I would fake being sick and get notes excusing me from gym class to try to avoid the whole issue.

On reflection, I was going through trauma. Imagine if you force a heterosexual little boy to shower with girls, at the same time telling him that if he looks at them and shows arousal and enjoyment, he'll be humiliated and chronically bullied. Putting a straight little boy in a shower with girls is clearly wrong. Yet what gay little boys must endure is never seriously considered—except inasmuch as that boy is wrong for finding the other boys arousing. Blame the boy, not the situation, is how it's handled.

Growing up gay and lesbian *is* traumatic! Even if you don't suffer the same experiences as Merrill or George, just hiding who you are inside every day—and hearing society's negativity and hate—is traumatic enough for gay children. So is hiding one's sexuality and core self and fearing that discovery might result in psychological and physical harm. And this trauma is chronic; it continues for a lifetime, starting from day one. School kids use the word *gay* in a pejorative way: no one wants to be near the "fag." Imagine sitting in a church or synagogue, listening to sermons that say you're bad and wrong. As a result, many gay and lesbian children grow up hypervigilant to make sure they're not detected. We are always looking around and asking ourselves, "Is it safe, or is it dangerous?" Is it any wonder then why gay men find it so difficult to maintain community and connections with one another as friends, much less as partners? We have had so much imprinting that causes us to run and hide from one another, and not to connect—an additional obstacle in our way in finding Mr. Right that has to be addressed and resolved.

Another factor that occurs during trauma is hyperarousal. "After a traumatic experience," says Herman, "the human system of self-preservation seems to go onto permanent alert, as if the danger might return at any moment. Physiological arousal continues unabated. In this state of hyperarousal, which is the first cardinal symptom of post-traumatic stress disorder, the traumatized person startles easily, reacts irritably to small provocations, and sleeps poorly." This is exactly why so many gays and lesbians have trouble coming out. In addition to surmounting homophobia, rejection, and adversarial reactions, we must each delve into our own personal *post-traumatic stress.* Coming out reactivates memories of the original abuse.

This explains why George was scared to enter gay social situations. Those male friends had traumatized him for being gay, so the act of telling others, even other gays, activated his physiological hyperaroused state, making him feel anxious, endangered, and literally terrified.

Herman and other trauma experts talk about how "trauma arrests the course of normal development by its repetitive intrusion into the survivor's life." So in George's case, he was stuck at the age of thirteen, worrying about everything that thirteen-year-olds worry about and reacting emotionally like a thirteen-year-old about making attempts at joining gay groups.

Post-Traumatic Stress Disorder

Symptoms of PTSD are another result of these covert assaults on our sexuality. The gay adolescent must keep his feelings and thoughts to himself. For fear of being outed, he has to be hypervigilant and isolate himself. He is anxious and mistrusts his environment, worrying that he'll be targeted as someone to be avoided, and his own family may shun him. To be accepted and loved like everyone else, he typically develops a false persona to pass as straight. Becoming the "good son" and an overachiever is his defensive posture to assure that no one discovers his "flaw."

If you're to find and keep a partner, these are important points to keep in mind. The trauma done to your developing sexuality as an individual by the attacks on gays as a group (which I call *covert cul-*

tural sexual abuse) can destroy your love mapping and erect more barriers in your relationships.

We need to make firm definitions of sexual abuse, distinctions between covert and overt sexual abuse of gay men, and to understand the covert cultural sexual abuse of gay men as a whole. In doing so, we can rid ourselves of the hurdles that prevent us from finding relationships and making them work. Not doing so may keep you isolated and alone, and even keep you from making friends—as in the case of George.

Sexual Abuse

My working definition comes from Wendy Maltz's book, *The Sexual Healing Journey: A Guide for Survivors of Sexual Abuse.*[11] She writes that sexual abuse occurs whenever one person dominates and exploits another through sexual activity or suggestion. The perpetrator uses sexual feelings and behavior to hurt, misuse, degrade, humiliate, or control another. This is always a violation of a position of trust, power, and protection. Often, it's inflicted on a child who lacks emotional and intellectual maturity, but it is not limited to children.

Overt sexual abuse involves direct touching, fondling, and intercourse with another against that person's will. A few examples would include French kissing, fellatio, sodomy, penetration (with objects, genitals, and fingers), and masturbation. Sometimes force is used and at other times psychological or emotional power (such as differences in age, status, or rank) is brought to bear.

Covert sexual abuse is more subtle and indirect. Examples include sexual hugs, sexual stares, inappropriate comments on one's buttocks or genitals, shaming someone for the kind of male he is (more about this in chapter 2), and homophobic name-calling.

Covert Cultural Sexual Abuse of Gay Men

I don't intend to minimize the effects of overt sexual abuse, which is abhorrent, but rather to emphasize the parallels between those who are overtly sexually abused and the dynamics of covert cultural sexual abuse of gay men.[12] Many covert forms of abuse need to be highlighted. First, most people in our heterosexist, homophobic culture equate gay with adult gay sex. Many heterosexist people, hearing that you're gay, automatically imagine some gay sex act. This is why they find it difficult to imagine a child being gay: the word conjures up *adult* sexuality. And yet gay no more equals sex than does *heterosexual.* Our society has no problem with a little boy holding a little girl's hand and kissing her. But if two little boys did the same, many would be outraged. This is covert sexual abuse, inappropriately sexualizing the child—and ignoring the love and romantic emotions that can occur between a little boy and girl, two little boys, or two little girls.

Any gay child experiences covert sexual abuse when forced by the dominant, heterosexist society to "play" a heterosexual role. The covert part is what's left unsaid. It's abusive not to let young people explore and discover their own sexual and romantic orientation, and to pressure growing adolescents toward heterosexuality, no matter their orientation.

Yet another form of covert abuse is telling young boys that homosexuality is wrong, a sin: that if you're gay, you're not a man. Others referring to you and other gay men as sissies, immature, or deviant (to name only a few such slurs) is a form of name-calling and gender-bashing.

Wendy Maltz's *The Sexual Healing Journey* describes some of the consequences of telling about one's original sexual abuse, which parallel what any gay man goes through when he comes out to others. For example, sexual abuse survivors and gay men don't want to be seen as victims. People make comments such as, "Oh, that's too bad. You're going to have a hard life." Often, gays just want to be seen as men, not marginalized. Yet people judge and label them for their sexual behavior alone, as they do survivors of sexual abuse. They'll embrace their own label before they accept the person.

Another parallel: both abuse survivors and gay men feel sexually embarrassed and ashamed. People sexualize and pigeonhole us into a category, so we carry the same burdens as do sexual abuse survivors. I agree with Maltz that being touched in a private place—whether physically or emotionally—is an intimate, very personal offense. Imagine the gay teacher, however, who's told that he's no more than a sexual predator—that if his school ever learned he was gay, they would (and indeed sometimes do) terminate his employment, lest he try to entice male students.

Like the sexual abuse survivor, a gay man must remember that he's done nothing shameful. The shame lies in the perpetrators who have judged him wrongly, based solely on their false beliefs. Like sexual abuse counseling, gay affirmative psychotherapy helps clients see that the problem lies in what was—and is—being done *to* them and not *in* them![13]

In addition, the sexual abuse survivor worries that he'll be viewed as less of a man. Many heterosexist and homophobic people claim that gay men are more like women. Even gays discriminate against effeminate men, saying, "If I wanted a woman, I'd have been straight." This all creates the mind-set that being gay—or at least, not macho—makes you less than a man. Similarly, the survivor of overt sexual abuse also fears what people will think of him because, as Maltz says, "our society gives boys the message that men should be able to stand up for themselves and fight off danger. They're also told that if a man gets hurt, he should go it alone instead of seeking help." Imagine the deep double bind of being gay *and* having been sexually molested! "Because most abuse of males is perpetrated by other males," Maltz writes, "heterosexual male victims may worry that they will be seen as homosexual if others hear the details of what occurred. Gay men may wonder if the abuse made them gay."

Another way in which covert cultural sexual abuse mirrors the dynamics of sexual abuse is being warned not to tell. We gay men get that message throughout our lives: "Don't talk about it." So when a gay man does come out, he must courageously risk having people threaten to harm him, vandalize his house, kill his pets, fire him, reject him—or all of the above. Usually, of course, when someone comes out, such things don't happen. But the same nightmare holds true for sexual abuse survivors, whose tormentors often threaten to harm them or loved ones if they ever tell. So they don't, giving power to the perpetrators.

Psychological and Behavioral Effects of Covert Cultural Sexual Abuse

Existing literature on sexual abuse talks about the thoughts and effects of sexual abuse survivors, which I believe parallel what happens to gay male children and teens who bring this into their adulthood.[14] These effects are:

1. Erroneous self-perceptions
2. Pretending that nothing is wrong
3. Keeping sexual secrets
4. Becoming a master of pretense
5. Disowning aspects of yourself
6. Confusion about one's sexuality

Erroneous Self-Perceptions

In their early stages of coming out, many gay men feel that they are hopelessly flawed. Before self-acceptance and formation of their full identities as gay men, they feel like damaged goods. This is where shame comes in, which is different from guilt. Guilt is "I *did* something bad. My behavior was wrong or bad." Shame is "I *am* bad. I am inherently wrong." While some religions and cultures state that gay and lesbian behavior is wrong, the message is that *we* are bad at the core, which makes us ashamed of ourselves.

Pretending That Nothing Is Wrong

All that has been discussed thus far contributes to being out of integrity with ourselves and others (more about that in the following chapter). Early in life, we learn to cover up anything that suggests in any way that we might be homosexual. I recall trying to spit better, like the other guys. My cousin spit like a real guy, and I always wanted to do it like he could. But when I tried to spit, it went all over the place or nowhere, so I stopped trying. Trivial as that sounds, I really tried my best—as do so many other gay boys and teens—to pretend nothing was wrong. All that achieves, however, is to make gay males live out of integrity—which persists even after coming out. Just because you come out and integrate your sexual and romantic orientation does not mean you start living in integrity everywhere else. The longer you live out of integrity with yourself and others, the more it hampers other areas of your life.

Many of us hope that someone will see through our pretend-ing—that someone will say, "I can see something is wrong; let me help you." But this never happens. So we nurture the hope that our partners will see when something is wrong inside us, but they don't either. In truth they shouldn't have to. We should instead tell them about our feelings. To maintain a relationship, you must tell your partner when something is wrong. If you don't, and simply hope that he realizes it on his own, he may never see that something is wrong because he simply doesn't know. Holding him accountable results from your own unresolved issues from when you were growing up, when others weren't able to see that you were hiding a precious part of your identity. This, as I'll address later on, is reflected in the atti-tude of those who say, "I shouldn't have to tell him, he should just know." False! You *do* have to tell him.

Keeping Sexual Secrets

Just like the survivors of sexual abuse, we keep secrets about our gayness, which has been labeled as nothing more than sexual. But in reality, being gay is more than just sex. As I say frequently, it's an affectional, spiritual, emotional, psychological, mental, and sexual way of life. But because we're taught that *gay* equals *sex,* the unspo-ken lesson is to keep it secret.

Learning to keep sexual secrets can also lead to withholding sex-ual information from a partner, as when you find that either of you is cheating and not coming forward with what you and he truly want sexually within your relationship. You may find, like the sexual abuse survivor often does, that you are even keeping sexual secrets from yourself. An awakening happens once you come out of the closet with your secrets. As AA says, secrets keep us sick!

Becoming a Master of Pretense

Wearing a false self so others won't detect your gayness becomes a way of life. This may explain why so many gay men—and straight men as well—are pretentious. A large number of gay men first intro-duce themselves by letting you know immediately how important they are in their activism, their jobs and the money they make, how ripped and buff their bodies are, even how well hung they are. We were taught, from childhood up, that who we are on the inside is a disappointment and something to be despised. No wonder we become masters of pretense! This only limits your availability for a serious relationship.

Disowning Aspects of Yourself

Cutting off your romantic and sexual urges becomes a habit. Your real self becomes a fugitive, and you tend to forget who you really are—not only in terms of being gay.

This is what the shadow is all about, as I explain in the following chapter. When we cut off and disown parts of ourselves, they go underground—they are not gone forever, just buried. They knock on the door of your consciousness repeatedly, throughout your life, trying to be freed. If you pay them no attention, they'll sneak out sideways—or camouflaged in ways you won't immediately recognize.

The best way to discover your shadow—those aspects of yourself that you've disowned or cut off—is to examine the very things that attract you to potential partners, your current partner, and your past partners. The things that drive you crazy about him, causing your greatest sources of pain, also reveal important information about yourself. As the saying goes, "If you spot it, you got it." Also, the things that you don't mean to do to your partner are indicators you are in shadow, and that a disowned part of you is sneaking out sideways.

Confusion About One's Sexuality

Perhaps the worst part of any form of sexual abuse or assault is that the victim is confused about his responsibility for the victimization—for which he has none. You are not responsible as a child for someone abusing you in any way, ever! But children do not know this and feel they are responsible for everything that happens to them. For example, plenty of heterosexual men and women who have been sexually abused wonder if they might be gay. They're not, but the abuse causes them unnecessary confusion, particularly if their perpetrator was of the same gender.

When an adult is sexually harassed, he wonders if he somehow provoked or even wanted it. For a person to be aroused by the harassment is normal and common, even if it's unwanted. Your body responds separately from what your mind wants or doesn't want to happen. Sexual abuse and harassment can cause not only identity confusion, but also confusion around sexual *interest*. If an adult wonders if he somehow wanted the sexual harassment, imagine how a child feels.

Because gay males have to surrender their sexuality to heterosexism, is it any wonder that they're confused about their orientation? Only when they finally get the nerve to go on their own hero's journey and reclaim their own sexuality does their confusion dissipate.

I often see these symptoms among gay men—but not because they've been overtly sexually abused in a physical way. Again, this is the result of covert cultural sexual abuse on an emotional level. The thoughts and effects are the same, but are initiated in different ways.

Gay men often feel hopelessly flawed. Using the Cass model, in the early stages of coming out, the homosexual man can't come to terms with the fact that he's gay, thinking he's flawed or "freaky."[15] One man, looking for reparative therapy, told me that he wished his Higher Power had not "scarred" him in this way.

As I always say, just because a man comes out of the closet doesn't mean that he stops pretending. At a young age, we gay men learn to pretend to be someone we're not. Over time, we even come to believe that we truly are the people we pretended to be. As a result, I hear gay men tell me they had no clue they were gay—or that they were even attracted to gay men!

The psychological aftermath of sexual abuse in adulthood again parallels the results of gay men impacted by covert cultural sexual abuse. These results include:

1. Affection inappropriately sexualized
2. Preoccupation with sex
3. Avoiding sexual arousal
4. Isolation from others and short-lived relationships
5. Settling for too little
6. Self-hate / internalized homophobia

7. Self-inflicted injury and suicide
8. Feeling responsible and to blame for causing the abuse
9. Affection inappropriately sexualized

Many men—not just gay men—inappropriately sexualize touching in general. In large part this is because people stop hugging and patting boys around age eight—a much younger age than we stop doing so for girls. No wonder, then, that touch-deprived males turn to sex for touch. Females have permission to touch men, women, and children and be affectionate without anyone thinking there's anything strange about it. Walking around airports, malls, and other public venues, I always notice that females—both children and adults—think nothing of touching one another's hair and clothes, even holding hands. Imagine any man walking up to a straight male friend and saying, "Wow, I love your hair!" and messing with it. Straight male friends often touch and affectionately wrestle when drunk or excited, perhaps at a football game. As men, we are socialized not to touch: all men, whether gay, straight, or bisexual, are socialized to sexualize affection— inappropriately.

Straight men are fortunate in that they have women to teach them how to "unlearn" this. Women require that men touch them with affection that doesn't always lead to sex. As gay men, this demonstrative outlet is typically blocked, which contributes to too much sexualization in gay male culture.

This also explains why there is often less physical affection between gay male couples than between lesbian couples or straight couples. We men are not allowed to demonstrate physical affection for one another in public. So from childhood on, we refrain until it becomes the norm—even in our romantic relationships!

Preoccupation with Sex

The overtly sexually abused child develops hypersexuality, which vandalizes his developing sexuality. As gay children, heterosexuality is superimposed on us just as the sexual abuse victim has the perpetrator's sexuality superimposed on them.

If we appear to be sissy boys, girlie boys, or anything that doesn't resemble standard masculinity, we get gender abused—that is, told we are bad and wrong for not acting like real boys. Later, this interferes with our relationships with partners and contributes to sexual acting—out outside the relationship, as well as vulnerability to sexual addiction, as I explained in my previous book.

Avoiding Sexual Arousal

Perhaps the saddest negative effect of all forms of sexual abuse is the deadening of all sexual feeling. Some men remain asexual and closeted, numbing and neutralizing their sexual urges. Or the only way they can give themselves permission to be sexual with other men is on drugs like crystal meth. Others are sexually anorexic. Patrick Carnes, who also coined the term *sexual addiction,* calls sexual anorexia "a disorder that parallels sexual addiction and compulsivity, based on childhood sexual trauma...an obsessive state in which the physical, mental, and emotional task of avoiding sex dominates one's life."[16]

The sufferer is preoccupied with avoiding sex and actually finds the idea and act repulsive—which is quite different from having a low libido or simply feeling neutral and not interested. The sexual anorexic's primary goal is finding ways not to link intimacy with sex. (More to come about this in chapter 10.)

Isolation from Others and Short-Lived Relationships

To ease their pangs of isolation, many gay men use alcohol and drugs. To achieve a sense of belonging, they may hang out at bars, clubs, and circuit parties. Or else they simply remain marooned in the closet—solitary guys, consoling themselves with porn and gay chat rooms.

Like sexual abuse survivors, gay males tend to enter into short-lived relationships, because their love map and capacity for intimacy have been vandalized, overlaid with someone else's sexual agenda. Again, sexual abuse of any kind always derives from the offender's needs and desire for power. If your ability to deeply attach in healthy ways has been negatively impacted, how can a relationship move to real love and endure?

Settling for Too Little

Like sexual abuse survivors, gays and lesbians adopt the belief that they don't deserve much of a life, that little is available to them if they do choose to live a life of abomination. It follows that anyone treated as though he or she were basically worthless will settle for very little. This can either prevent you from attempting any relationships at all, or lead you to men who treat you as an inferior and whose verbal, physical, and psychological abuse contributes to your low self-esteem.

Self-Hate / Internalized Homophobia

We internalize the hate that we see in the media, read about, and watch others inflict against other gays and lesbians. Those less fortunate who cannot pass as straight receive it directly. We learn self-hate at an early age. This, I believe, contributes to self-destructive acting-out behaviors such as drug use, unsafe sex practices, alcohol abuse, and sexual addiction.

Self-Inflicted Injury and Suicide

Victims of sexual abuse often will cut themselves at some point. One of the many reasons is that they're trying to bringing their inner pain to the surface. I believe that barebacking sex and risking HIV exposure is analogous to cutting. So-called bug chasers try to achieve a sense of belonging by purposely contracting HIV. (This will be examined further in the discussion of the sexual shadow in chapter 7.) Some gay men purposely infect other men with HIV without their victims' knowledge. Anger and rage that derive from the self-hate they experience stems from covert cultural sexual abuse as well.

The rate of adolescent suicide in gay and lesbian teens is 30 percent, a commonly reported number whenever suicide is discussed among gay and lesbian teens. Many say the percentage is inflated; some say it's higher. But this is a fair number when you consider those who attempt suicide and, fortunately, don't succeed. This percentage most likely includes straight teens as well, who, because of homophobia, worry that they might be gay. Prepubescent boys often experiment sexually with one another, but that curiosity does not make them gay. Lastly, if a male sexually abuses another male, the victim often is concerned that the perpetrator either could tell he is gay or the abuse will make him so. Do you feel responsible and blame yourself for making others abuse you?

Thus many of my clients feel that *they* are the reason why friends, family, and colleagues won't accept them. They say things such as, "If I hadn't told them I was gay, everything would be okay" or "They don't tell me what *they* do in their sex lives, so by not telling them I'm gay, I show them the same respect." Once again, they're equating *gay* and *sex*. Sexual abuse survivors need to understand they are *not* responsible for the abuse they suffered and that they did nothing to provoke it! If others have a negative reaction when told about it, this is *not* the fault of the survivor.

Feeling Responsible and to Blame for Causing the Abuse

Covert cultural sexual abuse of gay men leads to four core beliefs, which I've adapted from Patrick Carnes's four core beliefs of sexual addicts:

1. As a gay male, I am basically a bad and unworthy person.
2. If people knew I was gay, no one would love me.
3. If I have to depend on others, my needs are never going to get met.
4. This world is dangerous to me as a gay man.

As a psychotherapist, workshop presenter, and author, my goal is to teach gay men that they're not responsible for any of the abuse they received as children and teenagers. Accountability rests on the guilty shoulders of those who did the abuse. But today, our responsibility as gay male adults is to get past all that. And as you'll see in this book, the best way to move on is accomplished by developing a relationship with a partner that moves on to real love, and to make tight-knit, healthy, and strong friendships. Having strong and healthy attachments helps gay men recover the birthright of their sexuality and heal the effects of covert cultural sexual abuse.

In addressing all of this and doing the work suggested in this chapter, you will be on the same playing field as potential partners and know that you belong. To quote Joseph Campbell, "We must be willing to get rid of the life we've planned, so as to have the life that is waiting for us."

Homo-Work on Belonging

1. As a child, did you realize you were gay?
2. As a gay boy or teenager, what did you do in order to feel safe around others who didn't suspect?
3. Did you tell anyone about your gay feelings?
4. Were you popular or unpopular in school?
5. Were you athletic and good at sports, or not?
6. What do you remember about having to shower with other boys in gym class?
7. Were you sexually abused as a child? If so, what were the circumstances—by whom, when, and for how long?
8. Who did you tell (if anyone) that you were sexually abused?
9. Did you ever think about or attempt suicide for being gay?
10. Where do you *belong* within the gay male community?

References

1. Robert Bly, *Iron John: A Book About Men* (Vancouver, WA: Vintage Books, 1992).
2. Joseph Campbell, *The Hero with a Thousand Faces* (Princeton, NJ: Princeton University Press, 1973).
3. Deb Price, "How to Be Gay: Male Homosexuality and Initiation," Gannett New Service, 3 October 2000.
4. Frank Sanello, *Tweakers: How Crystal Meth Is Ravaging Gay America* (Los Angeles: Alyson Books, 2005).
5. Harville Hendrix, *Getting the Love You Want: A Guide for Couples* (New York: Henry Holt, 1988; reprint, Owl Books, 2001).
6. George Weinberg, *Society and the Healthy Homosexual* (New York: St. Martin's Press, 1983).
7. Joe Kort, *10 Smart Things Gay Men Can Do to Improve Their Lives* (Los Angeles: Alyson Books, 2003).
8. Gabriel Rotello, "The Enemy Within," *The Advocate,* 1 April 1997, 80.
9. Judith Lewis Herman, *Trauma and Recovery* (New York: HarperCollins, 1992).
10. Esther Giller, "Passages to Prevention: Prevention Across Life's Spectrum," Sidran Foundation, May 1999.www.sidran.org.

11. Wendy Maltz, *The Sexual Healing Journey: A Guide for Survivors of Sexual Abuse (New York: HarperCollins, 1991).*

12. Joe Kort, "Covert Cultural Sexual Abuse of Gay Male Teenagers Contributing to Etiology of Sexual Addiction," *Journal of Sexual Addiction and Compulsivity,* vol. 11(4), November 2005.

13. Joe Kort, "Queer Eye for the Straight Therapist," *Psychotherapy Networker* (May–June, 2004).

14. Maltz, Sexual Healing Journey; Mike Lew, *Victims No Longer: The Classic Guide for Men Recovering from Sexual Child Abuse,* 2d ed. (New York: Perennial Currents, 2004).

15. Vivienne Cass, "Homosexual Identity Formation: A Theoretical Model," *Journal of Homosexuality,* vol. 4(3), 1979.

16. Patrick Carnes, *Sexual Anorexia: Overcoming Sexual Self-Hatred* (Center City, MN: Hazelden Press, 1997).

Chapter 2
Become the Man You Were Meant to Be

When I was in the military, they gave me a medal for killing two men and a discharge for loving one.

—epitaph of Leonard Matlovich (1943–1988),
Vietnam veteran

This quote sets the tone for the punishment gay men suffer at the hands of a patriarchal society for having the natural desire to have real love for another man. This chapter surveys the obstacles we must overcome to remove anything in the way that was imprinted on us for not following the rigid male roles that patriarchy insists upon. We are taught to be out of integrity with ourselves for the kind of males we are—whatever that is—right down to being men who love men. From the beginning of our lives, we are taught that our love is wrong.

"Would the small gay boy you once were look up to the gay man you've become?" was my key question in *10 Smart Things Gay Men Can Do to Improve Their Lives.*[1] That's a question you must answer for yourself. And will the small gay boy you once were look up to the gay man you've become in your relationships?

In his book *The Hero with a Thousand Faces,* mythologist and author Joseph Campbell talked about the Hero's Journey.[2] I think that every gay man travels his own hero's journey in order to discover himself as a gay man and find a partner and real love. Campbell wrote about the "archetypal adventure," in which one must be initiated in order to progress from one life phase to another-from child to youth, adolescent to adult. In *10 Smart Things Gay Men Can Do to Improve Their Lives,* I tried to help move you from being a closeted gay boy to an openly gay man. In this book, I will show what it means to be a man who happens to be gay.

Adult love relationships, in and of themselves, are a hero's journey and another means to self-discovery for moving from child to adult—boy to man. Even if you've decided not to have a romantic relationship, close, tight-knit relationships with friends and family take you on a journey and adventure you shouldn't miss either.

In *The Power of Myth,* Joseph Campbell writes that in order to find a new way of life one must "leave the old and go in quest of the seed idea, a germinal idea that will have the potentiality of bringing forth that new thing."[3] He says we need rituals and initiation ceremonies to pass from boy to man, from child to adult.

Girls have rituals to mark their progression as women. When they reach menarche, usually their mothers or some female adult teaches them what this means and how to care for their bodies. It marks the end of one stage of their life and the beginning of another. Going with their mothers to buy a bra marks another point in their developing femininity.

We boys don't have the same markings of masculinity. When pubic hair starts growing and our penises develop and we get erections, no one talks to us about it. And at age eleven or twelve, we're certainly not about to bring it up. No one explains to us how and what to do. Without help in knowing what it means to be a male and understanding our masculinity, we feel lost.

The difference between the immature and mature masculine is that the immature masculine is usually patriarchal, involving male dominance and hypermasculinity—or its opposite, where a male is basically truncated and emasculated, having turned his balls over to someone or something else. This chapter is about coming into your own gay masculinity and getting your testosterone back. Gay male relationships can help you do it!

The Doubling Factor

When two males enter into a relationship, there's the impact of bringing their gender roles and socialization traits along with them. Working with male couples, I notice their difficulty with—or even absence of—relational skills. Often, I have to teach gay clients how to be in relationship with one another, in terms of interpersonal skills, dependency, intimacy, and expressiveness. Men—gay and straight alike—disengage emotionally as a way of coping with relationship pressures.

It's different with lesbian couples. By the time they enter therapy, they're so overinvolved and fused with each other that I joke that I'd need the Jaws of Life to pull them apart! They laugh because they know it's true—plus the literature supports this. Women in general are so relational that for them, the doubling factor can create too much closeness. But for male couples, there isn't enough.

We men are socialized to be the breadwinners, taught to be sexual predators whose conquests are cause for pride and status. We're taught not to show strong emotions, making for difficulty in expressing our anger, hurt, and vulnerability in healthy ways. Consequently, conflicts in gay relationships frequently involve money, jobs, sex, jealousy, and emotional closeness. Women teach straight men how to do this, and if straight men are willing, they can learn. This is why so many gay men who have once been heterosexually married have better relational skills than gay men who've never lived with women. (More about this in chapter 8.)

In your relationship with your partner or boyfriend, you need to discover what's *right* about being in a culture of males who desire other males as sexual partners, romantic partners, friends, and otherwise. We have to explore how our masculinity was shaped, in order to see how we view it today in ourselves—and in each other. By staying focused on this goal, we can lead healthy and fuller lives and enjoy better social and romantic relationships with other gay men.

As members of a subculture, we gay men are traumatized in the worst way by being called *faggots, perverts, pansies, sissies, mother-dominated mama's boys,* or referred to as "more like women," "immature," "underdeveloped in their masculinity," "less than a man," "stuck in their adolescent stage," "weak," "innately vulnerable," "cowardly," "unable to control themselves," and "deserving what they get."

In gay culture, the drive to escape this self-image manifests as the desire for the "straight-acting" male, as can be seen in a sampling of gay personal ads on the Internet. Anything less ("no fats, no fems") is not desirable as a partner or friend. I see gay men cringe at the idea of inviting gay friends to mingle with their straight friends and family, for fear of being judged negatively or appearing "too gay." As I point out in all my lectures, workshops, and writings, this is internalized homophobia. Being treated this way—and perpetuating such treatment among ourselves and each other—cripples us emotionally and literally kills any possibility for relationships requiring true intimacy.

Being raised male in the heterosexist culture means avoiding and distancing yourself from being viewed as gay in any way. *Gay* is synonymous with *effeminate*. This is inherent sexism, as if being associated with anything female would denigrate you. In our culture, being male is a privileged status, and anything else is viewed as inferior. A number of times I've had a straight man notice my wedding ring and ask if I'm married. I'll say, "Yes," because I am. When he asks my wife's name, I pleasantly correct him and tell him that I'm married to a man whose name is Mike.

Often, the guy steps back and immediately exclaims, "Dude, I'm not gay!" He may then proceed to ask, "Why did you choose to tell me you're gay?" as if I had a sexual motive, or tell me he was "grossed out" by the idea. Now, I never implied that he was gay by telling him I was, nor did I have any ulterior motive. I was simply correcting him, just as when people wish me a Merry Christmas. I nicely tell them I am Jewish; whereupon they usually respond politely by saying, "Oh, sorry! Happy Hanukah!" I've never seen anyone back away, exclaiming, "Dude, I'm not Jewish. Now all I can do is imagine you in a yarmulke in synagogue and I'm grossed out. You're trying to convert me?"

But if anyone did, he'd be expressing his shadow—as I'll explain shortly.

On learning that another man is gay, the straight guy proclaims his heterosexuality to ensure that the gay guy perceives him as straight and so won't hit on him. Since the word gay is often synonymous with sex, men often only hear "I get it on with guys—and you could be next!" And straight men have not learned how to fend off sexual advances from another man. For women, this becomes a natural part of their lives, as heterosexual men commonly make advances. So although a gay man telling a straight guy "I'm gay" is not a sexual advance, the straight guy worries that it will lead to that, and therefore must establish his heterosexual position quickly—and aggressively. He knows no other way. This is immature straight behavior, of course, as will be seen in the discussion about mature and immature masculine archetypes that follows.

Straight and gay men alike feel pressured to behave in "masculine" ways. But our society's concept of masculinity, handed down from archaic patriarchal times, is actually an immature one, in that it relieves men from being accountable and responsible from the very actions that harm others and themselves. It anesthetizes feelings, leaving men numb and stunted both psychologically and emotionally.

Historically, most of the religious and psychological disparagement and attacks on homosexuality have been directed at men. Groups such as NARTH and reparative therapists, all trying to "heal" homosexuality, target their literature and information for the most part at males. There has to be something behind this-these groups have a shadow of their own.

With regard to men being ostracized by male society, Terrence Real, psychotherapist and author of *I Don't Want to Talk About It: Overcoming the Secret Legacy of Male Depression,* writes,

> Boys and men are granted privilege and special status, but only on the condition that they turn their backs on vulnerability and connection to join in the fray. Those who resist, like unconventional men or gay men, are punished for it. Those who lose or cannot compete, like boys and men with disabilities, or of the wrong class or color, are marginalized and rendered all but invisible....The exclusion, isolation, of a failed winner is so great, it as if he never existed at all.[4]

I agree. For us gay men, the punishment for not being the privileged type of man is *brutal*—as I know all too well. Before I reached the age of eight, I would play dress-up in a dress and high heels with my sister and female cousin, and pretend I was a woman. Girls are allowed to be tomboys, but boys have no permission to be sissies. Yet so many boys are—and I was one of them. I remember having fun with my sister and cousin, but also the disapproving glances from my male cousins and the adults around me.

I recall my grandmother telling me, around age five, that I could no longer dress up as a girl and had to stop. "Boys do not do this," she said, not in a mean or shaming way, just factually and sternly. I felt incredible shame and of course stopped playing publicly with the girls. Privately, however, I continued—having learned that this was something to be ashamed of and to hide.

Perhaps the best example of the brutality of what a man should be and should not be was portrayed in the comedy movie *In and Out*. Kevin Kline plays Howard, who does not realize he is gay and is engaged to be heterosexually married. A former theater student of his has won an Academy Award for playing a gay man and, to Howard's horror, cites him on national television as a positive role model of an out gay man. Deciding to prove to his fiancée, family, and friends that he is not gay, he buys an audio tape called "Be a Man: Exploring Your Masculinity."

In this crucial scene, he listens to tape number one, "Getting a Grip," which teaches him how to be a man. This scene made me laugh so hard I cried, and after it was over, I wanted to stand and cheer; it was the most excellent comment I've ever seen on how we are taught to men.

The audio tells him how to dress, stand a certain way, and how to speak. He fails miserably at getting a grip on real men's language and posture. Then finally the tape tackles "the most critical area of masculine behavior—dancing!" The narrator explains, "Truly, manly men do not dance; under any circumstances! This will be your ultimate test. At all cost, avoid rhythm, grace and pleasure." It then launches into Diana Ross singing "I Will Survive"—a gay disco anthem.

In the background, the song plays louder and louder, while the audio shouts "Men do not dance! They work, they drink, they have bad backs. They do not dance!" Ultimately, Howard can't contain himself and begins dancing uncontrollably. The voice on the tape begs him to stop, calling him a "pantywaist" and a "big ballerina." It tells him to "bite someone, to kick someone, bite someone's ear!" At the end, the tape asks, "So how did you do, pussyboy?"

This scene is a great dramatization of how our culture treats men who don't follow a traditional male role. At a very young age, little boys, both gay and straight, are still taught to be this way. Yet we gay boys suffer several other wounds that vandalize our sense of belonging and exclude us from the male fraternity. Perhaps the first—if not the largest—is being told that we are not really men or aren't the right kind of men. If we come to believe that, then how can we ever feel good about ourselves and other gay men and be able to date and maintain healthy relationships?

Our efforts to conceal our pain and basic identities take many inappropriate and self-defeating forms. No wonder so many gay personal ads seek straight-acting guys only! We've been taught that anything else is inferior and unattractive. This explains why some gay men pursue straights, even preferring them to gay men and trying to win them over sexually: wanting straight men's acceptance and love becomes sexualized, as I'll explain in chapter 7, which deals with your sexual shadow. Other efforts to conceal pain and identity include excessive use of drugs and the obsessive pursuit of a hyper-masculine body.

My family was always trying to make a man out of me. My father left us to start another family when I was three, and focused his attention there. Meanwhile, my mother put me together with my uncles, who all tried to intervene and include me in sports—which I was not at all good at. In fact, I hated sports, but to please the adults in my family, I valiantly soldiered on in their campaign to help me become a man. I recall my athletic inadequacy meeting with disapproval from my uncles and other males. I was always the last to be picked for teams; the other boys basically ignored me. I hated it. To this day, I cannot pass a baseball game without feeling shame and inadequacy in the pit of my stomach.

I knew that my male cousins disapproved of my sissy behavior. One male cousin, two years younger than I, was very athletic and spent a lot of time with me. He and his sister were close to me and my sister in ages, and our mothers had been close as children, so we were often together. He played baseball, hockey, football; I was impressed with his athletic prowess and remember craving his acceptance. He and his brothers had scores of trophies lining the shelves in their bedrooms, which only reminded me of how inept I felt to not be the right kind of boy.

He patiently tried to teach me how to throw a ball and welcomed me onto his baseball team. But one day, he dared me to stop playing house with his sister, telling me he didn't think I could stop. I told him I could and promised him I would, but within a week I was back to playing house with his sister. He was right: I couldn't stop; I didn't want to stop—I enjoyed it! What is wrong with that? Certainly not the behavior; rather, what is wrong is how boys' play is negatively judged. We expect little boys to grow up to be good fathers and husbands, yet shame them out of playing house—which is all about preparing for that time in their lives. No wonder so many men have trouble when they try to raise a family!

Not surprisingly, research shows that effeminate or stereotypically gay males are more likely targets for other men's abuse—even rape. Yet ironically, men struggling with homosexual impulses or who have been sexually abused in childhood are more likely to bully another male who appears gay. Even if he's not, mere suspicion is the bully's justification for abusing him.

Perhaps the worst thing that happened to me as a young boy was a canoe trip I suffered with my mother's brother. Uncle Alvin was overweight, uneducated, sexist, and patriarchal—married with three children, he was a blue-collar type who never really achieved much status in life. At family gatherings, he teased everyone mercilessly. My other male cousins and I were in Hebrew school, and during the High Holy Days, we would begin the services with what we had learned in prayer. He would laugh, throw food, and belittle us as we tried to read the prayers and sing. Eventually we would be forced to stop, and everyone would begin eating. No one stopped his bullying.

When I was ten, my mother told me that I would be going with my uncle Alvin and his two sons on a sort of Boy Scout trip with boys and their fathers. I recall dreading it, since I knew this uncle didn't like me and disapproved of my sissy behavior. I remember him talking to my mother and the other adults about me, and most of them in fact agreeing with him! My own family referred to me as a mama's boy. So to please my mother and those trying to "make a man out of me," I went on this trip, which turned out to be one of the worst experiences of my life. For the canoeing part of the trip, everyone was paired up except me. Somehow I was separated from my uncle's boys and got partnered with Uncle Alvin himself.

I recall both of us in life jackets, and feeling the boat tip one way and then the other as my uncle shifted in his seat behind me as he paddled. Being that I was a skinny ten year old and he weighed at least 300 pounds, my uncle's weight rocked the canoe. I became frightened. Most of the time, I couldn't see the bottom of the lake. We were alone, with no other canoes in sight. Sure enough, he leaned too far to one side and we tipped over.

I went under. When I surfaced with the help of the life jacket, I saw the canoe overturned and my uncle trying to right it. I knew we were in deep water, since I couldn't touch the lake bottom, and I was afraid I would drown. My uncle looked afraid and not in control, which only scared me more. The next thing I recall is both of us back in the canoe, and my uncle yelling at me because I was crying from being scared. For what seemed like hours, he said cutting things such as, "You will never amount to anything. You are a sissy! All you like to do is play house and play with dolls! You are a crybaby, a mama's boy!" He shouted these patronizing, contemptuous epithets at me, over and over.

As a child you believe what adults say. To a child, adults are always right; so the child makes himself wrong. If the child is right, then the adults in charge must be wrong—and to a preadolescent, that is too overwhelming. So the child unconsciously agrees to be wrong in order to get along with the adults. When we arrived back on land, I was too humiliated to tell a soul about Alvin's barrage of verbal and emotional abuse. It was as if he'd said aloud what I knew others thought about me—and, in fact—what I felt and believed about myself. I had been crying hard, and my cousin, Alvin's son, still tells me how shaken I looked when we returned. All I wanted was to get away from him and everyone else.

For years afterward, this incident was the topic of much of my own therapy. Initially, therapists thought this had contributed to my homosexuality—that Alvin's verbal abuse contributed to and cemented the homosexual identity taking place during my early years.

Today, reparative therapists (and even some other professionals) would say that all of this trauma made me gay; but this would mean that you can shape sexual and romantic orientation. If so, then Real's *I Don't Want to Talk About It* would deal with gay men only. But it doesn't, because this type of mistreatment happens to any male who doesn't fit the image of how men should look and act; it doesn't shape his sexual and romantic orientation. What it does create is *father hunger,* which will be discussed further in chapter 4.

The fact is, gays and lesbians who raise their own (or adopted) children almost invariably have sons and daughters who grow up straight. Growing up in gay or straight families doesn't impact children's sexual orientation either way—but mistreating a gay or effeminate little boy certainly creates low self-esteem, which makes him feel less than a man. Again, this is separate from one's sexual interests. What makes things worse for gay men is the covert cultural sexual abuse that allows men to be violent to gay males as if we were less than human.

Trying to heal that abuse from my uncle and male peers in therapy did not make me straight. But it did help me understand how those incidents traumatized my masculinity, not my sexual orientation; these are two related but separate entities, as will be explained further.

In 1999, I was finally able to put to rest the episode with my uncle by attending a men's retreat called the New Warrior Training Adventure by the ManKind Project.[5] Here was a group of men, mostly straight, whose mission in life is to help men become better and more mature. Still, I went to this workshop not knowing what to expect—and I'm glad I didn't! That is exactly what made it so powerful for me. This workshop changed my life, liberated me as a man among men, and opened up new possibilities for me.

Here I was, able to have straight men love me, hold me, and help me feel part of the male culture. It is what I'd wanted and waited for all my life. I can hear a reparative therapist right now saying, "See, it was too late. If Joe had had this experience earlier in life, he wouldn't have turned out gay." The truth is that as children, the other men attending also had suffered at the hands of male peers, and most were not at all gay. To believe that mistreatment makes you gay, you would have to go back and look for the reasons why—first assuming that there's something wrong with being gay. When heterosexual males suffer mistreatment, no one bothers trying to establish through research that it made them straight. Real writes that bullying leads to depression and other disorders, particularly those that keep men from being able to connect with others in close relationships.

This is why I believe that in order to find real love with a partner, it's so important to identify any negative imprinting surrounding your own masculinity. Typically, we gays have difficulty in connecting to others, particularly other men. And here we are, trying to be intimate with men, when all our lives we were taught not to be! As males, we learned to disavow anything feminine and to avoid other gay males. Yet now we have to call on relational skills that we have not learned and therefore do not possess.

Real's book explains how we as males are socialized to reject the feminine and anything associated with it. He writes about how "boys are pressured to yield attributes of dependency, expressiveness, affiliation—all the self-concepts and skills that belong to the relational, emotive world...the price of traditional socialization for boys is disconnection—from themselves, from their mothers, from those around them." We gay men need to examine our disconnection with ourselves and one another. Emotionally, we restrict ourselves with other males, yet we have been able to connect with women—more than is permitted our heterosexual male counterparts. Along with being disconnected from women, they are restricted from connecting with other men for fear of being labeled gay or homoerotic. So we see portrayals like the title characters in *Will & Grace*, where the gay male is able to have a strong relationship with a woman.

It's wonderful that so many of us have a Grace in our lives. Many gay men enjoy wonderful relationships with their mothers, providing us, as adults, with a template for intimate relationships with women. Yet over and over, I see gay men who can't maintain friendships and romantic relationships with other men. They have limited relationships even with their fathers—a problem I will address in the following chapter.

When women get together, they touch each other easily, go the restroom together, cry together, enjoy a full range of contact with one another—and no one puts them down for it. Imagine for a moment that it is guys' night out at a sports bar, and Larry says to one of his buddies, "Steve, I gotta take a leak. You wanna come with me?" When I tell that to straight audiences, they roar with laughter. Yet, if you think about it, what is so silly about that?

Historically, psychotherapists have taught that homosexuality is a result of stunted sexual development, causing immature youngsters to turn gay. These assertions were almost always geared toward males and only rarely toward females. In fact, whenever a theory about homosexuality was developed, it first tried to explain how males become homosexual. Then the theory would be extended to females, with no clinical research to support its validity. Teachings about the etiology of homosexuality were purely anecdotal, not scientific or based on research. As the result of sexism and patriarchy, men are taught to be nothing at all like women and rather everything like a stereotypical, traditional man.

There remains a body of literature that continues to advance this out-of-date misinformation. Reparative therapists firmly believe that those of a homosexual orientation can transform themselves into heterosexuals. Their literature is filled with sexist overtones and patriarchal beliefs. It's absurd to believe that if boys would just play sports and avoid girlish pastimes and behaviors, and if girls would just wear makeup and act more feminine, their innate heterosexuality would come through. The best examinations of these reparative attempts and teachings are in Wayne Besen's book *Anything but Straight* and the documentary *One Nation Under God*.[6] I highly recommend both.

Reparative therapy promotes antiquated beliefs and theories about homosexuality and, quite selectively, uses sexist and outdated psychological views of what a man should be like. In the previous chapter, I explained how sexual abuse can be covert and take the form of degrading one's own gender. Reparative therapy's inherent abuse is telling those with homosexual desires to feel ashamed for being the kind of male or female they are. That's gender abuse, a form of covert sexual abuse.

Probably the most abusive book toward gays and lesbians is *A Parent's Guide to Preventing Homosexuality* by Joseph Nicolosi and his wife, Linda Ames Nicolosi.[7] In its veiled way, this book evades the American Psychological Association's warning that trying to help gay people suppress their sexual and romantic desires may lead to a lifetime of depression. Nicolosi's book on preventing "homosexual" orientation in the first place—by focusing primarily on male children—is therefore nothing more than child abuse.

Nicolosi and others in his extreme makeover camp have gotten wise to the criticism of their approach and so have disguised it. They've softened their terminology, telling parents to correct children, but not shame them for playing with opposite-gender toys. If your son plays with a doll, they advise taking it away and telling him you're giving it to a little girl who needs it. To me, this is abominable. They want men to be good fathers, but stop them from playing with dolls—which is one way to learn how to parent. Nor will playing with dolls make a boy homosexual or lead to orientation problems. Removing toys, whether you do it nicely or in a shaming way, will only wound a child's self-esteem.

A Parent's Guide to Preventing Homosexuality tells mothers to "back off" and turn away from their sons, giving the example of a mother who was disgusted by her son's asking to use her makeup. The only good advice they give is for fathers to get more involved. I couldn't agree more: fathers abandoning their sons, gay and straight alike, has caused much of the anxiety and depression in men today. More involved fathers can help their sons grow into more mature men, but cannot make them straight or gay—as you'll see in chapter 3, on gay men and their fathers.

In your relationships with other men, it is important to find your own path toward masculine maturity. It's inappropriate to look to others to make that happen. This is your journey, no one else's. Relationships with other men can help you attain your mature masculine.

Infantilization

As gay men we are infantilized—not allowed into the male adult fraternity. This contributes to why so many gay men act like boys and teenagers. In *Gay Warrior: Transforming Betrayal into Wisdom,* authors F. Jim Fickey and Gary S. Grimm talk about the *Puer,* "the archetype within every man that represents his eternal youth. The *Puer* (pronounced poo-air) is the psychological component of a gay man that still behaves, thinks and reacts to his world like a child, and it is the same part that most often keeps him from being able to fully embrace his manhood. As with Peter Pan, a familiar character for many of us from childhood, the *Puer* expresses the same longing— to never grow up."[8]

The truth is that as men and as gays, we are discouraged from seeking adulthood. Men find rewards for remaining immature, as Real talked about in terms of male privileges. The tragedy is, this stunts the relational skills necessary for long-term romantic relationships and friendships. We gays are shut out from adulthood simply by not being able to marry. For most men, the prospect of getting married someday is a milestone that separates childhood from adulthood. In Jonathon Rauch's book *Gay Marriage: Why It Is Good for Gays, Good for Straights, and Good for America,* he states, "Marriage confers status: to be married, in the eyes of society, is to be grown up." Marriage, he goes on to say, "is the great domesticator, but so is the prospect of marriage. If you hope to get married, and if your friends and peers hope to get married, you will socialize and date more carefully...if you're a young man, you will reach for respectability. You will devote yourself to your work, try to build status, and earn money to make yourself marriageable (often true of women, too)."[9]

Rauch explains how getting married—or at least the prospect of marriage—prompts people to "settle down" not only in terms of making themselves a home and becoming more stable, productive, and mature, but also less self-obsessed, impatient, and anxious. In America, gay men and lesbians are shut out from any such possibility. Preventing us from legal marriage creates a cultural shadow that eclipses us; we won't be able to move forward in our relationships with each other.

The Shadow

"Not that there's anything wrong with that!"

This afterthought was repeated over and over in "The Outing" episode of *Seinfeld.* The reason it's become a catchphrase is because it's accurate. Shakespeare was expressing the same idea when he had Hamlet say, "Methinks the lady doth protest too much." When anyone says, "It's not because of—" we know their protest really means, "It is because of—"; so every time Seinfeld says that, he really means, "I'm not gay, and I do think there's something wrong with it"—at the same time satirizing those "closet bigots" who want to be seen as tolerant and open-minded, and so wear their tolerance on their sleeves. This is otherwise known as one's shadow.

The shadow in psychology is a Jungian concept. All of us—gay and straight—project onto others what we don't want to or can't address within ourselves. Jung looked at the shadow as being the "dark side" of one's self that has been repressed and/or suppressed.

Carl Gustav Jung (1875–1961) changed the way we think about the human psyche, or personality. He originated the concept of the shadow and coined now common terms like introvert and extrovert to describe people's dominant approach to the world. He used *persona* to describe the mask each of us wears to hide our private self from the world, and *individuation* for the process of integrating our unconscious vitality into our everyday lives and becoming fully conscious.

Jung used the term *shadow* to describe the side of the human psyche that is hidden from conscious awareness—sometimes deliberately. As he himself realized, he had to try to gain power over his fantasies; otherwise, he ran the risk of their gaining power over him.

Jung defined four archetypal energies or drives that inhabit everyone's unconscious: the Magician, Sovereign, Lover, and Warrior.

More recently, the shadow has been discussed by Robert Bly, author of Iron John and other books about men.[10] In *A Little Book on the Human Shadow,* Bly defines it as "the long bag we drag behind us."[11] In that bag go the aspects of our parents we don't like, desires to hurt them and our siblings, and parts of ourselves that our parents and caretakers found unacceptable. At school, we learn what is socially and culturally unacceptable—which also goes into that bag. Bly writes that we "spend our lives until we are twenty deciding what parts of ourselves to put into the bag, and we spend the rest of our lives trying to get them out again."

This baggage or dark side—our shadow—includes the parts of ourselves we don't want to claim because we believe them unacceptable to others and, therefore, unacceptable to ourselves. So we have rejected it, consciously or unconsciously.

The way to find your shadow is through projections. If you react strongly-either positively or negatively—to an aspect of someone else, then that's a trait of the shadow that lives within you. The rule of thumb is, "If you spot it, you got it!"

Debbie Ford writes about the shadow in the same way as Jung and Bly, adding, "If you are human, you have a shadow." In her wonderful book *The Dark Side of the Light Chasers,* Ford says that discovering your shadow is "not an intellectual process; it's a journey from the head to the heart."[12] It is about becoming whole, about reclaiming parts of your birthright that you've disowned.

What I like about her work is that her books and talks expand as well on the positive side of the shadow: when you see the good in others and idealize them, you're seeing your own best attributes in them. Ford says that over the years, the positives of who you are also go into that bag:

> When we admire someone, it is an opportunity to find yet another aspect of ourselves. We have to take back our positive projections as well as our negative projections. We have to remove the plugs we've attached to others, turn them

around, and plug them back into ourselves. Until we are able to retrieve our projections, it is impossible for us to see our full potential and experience the totality of who we really are.

Relationships—romantic, familial, friendship, or otherwise—bring about a more acute awareness of your own shadow. You must have strong attachments to people or to something about them to discover your shadow. The closer you are to the person, the more your shadow will surface. Or you can ask friends, family, and your partners about their perceptions of you. You will discover things about yourself that you're either not aware of or consciously knew but preferred to ignore.

Maintaining a shadow means suppressing parts of yourself that you don't want to face, things you want to say or do but that you have learned are unacceptable to others and even to yourself. But when you bury and suppress them, they are forced into the unconscious and get squeezed out sideways. You'll still do, say, or even think the very thing that you're trying to suppress, but it will come out disguised—even to you. (See chapter 7 for how suppressed impulses emerge in disguise, letting you work on the very issues you've tried to block out.)

Consider the following example. In Provincetown, Massachusetts, I bought a lamp in the shape of a male torso with a switch where you'd expect the penis to be, and took it to my office. I am in a more sex-positive and body-positive mode these days and am enjoying art with these overtones. That week, I was running a group therapy, and one member spoke up. He said he was angry I had brought the lamp into the room, because he knew I have straight clients and was concerned the lamp would feed "heterosexuals' perspective that gay culture is all about sex."

On further investigation, we discovered that this client had spent his life trying "not to fuel stereotypes," to the point of diminishing his own sexuality. He is out to his friends, family, and at work, but is not as affectionate around his partner as he would like to be. He minimizes talking about his life at work and with nongay friends so as not to "overwhelm them." He began to get emotional about this, and as a group, we helped him track this back to the family in which he grew up. Their messages of "Don't be different" and "Don't stand out" were now leaking out into the rest of his life.

It's important to remember that just because you spot the shadow doesn't always mean that you have it yourself. The trait may belong to someone in your childhood or from a past relationship. If someone's trait had a strong negative or positive impact, or if it speaks to your character or personality, you might be trying to claim it as your own. That trait could be from another person and not something you adopted at all. And your reaction is meant for that other person and not for something that is about you or your personality.

And be prepared! Once you resolve one shadow, another one comes up. Just like coming out, illuminating your shadows is a lifetime of work. When you have spent so much of your life suppressing material, the unfamiliar task of bringing it forth takes consciousness, maturity, and work. Also, just as American culture does not support your gay orientation, neither does it encourage living openly and honestly. It supports living in shadow and offers everyone privileges for suppressing the essence of who they really are.

Again, just because you recognize your shadow and work on it doesn't mean it won't emerge again in some other disguised way. But the more you recognize your own projections, the better your life will become, directing you, not diverting you, on your journey toward wholeness. As a gay man, your job is to move out of the shadows and claim your mature masculinity. There's a lot of darkness about being male, and plenty of ways to uncover it. Shadow work is one of them.

Of course, life itself can throw help your way. For example, until I was in the fifth grade, the kids used to tease me by singing a line from the Beatles' song "Get Back": "JoJo was a man who thought he was a woman, but he was a friend of mine." The more I cried, the more they'd tease me. Even my cousins would tease me by playing the song on the turntable. Eventually, to stop them, I broke their record. (As I learned later in life, the actual but commonly mistaken lyrics are: "JoJo was a man who thought he was a loner.") Nevertheless, it hurt to hear kids sing that to me over and over.

Throughout my life, I could easily tap into this extremely hurtful memory and feel the pain afresh. I avoided even thinking about it. Then when Jacob, my first nephew, began to speak, he had a stuttering problem. I'd planned for him to call me Uncle Joey—a nickname still used by people who've known me from childhood. But he couldn't say my name without stuttering and calling me "JoJo." That name again! Only now, it came from an honest, loving attempt to say my name.

He overcame his stuttering three months later, but my three nephews call me JoJo to this day. I love it and no longer have any negative attachment to that name. I am healed! But you can't guarantee that life will offer these corrective experiences. If they don't occur, then we're doomed to suffer through—or repress—the original hurt. This is where shadow work can be so helpful.

Archetypal Integrity

Aside from rites of passage like underground sexual behavior, which aren't healthy or in our best interests, I have learned some ways to help you move into your mature gay masculinity that will help you in relationships—whether romantic ones you're already in, your dating trial runs, or nonsexual relationships with family, friends, and coworkers.

Carol S. Pearson, president of the Center for Archetypal Studies and Applications (CASA) and author of *The Hero Within* writes,

> In today's fast-paced world, no matter how successful we might be, we sometimes may feel "at sea." Like sailors navigating stormy waters, individuals, groups, and organizations need some means to orient themselves—the equivalent of the north star, a compass, or radar. Otherwise, how will they find their way home? ("Casa" is the Spanish word for "home.") Archetypes are patterns natural to the human mind and heart that orient us and help us know what to do and where to go. Understanding them also can warn us of

dangers and help us avoid pitfalls.[13]

Understanding archetypes can enable individuals and organizations to find—or create—their own Promised Lands: those places where they can thrive by being fully who and what they are meant to be.

Archetypal discussions are valuable because they remove us from our conventional ways of thinking—away from logic and what normally makes sense or doesn't—giving us a new language and fresh way of looking at things. In large part, this is what psychotherapy is all about: helping people to think differently so that they can achieve paradigm shifts and awakenings they couldn't achieve by themselves in everyday life. Archetypal discussions can also move us into exploring our emotions in addition to our intellectual understanding.

In other words, when we grow accustomed to the same things over and over, our minds go to sleep. If we can hear and express things in different ways, then we open ourselves to new possibilities, positive changes, and growth.

In *King, Warrior, Magician and Lover: Rediscovering the Archetypes of the Mature Masculine,* Robert Moore and Douglas Gillette discuss the male archetypes that can help any gay man not only find the kind of man you want to be with, and but how best to live your life generally—even if you don't enter into a relationship.[14]

With our culture celebrating and rewarding so much immature masculinity in both gay and straight men, these four archetypes are excellent doorways into mature masculinity. The lack of responsibility, accountability, and integrity in so many men results, ironically, from the patriarchal ideal that allows men to be insensitive and hurt others.

Of course, these four archetypes have significant meaning for us gay men too, and have important implications for psychological health. They dispense with terminology associated with pathology, honoring us instead by granting us entrance into the male fraternity as men among men. These archetypes separate the boys from the men. As boys, we're told what our lives will be like by those who raise us. But as men, we must take control of our own lives and decide what works for us—and what doesn't.

Your King helps you attain what you want, individually and in relationships. Your Lover expresses your sexuality, emotions, and passion. Your Magician directs rational thinking toward making effective decisions. And your Warrior lets you put your visions, passions, and plans into action—with clear boundaries and intentionality.

The King

This archetype is the sovereign part of yourself that rules your life—the visionary, goal—oriented part of you that plans five years ahead and writes a living will. It holds a clear (though not necessarily a nourishing or accurate) picture of how you want your relationships (and thus, your life) to turn out in the long term. According to Moore and Gillette,

> The King archetype in its fullness possesses the qualities of order, of reasonable and rational patterning, of integration and integrity in the masculine psyche. It stabilizes chaotic emotion and out-of-control behaviors. It gives stability and centeredness. It brings calm...maintenance and balance. It defends our own sense of inner order, our own integrity of being and of purpose, our own central calmness and certainty in our masculine identity...with a firm but kindly eye. It sees others in all their weakness and in all their talent and worth...guides them and nurtures them toward their own fullness of being. It is not envious, because it is secure, as the King, in its own worth.

This part of you lets you honor yourself and others, helps you feel grateful looking back on your life as a whole, and forward toward your future goals. We have to appreciate what we have before we can appreciate getting what we want. Gay men have absorbed the King but mostly express him through sexual activity. They tend to have a sexual vision of what they want in a partner before they have a relational vision. (I once read somewhere, "We quickly talk about our favored sex position before reading the wine list, and just in case this guy we are with does not work out, we make meaningful eye contact with the waiter—just in case!" When I quote this at my talks and workshops, gay men laugh knowingly.)

Each time I give a talk, I emphasize how sexualized our culture is. Being gay and male is about being rewarded for our sexual prowess as men. It's about a culture that doesn't place boundaries around sexual expression in terms of time and place. Gay male culture does, however, have a good understanding of boundaries in the sexual realm. The S&M community, the bear community, and others are very intentional, safe (by having agreed-upon rules between consenting partners), and appropriate in expressing their sexuality.

Lesbians express their King (or Crone) energy more through both activism and relationships. We gay men can learn from lesbians how to create greater balance in our lives, with less emphasis on sex.

In this, gay men have predominately the same dilemma and goals as straight men—namely, needing to attain mature masculinity. Unlike heterosexual men, though, we don't have women to help balance our relational selves. Generally, women focus on their vision of a family and raising children. We men are starting to do more of this, forming families of our own, and inviting our gay Kings to become good husbands and fathers.

The Shadow King

But so far, among gay men, I see mostly the King's shadow side, which seeks to become the Family Hero—a role developed in childhood in one's family of origin. The Family Hero can also be the Little Parent and the Caretaker. We carry the vision for the family as a whole. As little boys, we unconsciously take on these roles to cover up our gayness and show our families that we're of value. Gay boys often become high achievers, seeking approval by following the rules, often described as the family's good child or, as in the title of Andrew Tobias's memoir, *The Best Little Boy in the World.*[15]

We can become overresponsible, bringing these characteristics into adulthood and relationships. I also see many gay men who are *codependent*—that is, enabling their partner's addictions, character flaws, legal hassles, and other problems that weren't theirs to start with. Codependency is a pattern of subordinating your own personal needs to someone else's. Again, this is a way of covering one's own diminished sense of value.

Doug came to me depressed, not knowing how to get out of it, because his life wasn't going in the direction he had dreamed it would. Openly gay, he had been with Lee, his boyfriend, for ten years. Crying, he said that during their relationship, Lee had had two affairs. They had separated, but now Lee wanted to get back together with him. Doug described himself as more of the giver in their relationship, thinking of ways to be romantic and take time to do things together as a couple. Lee, though, was more interested in his work and going out drinking. Doug would often join Lee at the bar, but feel left out when Lee focused more on socializing with his friends than on him. He often complained about this, and Lee would try to bring Doug into their conversations—but still Lee's friends would focus on Lee.

Doug was successful in his own right, owning an ad agency that was growing in employees and billings. But he didn't like to talk about it much, even to me, out of concern that others would think he was showing off. He owned nice cars, clothes, jewelry and a house, but didn't feel very proud of himself.

He described himself as the type whose many friends came to him for guidance and help. When I asked if he ever asked for help in return, he said no. Even though he felt used and taken advantage of, he felt it was the right thing to "be there" for his friends and employees. He had no one to talk to about his partner's affair that had caused the breakup, so turned to therapy and came to me.

Doug's parents were alcoholics. His mother worked outside the home and gave all her kids chores to do around the house. As the oldest, Doug was in charge. He made sure everything was going smoothly when his mother came home, changed, poured herself a drink and sat down. While Doug prepared dinner, she came into the kitchen to inspect, letting him and his siblings bring everything to the table and clean up afterward.

That was the extent of his relationship with his mother. So as a boy, Doug learned to be the Little Parent, doing the things in the home that his mother and father should be doing. Neither his mother nor his father paid him much attention or looked after him. So Doug coped by depending on others' wants and how they judged him; it made sense that he'd partner with a man who didn't either, since Doug had a high tolerance for being treated this way. To be noticed, he developed into the Hero and Caretaker. Through therapy, however, he realized that he had done things not for himself, but for others—what he could be for them—just as he had during his childhood.

Socially, he was playing out exactly what was done to him in terms of feeling lost and left out. When he tried to talk to Lee about his affairs, Lee grew angry. Doug would fall silent and find himself tiptoeing around Lee so as not to upset him. This didn't work, and they eventually chose to separate. But Doug was miserable, since he wanted a relationship with Lee. Moreover, Lee still loved Doug and wanted things to work out, but didn't know how to convince him that he wanted to make amends and move past what had happened. Doug, for his part, didn't know how to ask for what he wanted, nor how to get past it himself.

Doug's inner King had become passive—a shadow King—blessing others and never being blessed himself. He was never taught how to take better care of himself, having projected his King onto others. About the passive shadow King, Moore and Gillette write that

> The so-called dependent personality disorder [is] a condition in which we project the King energy…(which we do not experience as within us) onto some external person. We experience ourselves as…incapable of action, incapable of feeling calm and stable, without the presence and the loving attention of that other person who [carries] our King energy projection.

Doug had done this, putting Lee in charge of how their relationship went. He had made Lee so powerful that learning about the affair was devastating, and their ultimate separation caused his psychological collapse.

Our work, then, was about helping him find his inner King. What was Doug's vision? How did he want his relationship to go, and how did he see himself in relation to Lee or anyone else? Why not take pride in his accomplishments and not hide them?

Mutual Relationship Vision

One basic teaching of Imago Relationship Therapy is that every couple should have a mutual vision of their relationship. Most couples don't have one, and if they do, they've adopted the desires of outside forces—what's valued by their families, cultures, or society. Both partners should create their own individual visions of their relationship, and combine them into one vision they can agree on. Only then can the relationship move in the right direction for both partners. In other words, couples have to access both their individual inner Kings and create a mutual relationship King that they work on together.

Doug's work became about accessing his inner King. Rather than turning it over to Lee, he reclaimed it for himself. This was very hard for Doug, but he had the right to get what he wanted out of life. He told Lee that if he really wanted to repair the damage he'd done to their relationship, Lee would have to come to couples counseling, or their relationship really was over. To stay true to what was best for him, he had to risk losing Lee for good.

Fortunately, Lee was receptive, and they attended my couple's workshop and started couples therapy. Lee stated he'd always wanted Doug to be more vocal in their relationship, firmer about what he wanted. For his part, Lee began to understand his childhood and how, by having the affair, he was reenacting things that were part of his upbringing in how he related to Doug.

While this was a successful ending, many are not. Doug could have easily lost Lee. But to stay true to his inner King and bolster his self-esteem and relational skills, it would have been worth it to have suffered loss.

To heal the shadow King requires that you receive blessings from yourself and others. Look at your own life and envision what you want it to become. Otherwise, you'll keep overvaluing others, subordinating your vision to theirs, and betraying yourself and partners on a regular basis. For anyone in the shadow King, letting yourself be supported and asking for help are big steps. Yet someone can go too far in blessing himself and becoming orthodox or rigid about his King energy.

My clients come into therapy with ideas of what they want and what they don't. Often, I have to teach them that their most desired goals are not always 100 percent attainable, but working toward them can be rewarding along the way. So when they say, "I want a partner, but he should be (fill in the blank)," I tell them to be open-minded and flexible along their journey to find their Mr. Right.

You may not be willing to stray from your required criteria for who Mr. Right should be. If you focus on your ideals too much, picking only those men who match them, you may well meet the man of your dreams—but then, pass right by him.

Boy Meets Goy?

In Yiddish, the word goy means non-Jewish. Gary, one of my Warrior brothers with whom I went to grade school, says he finds himself mostly looking for "Mr. Right-stein" and often overlooks Mr. Right. In my practice, in workshops, and among my personal friends I see so many guys with rigid, closed visions of what they want in their relationships. Their King is inflexible. Often, men say they like a certain type—and anyone who strays from that turns them off. This is the King's dark side or shadow. The idea that you should connect with only the type you're looking for sabotages and limits the number of available men out there who would make a great partner for you. I've counseled couples who admit—usually in front of each other—that they're not each other's types. Each is much of what the other wanted, and they understand that any type is idealistic, more of fantasy—yet they're able to move it into that realm and happily accept what they have found.

The truth is, most people never get *all* of what they want in any relationship. You have to make a list of what you want, access your inner King, and prepare alternative lists of what you can and can't live with—and without. Consider whether you're a "rice queen" (attracted only to Asians), a "size queen" (only to men with larger endowment), looking for only straight-acting males (butch and masculine men), or even only Bears or Arabic men. Make sure you're not sabotaging your efforts to find real love. Suffering gay men come into my office, say they are looking for a partner and complain of not having a relationship; then we discover their preference has become an insistence that's standing in the way. There may even be a secret logic to why you are drawn to certain types of partners, which we will address in the sexual shadow chapter.

If someone persistently pushes for some goal, strongly tied to his opinion and outcome in an overreactive way, likely it's something he's not ready for or doesn't really want. Some clients tell me how much they want a relationship; how they have to find the right partner-and inevitably end up sabotaging their relationships over and over, so that they do not keep Mr. Right. In other words, they're not ready for what's involved in relationship, or perhaps they really don't want one. Our culture has seduced them to think that being partnered is the better way—and perhaps the only way—to live. They cannot admit, even to themselves, that it is not time for them or that they may not want one at all. This will be explored more fully in chapter 10.

The Lover

The Lover embodies emotion, sexuality, the erotic, passion, and romance, helping you feel and express your heartfelt emotions—and others'. It is your creative aspect. The downside is infatuation and love addiction: being in love with love, an endorphin junkie. Without a fully developed Lover, you'll choose men who you wouldn't date otherwise. You won't realize that you've chosen Mr. Wrong until you are far along in the relationship—either dating or committed.

Moore and Gillette state that the terms *Eros,* lover energy, and *libido* are "not just about sexual appetites but a general appetite for life." They say that the lover's drive is to satisfy the "primal hungers...sex, food, well-being, reproduction, creative adaptation to life's hardships and ultimately a sense of meaning, without which human beings cannot go on with their lives." Our spirituality resides in the realm of the Lover, where you access your Higher Power.

Religious Abuse

The Lover energy can become a source of pain for gay men. As a young child or adolescent struggling with your romantic and sexual orientation, it is religious abuse to be sitting in church or synagogue and hear a clergyman telling the congregation that you are an abomination. What religion is to African Americans, therapy is to gays and lesbians. In other words, African Americans were able to turn to spirituality for solace and safety, validation and support; but gays and lesbian couldn't because of the negative, critical, intolerant stance that has characterized most organized religions.

This is where we gay men receive our deepest wound. From infancy, we're taught to keep our homosexual and homoerotic selves buried in rubble that gets taller with time, only to fall like an avalanche and bury the core of our sexuality, sexual aliveness, creativity, and spirituality. We are taught to be hypervigilant about our surroundings, to block our Lover energy and create a false self.

The Shadow Lover

While we're growing up, the Lover's shadow becomes the family's Lost Child, the introvert who remains quiet and thoughtful, keeping his emotions to himself so as to keep the family peace. Outwardly, he is shy and attaches to things, not people. An adult's Shadow Lover keeps the peace in relationships by going along and not speaking up for himself—or even knowing himself well enough to speak up in the first place.

In chapter 7, I'll explore how to understand, manage, and live your sexual Lover energy as best you can. Here, I want to explore what happens when you shut it down and bury it. This can block your connection to others. Erectile problems that are not physical, for example, often result from a Shadowed Lover archetype. The individual is cut off from his emotions and can't identify his own feelings. This is the client who tells me about horrific situations in his life with a smile on his face. It's a way of blocking emotional pain, but the price paid for this blockage can be very high.

Mike was a forty-eight-year-old engineer with one of the automotive companies. He was in a twenty-year relationship with Sam, whom he said he "loved" but was "never in love with." He came to me because several years ago, he and Sam decided to have an open sexual relationship. They had tried to be sexual with one another—unsuccessfully. After not being sexual with each other for at least five years, they felt they loved each other enough to maintain the relationship, and thought that opening it up would help meet their sexual needs.

Mike spoke in a monotone and with no emotion. In our sessions, he would report his pain, but not relive it or experience it. In an almost disembodied voice, he told me he was no longer able to feel sexual with his partner, and hadn't for years. Also, he no longer felt emotionally or relationally connected to him—or, for that matter, to anyone else. He had thought that becoming nonmonogamous within his relationship might reignite his sexual and romantic feelings for his partner.

For Mike, however, nonmonogamy brought him to other realizations. He described himself as a stable, loyal guy who enjoyed life with his partner. Externally, they had a nice life together. They had a big home, took vacations in all the right places, attended all the right gay events and even thought about adopting children. But since opening their relationship, he began meeting men to whom he felt sexually attracted—and realized that from the very beginning he had been only somewhat attracted to Sam. He had attributed that attraction to the novelty of being with Sam, since it wore off after eight months together. During the last year of their sexual openness, he had fallen in love with a different man in a way he had never done so before. This worried him, as he began to realize that his sexual relationship with Sam hadn't been there to begin with.

Although he loved his partner, Mike told me that he was not and never was "in love" with Sam. On reflection, during therapy he realized that he had led life with his head, not his heart. He strived for his planned vision, achieved it, and repressed his heart and emotions. He thought he was happy. In short, he didn't feel passionate about much of anything in life—and attributed that to his "engineer mind and personality." But as his past unfolded in therapy, it became apparent his undemonstrative parents had discouraged him and his sister from feeling emotions. Instead, they encouraged and rewarded setting goals and looking to the future. They loved him, Mike knew. But if he expressed any negative or emotional feelings, his parents would get upset and send him to his room. If Mike brought home grades less than A's and B's, or if he didn't win school elections, his father would tell him, "What a disappointment you are!" He spoke contemptuously to Mike and shamed him for not making "the right decisions." His mother would tell him and his sister, "Keep your negative thoughts to yourselves or tell me, but keep them from Father." If things didn't go well in school, again she warned them to not tell him. So they didn't, and Mike learned to keep his emotions at bay.

Their eye was always on the end result, not the process or journey of getting there. Mike's whole family buried their Lover energy and so became Magicians and Kings. Mike never told his father that he was gay. It was a Don't ask, don't tell situation—again, not to provoke his father's disappointment in him. Mike would bring his partner around, and everyone understood they were together. But actually saying aloud, "I'm gay, and Sam is my partner" was even more than Mike could bear.

He and his sister were consistently rewarded for keeping their feelings inside, so Mike entered his relationship using only his Magician and King archetypes. Quite unconsciously, that little boy whose father told him, "You're very disappointing" decided to avoid disappointments of his own by never opening his heart. He entered relationships with his intellect leading the way. In his effort to make the right reasonable choices always, he buried his emotions. Yes, he loved his partner; the only problem was, he wasn't in love with him.

During their five years of sexual openness, Mike tried gay bathhouses, group sex, and kinky role-playing such as master/slave. Since he was more of a top, he even experimented with being a bottom. Each new experiment would bring him into my office excited and emotionally charged about discovering different parts of the Lover aspect of himself, which he had never explored or experimented with while growing up, since his family ruled it out.

During the last year, he had a sexual encounter with a man that turned into a romantic affair—not part of the open relationship that he and Sam agreed on. This man had captured Mike's Lover energy. He did realize this would hurt his partner deeply and that he himself might get hurt. But he had to go into his heart and let his emotions express themselves. Now Mike was really in a bind. He found himself not wanting to disappoint his father or his partner. But he knew that doing what he wanted—to leave Sam to pursue his newfound Lover energy—would mean facing the very thing he had spent his whole life avoiding: disappointing significant men in his life. Until now, he had always chosen to disappoint himself before disappointing another. (In chapter 8, I talk further about the struggle to keep a balance between getting validation from yourself versus validation from others with the King energy.)

Sam was very much part of Mike's family and was even close to his father, who enjoyed Sam's business acumen and logical, commonsense thinking. Here it came again: Mike disappointing his father by ending a relationship with someone his father truly liked.

Mike's difficulty in stepping into his Lover energy is exactly what brought him to therapy. He had strong King and Magician energies, but needed therapy to help strengthen his Lover and Warrior, which both ruled his life—but in an unbalanced way. He was never taught how to use his Lover energy. Mike really embraced this new archetypal terminology, since it gave him a new perspective on how to look at his life. And he was much happier once he began to move into his Lover energy.

The idea here is not to have you change your nature as a gay man. That won't necessarily happen. But by examining your archetypes, you'll discover which is missing and out of balance and can move toward greater alignment.

Mike's next step was to confront his father, which he wasn't prepared to do. He left therapy secure with his Lover archetype and decided to leave his twenty-year relationship and forge a new one with his newfound man. I urged him to deal with his father dynamics, inasmuch as I predicted they would surface in his new relationship. But Mike was not ready, and I honored his decision not to. More about confronting the Father Within in chapter 4.

What happens when you let your Lover lead the way without consulting your other three archetypes? You'll pick the wrong partners. You won't be able to choose those who are your best matches.

You'll lead with your heart only, without your intellect guiding you to ensure that the guy is safe and can be available to you in healthy ways. Joe is a good example.

He was thirty years old and engaged to be married to his child-hood sweetheart. He'd spent the last ten years working on his medical degree and was just beginning his career as a physician. During his residency he met Don, an emergency room nurse. They hit it off, and Joe found himself sexually attracted. "It's the best sex I have ever had in my whole life," Joe told me. After two weeks with Don, he felt he was in love.

Joe had realized he was gay a while back, but thought that he had to repress it and would never find the love of his life. He loved his fiancée, but he knew he wasn't in love with her as he should be, but wanted to make it work. Now, after meeting Don, he knew the difference and wanted to pursue that part of himself. He told his fiancée he was gay and ended their relationship and engagement.

I educated Joe on the coming-out process, warning him that the high level of passion and sexual desire might likely be more of a stage of coming out and to avoid making major decisions at that time. He listened to me, and did not make any major decisions. Six months later, he still felt the same way for Don.

I also told him about romantic love and how the first six to eighteen months of a relationship is usually nothing more than romantic love, and also is a stage that is very compelling and feels very real. It often can turn into something long term and everlasting, but it takes more time to get to know the person. This time Joe didn't listen to me and decided to move in with Don and set up house.

After one year together, Joe started noticing things about Don that he didn't like and started comparing Don to his former fiancée. This could be part of the second stage of any relationship: the power struggle. Joe tried everything he could to make the relationship work; Don was cooperative and willing to go through the steps to fix their problems. Ultimately, however, Joe realized that he really had acted too quickly, and while he still felt wildly attracted to Don, sexual attraction was all it was.

One of the Lover's other shadows is addiction, which tend to land on those who suppress their feelings and authentic selves. It basically tells them, "Hey, I can help you not feel pain or anything at all and bury that pesky core self of yours." Thus the Lover archetype's inherent risk of being hurt can be masked by any variety of addictions, including love addiction, compulsive use of recreational drugs, excessive exercising to the point of using steroids, gambling, shopping, workaholism, compulsive cruising, and compulsive dating. Sexual addiction is not limited to the gay community, of course, but as our culture's sexual shadow, it needs to be addressed as a wound, if not the largest wound, we gays have suffered individually and collectively in our Lover archetype.

Because this core self gets repressed, people engage in addictive behavior to "colorize life"—as a reminder that they're alive and well. The unconscious is knocking on the door of their psyche, saying, "Notice me! I'm in here and I want out!" But their conscious mind is ignoring the call.

The Warrior

This is your doer, go-getter aspect. Craving action, it achieves the outward (not necessarily the most nurturing) things you want. It sets boundaries and is clear. Cliff Barry of Shadow Work Seminars states, "The Warrior loves action, sometimes for the sake of action....[It's even] willing to kill what needs to die in order to make room for something new to be born."[16] For gay men this means killing off our own internalized heterosexism and homophobia. It takes a true Warrior to come out in a society that insists, "Stay in the closet!" let alone a military that admonishes, "Don't ask, don't tell!"

Moore and Gillette describe this archetype as helping you be mindful, alert, discerning, clear in thought, and knowing how to focus on your mind and body. The Warrior is about decisive action and understands that hesitating to go forward can lead to doubt. The Warrior has a positive mental attitude, courage, and self-discipline. It doesn't react, but acts intentionally.

QTIP (Quit Taking It Personally)

When you are out there dating and even in a long-term committed relationship, you need to put up your shields and not take things so deeply to heart. Make sure your inner Warrior is strong and active. The QTIP concept understands that if a guy is not interested in you, even after some time dating him, it's less about you and more about him and what he's looking for. I know this is hard to remember, particularly when you're dating—which can be rejecting, judgmental, detached, and illusionary. As you bond and deepen a relationship and enter the power struggle (about which more in chapter 3), you'll feel as if your partner's actions are all about you. But they're not; they're about him. If it helps to keep your shield up, consider keeping a cotton swab (brand name or not!) in your pocket to remind yourself that what your partner is doing is not about you.

It is very important not to take things personally in relationships, because if you do, fighting escalates and people say and do things they don't mean to—which usually takes them off course from the actual argument.

The Shadow Warrior

Another dark side of the Warrior becomes sadistic and masochistic (not necessarily in sexual terms), where there is a disconnection from human relationships. Your Shadow Warrior can be mean and hurtful to others—or allow them to be mean and hurtful to you. It can leave you feeling unattached to anyone, even yourself. Moore and Gillette describe this shadow archetype as "angry" and "frightened" and that the one repressing this can become "hateful of the 'weak', of the helpless and vulnerable." The truth is, we all have parts of this in ourselves, but when it interferes with our lives, we need to take notice.

In *Gay Warrior*, F. Jim Fickey and Gary S. Grimm write about the "oppressor," who resembles the Shadow Warrior in that he has "forgotten about his early wounding and specifically how he was hurt by others, has become one of those people who now oppresses others. Gay men who have not found a recovery process through which to heal their early wounding, will often become as severe an oppressor as those who once oppressed them." I completely agree. Gay men, formerly bullied as boys, have now adopted those bullies as role models and perpetrate abuse on one another.

During childhood, the Shadow Warrior creates the family scapegoat—usually the boy who is angry, rebellious, defiant, breaks rules, and lands in all kinds of trouble. In an alcoholic and dysfunctional family, he draws attention away from the adults' problems and focuses it on his own bad behavior. The same dynamic can survive into adulthood.

Among my gay clients, I see a lot of Shadow Warriors. Examples are men who are:

1. Fully engaged in the drug scene, and medicating their anger by anesthetizing and numbing themselves;

2. "In your face" about being gay, in negative ways that don't serve the gay man himself or the gay community;

3. Harboring unresolved hostility and anger for all straight people, not just those who are heterosexist;

4. Overemphasizing getting big and muscular, not so much to be fit as to "work out their anger" and look more like a "bully";

5. Competing with other gay men in superficial ways, such as showing off a tight, buff physique, a bigger dick, ripped abs, a snazzy car, and glamorous career—to name a few.

Josh came to me after his romantic relationship from college didn't work out and he was humiliated at having to move back home from New York. Extremely attractive, lean, and muscular, he kept his jet-black hair cropped short on the sides and spiked at the top for a contemporary look. Boyish and very charming, he seemed even younger than his twenty-three years. Josh and his former partner of the same age had been college sweethearts at a Michigan university. They'd visited New York together, where they received a lot of attention. Following his partner's graduation, they decided to live there, where Josh would finish college. But he couldn't make it in New

York, since he couldn't find part-time work. And after his former partner landed a high-end modeling career, he tossed Josh out.

Living back home with his parents, Josh was feeling depressed, isolated, and lonely, which is what brought him to me initially. Each week when he came to see me, he talked and wept about leaving New York and wanting to make a life there as a model. But he was always respectful toward me and appreciative of our work together.

Then one time he came into my office hungover, looking disheveled and not dressed in his usual fashionable way. He told me he had gone to a "Tina" party where gay guys were doing all kinds of drugs, but primarily crystal meth. He told me he'd done crystal from time to time in college and in New York and recently had found some local gay men who did it, along with Ecstasy, Special K, and cocaine, among other drugs.

When I expressed concern, Josh became defensive and said that primarily he sold crystal to earn money. He'd begun selling drugs in New York and back home had found the drug crowd at a local bar. Within weeks, he became the top seller and made a lot of money. "I know what I'm doing," he told me, "and how to sell this shit." This was a side of him I hadn't seen during our first six months of work.

I talked to him about integrity, in terms of selling drugs to gay men who mostly abuse them. I also talked about the legal ramifications of this activity. None of this mattered to him, he explained. He thought that drugs were all a matter of control, and if these men didn't have control that was their problem, not his. He went on to complain that Detroit was an awful place to live—a "pit," he called it.

In working with Josh over time, I noticed a change in his appearance and commented on how increasingly muscular he was getting, and how quickly. He was working out five times a week and, he admitted, taking steroids. "They accelerate the rate of getting bigger, and I want that." He talked about how "flabby" men and older men—"trolls" as he called them—would stare and goggle at him as he worked out. He talked about the size of other men's penises in derogatory ways and flattered himself that down there he was "perfect."

When he began negatively commenting on my body and the way

I dressed, I gave him feedback on how that made me feel, so that he could gain firsthand insight into the impact he must be having on others. I also asked how he wanted me to feel; that it seemed to me he was in a "one-upmanship" mode. I wanted him to realize that his personality was changing, that he'd lost touch with his feelings toward himself. He would hear none of it and became increasingly critical of me. He talked about the gay "common people" who had no higher aspirations in life, let their bodies go, and made little money.

From selling drugs, Josh eventually accumulated enough money to move back to New York, resume his search to become a model and live the glamorous life he dreamed of. There was nothing wrong with his desire to be a model and make a lot of money. Sadly, after he left therapy and moved, I never heard from him again. I still wonder how he is doing and if he's yet emerged from his Shadow Warrior.

In many ways, I find Josh's mentality common in the gay community. The mind-set is to look the best, be in great shape, put down other gay men in contemptuous ways, harshly judge their sexual behavior, relationships, genital sizes, and so on. In *I Don't Want to Talk About It*, Terrence Real writes about male privilege being in the "better than" position, compared to others. He states, "Relational impoverishment creates the insecure base for the feelings of shame, worthlessness, emptiness that haunt many men . . ."

This is the very problem that interferes with gay men's relationships with ourselves and others. We are cut off from relating to others both by being male and being gay. The wounds are severe and until we examine them and recover from them, we won't be able to find Mr. Right on the outside or the inside.

I see so much attitude at gay clubs, on gay cruises, and other places where gay men gather. How are we going to mingle and mix and find Mr. Right if we can't even relate to one another and feel we must compete in even the simplest social situations?

Real also writes about men learning to be warriors by adopting a tough image: "toughness requires...the capacity to separate from one's own experience: to ignore fear and pain, in the service of doing what needs to be done, despite severe hardships. Boys' initiations culminate the toughening process that begins early in childhood. They frequently mock and shame the boy."

Isn't this what we gay men are doing to one another? It was done to us first as boys (see chapter 1), and now we are rewounding each other. Even in West Hollywood, New York, and San Francisco, gay men are still lonely because of the attitude. Their Shadow Warrior— whose main purpose is to distance feelings and connectedness— keeps these men in false arrogance and grandiosity.

The Magician

The Magician is your thinking, intellectual component, the part that uses common sense. It can be helpful, if used for good (other men's as well as your own), since it has insight and awareness. The Magician helps you reason and not overreact. Your overreaction to anything generally arises not from the immediate person or event that you think is the source but rather from someone else from another time and place. Relationships largely depend on using your Magician; by ignoring him, you'll find yourself in a scary defensive place in relation to others.

Moore and Gillette say that the Magician, "along with the observing ego, keeps us insulated from the overwhelming power of the other archetypes." So I often tell my clients to rely on their Magician to examine logically what's going on before they act on their feelings.

When a child plays the role of Magician in dysfunctional ways, he becomes what ACOA (Adult Children of Alcoholics) refers to as the Mascot—the hyperactive clown of the family, the trickster or comedian who does cute things. He is constantly in his head, thinking up ways he can entertain family members so as to distract them, moving their focus off their problems and restoring a temporary peace.

When this archetype is in shadow as an adult, it can cause great damage to oneself and others. The bipolar aspect of this is either being on a power trip by manipulating others, or else endlessly repeating "I don't know" and "I'm confused." I see more of the latter type in therapy.

Matthew came to see me after watching a movie about childhood abuse. He had inkling that he might have been abused and that things in his family weren't as good as he had assumed, but he couldn't put his finger on the actual problem. He just knew he was depressed and not experiencing any joy in his life. He had come out about three years earlier and last year met his current partner, who he wasn't sure was the right guy for him.

In fact, Matthew wasn't sure about much in his life. He reported being out of touch with his feelings, his thoughts (he claimed that he never knew whether he was being genuine and honest), and his own sexuality. Matthew's intuitiveness was entirely blocked, with his Magician in a dark shadow.

Matthew told me he was one of four children raised in an alcoholic home, where his father drank and his parents fought constantly. Matthew would hide in his room and listen to windows breaking and furniture being thrown. He feared that eventually his father would come to his room and bring him into the conflict. This never happened, but Matthew was traumatized by hearing his mother's screams and his father's anger echoing through the house. When they were finished, Matthew would wait a while, then go downstairs to find the living room in shambles and his mother asking him, "What would you like for dinner?" as if nothing had just occurred. Other times, he would come home from school and see bloodstains and furniture strewn about the house, and his parents would never talk about it. If he or his sibling tried to talk about it, either parent would discourage them and change the subject.

When Matthew was ten years old, his parents divorced. His father remarried and adopted his new wife's children, demanding that Matthew refer to his stepsiblings as his real brothers and sisters and call his stepmother "Mom." If Matthew pointed out anything his mother, father, or stepmother said that contradicted their behavior, they would shame him by saying he was "bad" for questioning them. Matthew's father, trying to get him to take sides, talked disparagingly about Matthew's mother; and his mother would do the same with regard to her ex-husband.

To keep the peace, Matthew learned to just agree with each of his parents. His mother would ask Matthew to tell his father he was a jerk, and his father would also use him to send his mother negative messages. This went on throughout the rest of his childhood, even after their divorce.

Early on, he learned to question his thoughts and feelings and to fool himself into thinking that things were not as they were. Growing up, children adapt constantly, making unconscious decisions on what to do to survive difficult situations. If they're raised in a healthy, functional home, these adaptations will be helpful when they go out into the world. In dysfunctional homes, the adaptive coping mechanisms serve to help the child only while the dysfunction lasts. After the child grows up and enters adulthood, the adaptation is usually maladaptive and does not apply to the person's current life situation. Yet the person continues to use this maladaptive coping pattern regardless.

This precisely describes Matthew. Throughout his childhood, he needed to remain confused and keep telling himself "I don't know" to ensure that he would never have to judge his parents as bad. Children will protect their parents at all costs, because the parents are in charge. Were a boy to perceive something wrong with his parent, he would know that his home wasn't safe and his life not secure. So Matthew adapted by declaring himself wrong and entering the state of confusion where he remained into adulthood.

Matthew's work in therapy lasted several years. Much of that time he spent in not trusting his own interests, motives, or agendas. He also felt mistrustful of me, and the government in particular. As long as Matthew never took a stand, he felt safe because no one could accuse him of being on one side or the other.

In group therapy, I urge members to voice their judgments. It gives them the opportunity to glimpse their shadows—of both the man in judgment and the man or men they're judging. One day, an irritated group member confronted Matthew and said he was like a "two-bit politician" for not taking a stand on anything. Matthew was insulted and enraged. "How dare you call me that?" The other man said, "I'm tired of hearing you be on the fence all the time on every issue." He had grown fond of Matthew, but called him on his

Magician Shadow.

Matthew stayed angry for two months and even considered leaving group because of this comment. I asked him what kind of man would behave like a two-bit politician? I asked him to take the accusation off himself for a moment and imagine that trait in someone else. Matthew was able to say quite a bit about that someone else—a man who never took a stand, who wasn't responsible or accountable, someone you couldn't trust. Immediately, he became aware that his family was like that. He had tried to talk to them about things that happened during his childhood as well as his father's alcoholism. His family blamed him for "bringing up things from the past" and told him not to do it again.

Matthew entered a new awareness about himself. He had been in therapy long enough to know that his reaction to being labeled a "two-bit politician" was more about himself than about the group member who called him that. He started to recognize that he acted just like his family—not that he *was* like his family, but he did act like them. He needed to act like a "two-bit politician" to protect them. Matthew started to realize that we learn from our family's behavior and modeling ourselves on them is one way of remaining close to them internally and externally and not having to deal with the awareness that they are different and "wrong."

Over time, as he was able to step into his Magician, Matthew's "I don't know" turned into "Now I understand." It didn't happen overnight, but about a year after his new awareness, he was more in touch with himself and his feelings. He still questioned himself, but increasingly he had more certainty about his interests and decisions and who he was on the inside.

And the more work he did, the more he realized how much he really loved his partner. For Matthew, that was no longer even a question. He discovered his Magician.

Yet another of the Warrior's shadows is being a trickster, using your cognitive skills to manipulate others for your own good and not theirs. This is what allows people to be mean and even cruel.

You can fool yourself that your desire for real life is sufficient, and you needn't do any work to have it. Also, you may be relying too heavily on your intellect to avoid the deeper feelings that surface about relationships and dating.

Archetype or Stereotype?

Some gay archetypes are often referred to as stereotypes, but there's a difference. *Stereotype* often has a negative connotation and, according to the online *Webster's Dictionary*, generally describes "an oversimplified mental picture of some group of people who are sharing a certain characteristic (or *stereotypical*) qualities...stereotypes [are] seen by many as illogical yet deeply held-beliefs that can only be changed through education."

An *archetype,* again as defined by *Webster's* online, is "The original pattern or model of a work; or the model from which a thing is made or formed." *Archetype* is often used in a positive sense, "as the first original model of which all other similar persons, objects or concepts are merely derivative, copied, patterned or emulated."

In his book *Beneath the Skins: The New Spirit and Politics of the Kink Community,* Ivo Dominguez, Jr., writes about three gay male archetypes that are more commonly viewed as stereotypes: the Drag Queen, the Leatherman, and the Teacher/Priest.[17] Reclassifying these figures as archetypes, Dominguez has removed their negative, pathological connotations to something that is of positive value in our community.

Drag Queen

Dominguez identifies the Drag Queen as "a divine Androgyne, a blending of male and female energies, but also a trickster." The Drag Queen is a magician (or these days, gender illusionist) in his obvious attempts to trick onlookers into believing he's a woman.

Leatherman

He represents the Wild Man—our wild and vigorous nature, which has been suppressed in modern males. We need to rediscover it to break out of our spiritual malaise. If we properly integrate this part of masculinity into our male psyche, it will be positive and creative. In his article Wildmen, Michael Flood writes that "the Wild Man is a spontaneous, forceful, primal being." The Wild Man represents the "nourishing and spiritually radiant energy" of the "deep masculine."[18]

In our culture, the Leathermen truly represent the deep masculine in their leather jackets and full mustaches. They often figure in "daddy fantasies" and look aggressive and authoritative. At the same time, these are sensitive men who are full of primal sexual energy, which emerges proudly in the masculine realm.

Perhaps the Leather Daddy and the Leather Boy—both of them adult men, of course—are metaphorically the Wild Man andthe Little Boy, who together reclaim the golden ball.

Teacher/Priest

Dominguez states, "He is the friend that listens, holds up the mirror of personal truth, and offers true counsel regardless of the temporal consequences. The Teacher/Priest recognizes the value of the individual within the context of the collective." Coming out as gay men demands that we truly be our own individuals in a bigger world of heterosexuals who are different from us and don't understand us. Proclaiming that you're gay demands a strong sense of trust and deep honesty. After you reveal this about yourself, others will often be honest with you about something *they* have been holding back.

Homo-Work on Masculinity Issues

1. As a young boy, what positive messages did you receive about your maleness?
2. As a young boy, what negative messages did you receive about being male?
3. Who were your male role models, and why?
4. How were men and boys viewed in your family?
5. How were men *treated* in your family?
6. What were the males in your family like?
7. How do you feel about masculinity in general?

8. What archetype have you fully embraced? Which one needs the most work?

References

1. Joe Kort, *10 Smart Things Gay Men Can Do to Improve Their Lives* (Los Angeles: Alyson Books, 2003).
2. Joseph Campbell, *The Hero with a Thousand Faces* (Princeton, NJ: Princeton University Press, 1973).
3. Joseph Campbell, *The Power of Myth* (New York: Anchor Books, 1991).
4. Terrence Real, *I Don't Want to Talk About It: Overcoming the Secret Legacy of Male Depression* (New York: Scribner, 1997).
5. The ManKind Project: The New Warrior Training Adventure (www.mkp.org).
6. Wayne R. Besen, *Anything but Straight: Unmasking the Scandals and Lies Behind the Ex-Gay Myth* (Birmingham, NY: Harrington Park Press, 2003[u1]).
7. Joseph Nicolosi and Linda Ames Nicolosi, *A Parent's Guide to Preventing Homosexuality* (Downers Grove, IL: InterVarsity Press, 2002).
8. F. Jim Fickey and Gary S. Grimm, *Gay Warrior: Transforming Betrayal into Wisdom* (San Francisco: GLB, 2002).
9. Jonathon Rauch, *Gay Marriage: Why It Is Good for Gays, Good for Straights, and Good for America* (New York: Henry Holt, 2004).
10. Robert Bly, *Iron John: A Book About Men* (Vancouver, WA: Vintage Books, 1992).
11. Robert Bly, *A Little Book on the Human Shadow* (New York: HarperCollins, 1988).
12. Debbie Ford, *The Dark Side of the Light Chasers* (New York: Penguin Books, 1998).
13. Carol S. Pearson, *The Hero Within*, 3d ed. (New York: HarperCollins, 1998).
14. Robert Moore and Douglas Gillette, *King, Warrior, Magician and Lover: Rediscovering the Archetypes of the Mature Masculine* (New York: HarperCollins, 1990; reprint, HarperSanFrancisco, 1991).
15. Andrew Tobias, *The Best Little Boy in the World* (New York: Random House, 1998).
16. Cliff Barry, Shadow Work Seminars (www.shadowwork.com).
17. Ivo Dominguez, Jr., *Beneath the Skins: The New Spirit and Politics of the Kink Community* (Los Angeles: Daedalus, 1994).
18. Michael Flood, "Wildmen," *XY: Men, Sex, Politics*, vol. 1(4), Spring 1991, (www.xyonline.net/Wildmen.shtml).

Chapter 3
Discover How What You Hate Can Help You Love

Love is a feeling, followed by a decision, followed by a behavior.

—Maya Kollman, Master Trainer, Imago Relationship
Therapy

Maya Kollman's statement is all about integrity—doing what you say you'll do, being who you say you are. It's about deciding how to behave in accord with your feelings and then how to act based on that decision. In other words, just loving someone else—or even yourself—isn't enough. You must follow it up by deciding how to show that love, then follow through in your behavior.

But we gay men are taught to do just the opposite—to keep our feelings inside, avoid homosexual urges, and forestall any gay behaviors. We learn, basically, to be out of integrity with ourselves, as men among men and with others, both gay and straight.

Larry, a forty-five-year-old draftsman, was heterosexually married. He came to see me after seeing a heterosexual therapist about coming out. Not completely sure he was gay, he felt that the therapist might be overlooking something in helping him decide to either leave his wife and come out or stay closeted and married. He decided to keep seeing his previous therapist along with me.

Ordinarily, it isn't productive for a client to see two therapists individually at the same time, since it can become confusing and work against the efficacy of the treatment—particularly if the other therapist's style is vastly different from mine. But Larry insisted that his insurance covered her services but not mine, and that he wanted to be seen weekly and couldn't afford to see me that often. I knew this wasn't his real unconscious reason, but decided that Larry needed to cling to his heterosexual privileges by seeing this other straight therapist along with me, so I agreed.

Larry had been married to his wife, Helen, for twelve years. He loved her and frequently called her the "salt of the earth." A year and a half before he came to see me, he had met a man from Seattle doing his internship in the architectural office where Larry did his drafting. Larry said he hadn't thought he was gay until he met Simon. Now he found himself looking at other men's bodies, and assumed it was just a desire to be more like them or simply appreciating their attractiveness, as women do with one another. One time when he and his wife were on vacation, a gay man made a pass at him, and Larry politely declined. He thought nothing of it, other than that the man must have found him attractive. But Simon was different; to Larry, there was something compelling about him.

During their time together, Simon expressed sexual and romantic feelings toward Larry, who responded excitedly, and they had sex. A relationship followed afterward that grew each time Simon came into town on business. Finally, Simon decided to transfer his internship to Michigan to be closer to Larry. Larry decided to tell his wife that Simon was here from Seattle for an internship, that they had become friends. Simon had nowhere to stay, given his meager salary, and could he live in their finished basement? Helen agreed, and Simon moved in.

Larry was a man of honor and integrity in all other areas up to now, so he was very bothered that he was lying to his wife. He was a man of his word at work and with Helen. People could count on him, and he always followed through. But in his therapy, we discovered that he wasn't up-front with his family of origin. As a young boy and later as an adult, Larry often lied to his overprotective mother and father to protect them.

When I asked what he meant by their overprotectiveness, he elaborated that his parents were "very Catholic," who attended church regularly and held rigid beliefs about appearances. When Larry's sister married an African American, his parents outwardly accepted this, but rarely called or spent time with the couple, as they did with their other children. In fact, they spend most of their time with Larry's other sister, Jill, who married a Catholic man and who was raising her children Catholic as well. They called this sister regularly every week, and if Larry was on the phone with them at the time, they would end the call with him so they could talk with Jill. Up till then, Larry hadn't felt that this favoritism had affected him that much.

In talking further, Larry recalled the time in his twenties when he dated a Protestant girl and could feel his parents' subtle lack of acceptance. They stopped calling regularly and asked fewer and fewer questions about his life. When he and his non-Catholic girl-friend moved in together, they both put their voices on the greeting of the answering machine. Larry's mother called, left a message and, thinking she had hung up, proceeded to tell Larry's father how disgusted and upset she was that Larry had made such a poor choice of girlfriend based on her religion.

Larry was angry and hurt to hear this from his mother and, on top of it, his father agreeing. His machine recorded much of their discussion about their disapproval. But finally he had overt evidence of his parents' attitude. Phoning them, he asked them point-blank how they felt about his non-Catholic girlfriend. They said they liked her and were glad he was happy—whereupon Larry then confronted them and played back his recording of their conversation. He said he knew the truth now, and while he didn't like their response, he wished they had been more honest. Their deceit bothered him more than their disapproval.

His mother went into a rage, blaming *Larry* for playing the message back. She never took responsibility for her statements on the machine and what's more, she and Larry's father punished him by not speaking to him for months after what "he did to them by playing back the message."

It took Larry a while—over a year in therapy—to tell me this. At the start, when I asked about growing up in his family and how things were now, he'd insisted everything was fine, except that his parents were just a bit overprotective. As a child, he'd made the decision most children make, to protect the family at all costs, even if it means hiding the truth—from himself.

So, unconsciously, he hid the truth about his family's rigidity and lack of acceptance—and also his own truth about being totally gay. He had compelling motives to live out of integrity—to protect his parents and, more than that, to avoid losing the acceptance of the very people he loved. He used the euphemism "overprotective" to hide his family's rigidity and closed-mindedness.

While Larry and Simon continued their relationship, Helen had no idea. They had sex in the basement at night, and Larry felt guilty about it. Ultimately, Simon's internship was over and it was time for him to go back to Seattle. So Larry began a long-distance relationship, flying back and forth to the Northwest.

Helen never said a word or acted suspicious. She liked Simon and didn't seem bothered by his "friendship" with her husband. But Larry felt "tortured" for many reasons—mostly for lying to and taking advantage of a women he loved and respected. "She doesn't deserve this," Larry would say. Agreeing, I invited him back into integrity, either by ending the relationship with Simon or telling his wife the truth about them. But Larry said he was not ready for that.

While Simon was back in Seattle, their relationship deteriorated and they began fighting. Conflict centered on Larry's reluctance to choose to come out and be in a full relationship with Simon. He was torn, since Simon couldn't find a job in Detroit, which meant Larry would have to move to the Northwest, which he was unwilling to do. Without telling Simon, Larry began looking for other men. He had sex with some and dated others as well.

When Simon became suspicious and asked questions, Larry would say that nothing was going on. When I asked why he lied, Larry explained that he didn't want to hurt Simon.

When I started to question Larry's integrity further, he began to cry. "Am I just a bad person altogether?" he asked. "And is coming out just shining a light on it? Is this who I really am?" What Larry is really asking is, "Am I just like my parents?"

I didn't think so at all. Often, when individuals behave in what we therapists call "ego-dystonic" ways—meaning against one's own values and morals—then I know something is being acted out. What was Larry acting out through his secretiveness and lack of integrity?

The next week, he came in and admitted he'd been with other men during his marriage to Helen. This was news, but he insisted he'd already told me. When I disagreed, it turned out he had told his *other* therapist. Now it became clear that Larry had been splitting himself between his therapy with me and his therapy with the other (straight) therapist—just as he had split himself romantically between Simon and his wife. I stressed how important it was that Larry choose one therapist over the other, emphasizing the need to be completely up-front and honest with one of us.

Some months later, Larry came out to Helen and told her about his affair with Simon. Only then did he decide to stop seeing his straight therapist and see me exclusively.

For Larry, this was a big step. He and Helen amicably divorced. But he was still acting out—keeping secrets as he did from Helen, not telling Simon about what he was doing behind his back. His pattern of hiding his true self was becoming clearer and clearer.

To call Larry back into integrity, I stressed his need to make some hard choices about his relationship with Simon and his interest in dating other men. He needed to be accountable and responsible for his own actions and desires. He agreed, continuously berating himself for his "shameful" behavior. Larry finally ended his relationship with Simon, then met Roberto, a man from across the state. As their relationship grew, Larry found that he wasn't telling this new boyfriend everything either—even neutral things that should be told. Roberto was possessive and felt angry and distrustful when Larry spoke about staying friends with both Helen and Simon. In an effort to not upset him, Larry avoided telling Roberto about his conversations with Simon or Helen in order to keep the peace.

Again Larry was out of integrity in his relationship. We started to refer to his behavior as codependent, in that he would suppress information in order to please others. This long-standing pattern went back to his childhood, where Larry knew his family wouldn't accept his thoughts and behavior. He knew his affair with Simon would hurt Helen. To spare Simon's feelings, Larry didn't tell him of his diminished interest in him and his dates with other men. Now he was keeping things from Roberto to spare him similar upsets.

Larry had to face his tendency to bury his needs so deeply and work to find ways to live in integrity with who he truly was. He began to see that his parents had demanded that their children be insincere in order to gain their acceptance, love, and attention. His parents themselves were insincere with their children, and Larry mirrored this insincerity, not only as a requirement for love and acceptance but also as a condition (hence the punishment for confronting them with their insincerity by playing back their true feelings in their own words), so insincerity in itself became a value as well as a demand.

Now Larry's work in therapy was to return to integrity and face his own consequences. He came out to his parents—who rejected and abandoned him, just as he had anticipated. This was devastating, and Larry spent much of his therapy crying and working through depression. But he saw the benefits of being accountable, responsible, and staying true to himself. Living in integrity with his feelings and himself became a priority.

For Larry, staying out of integrity was a way of protecting his parents. Remaining out of integrity and believing he was a bad person allowed him to avoid seeing that in fact his parents are out of integrity. This is hard to accept because it is a huge disappointment and involves a lot of grief. While being in integrity with oneself is a lot of work, however, it's well worth the effort.

As you can see, coming out of the closet doesn't automatically bestow integrity. That's something we need to teach ourselves to do to ensure that evasions are not popping out elsewhere—and if they are, to take care of them.

Integrity

The *Stanford Encyclopedia of Philosophy* defines *integrity* thus: "On the self-integration view of integrity, integrity is a matter of persons integrating various parts of their personality into a harmonious, intact whole. Understood in this way, the integrity of persons is analogous to the integrity of things: integrity is primarily a matter of keeping the self intact and uncorrupted."[1]

Integrity is a lifestyle of congruency; it means being outwardly who you are on the inside. Yet from childhood, we gay boys quickly learn that being out and open means ridicule, negative judgments, and lack of emotional and physical safety. So we spend our most formative years learning to live out of integrity, even in relationship with ourselves.

For children of any orientation, integrating all the parts of oneself is impossible. Family rules as well as socialization norms call for children to disown aspects of themselves. For gay children, an additional part gets disowned—our gayness. This corruption happens very early, when we detach from our gay selves in order to adapt. We are taught to disconnect in relating to ourselves and others.

In fact, we're rewarded for doing so. Heterosexual privilege and plentiful rewards await the closeted gay boy and man. The loss of that privilege is so big a danger that many gay men cannot even admit to themselves they are gay. So we all remain out of integrity until eventually—hopefully—we come out. The process of coming out is about integration, becoming congruent with oneself and with others.

Of course, we gay men and lesbians don't corner the market on living out of integrity. Heterosexuals get through childhood by burying and disowning parts of themselves that are not acceptable to their families or cultures. Gay and straight alike, we must all come back into integrity—which is often what a midlife crisis is all about. I prefer to call it a midlife awakening: finding out who you really are and moving toward it.

Larry *is* a man of integrity. He didn't think so, based on his behavior, since he cheated on his wife and then his boyfriends. I explained to him, however, that integrity is a lifestyle, just as being out of integrity becomes a lifestyle for those of us who have to live in a closet. It is our cultural shadow as gay men—living out of integrity. Coming out, being above ground, means changing not only your actions but also your thoughts, feelings, and beliefs. We lead lives that wander out of integrity because of how we're taught real men should be. Coming out of the shadows is about examining every area and behavior of our lives.

One common way we fall out of integrity with ourselves as men is in trying to act the way a "man" should. I recall being told not to cross my legs a certain way so as not to look effeminate, how to walk more like a man, even how to talk like one. Other boys in school singled me out, a little gay boy, as an object of disdain and punishment. I was spit at, punched, called names, humiliated, and threatened to the point that I would have my grandmother pick me up from school to avoid bullies beating me up. I had nowhere to turn, since the schools did nothing to protect me. My sixth-grade gym teacher told my classmates that my best friend and I must be "fags" because we spent so much time together.

Coming out is your first step toward integrity as a gay man, about integrating who you are inwardly and outwardly on a psychological, emotional, affectionate, relational, and sexual level. But just because a gay man comes out and gets back in touch with his sexual and romantic orientation doesn't mean he can easily achieve total integrity. Pretending, even to oneself, has become a habit. To come back to integrity, gay men need to look at every aspect of their lives, in addition to their sexuality.

Coming into integrity means maintaining your own beliefs, values, and behaviors in the face of opposition. And as gay men, do we ever face opposition! We have to take the stance of Warrior, as discussed in chapter 2.

Personal Integrity

Personal integrity is what you do when nobody's watching. It's behaving toward yourself in accord with your inner beliefs and desires. It is keeping promises to yourself, becoming aware of your personal thoughts and beliefs and behaving toward yourself the way you would like others—acting in your best interests—to behave.

Not that being out of integrity with yourself is always a negative thing. Second thoughts are often healthy—you may think you wanted something (or someone) but then, after taking verbal or physical action, decide that doesn't work and want to set yourself new priorities. So from being out of integrity, you learn to change the promises you make to yourself, so that you can keep them. Or you real-ize, as many of us gays and lesbians must, that we aren't at all who and what we thought we were. You then have to go inside and dis-cover who you really are.

Examples of personal integrity include wanting to maintain a cer-tain weight and eating a diet that keeps you fulfilling that desire; resolving to keep yourself structured and more organized; and main-taining an exercise program to keep your body in the shape you would like. And for us, personal integrity is about being congruent from the inside out about who we are as gay men. Just because we stop pretending to be straight doesn't mean we stop pretending. Since childhood we have learned how to pretend.

Personal integrity begins almost automatically when you come out of the closet and get to know your real self. You begin to appre-ciate yourself for deciding to come out and follow that up by com-ing out to yourself and others. Relationships with others force you to come out to yourself even more. As mentioned in chapter 2, your shadows lie in the space between yourself and those around you, and your positive and negative selves are mirrored in tem.

Research shows that falling in love is more likely to coax gay men to come out than will just having gay sex. In my practice, I see this all the time. A client can have sex with another man and call it "kinky" or "freaky" or a "onetime thing." But if in fact he's gay, for him to fall for another man emotionally *and* sexually prompts the coming-out process.

From Closeting Oneself to Personal Integration

In the early 1980s, Eli Coleman—psychologist, sex therapist, prolific writer, and professor at the Medical School of the University of Minnesota—developed a five-stage model for coming out that ends in integration.[2] I like his model as well as that developed by Vivienne Cass on the stages of coming out.[3] But what makes Coleman's relevant here is that he conceptualizes a stage of coming out that involves first relationships—that is, when gay men fall in love.

1. Pre-Coming Out

Individuals at this stage aren't conscious of any same-sex feelings, even though they may feel different from their peers. Coleman states that during this stage, because people are in denial and suppressing their true selves, they will develop psychosomatic illnesses, suicidal attempts, depression, and chemical dependency—to name just a few behavioral problems. Therapists know that if a person is suppressing or denying something about himself, he develops symptoms that he comes into the therapist's office complaining about. But those are rarely the real issues, and our work begins with what underlies those symptoms. In other words, the client is in shadow as to who he really is and out of integrity with himself.

In this stage, the person first comes out to himself, but keeps his thoughts and feelings private to avoid rejection, ridicule, and abandonment.

2. Coming Out

The person is aware that his yearnings, thoughts, and fantasies indicate same-sex attractions. He may start to tell other people, or at least seek contact with others who might understand. He's still not yet ready to label himself as gay, so he remains out of integrity and in shadow.

If telling others goes well, he can move more easily into the exploration stage. If responses do not go so well, however, the person can move into more shame and internalized homophobia about being gay.

3. Exploration

Still not self-identifying as gay or lesbian, the person starts interacting with more gay people and begins to explore a new homosexual sexual identity. *Homosexual* has a more clinical, negative connotation, whereas *gay* is more affirmative. Here the person will develop skills in relating to other gays and lesbians, who were absent (that is, socially invisible) in his or her childhood.

Here, a gay man starts to develop a sense of personal attractiveness and sexual competence. Developmentally, this parallels what an early heterosexual pubescent goes through, when he starts feeling attracted to girls and wants to look nice and experiment sexually and romantically with them. Since gay boys aren't allowed to express themselves this way, their impulse gets buried, only to surface in this stage of Coleman's coming-out model.

Another part of this exploration stage parallels Cass's six-stage coming-out process, wherein the gay man develops his positive self-concept by reverting to immature, immoral, or promiscuous behavior, as a teenager would. This is where someone's gay age doesn't matching his chronological years. His behaviors are very adolescent, but this is only a stage.

4. First Relationship

After some sexual and romantic experimentation, the person may want a more stable relationship that is physical and emotional. But first relationships seldom last long, since the person has not yet fully dealt with coming-out issues and tasks. This is similar to a teenager in high school or earlier falling in love for the first time. Imagine if he and his squeeze were allowed to run away and live together, or get married right away. They would be finished with each other in a very short time. First loves are often based on sex and sexuality, and the developmental task of learning intimacy skills.

Ron, a twenty-six-year-old graduate student going for his MBA, was living with his parents and wasn't out to them or anyone else. After realizing he might be gay, he began going to gay bars and, after some months of going to one regularly, he became known to the patrons and the bartenders.

One night, he met Mr. Right: Zack. Ron had extremely strong feelings for him, more than he had ever had before for a man. Zack had been out of the closet for a while and had enjoyed other relationships. That initially contributed to Ron's admiration for Zack's having his "act together"—or so Ron thought.

The two of them had better sex than Ron had ever experienced. They began spending lots of time around each other. Ron's parents asked where he was all the time, and he would lie, saying that he was studying with his graduate-school friends. Actually, he'd been skipping most of his classes to spend more time with Zack—who stayed at his parents' when he came to Michigan during his business trips.

Zack decided to purchase a house so that he and Ron could have a place to go when he was in town. Since Ron was in college, he didn't have much money, but over several months he spent time helping Zack fix up the house. They were both hopeful that this would eventually be their home together. Ron began to miss more and more classes. Finally, in an adrenaline high from his new love, he told his parents, siblings, and friends that he was gay. He dropped the number of classes he was taking and moved in with Zack so that they could spend more time together.

Ron's parents weren't supportive of his being gay and warned that if he didn't move back home, they'd stop paying for his schooling. They were troubled not so much by the fact that he thought he was gay, but that he seemed to be moving too quickly into a homosexual relationship. Also, after he came out to them, Ron lost two close male friends with whom he'd attended football games and played cards. All of this hurt him, but he didn't care since he felt he was in love.

These events occurred in the space of a year, during which time Zack's sex drive diminished considerably. Ron suspected he was cheating, but Zack insisted he wasn't and that his job was becoming busier and more demanding. Ron found himself going back and forth from his family's home, which was closer to the university than Zack's home, which was fifty miles away. There, he busied himself working on the house but found himself alone a lot since Zack was often away on business. He tried to discuss things with Zack, who wouldn't open up. They spent less and less time together, had sex less and less, and had little communication.

Ron began to feel that Zack had everything his way and wasn't interested when Ron voiced *his* needs. After finding himself depressed about going through so many changes in such a short time, he decided to start therapy with me.

We talked about his having moved too fast on his feelings toward Zack. His emotions had been so strong that he felt he had to follow them, but now he was embarrassed. He had withdrawn from some of his classes and almost dropped out completely. He'd come out prematurely to his family and friends, some of whom abandoned him. During his therapy, he returned home to face the mess he felt he'd created.

Eventually, he ended his relationship with Zack, who wasn't interested in doing any work to repair their relationship. He wouldn't even consider coming in for some sessions with me to discuss it.

Ron was reassured to understand that according to Coleman's model, he was in stage 4 of coming out. In other words, this explained his feelings and emotions and made him feel more normal. His therapy work then became about *why* he acted on them—and what this meant about him that he moved so quickly. Others may have similar strong feelings and not act on them, even though they might want to.

5. Integration

As a person's private and public lives begin to merge, he leads a fuller, more integrated life that's not so compartmentalized; he begins to move between gay and straight cultures seamlessly, being out and open without having to hide, be secretive, or change anything about himself. Of course, this won't be the case if coming out entails danger on the job, or anywhere the individual could be threatened psychologically and possibly physically.

Coleman and Cass don't assume that all gays and lesbians go through these stages in order, or that they complete all stages. Some may get locked into one stage and never progress. After Ron's relationship ended and he moved back home, he couldn't bear the rejection from his family and went back to stages 1 and 2. Ron knew he was gay but to appease friends and family he remained celibate and away from any gay socialization. To his credit, he stayed in therapy and worked on his internalized homophobia.

Coming out is a continuing process. You don't come out one day and that's it. It is a lifelong process on many levels, just as knowing your shadows are a lifelong process. Shadows and integrity are a normal part of life, but if you can learn how to identify them and make them conscious, you can continue to come out of your shadow and live in integrity with yourself and others as much as you can.

Being out of integrity can generalize to other parts of life without our even being aware of it. One gay man in one of the gay men's groups I facilitate didn't tell us that he'd begun the process of adopting a child—a milestone in anyone's life. But he was so habituated to withholding vital information that he wasn't even conscious of not sharing something so important with our group. Larry is a good example of how successfully emerging from the closet doesn't stop us from pretending and lapsing out of integrity with ourselves.

A Partner Provides Ballast

We human beings are wired for attachment, programmed to gather in groups, and fare better when we live in relationship with others. In fact, research shows that partnered people do better in school and business and even live longer! Newborn birds and mammals need caregivers to get them through childhood or they cannot survive. In addition, nature encourages diversity, which explains why opposites attract—why we are often drawn to those so different from ourselves. Nature disguises the incompatibility of such partners under the canopy of romantic love, forcing us to do the work necessary to heal our unresolved issues from childhood. You can do this only with a partner or close friend who's very different from you.

Custom-made Love

Just as the stages of coming out can impact your relationships, you should also be aware of the stages of love. It's no accident that you partner with the men you do. Truly, you pick the partner who's best for you—whether or not you think he is.

Harville Hendrix identifies three stages of love in Imago Relationship Therapy: romantic love, the power struggle, and finally, real love.[4] The first two are unconscious; only the third one—real love—is conscious.

When you find yourself falling in love with another guy, there is a lot going on an unconscious level. Imago Relationship Therapy calls it your *Imago match,* when you are attracted to someone who carries both the positive and negative traits of your primary caretakers, usually our mother and father. Others from childhood—older siblings, an aunt or uncle, grandparents—can also imprint and impact us in strong ways, positively and negatively. This is a normal psychological process. You scan a room of guys, many of whom you might find attractive and hot, but only some of them stand out for you. Something about them—they way they dress or stand, their facial expressions—reminds you unconsciously of those who raised you. This is familiar love.

Another aspect of the imago match is that we're drawn to people who can express the very things we were taught not to express. A guy can express traits and behaviors that you've unconsciously suppressed or denied. Growing up in your family, culture and surroundings, you weren't allowed to express them. If you were told *not* to horse around, you'll be drawn to playful people. While it is true that opposites do attract, you'll eventually discover that you two are not really opposites, that each of you has inside what the other possesses outwardly. As discussed in chapter 2 on the shadow, love takes you on a hunt for the buried treasures within you and your partner.

During romantic love, you find yourself drawn to both the familiar caretaking traits—as if reunited with your parents—and your own buried traits: various parts of yourself that you might have decided to speak about no longer. When you enter a relationship that is a true imago match, you're on the *reunion tour* with yourself and your family of origin.

Some folks don't like or accept the idea that relationships throw you back in time and bring out unresolved issues from your past. They think I am telling them to dwell on the past or that they can change their past. I am saying neither. What I do see are people recreating their past in the present. Unconsciously you will recycle, reexperience, and recreate your childhood, and the negative parts will cause trouble in your relationships. I am not saying that your childhood seals your fate. Some people have incredibly difficult childhoods, but not all of them spend their life being unhappy and having troubled relationships. What I do know is that the more conscious you are about yourself and your past, the less likely you will recreate the past in negative ways.

Once you have found him and start moving in his direction—and he in yours—what happens next? How do you move through the essential stages of love you must go through? What happens as you start liking each other more and more and want to spend time together? To explain, I'm borrowing from the work of Pat Love, an Imago Relationship Therapist whose work has been important to my thinking. She describes the stages of love as the Call of the Wild, the Call of the Child, and finally, the Call of the Mild. The first two of her calls are totally unconscious and in shadow—just like romantic love and the power struggle—while the third deals with conscious, intentional love: real love.

Call of the Wild

This is stage 1 of falling in love—that is, unconscious. Our society focuses primarily on romantic love and calls it *real* love. Movies, books, popular music, and television all make us feel that if we cannot sustain this feeling, then we've fallen out of love. Many believe that this rapturous emotion should never end and that keeping the high of the connection going should require little to no work at all. That's just not so. If you two are lucky, this physiological and psychological state of infatuation lasts from six to eighteen months, tops.

For most people, romantic love is the best part of their relationship. With the selection process in the hunt for love seemingly over, it's so easy to just lie back and enjoy the ecstatic feelings and the bonding experience. But as an emotional experience, romantic love is simply the doorway to any relationship. Its main purpose is to bring two people together in an emotional time out when both partners can feel their sameness, overlook their differences, and experience a feeling of euphoria.

The purpose of the Call of the Wild is attachment, which is designed promote attachment to a partner. This call can entail a truly wild emotional, physiological, and psychological experience.

Emotions

During the Call of the Wild, an individual becomes emotionally attached to his partner and experiences strong feelings of attraction, infatuation, and euphoria. Both partners feel a state of hyperarousal emotionally and sexually. They each hope to have found the man of their dreams, who promises to sustain the illusion that life is now fulfilled and complete. Both strive to identify their similarities and reinforce a symbiotic mind-set, making every attempt to find everything they share in common. Here, their psyches are trying to find wholeness. So they talk for hours about anything and everything they can find that they have in common.

Here the partners identify with each other's similarities—and often make the mistake of assuming they're essentially identical ("You think the way I think; you feel the way I feel"). Some normal symbiotic descriptors include: you want what I want; you see what I see; you hear what I hear; you experience what I experience.

One episode of the first season of *Queer as Folk* is the best scenario of romantic love I have ever seen for gay men. Emmett meets Mr. Right across a loud, crowded dance bar with gay guys everywhere. Once these two lay eyes on each other, all the other men in the bar draw back from them as if in a dream sequence. The loud house music fades out to something more romantic. Emmett and this newfound love get physically closer, and when they speak to each other, they finish each other's sentences:

EMMETT: I can't explain it. It is as though...
BRENT: We have known each other all of our lives.
EMMETT: Exactly! As if you have been waiting for me...
BRENT: And I've been waiting for you.
EMMETT: Two halves of the same soul...
BRENT: That finally met.

Then Emmett asks Brent, "Would you mind if I...?" It looks as though they will kiss. But the next scene cuts to the back room of the bar where Emmett is giving Brent a blow job. It is fast and intense, so charged and exciting that when they are finished, the other men in the back room applaud them.

This episode dramatizes the intensity of romantic love. Romantic love triggers lust. During romantic love your sex drive goes up. This is not only about gay men, since movies feature many scenes where men and women feel and act on the same urgency. *Fatal Attraction* is the perfect example where Michael Douglas's character meets Glenn Close's character, and they literally can't wait to get into the bedroom. The next scene cuts to them at her house having intensely passionate sex right on her kitchen stove.

In her book *Why We Love,* Helen Fisher writes, "Why do we feel lust when we fall in love? Because dopamine, the liquor of romance, can stimulate the release of testosterone, the hormone of sexual desire. This relationship between elevated levels of dopamine and sexual arousal, frequency of intercourse, and positive sexual function is common in animals."[5]

After Emmett and Brent finish their sexual activity, Emmett tries to introduce him to his friends, and both realize they don't even know each other's names. Asked how long they've known each other, they share what they have in common. Emmett responds, "In this life, only a brief while, but I believe we have known each other in many past lives before."

> BRENT: It is the only explanation for why we have so much in common.
> EMMETT: You can't believe it. We both love Brad Pitt.
> BRENT: Clinique for men.
> (*both together*): Especially when they're having a sale!
> EMMETT: Green-onion-flavored potato chips.
> BRENT: And our favorite song is "Somewhere Out There."

"Uncanny! " their friend Brian exclaims sarcastically. This couple is stretching for things they can find in common. This is a universal tendency, as these scenes in Queer as Folk dramatize brilliantly.

The Love Drugs

Romantic love is nature's anesthesia. During this stage, people often say they feel drugged. If depressed, they report being less so. If suffering from an addiction, they will experience a diminished craving or feel entirely "cured." Love's a stimulant, too: someone who needs a lot of sleep finds he can suddenly operate on less; and it will ratchet up a sluggish sex drive to match a partner's higher libido. Romantic love might turn into real love at some point—if you do the work, which we will further explore.

The elation, exhilaration, and euphoria that new lovers feel is mostly due to their bodies producing a natural amphetamine called phenylethalimine (PEA). So, yes, if you feel drugged, it's because you *are!* Most people don't know that as we fall in romantic love, nature floods us with chemical cousins of amphetamines such as PEA, dopamine, norepinephrine—all natural stimulants and painkillers. When PEA is first released, it is actually at its most potent state, which is why people never forget their first loves. PEA eradicates pain, lowers people's anxiety states, and makes the world seem bright and renewed.

In *Why We Love,* Helen Fisher has researched the other natural love drugs involved: dopamine, norepinephrine, and serotonin. Dopamine is often called the "morphine of the brain" because when released in our bodies, it relieves pain. In elevated levels it also produces extremely focused attention—and fosters dependency, which is why it is associated with all the major addictions, and can explain why such a strong dependency is created in the beginning. Fisher goes on to say that this is also why lovers can remember so many details about their partners, and why people say later in relationships during the power struggle, "I didn't have to tell you in the beginning—you seemed to just know then!"

Fisher points out that elevated levels of dopamine increases levels of testosterone, fueling the craving for sex. This explains the increase in libido most couples report when they first meet, and may even explain sexual addiction, since the person is really addicted to the brain chemicals released when acting out.

Also contributing to the lover's high, Fisher believes, is norepinephrine, which is derived from dopamine. "Increased levels of this stimulant," she writes, "generally produce exhilaration, excessive energy, sleeplessness, and loss of appetite—some of the basic characteristics of romantic love." When you're near the one you're attracted to, norepinephrine stimulates the production of adrenaline and makes your blood pressure soar. That's why you might experience a pounding heart or sweaty palms at the sight of someone you're attracted to.

Low levels of serotonin cause depression. This is exactly why serotonin-reuptake inhibitors (antidepressants) such as Prozac and Zoloft are prescribed for those suffering from depression; these medications help increase their low level of serotonin. Fisher believes that low serotonin also contributes to the obsessive-compulsive quality of romantic love, when lovers obsess over each other and constantly need to be in one another's presence. She hypothesizes that "as a love affair intensifies, this irresistible, obsessive thinking can increase—due to a negative relationship between serotonin and its relatives, dopamine and norepinephrine."

It's vital to understand this, so you have some perspective when these chemicals stop working—as you'll read about in chapter 7, on your sexual shadow, and chapter 9, on breaking up.

These chemical changes are not meant to last, since their only purpose is to connect two people to begin the bonding process. We gay men cherish this time even more than our heterosexual counterparts do, since we're so often warned that we'll never find love, that the gay culture is based on promiscuity and short-term hookups. So when romantic love hits, it's like discovering that a long-forgotten uncle remembered you in his will.

Alas, the rush of first love is only a temporary state that's supposed to end. But people, not knowing this, do all they can to keep it from ending. Some people break it off just to make up again and reactivate those early feelings, plus the PEA. Others use drugs and alcohol to try to make the feeling stay around—or at least replace it. Still others decide that relationships shouldn't be so much work, so they dissolve it in disillusionment—or else they seek sex with others, to bring back that PEA feeling. Too many gay men see the inevitable twilight of romantic love as confirmation of the myth that we cannot enjoy sustained love, that the heterosexists and homophobes were right. But this is another misconception.

Some cultures (India's, for example, where arranged marriages are still the norm) don't even aspire to romantic love, because they're aware that it's not based on reality. If you find a guy who you think is the man of your dreams, just understand that real love involves three stages; your first two years together are not necessarily a positive indicator that he's the right one for you. And when romantic love ends, it's not an indicator that he's *not* right for you. It's fine to enjoy PEA and the other love drugs, as long as you understand that it isn't what real love is all about. This is important because if you go with your feelings while high on PEA, when the stage of romantic love ends, you could walk away from the relationship of your dreams.

This is also what promotes addictions to sex and love in people who are constantly seeking this natural high. The problem, just as with most other addictions, is that each time these natural chemicals are released, they become less and less powerful and last for a shorter period of time.

Psychology of Love

During the Call of the Wild—perhaps the most important part of a developing relationship—what you're experiencing is a regression. You're going back to the time in childhood when you were totally dependent and you needed to idealize those who loved you. During romantic love, your psyche reverts to an infantile state and believes that it has found Mommy, Daddy, or whoever your childhood caretaker was.

In Imago Relationship Therapy we say that when you're looking for a partner, your unconscious is seeking for both the positive *and* the negative traits of your primary caretakers. Since you don't know this consciously, instead you say to yourself, "I like that guy's body" or "I like his smile," or are attracted to his personality; but more is going on: part of you feels you've come home and found these lost caretakers.

During the Call of the Wild, you have also come back home to yourself—the part of yourself that you buried or repressed because your family, culture, or social group found it unacceptable. Your romantic partner is very often someone with those very same traits. So if your family admonished you to never show anger, then you are going to be drawn to angry men. In the romantic phase, however, you don't see a guy as a hothead, you call him "assertive" or "passionate" about what he wants and believes.

Your psyche disguises the lost traits—the buried treasure—that is, aspects of yourself that are precious and specific to who you are, but that you had to bury in order to adapt. So when you fall into romantic love, these traits are exhumed and brought to light. You're finally able to tolerate them, at least in terms of allowing for them in your partner. This is important to know and explains why so many romances are doomed—a love-hate relationship is built in!

The Shadow in the Call of the Wild

In shadow terms, we project our idealized parents—and our own lost and buried selves—onto our partners. These are the shadow's *positive* aspects—the gold, if you will. You have projected your parents' best traits onto your partner and can see them clearly, while the bonding is taking place. In other words, the loving feelings you have toward your partner are a projection *onto* him, not so much a reaction *to* him.

The problem, obviously, is that you're not seeing him for all of who he really is. Yes, you will get glimpses of his real self, both positive and negative. But when you see the negatives and don't like them, you simply overlook them or tell yourself you'll work on helping him to change. Unfortunately (or fortunately, depending on your outlook), these negatives rear their heads during the Call of the Child—the second stage of love, otherwise known as the power struggle. The truth is that although the second stage feels bad, you are both growing toward real love—if both of you can survive it.

During the Call of the Wild, primal urges are heeded. We want to be loved, thought about, cared for—and we feel that finally, we've met that person who will do it all. But there is no such person other than you.

In *Owning Your Own Shadow*, Robert A. Johnson writes, "To fall in love is to project that particularly golden part of one's shadow...onto another person."[6] Until you can understand this and examine what those projections mean about you, your relationship won't get very far. Accomplishing this work will move you through the second stage of any relationship.

The Call of the Child

This is stage two of love—the power struggle—and it too operates on an unconscious level. It is supposed to happen and supposed to end, just like the Call of the Wild. How and why the relationship gets to this part remains a mystery to most people. During romantic love, similarities connect us. PEA helps us bond—for a while. But once the power struggle begins, we're disconnected by the very factors that we thought we could overlook. Differences start to show up between you and your partner, and the things you thought you could overlook you no longer can.

At this stage your partner ceases to resemble your idealized snapshot of the perfect partner, which means that you are beginning to see he's not the image of the idealized caretaker that you've projected onto him. You start to realize that he's *not* going to meet all of your needs as you once thought—or as he promised. The picture of him being the perfect fit with you comes crashing down. You begin to recognize that you do *not* think or feel alike, want the same goals, or experience life the same way.

We begin to feel a sense of entitlement during this stage in our relationship: "I have a right to what I want." We say things like, "I shouldn't have to ask you to do that"—as if our partner is under an obligation, that he *owes* us. We want to hold him to his promises, and expect no less. We begin to find him different; qualities of his that we once adored we now cannot bear.

I remember telling my partner, Mike, how I adored his calmness and serenity. Being with him felt so peaceful. But eventually, I started asking him things like, "Are you alive in there?" and "Do you ever feel anything?" Initially, he loved my passion and emotionality. In the Call of the Child, he started saying things like, "You're scaring me. You're too emotional. Give me some space."

Because this is all unconscious, most people don't realize what's happening other than they no longer feel in love with their partner. The truth is, they're no longer in romantic love after the Call of the

Wild subsides and nature shuts down the internal pharmacy. Suddenly you realize you're not going to get all of your needs met as you originally thought. The Call of the Child is the time in any relationship where your inner child comes out calling for healing—and he isn't happy. The small child within wants what he didn't get in childhood. Now the negative traits from your parents are projected onto your partner. No longer anesthetized, you fight like a child having a temper tantrum to get what you want, what you think is your right to have.

Disillusionment arises. Conflicts arise. You become acutely aware of the differences between yourself and your new partner, and fear that these differences aren't good for your relationship—when in fact, they are!

This isn't true, however, if one or both won't seek help for domestic violence, or active addiction exists. If you begin to have concerns for your safety—emotional, physical, and otherwise—serious therapy intervention is necessary. Couples therapy is out of the question here and will only make things worse. If the abusing partner is unwilling to seek help, then the other should consider leaving the relationship. Left untreated, this kind of tension can only harm both of you.

Once the power struggle begins, most couples—gay and straight alike—will unconsciously wish to end the relationship, because what felt so good now feels painful. But this power struggle stage is required for those who want to get to real love and achieve a full and lasting relationship. If your goal is short-term love and you do not want to get in this deep, this is the time to end the relationship.

As soon as both partners decide to make more of an investment in each other and the relationship, the Call of the Child arrives and the PEA wears off. If one partner was depressed before, back he goes to his depressed state. If he enjoyed a higher sex drive during PEA, he reverts to his natural lower libido. Most people, unaware of this unconscious process, blame themselves—or more often, their partners—for the return to their natural states.

The power struggle, or Call of the Child, begins when partners begin saying things like "Let's only see each other and stop dating anyone else" or "Let's take a vacation" or "Let's tell everyone we are a couple" or "Let's move in together—or talk about it" or "Let's get married."

Why do these commitments provoke the Call of the Child? Because they throw you back to the time you were first dependent on another human being—that is, childhood.

Very few other relational commitments are as dependent and demand as strong attachment as adult love relationships. But a part of your brain doesn't know the difference and thinks it's back with someone who feels the same as those who raised you (more about this in chapter 6 on communication and the brain). Your partner now becomes the stand-in for your parental caretakers or those who were influential during your earliest years.

Couples usually argue over things that are not the core issue at all. The unconscious finds a way to mask the real problems with more innocuous, seemingly unimportant matters. This power struggle, the second stage of relationships, is also supposed to happen and have an end—although many couples never achieve that end because they don't know how to navigate their way through it. The power struggle has an enormous amount to tell us.

Like a detective successfully solving a mystery, you will find disguised information waiting to help you to know yourselves better—as individuals and as a couple embroiled in the power struggle. Most of the emotions we attach to any current problem are connected to the past—typically our childhoods, with our Inner Little Boys calling out what wasn't resolved. Once you and your partner can see that, you'll both be more willing to address the present situation differently. That isn't always the outcome, but there's a much better chance of handling conflict.

Back in the Call of the Wild phase, your partner may have even promised to meet all your needs. But with the realization that he cannot or will not, as you originally expected, the Call of the Child begins in earnest. Old hurts and resentments get activated. Mostly, these old hurts are from childhood, but they can also arise from unresolved conflicts from past relationships.

The goal of Imago Relationship Therapy is to establish committed, conscious, intimate relationships by aligning the conscious mind (which usually seeks happiness and good feelings) with the agenda of the unconscious mind, which seeks healing and growth. IRT puts a positive spin on relationship problems that can otherwise seem impossible. As Hendrix says in *Getting the Love You Want,* "our partners become blank screens for our home movies." We burden our partners with our unresolved childhood issues and they do the same to us. We project the blame for these traumas onto each other and it is done unconsciously.

Some theorize that we tend to recreate our first adolescent crush. That first release of PEA can be so strong as to imprint another template onto your Imago ideal. That person then becomes our type, and we tend to be attracted to men who look like, or behave like, him. If that crucial first infatuation ended badly, there's a good chance that unconsciously, we'll try to resolve the kinks of that first relationship with any later stand-in-again, an unwitting screen for our home movies.

During the power struggle stage, you finish each other's sentences, much as you did during the Call of the Wild. Only now, you are making up stories, and the sentences are judgmental and critical of your partner. You'll hear and say statements such as, "You know what I need! I don't want to tell you, and I shouldn't have to!"; "You have what I need, but you won't give it to me"; "You meant to hurt me"; "You don't care about me. You only care about yourself!"

Sex and Sensuality

After the romantic period ends, of course, sex drives fall back to normal. The person with the higher libido may say, "You were more sexual when we first met. It was just a ploy to get me to move in with you." In other words, *you have what I need, and you won't give it to me.* This want usually reflects some unmet childhood needs—not sex, of course, but usually a caregiver's attention and responsiveness.

But when love is young and fresh and you're infatuated, you feel high on internal chemicals like PEA and dopamine, which increase your libido. So people with lower sex drives can usually keep up with their partners higher sex drive. For a while, both of you feel you're getting your needs met. The person with the higher sex drive (high-testosterone or high-T for short) thinks he's found someone who can keep up with him. Meanwhile, the partner with less of a drive (low-T) believes he's found someone who can raise his libido and move him to be more highly motivated.

In *The Truth About Love,* Pat Love writes, "Scientists have known for decades that male sex drive is correlated with testosterone...a hormone produced in the testes and adrenals...testosterone has been conclusively shown to highly correlate with male libido."[7]

Because opposites attract, Dr. Love goes on to explain, it's highly likely for high-T and low-T people to be drawn to each other. During their infatuation stage, they are matched with the help of, in her words, nature's "time-limited plan"—that temporary whirlwind of romantic love that bonds two people together. But after it drops them off, they begin the power struggle and revert to their normal baseline libidos.

Because few people know about these physiological changes, couples compare this second stage unfavorably to their romantic love. They blame the problem on their partner. "You turned me on in the beginning," says the low-T partner. "Why aren't you turning me on now?"

"You liked what we did in the beginning," counters the high-T partner, "but now you're holding out on me!" Many couples view this as the beginning of the end, but both low-T and high-T individuals need to cooperate and understand where the other is coming from.

During the Call of the Wild, we began to feel a sense of entitlement to whatever we want from our partner. Again, this is a regression to the blissful days of infancy, when an ideal caregiver was quick to answer our every complaint. We expect more of the same, as if our partner explicitly promised it to us—and even if he didn't, we intend to hold him to it! Now, though, we find our partner different than we thought he was—and for that, of course, we blame him.

If you've been repressing any traits or aspects, keeping them in shadow, you will recognize them not in yourself but in your partner, where you can tolerate them for only a short while. Then, unconsciously, you'll seek to kill off these long-avoided traits. But all too often, your relationship is the first to die.

Shadow in the Call of the Child

By going through the Call of the Child with a partner and letting your shadows surface-as well as his—you'll get better at it. Deeper layers of understanding will reveal themselves about you, your past, and that of your partner. As a result, you'll reimage your partner as a separate man with a past and lingering hurts of his own. When he has a strong reaction to something, you can have more compassion for him. You can allow your partner to reimage you as well, see you afresh and get out of your mutual shadows that have caused the ruptures in your relationship. "The shadow," Johnson writes, "is very important in marriage, and we can make or break a relationship depending on how conscious we are of this. We forget that in falling in love, we must also come to terms with what we find annoying and distasteful—even downright intolerable—in the other and also in ourselves. Yet it is precisely this confrontation that leads to our greatest growth."

During the Call of the Wild, one shadow that gets acted out is the *exit*—things you do, consciously or not, to relieve the pressure of the power struggle. Exits are feelings being spoken or expressed outside the relationship. (For example, if you can't express your anger toward your partner, then you'll act it out away from his presence, or sideways through being passive—aggressive toward him.) Doing this doesn't mean you're a bad person; it simply means that you are frightened and in shadow.

Some partners find themselves working more hours, focusing more on children or pets, and involved in many other outside interests, behaviors, and addictions. This shadow can even manifest in the *absence* of behaviors—stopping things you used to do or say to your partner to relieve the difficult and painful Call of the Child.

These behaviors and exits don't indicate that you're a bad person; rather,they show that you know no other way to manage the power struggle. But these shadow exits can either cause a lot of turbulence in your relationship or even end it. Without proper help and guidance, it destroys—as any shadow can, if not brought into the light. And it can cause breakups, as you'll see in chapter 9.

The Call of the Child can help you deepen your commitment to your partner, gain knowledge about yourself and him, transform your relationship into real love—otherwise known as conscious love and mature love—and gain an awakening to what healthy relationships are all about. You understand this more fully in the third stage, the Call of the Mild, otherwise known as real love.

Call of the Mild

When couples make it through the power struggle, they reach the third, final stage of mature love—and this one *is* conscious. This is what love is supposed to be—Real Love, as we call it in IRT, based on *reality* and not shadows and projections.

The Call of the Wild's only purpose was to bring you two incompatible people together and bond you, to make you willing to do the healing work you needed to do in relationship. The Call of the Child's purpose was for you both to understand and heal your unresolved childhood wounds, deepen your commitment to each other, gain knowledge about yourself and your partner, and transform your relationship into the one you wanted, awakening parts of yourself that were buried long ago.

The Call of the Mild doesn't imply that your relationship is boring or that everything will be dull and even. On the contrary, the Calls of the Wild and of the Child will still rear their heads. You will have to be more intentional, however, to make the Call of the Wild happen. Think back to your early times. What things made you feel cared about? If they have stopped, bring them into the present. Conflicts will still occur, but you and he will know better how to handle them and decode them more quickly.

In this final stage, each partner knows his own shadow and has an idea of his partner's. They still don't know everything about each other, or themselves, but enough to handle conflicts without much damage to their relationship. Conflict does not evaporate, which many people believe should be the goal. Rather, the goal is for there to be less conflict than there was throughout the Call of the Wild.

During the Call of the Mild, conflict does not cause as much rupture, and you'll begin to see yourself and your partner as two men who want a healthy love relationship and are committed to each other's personal growth and healing. Real love is about nondefensive relating, as chapter 8 will explore. Being defensive causes further fighting, conflict, and rupture—but knowing this, couples who want their relationship to endure can reduce their level of reactivity.

The Platinum Rule:
Do Unto Others as They Would Like You to Do Unto Them

In childhood, most of us we learn the Golden Rule: *Do unto others as you would like them to do unto you.* A good rule of thumb that works in many, but not most, situations; but your relationship will be out of balance without the Platinum Rule.

Everyone has his own love language: in the Call of the Mild, you come to understand what your own is as well as your partner's. What if you like roses, cards, and thoughtful e-mails and phone calls and your partner doesn't? If, instead, he wants to spend time with you and help with your daily chores, likely you will initially feel unloved. You'll be sending him the cards and flowers *you* like to receive, but he—trying to spend every day with you and help you with your daily living—won't feel loved either.

You learn to appreciate how he demonstrates his affection for you and recognize it as his love language. Meanwhile, your partner learns to appreciate your love language and how *you* demonstrate your affection for *him*. During the Call of the Child, most of the time you're angry for not getting the type of love you recognize and want, and you dismiss his personal ways of loving you. But now you learn to appreciate it, enjoy it, and feel loved by it. At the same time, you can teach him how you prefer to be loved. During the Call of the Mild, he will learn to do those things for you, just as you will for him.

This giving is cooperative and unconditional. You give to your partner willingly, without expecting anything back. You trust the process, and that it all balances out in the end. In other words, at times you'll be giving more to him than he is to you and vice versa. But over time, you will no longer have the tit-for-tat mentality of "I will do this for you, if you do this for me."

The Call of the Mild tests your ability to connect to someone else on a very intimate level. You have the chance to heal any problems you have in attaching romantically to another guy. But this takes a lot of relational work, and you must believe that the effort is worth it. It takes faith, self-respect, and good will for each other.

Also, this will force you to look at how you *receive* love. You must learn how to abandon your defenses that block real love.

Other-Validated Versus Self-Validated

This is another very important feature of what the Call of the Mild involves. David Schnarch, a prominent couples therapist, has written extensively on helping couples, and his book, *The Passionate Marriage,* examines the difference between other-validation and self-validation.[8] Self-validated intimacy is "maintaining your own sense of identity and self-worth when disclosing with *no* expectation of acceptance *or* reciprocity from your partner"; while other-validated intimacy is "expectation of acceptance, empathy, validation or reciprocal disclosure from one's partner." In other words, if you are self-validated, you can maintain yourself and your beliefs in the face of a partner's differences and judgments. When you are other-focused, you need him to validate your experience and don't feel complete or satisfied without his empathy and validation.

According to Schnarch, couples need a balance of self-soothing and being other-validated. I couldn't agree more. He goes on to explain the differences:

> Other-validated intimacy sounds like this: *I'll tell you about myself, but only if you then tell me about yourself. If you don't, I won't either. But I want to, so you have to. I'll go first, but you have to make me feel secure. I need to be able to trust you.*
>
> Self-validated intimacy in long-term relationships sounds quite different: *I don't expect you to agree with me; you weren't put on Earth to validate and reinforce me. But I want you to love me—and you can't really do that if you don't know me. I*

don't want your rejection, but I must face that possibility if I'm ever to feel accepted or secure with you. It's time to show myself to you and confront my separateness and mortality. One day when we are no longer together on this earth, I want to know you knew me.

Schnarch's work encourages you to hold on to yourself and not collapse in the face of differences or negative judgments coming your way from your partner or indeed anyone else. He stresses the need for self-validation to maintain your sense of self, especially when you are emotionally and physically close to others. While this is important to do in families, it's crucial to do with partners. And like shadow work, this is a lifetime process that takes a lot of practice.

We gay men have received many messages that our being different is bad and wrong. Negative judgments about ourselves, and having rights and privileges taken or withheld from us, can make this self-validation very difficult. But by so doing, you can see the healing it will provide, both for you and for your relationship.

Shadow of the Call of the Mild: Receiving Love and Reunion Grief

Surprisingly, receiving love can be very hard to do. Imago therapist Pat Love talks about what she calls *reunion grief:* "When you long for something and do not get it, it becomes a source of pain. Therefore, getting it is painful." In other words, the very thing you longed for now has pain associated with it, so that getting it now feels unpleasant. When the grief begins, it takes a lot of effort for you to stay with it and enjoy it. If you're not aware of this dynamic, when you receive the type of love you have longed for, you may well resist it and defend against it, even though it is the very thing you have wanted.

Jeff was a psychotherapist, and Bob, a probation officer. They came to see me after Bob had an affair with another guy. Jeff was angry and couldn't get over the betrayal. He felt that Bob wasn't doing his own work in terms of understanding why the affair occurred in the first place and feared that if Bob didn't figure it out, he might do it again. Jeff complained that Bob didn't share much about himself and when he did, it was "superficial and not deep enough."

Ironically, Jeff and Bob's relationship began with their own affair, when Jeff was single and Bob was in a committed relationship with another partner. Now Jeff was focused on Bob's "bad" behavior and wanted him to fix it.

Bob agreed he did have issues, but didn't understand why he had affairs. I suggested that he enter my Men's Sexuality Group, which deals with sexual addiction, affairs, sexual abuse, and other issues where men cannot maintain their sexual and romantic boundaries. Bob agreed, and I continued working with both him and Jeff in couples therapy. Meanwhile, Bob came weekly to group, where he worked hard and discovered that his problems stemmed from his critical mother, who judged him harshly and with whom he felt he could never get anything right. She criticized and belittled his efforts if they did not conform to her standards. His father never protected him from his mother's attacks, and Bob felt on his own.

It became apparent that Bob was having affairs when he felt he was being judged in his relationships. His only way to cope was to exit emotionally and physically and start up "new loves" to avoid pain in the existing relationship. Once he understood this, he was increasingly able to open up about himself, and gained new awareness and insights about himself. He began to feel confident that he could begin working on feeling criticized and judged within his relationship and not have to "exit" in order to cope.

In couples' therapy, he began to talk to Jeff about this. He shared his deeper work with Jeff and began talking at length about his childhood. But Jeff was not impressed. He said that since he already knew about Bob's family background, Bob would have to "come up with something better than that." Jeff still did not trust Bob. He didn't know what it would take for his trust to return, but knew that Bob still had more work to do.

It now became clear to me that Jeff had some work of his own to do. He was getting the love he wanted, with Bob doing his own work and sharing his issues deeply, but Jeff was not accepting it. Bob said he could finally make Jeff his number one priority they way Jeff had been asking for all along. Bob felt liberated in his ability to finally meet Jeff's needs and wants. Jeff rolled his eyes and stated he did not believe Bob. He spent months discounting Bob's disclosures about the insights into himself he was making in his therapy. Finally, Bob began to tire of Jeff's denial about his progress and negative remarks about his therapy work and considered leaving their relationship.

Jeff stated that in his parents' love for him, his older brother came first. His mother and father valued his older brother's athletic abilities, went to his sporting events, paid for his athletic gear, and provided him with every accolade he could want. Jeff, however, was more interested in music and choir. His parents would not buy him musical instruments and instead rented ones of such poor quality that Jeff became discouraged and eventually stopped playing them. His family was "too busy" for his choir presentations in school and rarely came to one.

Jeff was always made to feel secondary to his brother, which fed his reunion grief. Jeff longed for his parents to make him a number one priority sometimes, as they did his older brother, but they never did. This longing became painful for him, and it therefore made sense that he would have chosen Bob, a man who was willing to have an affair with Jeff while he was still in another committed relationship.

Jeff felt secondary to his former boyfriend's job and children. Now his work in therapy was to accept that finally he'd picked a partner who could make him a priority—but becoming *willing* to accept this form of love felt strange to him. This was his reparative work. In his reunion grief, Jeff was finally getting from Bob exactly what he had been asking for, but was blocking it and defending against it.

In reunion grief, you may say things like, "You must do everything exactly the way I want you to or it won't mean anything to me." Or else you'll want intimacy to the point of being insatiable and therefore tire out the one who wants to give you love. Both ways sabotage your receiving it.

The Promise of Real Love

Reaching the Call of the Mild—real love—takes a lot of work

and time, but a fulfilled promise awaits you and your partner together. When I prepare flyers to announce one of my weekends, I usually describe the event as, "A Couples Workshop for All *Three* of You: You, Your Partner, and Your Relationship."

The truth is that the Call of the Mild can be sustained, but the Call of the Wild and the Call of the Child cannot. Attachment and mature love demand that many things start to happen.

Real love based on reality, the Call of the Mild, embodies the following traits.

Intentionality. This involves remaining conscious and deliberate about how you speak to your partner as well as how you listen to him. This is no easy task, and remaining intentional 100 percent of the time is not realistic. It is about working toward intentionality all the time, not having to be perfect. Being intentional means being accountable for what you say and do. If you make a mistake, inadvertently harm your partner, or feel wounded by something he says or does, then it's up to you to correct it and not wait for him to become aware of it. Intentionality involves staying conscious before *and* after things are said and done. At the very least scanning your behaviors on a regular basis to keep yourself in check. This will strengthen your inner Magician.

Accepting differences, which can be threatening to all couples, but particularly to gay and lesbian couples. Our society treats us badly for differing from the norm, imprinting on us that differences are not okay. That in turn makes us more sensitive and suspicious at having to change for anyone again. So when these differences and conflicts arise for any gay or lesbian couple, it can trigger these old feelings.

Empathic and compassionate connection to your partner can be difficult to maintain, particularly during times of conflict and difficult differences. But the more you do this, the fewer ruptures you'll have between you. This will strengthen your inner Lover.

Quick rebound from conflict. Over time, where before it would have taken hours, days, and sometimes months to recover from a conflict, you will find that the recovery time takes only minutes or at least a much shorter amount of time than it historically would.

Appropriate communication methods. Using dialogue and clearings (as will be addressed in chapter 6) and making time for clearings is guaranteed to keep negativity from developing between you.

Nondefensive relating. Responding to your partner in a nondefensive way involves not taking things personally. In chapter 6, I'll expand on why this is extremely difficult yet extremely important—and how to do it.

The Platinum Rule. Essential for The Call of the Mild is to Do unto them the way they want to be done unto. In other words, show your love for your partner the way he wants to be shown love.

Reimaging your partner. This involves seeing your partner as the wounded child he once was. It's realizing that when he's reactive—and especially overreactive—usually he's regressed to another time and place that had nothing to do with you. Reimaging him as young and small makes you react less. Usually people react to a child much less strongly than to another adult, because of your expectations. Since we cannot expect children to think like adults, we give them more slack. Reimaging allows you to do this with your partner.

Mutual relationship vision. This entails envisioning what you both want, not just what you want. It demands that you sit down with your partner and discuss what each of your visions for the present and future is and then create a joint one. Here, you two will be utilizing both of your Kings. Most people I work with in psychotherapy start working on a mutual vision only after years together. Obviously, it's best if you can do this from the start.

Accountability. Living in integrity means being accountable for the choices you make—accepting the consequences, and owning your own emotions rather than blaming them on others. To be accountable means saying, "I acknowledge the consequences of my actions, as well as the choices and the intentions behind them." Being a mature adult means being accountable, but our society encourages everyone to blame other people and avoid responsibility for their own lives.

Accountability Versus Blame

Holding others accountable for their actions can be as hard as doing the same for yourself. In fact, most people who enter therapy seem more inclined to declare themselves responsible and accountable for the actions of others. Most of them fear that the therapist will ask them to blame their folks for whatever's gone wrong in their life. So at the outset, they state clearly, "I don't want to get into the past. I don't want to blame my mom and dad." I don't believe in blaming anyone for anything, since that makes you a victim. But with that in mind, it is important to hold others accountable for their words and actions.

We have no trouble admitting the advantages we received while growing up. The other night, I watched a politician thank his mother and father for all the good they did for him, letting him pursue his dreams of running for high office. Cut to shots of his audience applauding and his parents with tears of pride in their eyes. Really beautiful, though those same parents must have behaved badly at times, and most likely the candidate did too. There were times not to be proud.

Why can we talk about only the good, and never the bad? Talking about the negative doesn't mean the good is wiped out, but that's what my clients believe—that admitting any flaws about your parents implies they have no good points. Nor does talking about the good wipe out or justify all the bad. To come out of the shadows, it helps to view what happened to you in childhood—and what you and your parents are doing in your life today—as simply data. Examine this information without judgment or interpretation. To relate things such as, "something my mother said to me growing up" or "something my father did to me in childhood" is simply providing information. Any discomfort you feel in talking about someone isn't about that individual as much as it is about how that person's words and actions impacted you.

You are sure to have both positive and negative feelings about the data that you share about your family. Therapy is the place to let those feelings surface—again, without judgment. It's simply information, and doesn't make your parents—or you—bad or unworthy. You must acknowledge things before you can repair them. If you don't, likely they'll be reenacted and recycled in your current relationships.

Relationship Integrity

Similar to personal integrity, relationship integrity reflects the reality that love is a verb, not a noun. Love demands that you take action and show how you love. To stay in both personal and relationship integrity, it is often important to use dialogue. You'll learn about this process in chapter 6.

Going back to the Golden and Platinum Rules: the Golden Rule assumes that other people want exactly what you want, and believe the same things as you do. The Platinum Rule requires that you talk to others to learn *their* points of view, not your own. Seeing the world through their eyes, you can treat them the way *they* want to be treated, not how *you* think they should be treated.

When Art and Raul came to see me, they'd been together for seven years, but they'd had little to no sex for the past five. There was a considerable age difference between them. Art was sixty-three and had been heterosexually married for twenty-five years before he met with Raul, now forty. They loved each other very much, and four years into their relationship they had a wedding ceremony. Neither man had any desire to leave the other or end their relationship.

In their sessions with me, Art stated he had "waited a lifetime" to finally come out and that in Raul had met the partner of his dreams. He grieved at not being able to enjoy sex with Raul because of Raul's disinterest. Raul stated he had "a low sex drive," and that even masturbation was minimal.

Often, couples have a discrepancy in their sexual drive and interest. And once the honeymoon ends, sex tends to taper off. But for it to decline to almost nothing is not within normal limits, nor can a romantic relationship endure with the absence of sex. So after further talk and some weeks in therapy, I asked Raul if he would be willing to be sexual with Art—at least for Art's pleasure. In other words, maybe Raul wouldn't get off, but perhaps he could at least help Art have some pleasure and find pleasure for himself in pleasing Art.

NOTE: It's often suggested to couples that even if you aren't interested, then pleasuring your partner and seeing him get aroused might sometimes get you aroused. Either way, it helps maintain a relationship to keep the sexual connection going, even if one partner doesn't equally want it as often. Not that you should perform certain acts simply because he asks or wants you to; that's different than, for example, performing sexually in ways that you feel okay with when you're not necessarily aroused, or turned off.

Raul would hear none of this. In fact, the very suggestion made him angry. Now the real problem started to surface. Raul began talking about how Art "always gets his way about everything in our relationship." I watched Art's total surprise as Raul talked about his belief that Art was purposely dominant and went "out of his way to keep me under his thumb." Raul was angry, but he was unaware of how much of his anger was coming out sideways at Art by withholding sex from him.

I've been working with couples for almost twenty years. When I see one partner listening and looking as shocked as Art did, I know there must be some projection on the part of the partner who's doing the talking—in this case, Raul.

Raul talked about his childhood and his "wonderful" family. He described his parents as loving and good providers who kept a nice house and gave him and his older sister a nice middle-class life. His parents owned a local drugstore in their rural hometown, and Raul and his sister worked there while they were in high school. Raul disliked it and preferred to be home with friends or getting a job of his own. But his parents wouldn't hear of it, promising that as long as he worked in their drugstore, they would pay for all of his college.

When his sister decided she no longer wanted to work in the drugstore, their parents allowed her to stop. Since they gave her a break, Raul made one more bid to quit, but they insisted he keep working there. His sister then went on to college and graduated, and Raul's parents paid her way. During his second year of college, the drugstore's sales declined, and his parents thought they would have to sell it. They told Raul he would have to return home because they could no longer pay for his schooling.

Raul was devastated. Unable to stay at college, he came back to help his parents at the drugstore until he decided to move out.

I asked if this angered him. "My parents did the best they could," Raul said. He didn't like having to stop college and come home. He felt it wasn't fair that his sister got a fully paid college education, had married, and never had to return home. But he believed he "did the right thing." I assured him that I wasn't challenging his decisions, simply asking his view of the situation—about which he felt highly defensive. I began to see from Raul's childhood that he was projecting how he really felt toward his parents onto Art.

Art, now genuinely hurt by Raul's comments about him, grew defensive and angry. "I never make you choose things you don't want to do. I thought you did what you wanted, and if we agreed on something, it was mutual. I never enforced or coerced any decisions on you!"

Raul said he felt that if he didn't go along with Art's wants, there would be too much conflict. Art kept arguing that he never wanted to coerce Raul into anything; he wished Raul would speak up more often and either meet his own needs or tell Art what he really wanted. Art stated repeatedly he never wanted a yes man for a partner.

Through therapy, it emerged that Raul felt Art did indeed want to dominate him—consciously and purposely. Clearly upset by this, Art denied it and gave Raul example after example of why that wasn't so. What did seem true for the most part was that Raul was being passive, dependent, and blaming Art for things that weren't Art's fault. Raul wasn't being accountable for his passivity. Nor was he holding his parents accountable for their letting his sister escape having to work at the family pharmacy in high school and paying for her to complete her education and not his.

Raul's insistence that Art was purposely trying to dominate and hurt him was a *fixed delusion*—a thought that becomes set in one's mind and cannot be changed. No matter what you do to prove that the thought is incorrect, one with a fixed delusion cannot absorb any evidence to the contrary. Not that Raul was psychotic or mentally ill. I see many neurotic people (myself included!) who have fixed thoughts about something that they either cannot or will not challenge.

In Imago Relationship Therapy, we recognize that a person with an unresolved childhood need from a parent or parent figure will often project this unmet need onto his or her partner. Sometimes that person sees the partner as having traits belonging to a parent rather than as he really is. Raul was projecting his own dominant, controlling parents onto Art and reacting in the same rebellious, even passive-aggressive way that Raul wished he could have done with his parents. Raul was holding Art accountable for what his parents did to him, and punishing him by withholding sex, the very thing Art wanted most.

Raul had no idea he was doing this. But once he recognized his shadow and saw how he hurt Art, he felt badly and could be accountable for doing that to him. Raul's work was to become more assertive for his needs, not being silently passive when things in the relationship didn't feel satisfactory. Being submissively silent was the strategy he'd adopted in childhood to adapt to his parents, who he felt controlled him. As his work in therapy unfolded, he became increasingly conscious of this.

Now that Raul was clear about the fixed delusion of his parental projection, he became more assertive with Art—whereupon Art's own shadow began to show. Although Raul was indeed projecting a good deal onto Art, there was a grain of truth to the frustration he experienced. Most projections and fixed delusions are founded on some fact, no matter how insignificant it may be.

Make-Ups

We all strive for being in integrity, but it's only human to get out of integrity. The way back to relational integrity is to apologize to the person you've let down. This isn't penance for having done wrong; it's saying to your partner, "I screwed up and I'm sorry, and to make up for it, I offer you _____." Twelve Step groups call it making amends. Step 8 is, "Made a list of all persons we had harmed, and became willing to make amends to them all." This is an important way to reinforce accountability and contribute to stronger relationships.

Art was raised in a family where he mostly had to look after himself. Both his parents worked and didn't track him very closely, letting Art enjoy much more freedom than do most children. All the years he spent living a straight life as a husband and father, he enjoyed heterosexual privileges. His wife was compliant and supportive and usually acquiesced to his needs and wishes. His children always obeyed him and never questioned him or gave him a hard time. He owned his own company, and since he was the boss, his employees never challenged him. So Art was used to getting his way in life and not having significant people challenge him.

Now that Raul began to assert himself, all this was changing. Art was used to making plans and telling Raul afterward, and Raul, out of his usual passivity, didn't complain. Art had grown accustomed to taking charge of their social calendar without consulting Raul. But now, during their therapy, Raul asked Art numerous times to keep him in mind when making plans with others, to stop and talk to him first.

Art did become more aware of this and wanted to comply, but made slip after slip, which made Raul furious. Each time, Art would say he was sorry, that it wasn't intentional. He would sometimes ask, "What's the big deal, anyway?" That made Raul feel further injured and disregarded. Art wasn't being accountable for failing to give Raul what he asked for after he had agreed to do so.

The fourth time Art did this, excusing himself by saying, "I didn't mean to," I stopped him and said, "Art, you may not have genuinely meant to hurt Raul. But you did promise to involve him in making social plans—and have now forgotten to, four times."

Art grew defensive. "What about all the times I did comply and did remember? Doesn't anyone want to give me credit for that?"

"Yes," I replied. "But without taking some responsibility and being accountable for the times you didn't and just saying, 'Oh, I forgot' isn't enough. Particularly because you did it more than a couple of times." I believed Art to be in shadow and I suggested he offer a make-up to Raul for making a promise he did not keep.

When I suggest this, I see my clients and workshop participants becoming uncomfortable. Often the question is, "Why do they have to be punished?" or "Isn't that a bit harsh, to have to make up for it when it wasn't intentional?" I don't think so, because first, it isn't a punishment. A make-up is simply saying to your partner, "I admit what I did, and to make it up to you, I will demonstrate by _____."

This contributes to the intentionality of the relationship. It's easy (and honest!) to say that it wasn't intentional, that "I just wasn't thinking." By promising and not delivering, you are rewounding your partner. Basically, this gives a shadow message that your partner isn't that important. Being intentional in any relationship means being responsible and accountable, owning up to errors.

Whichever partner didn't keep his commitment or his part of the bargain and is out of integrity needs to be the one to offer the make-up. If his partner declines, then he must think of something else to offer. In Imago, we call these *behavior change requests,* where one partner asks the other to act differently.

In one instance, Art failed to consult Raul on some handiwork being done to their house. This upset Raul—all along, he had told Art that he wanted to be consulted. So as a make-up, Art offered to pay more of his share of the bill for the handiwork—an offering Raul accepted.

Initially, Art felt defensive at doing this, that he was being "punished" and put in the dog house to make up for his sins. But in the next session, he said it really forced him to see the issue through Raul's eyes, to understand what it meant for Raul to be involved. It would ensure that he'd be more intentional in future.

No one is perfect. Yes, mistakes will happen. In the meantime, accountable behaviors validate the importance of your partner's needs and requests. No matter how small or big *you* may think it is, more important is that you've committed to something. Your partner has the right for you to own the consequences. How can you maintain relationship integrity and be in it for the long haul?

Homo-Work for the Shadows of Love

1. If your partner were to state what he was frustrated with you about in the relationship, what would he say? Be detailed and itemize a list of all that he would say.
2. What are the things that attracted you to your partner?
3. What are the traits that most infuriate you and frustrate you about your partner?
4. What positive and negative traits does your partner have

that are the same as those of the mothering and fathering caretakers who raised you?

References

1. *The Stanford Encyclopedia of Philosophy.*
2. Eli Coleman, "Developmental Stages of the Coming Out Process," In J. C. Gonsiorek, ed., *A Guide to Psychotherapy with Gay and Lesbian Clients* (New York: Harrington Park Press, 1985).
3. Vivienne Cass, "Homosexual Identity Formation: A Theoretical Model," *Journal of Homosexuality,* vol. 4(3), 1979.
4. Harville Hendrix, *Getting the Love You Want: A Guide for Couples* (New York: Owl Books, 2001).
5. Helen Fisher, *Why We Love* (New York: Henry Holt, 2004).
6. Robert A. Johnson, *Owning Your Own Shadow* (New York: HarperSanFrancisco, 1993).
7. Pat Love, *The Truth About Love* (New York: Fireside, 2001).
8. David Schnarch, *The Passionate Marriage* (New York: Owl Books, 1998).

Chapter 4
Go from a Gay Boy to a Gay Man with Your Father

A king had fallen out with his son. Very angry, the son left his father's castle and created his own kingdom, many miles away. Over time, the king missed his son and sent a messenger, asking him to return, but the son declined his father's invitation. This time, the king sent the messenger back with a different message: "Son, come as far as you can, from your kingdom to mine. And I will meet you the rest of the way."

—The Talmud

I love this story. The father's attachment is strong enough for him to stretch out of his comfort zone and do whatever it takes to reunite with his son. If you're lucky enough to have a father like this, you're more likely to have healthy relationships with men. The good father blesses your uniqueness, your masculinity—and your being gay.

This particular story is about a straight father and son. A strained relationship with one's father doesn't make you gay, as some today still believe. It doesn't even make you more or less masculine. It does interfere with your inner King and relationships with other men. And for men who want relationships with other men, this is significant. Our fathers were our first encounters with masculinity. We men need their blessings to become men and go out into the world to find male relationships. Lacking their blessing, we remain Princes without access to our inner King.

It's normal to bring unfinished business with your father into relationships, and your work in the relationship will help you resolve those old issues. Your partner becomes a stand-in for your father. But if you don't understand this, you will hold your partner accountable for things that aren't his fault. I've seen countless people demand from their partners what they failed to get from their parents—which is not only inappropriate, but impossible. No partner can ever make up for what you never got—or didn't get enough of—from your father in childhood. He can, however, help you resolve those issues within yourself. You just need to know what to do.

This whole process—demanding from your partners what you didn't get from childhood—is often unconscious, so becoming consciously aware of it is the only way to stop its preventing you from getting and keeping a partner. That you unconsciously project your father onto partners seems like bad news—but isn't. Being conscious about this projection allows you to heal this with your partner's help. He is the one who can be most helpful to you, as you will see.

Here again, repeatedly you will return to the scene of the crime until you solve it. This dynamic is gender-neutral and can also happen with straight men in their relationships with female partners: you bring into relationships unfinished business with whichever parent who was more dominant in negative ways. For us gay men, our father is often the problem parent we project onto our partners. With this in mind, let's examine the various ways dysfunctional relationships with your father can seep into relationships.

John Lee is a pioneer in the field of men's work. In his book *At My Father's Wedding,* he writes, "By letting the father sit on the throne of our psyches and souls, we keep ourselves from living."[1] His impact will have vandalized your love maps, and your Lover archetype will be running loose—or with your *father's* vision, not your own. Without this secure King archetype to bless healthy relationships, your Lover archetype will fall in love with the wrong man, again and again.

Remember, your imago match consists of both the positive and negative traits of your father or fathering caretaker. Many of the traits your father figure imprinted on you are the same ones that your partners will possess. They are stand-ins for your father; you hire your partner to rewound as your father did, so that you can resolve those issues. Without this knowledge, unfortunately, you will project these negatives onto a partner and punish him for something that may not be his fault. And doing so, you might well walk away from the very man you were meant to be with.

Unfinished business with your father will also crop up in your relationships with straight men. Looking for that straight-acting partner or for straight men only is often about overvaluing the heterosexual male archetype. Again, looking for father does not make you gay; it simply stems from father hunger, which anyone—male or female, gay or straight—can suffer from. So many straight men are stand-ins for our fathers, and poor substitutes at that. In chapter 8 on heterosexually married gay men, I'll explore how many gay men may be seeking their fathers and playing at winning him over to get daddy's acceptance.

Seeking men who are fathers themselves can be another way of feeding father hunger. There's nothing wrong with dating a man who has children or looking for men who are straight acting (*acting masculine* is what gay men really mean), if they're your type. But if you become rigid—if your man *must* be a father or appear heterosexual, to the exclusion of all others—then you may have trouble finding a partner.

Your inner King leads you to the right man—the one who is healthy for you and can best bless you. In *The Prince and the King,* Michael Gurian observes that the "father-son relationship activates the King more than any other, and if we have dysfunction in that relationship, our way of loving is affected in profound ways." Thus, in archetypal terms, if your father (King) didn't bless you (his Prince) and help you gain a vision for who you are as a man, then you'll have a weak vision for your life—or none at all. Gurian adds:

> The Lover is easily swayed this way or that, easily tempted, and so when a King is not developed within a man, the Lover will often love the wrong [person]; it is the King that guides the man toward the [person] who is most healthy for

him, the one who will best bless him. The King is capable
of judgments that the Lover, passionate and unreserved, is
not.[2]

Unresolved and unacknowledged issues will interfere with your
finding and keeping a partner by making you try to:

- get a partner or boyfriend to "father" you and care of you;
- take care of or "parent" him;
- change his personality and transform him into what *you* want.

Issues related to your father can also lead you into dating and
partnering with men who cannot be there for you the way your
father was not there for you. These men:

- are untrustworthy;
- won't be accountable or change their behaviors;
- don't stay;
- won't leave;
- cheat on you.

For many gay men, unresolved father issues create a rigidity that
prevents them from being attracted to anyone except a certain type.
Their unconscious won't let them rest until they find *that* Mr. Right.
But that's no solution, of course—the underlying problem remains.

In order for sons to improve their relations with their fathers,
Robert Bly invites them to meet their fathers on *their* own terms. For
example, if your father is watching television away from the rest of
the family, Bly advises the son to go join him.[3]

I think this is great advice, but some men, gay and straight alike,
have problems with this approach. Every gay son should *try*—but
what if his father keeps on rejecting him? What's a healthy, effective
way to deal with an unresponsive dad?

Overall, most gay and straight men haven't received much contact or mentoring from their fathers. So there's really little difference,
except that gay men must face the additional baggage of not being

the kind of heterosexual son their father always hoped for.

Some fathers are emotionally, physically, and even sexually abusive. Many more are simply neglectful and absent. As you remember your father from your childhood, did he seem safe or dangerous? Was he kind or abusive and cruel? Was he involved with you or too busy? Was he loving and nurturing or distant and unaffectionate? Could you trust his word? It's important to know *your* perceptions of him—as well as the reality—because this will dictate your search for the right partner for you.

Don't resign yourself to your expectations from childhood. If Dad wasn't available before, how can you believe that men will be available now to offer you relationships? Without trust, you'll seldom enjoy any close male friends, or just drift from one superficial relationship to another. Your task is to mourn for your lost childhood and the father who never was, so you can begin nurturing yourself and trusting other adult men—not as would-be father figures, but as partners and friends. This can also improve your current relationship with your father, if that's what you want.

But you shouldn't stop looking for fatherly men, if that's what you like. Among gay male relationships, there exist many who are fatherly toward each other. The problem lies when your inner Little Boy seeks a partner to literally father him—that's inappropriate.

"The son wishes to remember what the father wants to forget."
This Yiddish proverb begins Terrence Real's book *I Don't Want to Talk About It.*[4] He writes about how when he was in high school, his father saw two boys drown, one trying to save the other. "A drowning person will grip you, if you get in too close," he told his sons. "They'll pull you down with them. You should throw them something, a rope, a life preserver." He gave them this advice without mentioning that he had known both boys; he didn't want to burden his sons with his personal history. Inevitably, however, Real's father did burden Terrence with his inner demons, and Real's work comes out of that legacy.

I admire Real's work for many reasons, chiefly because he writes mostly about heterosexual men and their fathers. It illustrates that straight men have problems with their fathers similar to those that we gay men face. In other words, the father issues we men face have little to do with being gay, but everything to do with being male. Again, the scientific explanation for homosexuality is that a weak father abdicates power to the mother. Thus the boy cannot identify with his father and separate from his mother, and the boy's hunger for a male role model becomes eroticized. "This myth," Real writes, "is repulsive."

What boys need from their father, Real argues, is "affection, not 'masculinity'." He rightly stresses that men need more emotion and vulnerability, which they need to learn from their fathers. By being gay, little boys experience even more disconnection from their fathers. Having a queer son can horrify a father. Yet how would he know if his son were queer? Perhaps a gay son is more clinging and emotional toward him, thereby provoking a harsh response, because he's worried that his son is effeminate. If men are so ingrained to reject anything "feminine," then imagine how a father reacts to an effeminate son or one who doesn't behave in gender-appropriate ways. The distance is more extreme and the disconnection more severe.

As gay boys, our first relationship with a man was usually with our fathers. Learning how to become male usually starts with him. But for so many of us, our fathers were not available. Typically, they did their best and meant well, but many other reasons—work, addictions, intimacy difficulties—may have prevented them from being there for us. So we had to accept father substitutes: uncles, grandfathers, coaches, teachers, and clergy who couldn't provide the affection and intimacy we needed from our fathers. If your father substitute could be there for you in a way that your father should have been, you were lucky.

Relationships force us to go into our own inner journey with our fathers. Gurian calls this process your *inner wilderness,* where you address the issues between you and your internalized father. In *At My Father's Wedding,* John Lee says that if we men "did not trust our fathers and they didn't trust us, it's difficult for us to trust any man fully. If you did not trust your father in general, then you can't trust him as a masculine role model." If that's the case, then how will we as gay men be able to have full relationships?

The way to develop trust is to begin exploring the father wound. Allow yourself to feel the pain. Look at the realities that lie between you and your father and how they've affected you. John Lee says, "The father-wound must be opened, descended into, and dealt with in order that [you] may someday trust [your] own maleness." Not having this trust in your maleness means being forced to relive over and over the negatives between you and your father with every man with whom you enter a relationship

My Relationship with My Father

The work I urge on my clients began as a result of my own work with my father. In chapter 2, I talked about how my female-dominated family was always trying to make a man out of me. They were concerned that all the women might feminize me and make me gay, so they would place me with other males such as my uncles and encourage me in sports—neither of which I liked. All I wanted was my own father—and I never got him.

Many times during my growing-up years, my father was absent from my life. When he *was* around, what affected me negatively was mostly what *didn't* happen and what *wasn't* said. As a child and teenager, I was very verbal and emotional, open about my feelings and thoughts. But early on, I became aware that my father wasn't okay with that about me, so to receive his love and approval, unconsciously I decided to be quiet and go with what I thought was his program. I sat up at night crying, wondering what it was about me that he didn't like as I did not feel loved by him. I thought that perhaps I was unwanted or was just a reminder that his first marriage (to my mother) had gone bad. I believed he really didn't love me.

But after I became a therapist and learned more about my father's formative years, I came to understand that it probably wasn't personal. Most likely, he gave to me all that he could—perhaps that was all he himself had received as a child. My father is the last of ten children, so I can imagine the neglect he must have suffered in such a big family; nonetheless, I had to deal with the marginal relationship with him and how that impacted my forming a male identity.

When I was three and my sister was one, our parents divorced.

One year later, my father remarried and later had a son with his new wife. As a divorced dad, he would take my sister and me for visits each weekend. I remember spending most of my time with his wife while he watched sports on television. To this day, I cringe inside when I hear a sporting event on television, especially on weekends.

As I grew older, I could no longer hold in the feelings and emotions I felt toward my father and tried to tell him. But I did not experience him as receptive; he either changed the subject or told me he did not want to hear it, saying he felt chastised and attacked. I was admittedly aggressive and hurtful at first. I lacked the skills to talk to him, but hurting him was the last thing I meant to do. Instead, I wanted him to hold me and tell me that it was okay to have my hurt feelings.

Once when I tried to talk to my father, he walked away from me physically. Another time he packed up my sister and me and took us home. Still another time I was driving us to lunch when I began to try talking about our relationship. He ordered me to turn the car around and go back home, which I did. Each time he stopped the conversation, I would avoid him until things seemed better between us and as if nothing had happened.

I wasn't physically afraid of my father, but I never wanted to make him angry or have him upset with me. I learned to avoid these types of discussions with him, and yet I wanted to have my truth out between us. I had so many questions about how he felt with my mother, about leaving me at age three and making a new family. One line in Eminem's song "Cleaning Out My Closet" refers to his father, who left him at a young age: "I wonder if he even kissed me goodbye." I wondered the same thing.

Those were the kind of conversations I wanted to have with my father. Even if they weren't things I wanted to hear, I wanted to hear them anyway because they still stood in my way of having a good and connected relationship with him. I wanted to talk them out because they were negatively impacting my relationship with him. I felt that I was holding on to things he had done and said, and needed to get them off my chest, because I knew they were impacting my relationships with other men, both straight and gay—and particularly on my finding a partner.

As I approached my thirties, I found myself still wanting to talk to my father, but I didn't know how to without him feeling chastised or attacked. When my sister started having children, I began to understand what it had been like for me at their young ages, not having my father around. I began to see how important my brother-in-law was to them as their father. I also understood how important I was to them and how they needed a strong connection to us as well as to their mother. Their mere presence flooded me with all kinds of memories and feelings I had as a child about my own father. I needed to get it all off my chest.

At thirty-six, I was initiated into ManKind's New Warrior Training Adventure.[5] In this men's workshop and in subsequent men's groups, I learned how to be around other men, particularly the straight men that I'd feared my whole life. I talked, wept, and dreamed of talking openly with my father about my feelings and thoughts and listening to his. I heard about other men having similar talks with their own fathers—some successful, others not.

I began to realize I was carrying part of *his* baggage, which he unintentionally passed onto me as a boy. I needed to give it back. So with the help of the men in my men's group, I worked on approaching my dad for a heart-to-heart talk. I met him for lunch, but once he realized this was one of those times where I wanted to talk on a deeper level about my feelings and our relationship, he said, "Joe, I cannot do this."

"Do what?" I asked.

"The past is over and done with. Can't you get over it? Can't we move on?"

"Dad," I said, "that's what I am trying to do. I just need to express my feelings, not just about the past but the *present* as well."

My father shook his head in disappointment and began to rise from his chair. "I'm sorry son," he said. "I cannot do this."

It was then I went from boy to man. Afraid and yet not afraid at the same time, I stood up and said firmly, "Sit down!"

He looked at me in disbelief. "What did you say?"

I wasn't going to cower to his disapproval this time. I felt myself coming into my mature masculinity and wanted to be man to man with my father.

"I said, 'Sit down,' Dad!"

Silence. The restaurant around us vanished, and mentally I was my twenty-five-year-old self who turned the car around when he demanded I do so, with my teenage and preteen selves standing beside me. This time, my mature masculine thirty-seven-year-old adult wasn't going to back down. Once more I said, "I am asking you nicely to sit down!" And to my total disbelief, he did.

Shocked, I calmly sat down and firmly began telling my father of my pain, my sorrow, my desire for more from him and *with* him. Many times as I was talking to him, I thought to myself that even if he wasn't listening, I had to do this for *me*. I had to give him back all his baggage he'd passed onto me so that I no longer carried it for him. Secretly, I hoped he *was* listening, that somehow my pain and my feelings would open up his, to let him connect with me as I'd always dreamed of.

He sat there and listened. He wept, and so did I. In fact, I realized that so much of what I was saying to him were the exact complaints I had with my partner, Mike. I had begun to realize that many of the issues I had with Mike were the result of the unfinished business I had with my father. I listened to myself tell my father things I'd said to Mike over the years. Now I saw that these things were clearly between my father and me, and I'd projected them onto Mike. I found it comforting that I could go to Mike after this and begin removing these negative projections that came from my fathering and exorcise them from our relationship.

After an hour, I was finished. My father had hardly said a word. I knew that for him, this had not gone well. He wouldn't and couldn't go where I needed to go with him. But that was okay, because I went by myself. I didn't attack or blame him, call him names, humiliate, or belittle him. I stayed with the data that existed between us—my feelings and judgments. I had done a clearing with him, as I'll describe in chapter 6 on communication. I had purged long-standing issues that prevented me from maturing from a boy to a man, not only with him but in other areas of my life. I firmly believe that on that day, I became a man. I blessed myself. That day, I activated my King.

That's why you're holding this, my second book, in your hands today. I found my vision and I also found myself. Hopefully, this chapter will help you do the same, or at least put you on your own road to finding your inner King.

Paternal Wounds

In our early lives, our fathers, male caretakers, and father surrogates can imprint our concept of males—for better or worse.

From family legends and fairy tales, we learn how to act as men. But when our own fathers have been inadequate, neglectful, absent, or abusive, we begin to long for an idealized father figure. As adults, we search for that good father in the partners we choose, political leaders, gurus and spiritual healers, heads of corporations, and others. We make these men surrogate father figures, and we regress in their presence, becoming little boys.

As adult males we each have an adult self and a little boy self. Leading with your little boy self and putting him in charge of an adult relationship with a partner is like pairing a ten year old with a forty year old. A little boy cannot be in an adult relationship. A grown-up and a child are developmentally unequal in too many ways. This creates unbalanced power between partners and causes much conflict. If your unconscious stays emotionally regressed at a young age, your partner will not only be turned off, he won't even want to help you or work with you on the relationship. Even if he doesn't fully understand that you are regressed, he will be turned off. He wants a man, not a boy. Becoming aware of this dynamic, you can recognize when one of your unmet little-boy needs arises, without expecting your partner to meet it or solve it, as you would have expected your father to do.

Your partners will embody your father's dominant negative traits as well as his positive ones. If your father was cold, distant, and unavailable, so might your partners be. Or your own behavior may unwittingly provoke them to behave like your father, eliciting these same traits.

As I have said, we men also live with our internalized father! Even after he's dead, we don't bury him emotionally. We may keep trying to get from him what he never gave, or try to become for him what we never were—and thereby face disappointments over and over. Another trap is to assume that now that your father's grown older and matured, he can give you what you never received as a child.

Jay, a thirty-five-year-old waiter at a local restaurant, was depressed and suffered from low self-esteem. He told me he was having trouble finding a partner. When he dated men he liked, he would always find something wrong with them. Men he felt attracted to weren't attracted to him. He was seeing another therapist, a straight male, and felt he couldn't tell him certain things. He felt that talking about his sexual issues and relationship problems would let my therapist down, so he edited out things he thought would disappoint or upset the man. He laughed, saying that he knew it was ridiculous to pay all that money while hiding things from the very person he should feel able to talk to.

He continued seeing the other therapist and me at the same time. He didn't want to leave his other therapist, he just wanted to be able to talk freely about what was happening in his life with me, as he did not feel free to do so with the straight male therapist. Clearly, Jay was in negative transference, projecting his father onto his therapist and reenacting old patterns between himself and his father. He could resolve these issues with his *internalized father* through the other therapist as the stand-in father if he chose to by talking to him openly about the things he thought would let him down. I told him so, but still he wanted to keep seeing the other therapist without telling him certain things.

I agreed to see Jay only if his other therapist knew that Jay was seeing me, and if there were things he felt that he couldn't tell him but could tell me, a gay therapist. Jay agreed with this and told him, and we all three agreed to this arrangement temporarily. It was clear Jay was scared and anxious, and the other therapist and I agreed it best to honor his wishes and let him proceed at his own pace.

Jay was frightened by old childhood issues with his father surfacing in his therapy, so he brought another therapist—me—into the mix. It isn't ideal to have two therapists this way. The best approach is to work out with one therapist the issues that might be uncomfortable for you. Jay was creating an exit. In other words, to minimize his discomfort at doing the work he needed to do with his straight therapist, he sought out my services. This was a glimpse into what his relationships were probably like—filled with exits. And in our work, this is exactly what surfaced.

Jay began telling me about his background. His father had died five years earlier and throughout the funeral, he told me, he never cried. He was raised in a middle-class neighborhood by a codependent mother and an alcoholic father who, when he drank, grew hot-tempered and fought with Jay's mother. He could hear them in his bedroom while he was trying to sleep at night. Sometimes his father would start drinking early in the evening and begin berating Jay about his weight and facial acne. His father harassed him about his weight constantly and called him "chubby," even though Jay didn't have a weight problem. Even his doctor told his parents that Jay was physically stocky but within normal limits of weight for kids his age. His mother never came to Jay's rescue. Jay's sister never received the same type of abuse from their father, so Jay assumed that his father hated him.

The day following his drunken stupors, his father would demand that the house be quiet because of his hangovers. Everyone had to tiptoe around. Jay hated his father for being so intimidating and controlling, but never dared say anything to the man. He tried to speak to his mother about him, but she would say, "He's still your father." This meant that she didn't want to hear it, nor did she want him to say anything, so Jay kept quiet.

One evening when Jay was thirteen, his mother went shopping with his sister and left him home alone with his father. Jay was watching television, and his father demanded he turn it off. Jay, smelling alcohol on his breath, chose to ignore him and kept on watching television. His father angrily shut the television off and began screaming, "You never listen to me, you little shit. I'm going to kill you!"

Jay remembers seeing his father rush toward him, grabbing his hair and dragging him into another room. He thought his father was only trying to scare him, but the man began punching him repeatedly in the face and did not stop. Jay thought that he was going to die. He tried to scream, but his father's strong hands kept punching and slapping him over and over. He struggled to break free, to no avail. He could see evil in his father's eyes, as if he were a man possessed.

When his father finally did stop, Jay fell to the floor gasping for breath and bleeding all over. His father went off to bed. When Jay collected himself, he went to his room, set a chair against the door to alert him if his father came in, and collapsed into bed. When he came downstairs the next day, his mother asked, "What happened to your face?" It was red, bruised, and swollen. Jay said, "I fell." His father added nothing, and Jay's mother asked no more questions. It was clear as I listened to Jay telling me this that she didn't want to know. Most mothers would find his answer unacceptable, seeing this type of swelling and bruising on her child's face.

Jay had forgotten this memory until I asked him what I ask all my clients in our first few sessions: "What were your best and worst memories of your father?" Jay didn't think his father *meant* to harm him: he must have been in an alcoholic blackout and didn't even know what he had done to him that day.

Still, I told Jay, whether or not the intent was conscious, his parent's silence about it the next day was abuse. They saw from his face that obviously he had been beaten. Often, for children, the lack of follow-up to an abusive situation is worse than the actual abuse. Jay had never been given the chance to talk about it, and that had traumatic effects for him. I suggested that he enter group therapy. There, I told him, we could work with his issues with men.

This is what makes group therapy so helpful. Other members stand in for family and friends. The issues in one's life get played out, and as a therapist, I get to facilitate the process as it happens, live and unplugged. In fact, skillfully guided group work is therapy at its best.

Jay agreed to enter the group, and after some time he began talking about his father. The group asked if he felt angry or hurt by what his father had done. Jay responded no, that if his father hadn't been alcoholic, none of this would have happened. The group challenged him appropriately: "But it *did* happen, he was alcoholic and you did suffer at his hands—literally!" They urged him to consider how his mother failed to protect him from his father. We could all see clearly that Jay's family of origin contributed to his inability to find healthy relationships.

In her neglect to protect him or teach him how to protect himself appropriately, Jay's mother helped to carve the template that men are dangerous; they're to be feared, and so you keep your distance. He was going it alone, and he was powerless.

Experiential Group Work

Since Jay lacked emotion about the incident, I suggested we do an experiential exercise. Experiential group work is when other men in the group role-play and act out scenes from one another's childhoods and present lives, and practice saying things to people that they want to say from their own lives, using group members as stand-ins for these people. It can involve shouting, screaming, and hitting pillows, but all within the safe group environment we create.

Jay picked another man in group who agreed to role-play his father. The setup I created was at Jay's father's grave. (His father had died five years earlier.) The volunteer lay on the floor, and we put a sheet over him. I told Jay this was his dead father and then suggested that Jay had unfinished business to talk to him about, in particular, how his father's drinking affected him as well as the time he beat and almost killed him. I also urged him to share with his father anything else he needed to tell him.

"I don't think this is going to work. This is acting," Jay kept insisting. "I feel stupid and embarrassed," he protested. The group assured him that it wasn't stupid and that it would be important for them, letting them open up to their father issues as well. Jay would be demonstrating how other men could begin addressing these issues. Ultimately, Jay agreed.

I asked, "What kinds of things would your father have said to you if you talked to him about hard issues and your feelings?" Jay told us that as an older man, his father had changed quite a bit—he had softened, was more affectionate and loving. So he might be apologetic and remorseful over what he had done. So I directed Jay's surrogate father to behave that way in responding to whatever "his son" said.

I had Jay sit down next to the pretend casket and lift back the sheet, as if his deceased father had come back to life and could talk to him. Then we began, with my coaching.

"Hi, Dad," Jay said. "It's been a long time."

"Yes, it has, son. How have you been, and how's your mother?"

"We're fine, Dad. I have some things to talk to you about . . ." Then Jay fell into tears. His head in his hands, he could not stop.

The rest of the group was silent, holding a safe space—a tight container, if you will—for Jay. Some had tears in their eyes watching the pain that he was expressing, but feeling their own father wounds as well.

"Dad," Jay asked, "why did you drink so much?"

"I didn't know any better. I know I drank too much, and I must have hurt you and the family."

"You did hurt me, Dad. A lot! You almost killed me one time." Now Jay was getting angry. "Do you remember that, Dad?"

Up to now, he hadn't shown feelings of anger or sadness about his father. But now he was, and more were coming. I set up these sorts of scenes in group and workshops so that every member will feel safe to do whatever he wants to physically release his angry feelings. Off limits, of course, was Jay's physically harming himself or anyone else, particularly the man playing his father.

Jay was overcome by a wave of anger. He started crying and shouting at his father over and over, "How could you do that to me? You almost killed me. I am your son! Do you hate me? How can you hate me so much? You are my father!"

As he expressed these strong feelings, I whispered in the stand-in father's ear to just listen and look at Jay. When he finished, he collapsed to the floor crying.

I asked Jay if he were willing to let his father apologize to him and hold him in his arms. Crying even more, Jay nodded yes. I had him move into his father's embrace. While Jay sobbed and sobbed, his dad whispered in his ear, "I am so sorry! I never meant to hurt you.

What was I thinking? I should have thought about *you* more. I should have been there for you. You're my only son, and I let you down. I *am* sorry."

As a group, we were offering Jay a reparative experience. Even though this was a made-up scenario and Jay's father never did tell him these things, it allowed him to experience the facts differently and change his relationship with his inner father—the one within himself. A reparative experience can take place in life outside of therapy, depending on the circumstance. You could meet a man who looks or acts like your father, and through your encounter with him have a healing experience about your internalized father; you never know, however, if or when that will happen to create this change for yourself. Group therapies accelerate the healing process by making such shifts happen.

After Jay calmed down and his tears stopped, I asked him to slowly pull away from his father, look into his eyes and say good-bye. I told him that he could put this experience into his heart, reflect on it, and do it again in group to learn how to do this for himself—to internalize the healing introspectively. Jay said good-bye to his father and lifted the sheet back over him.

When you do this type of experiential work, you are really *there*. Group members always report that the rest of the group disappears while this work is being done. So to finish a role-play like this, I coached the stand-in father to look at Jay and say, "I am Howard, your group peer, not your father." I then asked Jay to look at him and say, "I see you as Howard, and not my father." This allows parts of the mind to distance themselves from the experiential exercise. Jay said it felt like he truly was talking to his father. The group members indeed had disappeared, and he was there with his father—his internalized father—and realized he had more feelings about his father than he'd thought.

Jay began to understand that because he hadn't resolved his father's not being there for him, he kept meeting men who would not and could not be there for him. This was standing in his way from finding real love with a partner. This was partly too a result of his mother's neglect, but that was another group and another experiential exercise.

Father Hunger

Father hunger—a phrase that comes from studies of straight men—is a yearning to know our actual fathers and what it means to be a real man. By "a real man," I mean a man who is mature and affectionately masculine. Other theorists of the men's movement have referred to father hunger as prompting fear, grief, and even rage. With this all unresolved, you'll again act out negatively in your unconscious search for the Good Father.

Patriarchal Father

A patriarchal father is the Shadow King. Recall from chapter 2 that he King in his most highly evolved form is loving, wise, powerful, and able to bless others, particularly his sons. But the patriarchal King competes with other men needlessly, in inappropriate ways, punishing other males—his sons included—if they don't behave and conform to his thinking and ways of behavior. He follows the strict male gender role of being unfeeling, unaffectionate, and demeaning to women and anything that resembles the feminine.

Cole and Tony had been together eight years. For the past three, they lived in a house they'd bought together. But since moving in together, their relationship had changed. Tony felt that Cole left everything around the house for him to do. Cole felt that Tony was trying to order him around. Both stuck to their stories and wouldn't budge. Cole was most upset that Tony was threatening to leave the relationship. He felt that they could work this out, but Tony said, "Not until you change your dominating ways."

As we learned in chapter 3, the more deeply partners commit to one another, the greater the power struggle becomes. I informed both Tony and Cole that after they bought the house and moved in together, it was normal for issues to arise. I told them what I tell others about relationships: that they had hired each other to resolve issues from the past. I asked Tony to commit to staying in the relationship until we could see what was really playing out between them. In other words, I asked Tony to close his exits (see chapter 9).

Tony agreed.

I obtained family histories on both of them. Tony had a passive father who made Tony do everything that the father should have been doing himself. If Tony's mother went out, he put Tony in charge to watch his siblings. Often, he corrected Tony at the dinner table or in front of his friends for not having accurate information. When his father realized Tony's ignorance on a subject, he'd spotlight it by asking Tony questions he couldn't answer; then when it became obvious that he didn't know, his father would correct him in front of everyone, making Tony feel stupid and humiliated.

In Cole's household, his father was extremely dominant. Whatever he said, went. His mother was passive and acquiesced to his every wish. He always felt loved by his father, but recalled not feeling accepted. Cole felt that he was a disappointment to him. Both Cole and Tony had dominant, patriarchal fathers.

Cole had one good memory of his father that brought him to tears. It seemed that Cole had trouble behaving in kindergarten, causing the teacher to reprimand him. She began by rewarding each student with a full set of stars, and for every misbehavior, one star would be taken away. If stars weren't gone completely, students would get one to wear home on their forehead. But each day, Cole couldn't cooperative in the class and got all his stars taken away. He'd go home feeling very badly about this, not knowing what to do. His parents knew about this and worked on it with him, but still Cole had trouble.

One day Cole came home from school, starless, to find that his father had made a large cardboard star, shiny with aluminum foil, and hung it over Cole's bed. Cole recalls being elated at feeling his father's love and support. As he told the story, he wept, saying, "I knew my father loved me. I just think he didn't know ways to show it." While most likely true, Cole still walked on eggshells around his father, even today. And now he was making his partner walk on eggshells, just as his father had done to him.

Yet Cole had always had trouble talking with his father. His father was not happy about his being gay and had never met Tony in the eight years since they were together. This was not totally unusual, since Cole's parents lived in another state. During holidays and visits home, Cole and Tony went alone to their respective families. This made it easier for Cole not to stand up to his father and force the issue that he was gay and partnered.

I could see that Cole's unresolved issues with his father were eclipsing his relationship more than couples therapy could handle. Cole disagreed. He didn't believe he was behaving that poorly to Tony, nor did he believe that he was acting in a dominant patriarchal way like his father. He wouldn't take any of my suggestions that he receive some individualized help with me while he did couples therapy.

One day they both came in to see me, with Tony very upset at the way Cole had spoken to him in front of their friends. Tony felt humiliated, and it was clear that Cole had been belittling Tony. While not purposeful or conscious, it was deteriorating their relationship and causing Tony to distance. Cole clearly did not want him to leave.

Even though it was clear to me what Cole was doing, I could see that Tony wasn't getting through to him. In this particular session, I let them argue they way they normally did at home. Angrily, Tony told Cole he was mean and insensitive and accused him of acting this way on purpose. Cole denied this and called Tony thin-skinned.

They had established a victim—perpetrator dynamic with each other. After watching this for fifteen minutes, I interrupted to tell them I could see that neither was getting what was going on between them. To better illustrate my point, I asked Tony to get down on hands and knees at Cole's feet and look up at him—and for Cole to tell him he was thin-skinned and ought to shape up.

They both looked at me in disbelief! But I knew exactly what I was doing. I wanted to shock them in some way, to interrupt the fixed dynamic of their dominant-submissive style of relating to each other.

"I am never going to do that, Joe!" cried Tony. "That's humiliating."

"But that's how you are responding to Cole," I said to Tony. "And Cole, that's how you are talking to Tony, as if he's your servant. So you might as well make him assume the subservient position."

Neither Tony nor Cole moved. For about ten minutes, there was silence in the room. Tears welled up in both of their eyes.

I'd worked with them long enough for them to trust me and to know that I wouldn't have suggested this if it didn't have some truth to it. Finally, I said, "Even if you don't physically assume the position, my point is taken. The only reason I made the suggestion was for you both to see, vividly, what you're doing to yourselves and to each other."

Tony entered group therapy to work on his father issues. Clearly, both of them had issues with their fathers that were surfacing, but Tony's were stronger, pushing Cole away and closest to breaking up their relationship.

Tony began coming to group. There, I could help him clear up the issue of his father and accelerate that process faster than his couples therapy with Cole would allow.

Letting Go of Your Negative Father

At the beginning of my workshops for gay men, I include material on father-son issues. I never expected the reactions I received at the first workshop. When I began talking about doing father work, the gay men grew quiet and their breathing became shallow. The further we proceeded with the exercise on fathers, some men started crying—slow tears at first, then for others, sobbing.

This part of the workshop is to address your issues with your father, and to do so you must get closer to your feelings and attitude toward him. This can bring up strong and unfamiliar emotions—feelings you have been suppressing much of your life. But you have to do this, if you want to resolve them and stop them from ruling your life and interfering with your relationships with yourself and your partners. If you don't want to recreate your father's negative aspects in your relationships, then I believe you *must* do this work.

Almost half the men passed on even doing the exercise in my first workshop, which I give them the option to do. I gently urged them to do the exercise, reminding them that they came here to achieve something, and what seems difficult might be the very thing they need to do. But if they insisted on not participating, I supported their decision.

Now, in workshops at the gay men's retreats I facilitate, I anticipate that some participants will have difficulty with father-son exercises. I tell them in advance that doing father work is part of the workshop and stress the importance of looking at our relationships with our fathers. In order to become the men we want to be, we must do this work.

John Lee calls this process metaphorically "killing the father":

> When a son rejects his father's fears that there is too little energy to go around and asserts himself, he begins to "kill the father" in another necessary rite of passage. If a son finds the courage and responds to the need to look his father squarely in the eyes until the elder looks away, he's done it. When the son finally allows himself to succeed in the areas in which his father failed, then he's accomplished it. The day the son breaks the pattern that has tied him to his father's psyche and soul, he's achieved it. These are just a few of the ways that the son symbolically and necessarily "kills the father".[6]

In doing any work on letting go of their fathers, men fear that this means one has to break off contact with him or brand him a bad man and hate him. That's not at all what this is about. As Lee states, "it is about letting go of the negative, not-good-enough, abandoning disappearing father." Letting go of the negatively imprinted father can help you begin to parent yourself in healthier ways than he did for you when you were a child. It will free you to find healthier partners and reduce your attempts at looking to be fathered by your partner.

This is *not* about letting go of your father's positive aspects, but about letting go of the negatives to better embrace the positives. Nothing will exorcise the positives that your father gave you; cherish those you have.

Here is an exercise that blends John Lee's work with Harville Hendrix's work on dealing with the internalized father, where a partner or another male in your life can stand for your father. In Imago

Relationship Therapy, partners do a version of this called the parent-child dialogue, where by taking turns, couples begin to understand how each of their parents influences the relationship.

Father-Son Dialogue

Two men sit comfortably in front of each other. You can do this with your partner (ideally) or in group therapy or with a close friend you trust. There is no touching of one another in this exercise. One man goes first, as himself at a young age. The other man plays the role of the father.

Pick an age you have clear memories of, or some memory of being young and small. Take deep breaths, letting attention leave your head and move down into your body. The man in the fathering role tells you, "Close your eyes and envision yourself being young and small," at whatever age you have chosen to be in this exercise. If you chose age ten, for example, say things like, "I am small, skinny. I have bangs in my eyes. I get dirty a lot playing outside." Notice that you don't say, "When I *was* ten." Say, "I *am* ten," to really transport you back in memory to that time and place.

The man in the fathering role now tells you to close your eyes and envision your father—or childhood caregiver—in your mind's eye. You picture your father of today as he looked then, not now. Describe him out loud, as if he were right there. See what he looks like, hear what his voice sounds like, smell his aftershave, cigarette, cigar, or alcohol on his breath. Imagine what he felt like—his beard or stubble, his hair, his clothes. For example, you say, "Daddy, you are tall and overweight. You look angry a lot and you smell like beer"—or whatever he was like. But say it as if he were there right now, looking the way he did *then,* not *now.*

Admit whatever feelings that want to arise. If there are tears, I recommend letting them stream down your face and don't wipe them away. Feel your tears—they remind you of the hard work you are doing.

When you are both ready, the man playing your father says, "I am your father. What is it like living with me as a gay little boy?"

The stand-in father doesn't respond to anything said by the man playing himself as a child. Instead he sits without saying anything and simply listens to the stand-in child who's talking. He keeps the other man in his gaze and doesn't interrupt or ask leading questions. He just listens. Often the stand-in father may get tearful and have compassion for the man doing his work; it may also bring up issues with *his* father. But it's not yet his turn. He is simply holding open a space for the other man to do his work.

When the stand-in child seems to have finished, the man playing the role of his father can ask him, "Is there more?" This may prompt him, but if he says, "No," move on to the next question.

> *"What was your best day with me, when you felt most connected to me?"*
>
> *"What was your worst day with me, when you felt most injured and wounded by me?"*
>
> *"What did you need from me most and never got?"*
>
> *"What did you need from me regarding your being gay?"*
>
> **"What did you do in order to feel safe around me?"*
>
> *"Say good-bye to me and let me go."*

This last sentence is *not* about completely letting go of his father—just the parts of him that have caused dysfunction in his adult life and current relationships with friends, other men in general, and with his partner.

The purpose of this exercise is to become conscious of the present undertow that might exist from unfinished business with a father.

*Notice this question, "What did you do in order to feel safe around me?" Remember, children are not necessarily conscious of what is happening around them. This question requires that you think back and assess today the decisions you think you made in order to adapt to your father. I, for example, was obedient, stayed out of my father's way, distanced myself emotionally, and adapted to what I thought he wanted.

After doing this exercise at couples workshops, I've heard hundreds of couples say, "Is *that* what we have been fighting about. It is about your father?" The listener recognizes that what his partner says during the father-son dialogue is about yesteryear, simply surfacing in their relationship the way it's supposed to, as imago therapy reminds us. This lets you, the listener, understand that any conflict on this issue is *not* personal. This issue is your partner's childhood wound, and the exercise allows you to feel compassion for whatever happened to him. The partner who plays the young, small version of himself can also recognize that whatever he is arguing about is not between the two of you, but between his father and him.

Doing this exercise with your partner can provide deep insight and healing. If you have no partner, or if he won't do this with you, then the next best thing is doing it with someone you know and trust, or in a group or workshop you attend.

Facing Your Father Head-On

As a therapist, my bias is that the greatest healing you can do is to go to your father directly. You can read a self-help book, attend therapy and workshops, and even do this father work with a partner. The most healing, though, will come from doing this work with your father himself, face to face. I have heard clients ask, "Why bring all of this up and hurt my father?" or "My father is old now. What good would it do *him?*" or "My father has changed. Why do this, if he's not like he was when I was a young boy?"

I recommend that they still do it, particularly if their early childhood issues are interfering with their adult lives and relationships. This isn't about bashing your father or making him feel bad, but rather lets you both have your own feelings that can connect the two of you. It's about doing a clearing-out of whatever lies between you two, as we will discuss in chapter 6, on communication. And if you don't believe there *is* anything between the two of you, be sure you haven't transferred it elsewhere. That transference can be your way of letting father off the hook, if you project your feelings and judgment onto someone else—particularly onto your partner.

Meeting Your Father

If you decide to do this work with your father face to face, I suggest doing it when you are calm, nonreactive, and can have a discussion, not an argument. It's important that you go to him without blaming or making yourself a victim. Also, there should be no expectation attached to the outcome. Let the dialogue with him be the first step to purge anything unresolved between the two of you.

If your father is an alcoholic or the type of man who would do physical harm or abuse you or anyone in a way that could be dangerous, then I don't recommend approaching him. Talk with a therapist, coach, sponsor, friend, or your partner before doing it, because it's especially important to practice what you want to say and how you're going to say it. This will help you anticipate different things that could surface when you do speak to him.

Welcoming the Good Father

There is plenty of positive fathering energy within our gay male culture and many gay elders who would like to share it. This is one way to father yourself by finding a gay man who has that energy. I encourage you to look around for it among gay males. Culturally, we tend to discard older gay men as though we had no use for them. But we need them to guide us in our relationships. We need their counsel on how to deal with relationship problems and resolve conflicts. They *are* our gay fathers and grandfathers. They need us as much as we need them.

Having male mentors, both gay and straight, can help. Do the imaginary father-son dialogue exercise from this chapter, adapted from John Lee's work, with a gay elder to help you let go of your father's imprints that have survived to interfere with your life.

Homo-Work on Father Issues

1. Write down your father's positive and negative personality traits as *you* perceived him as a young child.
2. Identify the worst memories from childhood that you've had of him.
3. Identify the best ones, along with a special time you had

with him in childhood.

4. When you were growing up, what was your father's view of the world? Did it change as you grew older, or did it stay the same?

5. What did you want most from your father, but never received?

6. When you are around your father, how old do you feel?

7. What is your perception of your Divinity or Higher Power?

8. What are your judgments about male-dominated corporations?

References

1. John Lee, *At My Father's Wedding* (New York: Bantam Books, 1991).
2. Michael Gurian, *The Prince and the King* (New York: G.P. Putnam and Sons, 1992).
3. Robert Bly, *Iron John: A Book About Men* (Vancouver, WA: Vintage Books, 1992).
4. Terrence Real, *I Don't Want To Talk About It: Overcoming The Secret Legacy of Male Depression* (New York: Scribner, 1997).
5. The ManKind Project: New Warrior Training Adventure (www.mkp.org).
6. Lee, *At My Father's Wedding*.

Chapter 5
Recognize the Difference Between Mommy Nearest, Mommy Dearest, and Mommy Queerest

The ideal mother, like the ideal marriage, is a fiction.

—Milton Sapirstein, *Paradoxes of Everyday Life*

Is your search being blocked by maternal inhibitions? Often, the other woman in a gay man's life is his mother, which can block you from intimacy in your relationships. This chapter explores how gay men get hung up on what their mothers would—or wouldn't—approve of for them. It also covers what a good mother offers to her growing son in terms of relational skills and the ability to comfort himself, and stay true to his own needs and wants in relationship while still being able to give to his partner.

How do you separate from a mother who relied on you, her gay son, as a surrogate husband? When a mother makes a son—gay or straight—her partner in emotional ways, she prevents him from being able to attach appropriately to future partners. There can be a psychological marriage to mom, typified by the understanding gay son in whom she might confide. This is emotional incest. While this does not make a boy gay, it does vandalize his ability to create loving romantic relationships. In fact, serious negative effects from this prevent healthy relationships.

A mother's overt and actual abuse of any kind impacts her gay son and his future relationships. Separating from her is necessary, but still learning from her is an even better idea! I will examine the positives you received from her, such as her relating and nurturing skills.

It's inaccurate to believe that you won't have to deal with your mother in any relationship just because you're a man with other men. Relationships are gender-neutral in terms of whom we pick and which parent's influences will predominate. Straight men can actually marry female versions of their fathers, and straight women can marry their mothers in men. The internalized parent or caregiver who was most negative to you, not necessarily of the same gender, will appear and disrupt your relationships.

This chapter also illustrates how to steal the key from under your mother's pillow—taking back your autonomy from your mother in keeping with the theme of the story of Iron John. I believe we should go to our mothers while they are still alive and address the issues, both positive and negative, that lay between them and ourselves. No matter how close the relationship, to be a man you need to separate and cut the umbilical cord—but not necessarily sever your relationship with her. Simply *change* your relationship with her to make room for real love with a partner.

Your mother, however, may be unwilling to have these conversations, and even if she is, she may not be able to let you unlock your inner Wild Man. This chapter teaches you how to do it, with or without her permission. It will feel dangerous at times, but it can be done.

Your next task is addressing your internalized mother. The way to honor but also exorcise this internal mother is to become conscious of the ways she manifests within you and your relationship. Is it working for you? If not, find a way to eliminate parts or most of it.

This chapter will cover diva worship as well; time and again I've seen how mother hunger contributes to it, which in turn interferes with those wanting to find and keep Mr. Right. Many gay men devote time and energy to their divas as replacements for their mothers, which distracts them from their partner or from having one at all.

Mommy Nearest

In this society, it is taboo to speak ill of our mothers, so we either keep silent or get judged negatively for doing so. By going against his mother, a man gets punished and called a misogynist. Perhaps, owing to the horrors of sexism, the culture has become too focused in one direction, looking only at what men have done to women. It may be time, however, to examine what women do to men—especially mothers raising the boys who ultimately grow up to hate women. Somewhere our mothers play a part in engendering this negativity.

When someone disparages his mother, why is our wondering whether she is at fault met with disapproval? We allow sons and daughters alike to criticize their fathers, and our discomfort over their negative talk is considerably less than the public outcry when the topic switches to Mommy Dearest.

Society reveres anything associated with mother: Mother Earth, Mother Nature, and the celibate, childless Mother Teresa. Especially in the mental health field, when we examine a child's early infancy, we focus on the mother, talking about the time and attention she devotes to nurturing her baby. During the child's first year of life, the father is rarely the primary caregiver. I am sure this will change as more fathers, particularly gay men, join in the care and rearing of their children, but until then, talk about child-rearing usually focuses on the mother.

Herein lies the source of the social mantra "Love your mother." No one wants to believe that a mother could not love her children. No one wants to hear about how a mother can lack maternal instinct. Those who speak out about their mothers abusing them or being indifferent maternally to any extent will often not be believed and find themselves accused of betraying their mothers.

Mother attachment runs so deep that in *Necessary Losses,* Judith Viorst writes, "A young boy lies in a hospital bed. He is frightened and in pain. Burns cover 40 percent of his small body. Someone has doused him with alcohol and then, unimaginably, has set him on fire. He cries for his mother. His mother has set him on fire."[1]

Viorst goes on to describe the difficulty of separating from one's mother: "[I]t doesn't matter what kind of mother a child has lost or how perilous it may be to dwell in her presence. It doesn't mater whether she hurts or hugs. Separation from mother is worse than being in her arms when the bombs are exploding. Separation from mother is sometimes worse than being with her when she is the bomb."

You can love your mother, not want to hurt her, and at the same time tell her how you feel about her even when it is not all good. Often, it's the father who leaves the children and the mother who sacrifices her life for them, so it makes sense that she's protected and often given a pass when she behaves badly. Our society even protects mothers who have mistreated or killed their own children; usually, a group joins to create a fund to help these mothers. Rarely is the same done for fathers who mistreat their children. But this makes sense, since a mother is often there for her children and the bond between them is very tight.

Males, particularly gay ones, rarely speak ill of our mothers. We honor and love her and, if gay, often worship her, too. It's not just cliché that we gay men are especially close to our mothers. It's frequently true. Because of our special connection to her, mother is usually the first person we come out to. We feel safer with her than with our fathers, perhaps because she has always been there for us. Gay men are usually protective of their mothers because the two are more in sync with one another. We want to ensure her welfare, since we're often more aware of her and what she needs.

"Maybe gay men tend to be particularly close to their mothers," said one workshop participant, "because we identify more with a straight woman rather than straight men. And our mother is usually a straight woman we've known our whole lives." Holding her in high esteem, we bond with her and often enjoy a better relationship with her than most heterosexual men have with their own mothers. Many mothers do deserve such positive regard.

Shawn, twenty-seven, came to see me because he was finding himself no longer able to cope with his partner's newfound fascination with the circuit party scene. Richard, his partner of seven years, the first and only love of his life, had started going to various parties and club events locally and across the country. He had begun dabbling with Ecstasy, moving to Special K and acid and finally to crystal meth. Shawn was unhappy with Richard's drug use, but it had been recreational and controlled. Now that Richard had started using crystal, his drug use was spinning out of control, and he no longer listened to reason about the effects it was having on their relationship. Nor was Richard keeping up his end of tasks such as cleaning the house, paying bills on time, and walking the dogs.

Shawn badly wanted to make things work with Richard, who was closed to coming to couples therapy or any therapy of his own. Shawn's friends were encouraging him to end the relationship, but because Shawn really wanted to stay with Richard, he thought therapy for himself might help.

Shawn wept as he told me about his mother's death two years earlier. He said he was close to her and that she had suffered with ovarian cancer for five years. Her cancer had been diagnosed when he was thirteen, was treated, and went into remission. While there was talk about her being ill, it was downplayed and minimized. "She was strong," he said, "and took care of it without troubling me or my brothers and sisters."

Then five years later, the cancer returned with a vengeance, and she was put on strong medications that often caused more problems than the cancer itself. "She never complained," he said tearfully. "She was there for me. She loved me and I knew it. She was great about my being gay and she loved Richard like another son." That probably made it hard for Shawn to leave Richard; she'd given him her blessings. Having just suffered one loss, how could he go through another?

Shawn was born in Argentina, and his family moved to the U.S. when he was a year old. His mother was lively, fun, and energetic. Speaking with her about his problems—mostly in Spanish, since she maintained her strong Argentinean identity—made him feel even closer to her. She never talked about being in pain and never talked negatively about her cancer to him or his siblings. "She just did what she had to do and simply wanted to live. And we all wanted the same."

Shawn entered my gay men's group therapy to work on making the right decision about Richard, but I suspected that the loss of his mother was mixed in with his grief about losing his partner. I believe that you never fully get over a parent's death, especially if the two of you were close. Instead, you learn to live with the loss and adapt as best you can.

In group, it quickly became apparent that since Shawn had received such good mothering, he was able to mother others as well. He immediately connected to the other group members, was exquisitely sensitive to their emotional pain, kept track of their stories, and week after week, asked how they were doing and took time for himself in the group on top of everything. They often commented on his maternal energy. It became increasingly obvious that he was caretaking and enabling Richard by shouldering all the tasks that he neglected and not letting Richard experience his own consequences. His maternal nature was now becoming codependent. Richard was taking advantage of Shawn's good nature by relinquishing his responsibilities and getting his partner to mother him.

Shawn's maternal instincts, which he'd learned to use so well and could give so lovingly, were now in shadow and were contributing to something in no one's best interest. He was *enabling* Richard's drug use, protecting his partner from his own consequences, and setting himself up for being hurt emotionally. Shawn now had to make a decision to mother himself and to not take care of Richard any longer. He read books like Melody Beattie's *Codependent No More* and Pia Mellody's *Facing Codependency: What It Is, Where It Comes From, How It Sabotages Our Lives.*[2]

In group I asked Shawn, "Tell us what your mother would say if she was alive and you went to her about this situation." This really got him emotional and started him crying. "'Honey,' she would say, 'you don't deserve to be treated this way. You love him and want the best for him, but this is not the best for you or him. If he's not going to listen or get help, you have to move on.'"

He started crying more. The group members started weeping with him, as did I. Then, as I often do with clients who speak another language, I asked him to repeat what she would have said, this time in Spanish. "But you all won't understand it," he said. "It is for *you,* not us," I replied, "and it's important."

He did it. His tears, which were riddled with pain before, turned into comfort this time. As he completed his work in group that night, I said to him, "Thank you for bringing your good mother into this room. It was nice to meet her!" And it was.

Shawn was lucky enough to have had a good mother, but many of us have not.

Unfortunately, many gay men don't have a good mother—or one who's good enough. Some mothers aren't there for their gay sons, or for any of their children for that matter. And sometimes this needs to be pointed out.

Wired for Attachment

Birds and mammals are the only organisms who *must* attach to survive. Without doing so we would die. How we *learn* to attach is usually from our mothers—if not her, than from another primary caregiver—and that sets the tone for how we will bond with others throughout our lives. This is important information in terms of how we attach to our boyfriends and partners. In Psych 101, most college freshman learn about psychologist Harry Harlow, who separated rhesus monkeys from their mothers in a number of controlled experiments and reared them in isolation, with surrogate mothers made of both wire and cloth. Even though the surrogate made of wire offered milk, Harlow found that the infant monkeys spent most of their time clinging to the cloth mother, although there was no nourishment to be gained. He suggested that monkeys needed the comfort of contact and found that if he introduced them back into the colony after three months, usually they were accepted and adapted well. After six months, however, the monkeys were severely withdrawn or violent, and also found it difficult to mate. If the females raised in isolation produced offspring, often they ignored them.

Harlow concluded that in all primates, maternal deprivation leads to distorted development, and suggested the importance of mother-child bonding. Not only do children look to their mothers for such basic needs as food, safety, and warmth, but they also need to feel love, acceptance, and affection from their caregiver. His findings show that delinquent or inadequate attentiveness to a child's needs can result in some long-term psychological physical effects.[3] As babies, we need touch to survive and as adults, need touch to thrive.

Wherever You Go, There You Are

Research shows that good mothers provide their children with a secure emotional base. Wherever they explore, they can feel safe and find others with whom to have relationships, and not have to self-soothe. This parental bond becomes an important part of the child's personality, serving as an internal working model or set of expectations about the likelihood of receiving support from available attachment figures during times of stress. This template becomes the basis for all future close relationships throughout childhood, adolescence, and adult life.[4] If the mother does her job, her child internalizes her and as he grows older, learns to find a safe, secure base in his relations with others and ultimately with his mate. According to psychological attachment theory, mothers need to be available to their babies at least 60 percent of the time, to touch them and attend to them in loving ways. Their children then grow up into healthy adults who can attach to others. Otherwise, problems occur, creating unhealthy attachments that we psychotherapists call (logically enough) *attachment disorders*—vandalized forms of the ability to bond to others through love and friendship. In its most severe form, the sufferer cannot form attachments and becomes isolated and a loner. This information is crucial to understanding what may be disrupting your attachment to men you date and with whom you form relationships.

From the gay men I've treated over the years, I repeatedly hear about three definite types of mothers:

1. The mother who's overly involved with her son, thus contributing to his becoming a "mama's boy";
2. The sexually abusive mother who uses her son as a "boy toy";
3. The narcissistic, self-absorbed Mommy Dearest with borderline personality disorder.

Mother Love

In *Understanding the Borderline Mother*, Christine Ann Lawson offers a superb comparison between what an ideal mother should be and a mother with a personality disorder—that is, one who exhibits abnormal thoughts and behaviors that impair her relationships with her children.[5] In referring to mothers with personality disorders, I mean those whose personal issues impair their overall mothering ability. In real life, to be sure, there are no ideal mothers. But overall, if a mother exhibits the following behaviors and character traits (listed in columns), she is more on the dysfunctional side and will negatively impact her children.

If you remain unaware of how your mother behaved and how she impacted you, you will unknowingly pick a partner who resembles her in some way. Positive influences from your mother are not the issue. My mother gave me a wonderful sense of humor that helps me in difficult situations. That doesn't interfere with my life; rather, it enhances it. Any negative influences, however, will interfere with your life, particularly your relationships with partners and friends.

Lawson lists the traits of an ideal mother alongside traits of the borderline mother (see chart on following page). Later I'll be addressing what *borderline* means, but for now, I'd like to examine what the personality-disordered mother generally looks like, since her traits apply to other types of flawed mothers as well.

If you're among the lucky ones, you received the benefit of having a mother closer to the ideal. No mother is perfect, but the closer she strives to tracking her child and doing what's right for him, the more self-esteem and relational skills he'll have to find a healthy relationship.

Smother Love

We gay men usually have very tight bonds with our mothers, who protect us from the homophobia out there. She's there for us from the beginning. If our dads distance themselves from their queer sons, Mom's arms are there ready to protect us. Mothers are usually the first to protect their children, and even when their children have committed crimes, will proclaim their children's innocence. We're often her favored child and have a special relationship with her. Therefore, it makes sense not to disparage anyone who protects us and makes us feel safe.

Some therapists, ex-gays, and even gay men will read this and say, "See, this proves this is why we are gay; we have a special relationship with our mothers!" But I beg to ask: Whoever established that cause and effect? Maternal closeness may cause other problems, but to anecdotally state it *makes* someone gay is absurd!

Heterosexual males who have equally close-binding mothers survive without any homoerotic impulses, but they still develop problems in their relationships with their partners, just as gay men do. For years, straight women have understood that if they date a mama's

IDEAL MOTHER	BORDERLINE MOTHER
Comforts her child	Confuses her child
Apologizes for inappropriate behavior	Does not apologize or remember inappropriate behavior
Takes care of herself	Expects to be taken care of
Encourages independence in her children	Punishes or discourages independence
Is proud of her children's accomplishments	Envies, ignores, or demeans her children's accomplishments
Builds her children's self-esteem	Destroys, denigrates, or undermines self-esteem
Responds to her children's changing needs	Expects children to respond to her needs
Calms and comforts her children	Frightens and upsets them
Disciplines with logical and natural consequences	Disciplines inconsistently or punitively
Expects that her children will be loved by others	Feels left out, jealous, or resentful if the child is loved by someone else
Never threatens abandonment	Uses threats of abandonment (or actual abandonment) to punish the child
Believes in her children's basic goodness	Does not believe in her children's innate goodness
Trusts her children	Does not trust her children

boy, they'll have to compete with the other woman—his mother. So these straight men's overly close relationship doesn't make them gay at all, though it can make them relationally handicapped.

The close-binding mothers may not create a problem for their sons. Many men have wonderful relationships with their mothers and are very close. But what if the mother's need supersedes his? What if she refuses to allow for normal separation and does indeed produce a mama's boy? It is a betrayal for parents to turn to one of their children to meet their own adult needs.

The mama's boy syndrome typically begins when the mother's relationship with her gay son's father grows conflicted or distant. She may turn to her son if she doesn't work things out with her husband or if she doesn't find another adult to meet her needs. Because the gay son is often more emotional, sensitive, and connected to her than is his father, that's the easy way for her to go. The gay son, needing the secure base of his mother's protection, feels he's in a privileged position and complies. But while this dynamic relieves the mother's anxiety of dealing with her relationship with husband, it causes many problems for her gay son.

Surrogate Husband

Surrogate spouse describes the emotional and psychological bond a child and parent sometimes establish that resembles the one between husband and wife. A son can become his father's surrogate following his parents' divorce or his father's death. Even if the mother does nothing to provoke such a response, her son may feel obligated or even want to assume this role.

I see this frequently when one parent becomes ill or dies. It's awful to watch a parent suffer, and children usually want to make things better by taking on the rescuer role. A son, feeling he needs to protect his mother, does the "manly" chores around the house, looks out for her best interests, and becomes a little version of the man she's lost.

For her part, it's a mother's responsibility to block her son from taking on these roles. In therapy, in fact, we teach a mother who has lost her partner to be sure to tell her sons they need not step into their father's shoes, that she can take care of things and will get adult help. I often must educate parents to let their children know they don't need to protect their mother. Her response should be, "I can take care of myself, and I'm glad you want to do this. That's nice of you, but just know that I'll be taking care of myself *and* you." But many mothers don't say this, don't know how, or are so preoccupied that they don't see that the son is stepping into a partner's role.

Gary—forty years old, openly gay, and single—was in an on-again, off-again relationship with Jeff, whom he had been dating for four years. Gary wanted their relationship to work but didn't think it could happen because of Jeff's temper tantrums. Try as he might to get Jeff to not act out his anger in yelling and screaming, he was unsuccessful—and started to realize he needed to end the relationship. Gary tried a number of ways, short of telling Jeff that it was over, but nothing worked. He didn't want to hurt Jeff's feelings, but by protecting him, was paying a huge emotional price. Where had Gary's protective instincts come from?

When Gary was ten and his older brother was seventeen, their father died. The following year, his brother left for college, leaving Gary home with their widowed mother. Even though she never asked for anything, he felt he had to protect her.

His brother had rebelled, as teens between the ages of thirteen to eighteen often do. But Gary never gave his mother any trouble, since he was protecting her from any further pain.

Gary told me his mother knew he was gay, but he'd never told her directly. When I questioned why he did not tell her directly, he immediately became defensive and protective of her. Over time, as his story unfolded, it became clear that a long time ago, when his father died, he made an unconscious decision never to upset his mother. Children don't usually make conscious decisions on how to behave in their families. In order to survive, they decide to adapt to whatever is going on in their family. Ten-year-old Gary's adaptation was to protect Mom, even if it meant hiding parts of himself that might hurt her.

Later, as an adult, Gary often grew upset and angry with his partner. But instead of saying anything to Jeff, he would hold it in and take it out on Jeff later, in a passive-aggressive way. And when Jeff had his usual temper tantrums, even if Gary felt hurt, sad, and even angry, he would be the one to attempt repair and bid for reconnection. Yet this upset Gary too, inasmuch as he felt that since Jeff created the rupture, then he should try to repair it. But this never happened, and Gary adopted the role of the fixer in their relationship, just as he had in childhood with his mother.

For him, this interpretation was eye opening. He found it easier to link his playing peacemaker to his childhood, when it did not involve blaming his mother or putting her in a negative light. Still, I told him her job was to ensure that he not take on this protective role and to learn to take care of herself. In a perfect world, she would be self-aware enough to be able to make this decision. But she wasn't, since the devastation of her husband's sudden death had left her incapacitated. Again, this wasn't her fault per se, but what needed to be addressed hadn't been.

Gary began identifying many areas where he had been the fixer—at work, with friends and neighbors—and how this played a very large part in his life. This had worked for him in childhood, but now it was time to fix this dynamic of his—especially since it was no longer needed or working.

Covert Incest

Covert incest can overlap—or be a continuation of—making a child the surrogate spouse. The severity of the effects depends on how far and how long the mother continues this dynamic with her son. The two become emotional lovers, which begins to enter the continuum of sexual abuse. It's not that the mother is actually behaving in any sexual manner; rather, she won't stop depending on her son for her adult emotional needs. The parental relationship becomes sexualized because making a child into a surrogate spouse is *romantic* in nature. Children of covert incest often feel "honored" and "privileged" by being depended on by a parent.

The difference between covert and overt sexual abuse is covered in chapter 1, but the emotional or covert form also occurs among family members, more commonly among parents and their children.

Kenneth M. Adams explains this distinction in *Silently Seduced: When Parents Make Their Children Partners—Understanding Covert Incest:*

> It is a distortion in perception to believe that the mother's [or father's] excess attention given in a covertly incestuous relationship saved the child. On the contrary, it robbed the child of the freedom to be autonomous and to feel worthy. Vitality is lost under the insidious, life-long trap that "I should keep being there for my mother; after all, she was always there for me."...the mother's preoccupation with the child is not a statement of love for the child, but a statement of dire neediness by the mother.
>
> The child's core needs are not served but rejected. The child feels like an object, not a person. The real needs for love, nurturing, security and trust are never met. Worse yet, the child is made to believe they are [being] met.[6]

Covert incest cannot be easily perceived. It is like sexual harassment, which is often more covert; in the form of lingering hugs, staring at someone's body, inappropriate comments on someone's body parts or their development, or sexual name-calling like *cocksucker* or *girly boy.* More subtle dynamics might be a parent denying privacy by entering the bathroom while their child is showering or having children leave open the bathroom or bedroom door.

Often victims of covert abuse feel "icky" and violated but can't put their fingers on the reason why. When they accuse the perpetrator, that person often denies it and will say things like "You're taking it the wrong way" or "How could you think that's what I meant?" Since the act is indirect and inconspicuous, the perpetrator finds it easy to deny it was intentional and thereby avoid accountability. Despite their strong feelings, victims are persuaded to believe that their thinking is faulty and give their perpetrators a pass.

Clients whose fathers were frequently gone or absent through death or divorce, often recall that their mothers called them "the man of the house" or "mama's little man." And even if they're not told these things overtly, inside they feel "special" and "chosen" and "privileged" to be their parent's rescuer.

If their child seems to be nurturing and caring for them, they mistakenly take that as a sign that the child is not just willing but able. The truth is that *no child can handle the emotional needs of a parent.* Parents need to find the strength within themselves to go to another adult, not their children.

Thirty-year-old Marty came to me over his troubled relationship with his partner, Lee. They'd been together for over two years, and the holidays were approaching. But Marty still wasn't out to his mother and couldn't tell her he was gay, let alone introduce her to his boyfriend. This had become a conflict with Lee, who wanted to meet Marty's family and not be kept a secret.

Throughout their two years together, Marty had celebrated every special occasion—such as birthdays, Christmases, job promotions, and his half sister's marriage—separately with his family. Finally, Lee had had enough and warned Marty that if he didn't include him, he was going to leave.

I asked Marty why he wouldn't tell his mother. He replied that she'd been very "sweet" to him throughout his life and could not hurt her like that. He felt that because she'd "sacrificed" her life for him, in return he wanted to protect her from any further worry. Marty insisted he had to be strong, or she might "fall apart." Telling her would hurt her more than *not* telling her, even though it was hurting his relationship with Lee.

Marty had two half sisters but was the only child from his father's second marriage. Throughout his childhood, his mother had been preoccupied with his safety. Until he was eighteen years old, she picked out the clothes he would wear every day. Throughout his grade school years, she drove him back and fourth to school, even though he could walk and they lived in a safe neighborhood. He recalls wanting to take the school bus to be with his friends, but his mother insisted on driving him. He would come home for lunch every day, and his mother would fix him his favorite meals. If his friends wanted him over for sleepovers, she would discourage him from spending the night at their houses; they had to come to his. At night, even into his senior year of high school, she would tuck him into bed.

He recalled his relatives saying his mother was overprotective, but he still didn't see it that way. He viewed her as a loving, caring mother who was interested in his well-being and whose devotion to him was unending. In terms of his parents' relationship, he said his father worked long hours, was away a lot on business trips, and didn't treat his mother very well. She complained to Marty that his father wasn't very attentive to or communicative with her. When his father was home, if his parents weren't arguing, there would be silence. Marty and his mother would go shopping, leaving his father home to watch television. They even took trips together without him.

His mother spent hours helping him with his homework. If Marty was sick with a cold or any mild illness that kids typically get, his mother would fret and often take him to the doctor, even when the doctor said a visit wasn't necessary. Sometimes she would even get sick too, with the same illness. He recalled his father arguing with his mother and accusing her of being a hypochondriac, of encouraging their son to be one too, and of loving Marty more than him. This made Marty hate his father even more. He did admit she would get a "bit overconcerned" but told me, "You know how mothers are." He grew resentful that his father didn't help him and spend time with him like his mother did. He also resented how his father treated his mother. He was glad to be there for his mother.

He saw how his father also seemed distant from his older children by his first wife and how his half siblings were very close to one another. Since Marty had no siblings of his own, he was grateful that at least he was close to his mother. He told me he didn't want to destroy the "special relationship" he had with her. I told Marty that if his relationship was as special as he said, and his mother's devotion as strong as it was, then nothing—not even his being gay—should destroy that. He told me that one of his half sisters was gay and he didn't think his mother liked it. Even though she never said anything overtly negative about his half sister, Marty had a feeling that it was unacceptable to her.

Marty recalled that after his half sisters left, his mother would say that she was glad he had girlfriends; that she wanted grandchildren and it was too bad that his lesbian half sister would not know the joys of that. The college Marty went to was about an hour from home, and he and his mother talked almost daily during his first year and at least twice a week thereafter for the next three years. She would often continue telling him about her problems with his father, and Marty would listen and give her advice. When his friends negatively commented on how close they were, he believed they were jealous of his relationship with his mother.

In his second year of college, he began dating a young woman his age named Denise. They became very close and he knew, even though he was gay, that dating this young woman would please his mother because he wouldn't be like his half sister—a *homosexual.* Denise was from Chicago, so while his mother knew about her, she met her only a few times when she went up to visit Marty and once when Marty brought her to his house for the holidays. He remembers Denise being a bit awkward around his mother. He felt as though Denise didn't like her but chalked it up to her being "competitive" with his mother for his attention.

Denise told Marty that she thought his mother didn't like her and was not very nice to her. Marty insisted that his mother liked her very much. When he asked, "What's my mother doing that makes you think she doesn't like you?" she couldn't identify anything tangible, but said it was in her actions and in the things she was *not* doing. Denise's reaction left Marty feeling this was her problem and that his mother wasn't doing anything at all.

As the two grew more serious, they began talking about where they would live after college. Marty knew he had homosexual tendencies, but thought if he got more involved with Denise, his sexual and romantic urges for men would go away. But they didn't. Then his mother discouraged Marty from moving to Chicago for the "first woman" he was involved with and told him he should consider others, particularly local girls. Marty decided to go along with her line of thinking as a good way out of getting more involved, and so ended the relationship with Denise—who was crushed and blamed his mother for intruding. But Marty thought she was simply jealous of his close relationship with his mother. In fact, he blamed himself, believing he'd decided to end the relationship because he was gay.

Now that Marty was back home, things went back to how they were before. His mother no longer tucked him in at night or picked out his clothes, but she bought all of his clothes, did his laundry, and cooked his meals. She went shopping with him and confided how troubled her marriage continued to be. She worried about his health even when he was not sick and asked him daily how he was and if he was taking his vitamins. He still felt her behavior was "sweet" and loving, and that his father deserved the distance his mother gave him for not being good enough as a parent. He was "glad" he could be there for her.

Then one day, Marty got up the nerve to enter a gay bar. His first night there, he met Lee. From that day forward, they had an electric connection that convinced Marty that he was gay. But how could he tell his mother? What would happen to her? Could she live with this? With these worries running through his head, he decided never to tell her and just live secretly with Lee.

But Lee tired of the charade and after their second holiday not being together, told Marty that if he did not tell his mother, he would break off with him. Lee would not live a secret gay life with Marty. Lee stated he felt as though there was "another woman" in the relationship—namely, Marty's mother.

This is the covert incest that Marty's mother committed. When her husband wasn't meeting her emotional needs, she turned to her son. But calling this dynamic *incest* can be problematic and troubling, since when most people consider sexual abuse, direct and overt acts come to mind. In other words, Marty and his mother were lovers psychologically and emotionally. Her relying on him the same way that she should have an adult partner set up a triangulation between the three of them—mother, father, and son.

To reduce the conflict with her husband, Marty's mother turned to him for emotional and psychological support. She played the victim, Marty was the savior, and his father the persecutor—a dysfunctional and extremely inappropriate dynamic. Family therapist pioneer Murray Bowen termed this *triangulation,* wherein another family member—usually a child—is used as a buffer to diminish conflict in a relationship.

In triangulation, the *victim* is one who suffers injury or loss, the *savior* is the rescuer in the drama, And the *persecutor* is one whose ill treatment harasses or oppresses another. Each participant who maintains this dysfunctional pattern receives a negative payoff. In this case of triangulation, the victim unburdened her problem onto Marty, the rescuer, to ease her own anxiety about the situation. It's similar to telling a friend about a problem you're having. To lessen the burden, you transfer your anxiety to him for the time being—a normal and healthy thing to do, unless it becomes a habit. Marty's chief problem was his mother's inappropriate use of him to meet her needs in her dysfunctional marriage. Until he became conscious of the triangulation, there was no hope for his own emancipation as an adult.

Marty's mother had made him her surrogate partner. She had not only engulfed him; more concerned with her own needs than his, she had used him to replace her husband. Since she couldn't get along with Marty's father or have him meet her needs, she tried to mold his replacement from the ground up. From birth, she molded Marty into meeting *her* emotional needs, not the other way around. This crosses an important boundary that parents should protect. No child is prepared or developmentally able to handle an adult's emotional needs.

Marty's mother was covertly incestuous with him in so subtle and indirect a way that he was unable to identify it. True, he had his own denials, as his friends and even his girlfriend tried to point out. But Marty's mother was not overtly pushy. She began leaning on him inappropriately in his childhood, when he couldn't have had the maturity to stop her from doing so. In his therapy, Marty was able to admit he felt burdened by his mother but knew that being there for her would make *her* feel better, so he was glad to do it. To borrow the title of Kenneth Adams's book, he was *silently seduced.*

Marty also spoke of his grief over his relationship with his distant father, whom he blamed all his life for not being closer to him. He did begin to identify ways in which his father had tried to bond with him, but recalled his mother interfering. One time, his dad planned to take him on a sleepaway Cub Scouts camping trip, but his mother said that Marty could get sick sleeping outside in a tent and forbade his going.

Marty's father should have stood up to his wife more strongly.

Marty's Journey

Now Marty had to examine this dynamic in his relationship with Lee or risk losing the love of his life. I supported his understanding that he didn't have to give up either his mother or his boyfriend. He began reading about covert incest as well as other self-help books and came to weekly therapy. But he was frightened by what lay ahead of him. Not only would he have to tell his mother he was gay, but he also would put an end to their daily conversations and ask that she no longer bring up her problems with his father.

"She won't like this," Marty said. In our therapy sessions, he often became defensive and angry with me for talking about his mother in dysfunctional terms. As a therapist, I knew that to protect his mother, he was projecting onto me anger that was really directed at her.

This is called *negative transference*. A client who feels anger at a parent but can't tolerate knowing this consciously will transfer it onto the therapist—as well as onto a partner. Surprisingly, this is a good sign that indicates the client is going deeper into therapeutic work. So I was glad to be the antenna for Marty's anger, knowing that he was moving it in the direction where it belonged: at his mother.

It was very hard for him to see what his therapy exposed: that his closetedness and difficulties with Lee stemmed back to his too-close relationship with his mother. As he began to understand, it wasn't so much that they were too close but that her needs overlapped his. She crowded him and superseded his developmental needs. She made him her psychological partner to meet her needs, which should have been met by another adult friend, a therapist, or Marty's father.

In the sessions, Marty typically blamed himself. "It's not her fault, it's mine," he would say. "If I didn't want it, I could have stopped it." This is a common response from those who've suffered abuse or neglect. In an effort to protect the perpetrator, clients blame themselves. But as a child, you couldn't have protected yourself; that was your parents' job.

I know the language I'm using could be off-putting if you are still denying that your mother may have done something like this to you.

Words such as *abuse, neglect,* even *perpetrator* might imply that I'm defaming mothers in general. My intent is to stay with the facts and the data, to judge where healing is necessary for mothers and sons alike.

Over time, Marty understood that his mother had molded him from the beginning and realized the dynamic she'd established between them. This didn't make her a bad or evil person; it's likely she wasn't even aware of what she was doing. He came to see that while he wasn't accountable for developing this pattern, he could stop it. He knew he would feel tremendous guilt, but it had to be done for him to achieve a separate sense of self and a full relationship with Lee.

Marty began to feel relief as he became aware that his close maternal relationship had been more of a *burden* than a privilege. He did love his mother and wanted the best for her, but also felt stressed at having to be available for her so often. I helped him see that if she were healthy or interested in becoming so, she'd want the best for both Marty and herself and want to examine these dynamics on her own.

In their book *Gay Warrior,* Fickey and Grimm write that "a mother betrays her gay son when she develops and maintains an unhealthy and inappropriately close emotional relationship with him and uses him as a surrogate husband and/or refuses to let him 'divorce' her."[7] Marty didn't have to hate his mother and stop all contact with her, but he did need to go through a divorce process from surrogate husband to son.

Marty finally told his mother that he was gay. Her reaction wasn't bad at all; in fact, she said she'd suspected it all along. She did tell him she was disappointed and worried that as a gay man, he could come to harm; but she said she would learn to support him, which came as a relief to him. She was willing to read the books and literature he gave her and even go with him to meetings of Parents, Friends/Family of Lesbians and Gays (PFLAG).

Yet that wasn't as hard for Marty as what he had to do next: ask that she no longer tell him what was going on with his father. He explained he could no longer listen to her troubles, because it affected him and his relationship with Lee, making him worry too much for her and want her to either work things out or seek some therapy. They both wept. She was upset about this, and did not understand. Here, on this issue, she began to state her confusion. She said things like "I don't get it" and "I don't know what you mean." Marty explained that he needed some distance to develop his own identity. That meant that for the next holiday, he would be going to Lee's family.

Marty's mother was enraged. She blamed his therapy for "pitting you against me," which made Marty feel very bad. "You're telling me I have been a bad mother after all I have done for you?"

He came to his next session angry at me (and himself) for telling his mother not to lean on him any longer. We talked about this, and I appealed to his reason. "What's wrong with an adult telling his mother to get support from someone other than him around her issues with his father?" Marty was entitled to enjoy a separate relationship with his father and be sheltered from whatever simmered between his parents. This was *not* about her bad mothering, but rather some bad dynamics established between him and his mother that needed repair.

It took Marty months to integrate this line of thinking. Even though he agreed with me, his mother's resistance—and his—was so strong that he consistently reverted to blaming himself and me. Finally, Lee, seeing Marty struggling to break the emotional umbilical cord, had the courage to tell him that his mother had been interfering in their relationship all along. Lee felt that Marty had been devoting his energy and attention to her when actually it was Lee who deserved his attention. He told Marty he had felt cheated by the amount of time she took away from their relationship. Marty had no idea Lee felt this way, and it really hit home.

Up until then, his mother had been holding his Lover energy. He needed to go in with his Warrior, reclaim this Lover energy, and decide for himself how and where he would direct it. He was, in fact, able to redirect his Lover energy toward Lee, his partner, where it truly belonged. This was truly a "man's job."

Over the next year, his mother did go to PFLAG without Marty, began therapy, and eventually entered couples therapy with Marty's father. As for Marty, he was able to move forward and work things out with Lee. His and his mother's roads to recovery weren't smooth. They had lots of relapses to their old ways, but both were able to move on and get back on track.

Marty was lucky. I've seen many a client whose mother didn't understand and was unwilling to listen to *any* reason. I have also seen mothers who, upon learning their son is gay, are secretly or openly glad there's no other woman to compete with her. They don't realize that regardless of whether his partner is male or female, the same Lover energy should be transferred onto that partner.

Mama's Boy Toy

For anyone who's had some sexual inappropriateness from his mother, this section might seem overwhelming, so out there and unusual that you react in disbelief. I suggest that you read slowly and stay gentle with yourself. If you feel overwhelmed, put the book down and return to it later.

No one talks, much less writes, about mothers who sexually abuse their sons. Quite a bit of research has focused on girls sexually abused by adult males, and—as you might expect—there are literally hundreds of books and research articles on fathers who commit incest with their daughters. Yet there's little if any information on females sexually abusing children—particularly boys—and especially not their own sons. I found one book, *Female Sexual Abuse of Children,* edited by Michelle Elliott, devoted to the dynamics, with an entire chapter devoted to the case of one woman abused in an incestuous relationship with her own mother.[8] Even in this book, information about mothers sexually abusing their sons is scattered and minimal. Enter *mother-son incest* in most search engines and you'll find very few legitimate entries, most of which direct you to the same few sites. The rest are all porn.

But thousands of legitimate Web sites offer information about fathers who abuse their daughters sexually. Also, an increasing number of journal articles, chapters in books, and pamphlets discuss mothers who abuse their daughters—but not those who perpetrate incest on their sons. Other than a story here and a case history there about a boy sexually abused by his mother—in books about male survivors of sexual abuse—virtually nothing is devoted exclusively to the topic. One pamphlet, titled *Mother-Son Incest: The Unthinkable Broken Taboo,* by Hani Miletski, is filled with much solid, valuable information, but has little if any information on gay male victims.[9] On her Web site, psychotherapist Kali Munro writes about mother-son incest in an article about female perpetrators of sexual abuse.[10] But even there, the mother-son piece is minimal!

Before we begin to explore the concept, it's important to reexamine the taboo of "outing" a mother sexually involved with her son. Because our culture idealizes mothers, we never want to think of them as behaving abusively or of harboring bad intentions toward their own offspring. Whenever a mother is accused of intentionally killing her own children, we want to believe otherwise. We give her the automatic benefit of the doubt, until we absolutely cannot because of incriminating evidence.

When a mother abuses her son sexually, it's most often covert. She's subtle and does it in such "loving" ways that even the son is left with questions as to whether the abuse really happened. Female perpetrators of sexual abuse commonly act in the indirect, covert ways examined earlier.

This makes better sense when you consider that research shows that most exhibitionists ("flashers") are male. Historically at least, men have not had permission to show off their bodies without being called perverted. Nowadays, of course, things have changed a bit with younger men wearing their pants below their pelvic bones. But women can be closet exhibitionists without anyone raising an eyebrow. They can wear low-cut blouses, let their bra straps and cleavage show, wear transparent clothing and open-toed shoes that some heterosexual men find very sexy, and receive positive attention—at least from males. Research would overlook these exhibitionists, who very well could be given a "pass" by men who find them alluring. Men are more direct, bold, and overt about their sexuality, while women are encouraged to be more subtle, hidden, and flirtatious. So when a mother becomes a sexual predator, it's logical that she would do it covertly.

Also, if you begin talking about pedophiles, people immediately think you mean male pedophiles. I've heard clients and colleagues say they would never have expected a female pedophile, particularly a mother. Again, we bump up against the thinking that mothers protect their children and would never harm them intentionally, especially not sexually.

Also significant is the fact that most males won't admit to being sexually abused by a *female* perpetrator, particularly their own mothers. Many heterosexual males brag about their "first sexual experience" with an older woman who had sex with them in their adolescence, when in reality an adult woman being sexual with an underage boy is sexual abuse! The heterosexual boys enjoyed it, so naturally they don't view it that way. But if we picture an adult male being sexual with an adolescent boy or girl, this abuse becomes obvious. No matter if the adult is male or female, it's still sexual abuse.

Boys are taught they can protect themselves—or should be able to. Girls are taught from an early age to be alert, to make sure they're never alone in public, to be prepared for any male predators who might try to harm them. We seldom train older boys to anticipate that molesters might come after them. A friend said to me that women couldn't sexually abuse male children because males could fend off the female. Many share that mind-set, but the truth is that young boys are just as susceptible as females to sexual abuse and rape.

For these reasons, males underreport being been raped or abused, having reframed it as their first experience. And when a mother sexually abuses her son covertly, you have the setup for a perfect crime. The mother goes unsuspected, her son has no tangible evidence, and it all gets ignored or covered up—even by the son. He'll repress the memories because he doesn't want to have to view what happened as abusive.

Overt Sexual Abuse

Stuart, thirty-seven, was a successful Web site designer. He came to see me after breaking up with Kevin, his partner of seven years. Weeping, he told me that he'd not been able to remain faithful, and Kevin finally had had enough. According to Stuart, his sex with

Kevin wasn't good, even though he had tried everything, including Viagra, to help maintain his erections even though he had no trouble when he acted out sexually at the baths or at sex parties and hooked up online. But with Kevin, it was a different story.

Stuart had come out in his twenties without any problems, and told me his healthy family had accepted him. His mother and father had stayed married, and he was close to both his parents and his one older sister. He spoke proudly about being an uncle to his niece and nephew, then five and one, respectively. He was close to his sister and her husband and saw his niece and nephew regularly.

Since he began his sexual development, Stuart told me, he'd been a frequent masturbator. While they drove on family trips, he recalled masturbating in the back of the van, where no one could tell what he was doing. In school locker rooms and at the local swimming pool, he would steal other guys' underwear and bathing suits and, smelling them, masturbate in a locker room bathroom stall or take them home. He frequented porn stores as soon as he was old enough to get in and spent hours there. Soon he was going to bathhouses and rest areas and, once the Internet arrived, having hookups at least twice a week.

I placed him in my sexual addiction group therapy. Stuart told me that as far back as he could recall, his father had been an alcoholic. When his father drank, he didn't grow mean or abusive; he would just get quiet and watch television. Often, he would fall asleep in front of the set. Stuart recalled how his mother would come into his bedroom to wake him and have him sleep with her in his parents' bed.

Recounting his family history, he thought nothing of telling me this and recalled sleeping with his mother until he was sixteen years old, when his father stopped drinking and joined his mother in bed. I asked how Stuart felt about his mother's getting him to sleep in her bed, and he said, "It didn't bother me then. It is a little weird as I think back on it now."

I asked, "How was your mother dressed in bed with you?" and he couldn't recall.

Stuart told me that his mother, a big-breasted woman, dressed in low-cut blouses and dresses that showed off her cleavage. Even at sixty-five, she never wore a bra. His male teachers and friends commented on how beautiful she was, and he thought the same. He described her as very "vain" and didn't know how many facelifts she'd had—she would never answer that question, even though everyone knew she'd had plastic surgery. During his childhood, Stuart said she often walked from bathroom to bedroom wearing only panties, seemingly oblivious to anyone around her. At clothing stores, she would bring him into her dressing room while she changed. He explained it was because he was young and there'd be no one to watch him if she left him out in the store. She brought him into dressing rooms with her until he was fifteen years old.

His mother would walk into the bathroom while he showered and even when he urinated. Until he turned fourteen, she would often insist on drying him off, which he recalled as "affectionate motherly love." He made sure to tell me she only dried off his back. "She never looked at me peeing," he said but added that she would joke that he was better endowed than his father.

How, I asked, would she know about his genital endowment if she never looked? He had no answer, other than maybe she looked at him through the mirror "by accident."

Stuart was glad to be gay, he joked, because otherwise he'd have had to be concerned about his mother's sexuality, which, he was able to say, was "out there." Once, when Stuart was in his twenties, he told his mother that she should cover up and not wear clothes that exposed so much cleavage. She became angry, said that was "his problem," not hers, and pouted for the rest of the day, giving Stuart the cold shoulder.

He couldn't say why, but during our work together Stuart began to be concerned about his mother being alone with his six-month-old nephew. What if something happened, he wondered, "leaving the baby uncared for?" There was no indication of any poor care on his mother's part. She'd baby-proofed her house and, when his sister came to get him, he was always changed and well fed. Stuart told his sister that he was having some disturbing dreams about his mother caring for his nephew, but she shrugged it off. He didn't believe in premonitions either, so he dismissed his dreams too.

It became increasingly clear that covert sexual abuse had occurred between Stuart and his mother. I started to investigate, but when I asked Stuart to talk more about his mother's sexualized behavior, he immediately became defensive. "I'm not here to discuss my mother! I'm here to talk about sexual addiction and my breakup and how I'll be able to move on from it!" He could talk at length about his father's alcoholism but not about his mother's sexual inappropriateness.

Shadowboxing: Projecting Disowned Parts of Self onto Therapy

I saw that Stuart couldn't tolerate any feedback about his mother's sexual inappropriateness with him, particularly from me, as he then would view me in a negative transference light, also known as shadow. In other words, I represented the part of him that *did* know that his mother was a sexual perpetrator. But without addressing what his mother did to him, he would likely continue his sexual acting-out behavior and might well lose any future relationship.

The benefit of group therapy is that it reduces tensions between therapist and client and lets the client process the information with his peers in the group. That is, I become everyone's "father" or "daddy," the client is the "child," and the other group members or "siblings" can be there for him. So I hoped that in group, Stuart could reduce his defensiveness enough to access his true feelings.

All group members shared their own stories, and two of the eight men had been sexually abused by their mothers. These two men were straight, which helped throw off Stuart's defensiveness about his mother. Then one day, in an individual session with me, he admitted that while talking about his mother, particularly around sexual topics both in individual and group therapy, his left leg got "tingly," as though it were falling asleep. When he stood up, he couldn't feel any sensation until he'd walked on it a bit. This occurred *only* when we talked about his mother's sexuality and the other group members talked about their mothers.

I encouraged him to have a checkup to rule out any medical or physical symptoms. He said he would but added that he knew I was right—that his mother's sexuality had impacted him negatively—and he began to tell me more.

His mother used to bring him into her bed and place herself over him as if spooning with him. Often, he would awaken in the middle of the night in a daze, with his mother on top of him. He remembered her against him, her arms and legs over him and not being able to breathe. As he told me this, his leg began tingling again, and he began to weep. His crying turned to deep sobs, and he began wailing in a high-pitched voice.

When recovering memories of sexual abuse, whether covert or overt, this kind of reaction is not uncommon. Stuart didn't yet know that in the process of working through his sexual abuse issues, he was right where he needed to be. And so it went: session after session, he could talk about his mother for only the first ten minutes. The rest of his time he spent weeping and talking about other topics, particularly his breakup with Kevin. Over time, he was able to take up the whole session talking about his mother as much as was necessary without so much emotional pain. It was becoming apparent that this abuse was not only covert but also overt.

I couldn't overlook one issue that needed more immediate attention: Stuart's nephew being alone in his grandmother's care. Stuart hadn't revealed any overt sexually inappropriate behavior in terms of her touching his genitals, so—on the surface—there seemed to be no immediate danger; but as we talked about how her pressing against him was overt sexual abuse, his concern for his nephew grew.

I asked Stuart to observe how his mother acted around his nephew, who by now was almost two. In the summer, he reported, his mother would wear bikinis exposing most of her large breasts, with her nipples visible through the fabric. His sister had asked her not to dress like that around her son—to no avail. Also, when his nephew and niece went to their grandmother's to spend the night, his mother openly admitted to sleeping with his nephew in one bed in a separate room, away from his father and his niece. Even his sister thought this was weird.

I urged Stuart to speak to his sister about their mother's dressing inappropriately around the children and have them sleep in their own beds. Stuart agreed, half disbelieving that his nephew and niece were in harm's way. His sister completely agreed with my recommendation. She too was becoming concerned about their mother's lack of responsiveness to her requests.

Stuart confided to her his discoveries in therapy, which made his sister very uncomfortable. She asked their mother not to dress in skimpy clothing around her kids and, if they slept over, to ensure that they slept in their own rooms, apart from their grandmother. Stuart's mother was upset, but agreed to this request. When Stuart's sister asked his father to oversee the situation, he agreed to do so but seemed confused by it all.

Then Stuart's sister phoned, saying she suspected that even though their mother had agreed to their terms, she wasn't really following through. One evening after she and her husband went out, she made a surprise visit at 1 A.M. to find their mother in a skimpy nightgown and no underwear spooning her now two-year-old grandson in her bed. Her granddaughter was sleeping by herself in the other room, where both children were supposed to sleep. Stuart's father was asleep on the couch in front of the television. Stuart's sister woke everyone up, yelling at both her mother and father for not abiding by her wishes and took the children home.

Enraged and weeping, Stuart talked about what was becoming increasingly clear: his mother was a pedophile. Over time, he was able to admit more of what his mother had done and came to realize that in fact she had abused him. He would awaken at night with her breasts pressed against him, and he recalled having erections as he got older. Since he thought he was enjoying the contact, he blamed himself. He never believed she knew what she was doing, and would move away so as not to wake her. "She was asleep!" he cried. "How could she know she slept like that?"

I kept reminding him that she should *not* have been sleeping with him in the first place. Also, as he hit puberty, his nocturnal erections would be normal and not a sign that he was enjoying his mother's contact. His mother's physical presence in his bed was abuse in and of itself, during a time when he needed privacy.

Stuart could barely tolerate the thought that his mother would fake being asleep and intentionally do anything to him. I made him understand that his mother could very well *not* have meant it in any "evil" sense. Most likely, she was reenacting the trauma of something that had happened to her.

Dissociation

I educated Stuart on what he experienced when he tried to talk about her abuse as well as on what his mother was going through. He was *dissociating*. Researchers and clinicians believe that dissociation is a common, naturally occurring defense against childhood trauma—sexual or otherwise. Unable to flee or fight overwhelming abuse, children flee psychologically (dissociate) from full awareness of the experience.

Disconnection from full awareness of self, time, or external circumstances exists along a continuum: from normal everyday experiences (such as daydreaming, highway hypnosis, or getting so lost in a book or movie that one loses a sense of time and surroundings) to events that can interfere with everyday functioning. The latter usually includes sexual abuse, accidents, violent crimes, natural disasters, and anything else that evokes an extreme response in order to survive a threatening situation.

Dissociation is one way to get through a trauma or terrible ordeal. Clients have told me that while they were being abused, they would pretend they were out of their bodies and on the ceiling looking down or out of the room or else numb themselves to not feel anything physically or emotionally. In traumatic situations, dissociation is an automatic process. The mind will never let you experience more than you can handle.

In this respect, dissociation is a survival mechanism. Many individuals have used it as children and adults to deal with abuse, to protect them in situations where they couldn't run or fight. For many of us gay men who were picked on or abused, it most likely helped us survive our childhoods.

Unfortunately, dissociation doesn't work so well in nonlethal circumstances. When we most need to be aware, we may find ourselves spacing out, unable to do what we need to in order to protect ourselves. Stuart's acting out and failed relationship were results of his dissociation. The very defense that protected him as a child was now destroying his life as an adult.

Since everyone dissociates from time to time, these experiences are normal and part of daily living. But as you become aware of the process, you can learn to control the dissociative response instead of allowing it to control you. Stuart, and others who enter therapy to recover from childhood trauma and abuse, work to control their own dissociation.

Dissociation-prone people often space out in a present-day situation they perceive to be dangerous. The numbing of Stuart's leg might have resulted from *body memory*: his leg went to sleep once when his mother pressed against him, and now did so again when he was "reminded" of his trauma. Or, since he felt unavoidably guilty about the contact, his numbness may have been akin to the cases of hysterical paralysis that Freud encountered, in which the mind tries to "amputate" or dissociate from whatever part of the body triggered the original guilt. (More about how your brain takes care of you in chapter 6.)

Stuart spent about three years in both group and individual therapy. As he worked on the sexual abuse he'd suffered, his sexual acting out reduced greatly. He made several attempts to talk with his mother, but she never admitted to anything, replying that she "couldn't remember" and that much of what he recalled, he was exaggerating. "About changing in the dressing rooms, what was I supposed to do, leave you out in the store?" She did not want to be accountable for her actions; doing so would mean having to accept her own abuse, which I suspect took place.

Important for Stuart was to confront his mother, disown any responsibility for her abuse, and place it back where it belonged— onto her. Whether she decided to accept it was her issue, not his. Stuart learned that if his mother wanted to join him in his recovery, as he hoped, that would have been a benefit. But even though she didn't, his recovery was still a success.

Mommy Dearest

In the movie *Ordinary People,* Mary Tyler Moore plays Beth, a mother who had a covertly incestuous relationship with her son Buck, now dead. She's not very fond of her surviving son, Conrad. When her husband tells her Conrad thinks she hates him, she loses her composure and screams, "Hate him? Hate him? Mothers don't hate their sons!"

Oh, but some do.

Ordinary People depicts how a mother can indeed betray her children by not acknowledging them or recognizing their individuality. These mothers might be diagnosed as having *narcissistic personality disorder* (NPD). A mother can be so clearly self-absorbed that she sees her children as extensions of herself. She blurs the boundaries of where she and her children start and stop.

Narcissistic mothers display arrogance, grandiosity, inflated self-esteem, and are easily wounded by any criticism, even if it's well intended and for their own good. A high percentage—about 75 percent—of those who suffer from this personality disorder are men, who portray their narcissism by flaunting their intelligence, power, aggression, money, or social status. Women are likely to emphasize their bodies, looks, charm, and sexuality, along with their feminine "traits" such as homemaking and child-rearing.

These types use everything around them to obtain their narcissistic fix. Children are more available to the female narcissist, since mothers are their primary caregivers from birth. It's easier for a woman to think of her children as extensions of herself because she once carried them inside her and because her ongoing interaction with them is more intensive and extensive. The narcissistic mother fights to maintain her most reliable fix: her children. Through insidious indoctrination, guilt formation, emotional sanctions, deprivation, and other psychological mechanisms, she tries to induce in them a dependence that can't be easily unraveled.

A narcissistic parent can be annihilating for any child who finds no room for his personality or sense of self. The child's sense of self is completely stolen by the NPD's need for constant attention and admiration. The son robbed of his personhood must conform and adapt to his mother's every wish and mood. A mother who isn't narcissistic would say, "Let me give you a kiss" and "I am so proud of you!" while a narcissistic mother would say, "Come give *me* a kiss" and "You make *me* so proud." The difference between these types of sentences can be subtle, but a mother with true maternal instinct would know to focus situations on her child to help him develop a good sense of self. A client once told me that his mother believed his birthday was *her* special day, since that was the day she gave birth to him! That's an obvious expression of narcissism. An NPD mother continually struggles with trying to fill the void of her *own* underdeveloped sense of self.

Borderline personality disorder (BPD) is often very similar to NPD. The difference is that the BPD mother has a pattern of intense but unstable relationships. In *Understanding the Borderline Mother,* Lawson states that "children with borderline mothers begin their lives with an insecure attachment to an emotionally unstable mother." If she is oppositional, aggressive, filled with rage, depressed, and sometimes violent, then her children will adopt these traits and behaviors. How have her traits contributed to and shaped your imago in terms of your selection of partners? An excellent book on relating to a BPD sufferer is *I Hate You, Don't Leave Me* by Jerold Kreisman and Hal Straus.[11]

Growing up with an NPD or BPD mother can alter your emotional settings so that later, as an adult, you hook up with men who are themselves narcissistic, constantly demanding your attention and taking the time and energy that you deserve and dragging it back to themselves. Or you may unconsciously agree with a partner to consistently meet his needs over yours. Over time, you'll come to resent this and blame him for never meeting your needs. But it won't be only his fault. You thought love meant minimizing your own dependency needs and catering to the object of your affection, as you had to do with your mother, so you hired him. Lacking this knowledge, you'll find yourself unfulfilled in relationships.

Covert Versus Overt Narcissism

In *The Wizard of Oz and Other Narcissists,* therapist Eleanor D. Payson uncovers the difference between overt and covert narcissistic personality disorder.[11] In terms of identifying a problem between you and another person, covert material is much harder to pinpoint and work with than the overt.

Payson describes the overt narcissist as "someone whose self-image or identity allows the more open expression of narcissistic needs such as admiration, power, control, etc....Whatever the self-image is, the overt type of NPD person uses his persona to directly take the spotlight and openly demand an endless supply of public attention such as admiration, respect, awe or perhaps even fear." She proceeds to explain how overt narcissists maintain a busy social life, surrounding themselves with people they've known for years who outwardly appear as friends but on closer examination are superficial and "require minimal emotional investment on the part of the narcissist."

Payson writes that the covert or "closet" type of narcissist mother "gains admiration, status and control through more subtle and indirect means." Payson says this mother's self-sacrificing self-image makes her "strive endlessly on behalf of her child and gain the need for attention and admiration through a martyrlike expectation of undying loyalty and appreciation alongside frequent reproaches to her child for not showing enough gratitude."

As a parental figure, the overt NPD mother gains attention and admiration, not always from her child but through her "mother" status in her community. She expects her child to worship her and adore her and, at the same time, meet her high expectations and needs whether or not they match the child's. Her standards may be impossibly high or change so often that the child can never meet them and is always left feeling incompetent.

The child of a mother like this may grow up into someone who competes constantly with others to gain the attention and recognition he never received from his primary caregivers. He'll find workaholic boyfriends and partners who are more attentive to their pets, workouts, and social lives, or who are so overinvolved in volunteering that he's constantly competing for their attention. Or, he might find "parental" boyfriends who constantly make him feel incompetent and inferior.

The Covert NPD Parent

Bernie, a forty-five-year-old elementary school teacher, came to me because his depression was impacting his relationship with his partner. For ten years, he and Dave had been together living with Dave's mother. Bernie told me he agreed with Dave's complaint: that over the past year, he'd become overly sensitive. He was easily agitated, even by small frustrations that wouldn't have bothered him in the past, and continually expressed guilt, particularly over his mother's welfare.

Bernie said he felt as if he were a "bad son" to his mother and was beginning to hate himself. His self-esteem was always low, and he had never really felt good about himself. But lately, things were getting worse. He was getting more and more depressed, and now he was feeling like a "bad partner." He would apologize to Dave like a child. Dave felt that he couldn't tell Bernie anything without upsetting him, or else Bernie would regress and become self-deprecating. Bernie was exhibiting classic signs of clinical depression.

Bernie filled me in on his last year. His mother, now elderly, had decided to move out of the family home where he grew up to a small apartment for senior citizens. She had been "cold" to him ever since he moved out to move in with Dave and his mother, ten years earlier. He suspected her emotional distance was because she suspected he was gay, which he'd never admitted to her. Now that her move and all the furnishings in the family home had to be discussed, he found his siblings being cold to him as well. He was surprised and confused: Why were they treating him so indifferently?

Bernie was the last of ten children, the rest of whom were now married with their own families. Bernie had been the "chosen" one to care for their mother. He had lived with his parents until he was twenty-five, when he decided to become a priest with both of his parents' blessing. But one year into seminary school, he realized this was not for him, and his parents welcomed him back home to live with them. At age twenty-seven, he decided to move into his own apartment. "How could you do this to me?" his mother asked. "I need you here. If you leave, you are a bad son and you won't get any help from us financially or otherwise." His father, hearing this, did nothing. Sobbing and guilt-ridden, Bernie moved out anyway. But when his father died two years later, he moved back home to help his mother.

At age thirty-three, Bernie met Dave, an only child whose father died years ago. They fell in love, which confirmed to Bernie that he was in fact a gay man. He could never tell his mother, since she was already so rejecting. After two years of dating, Dave asked Bernie to move in with him and his mother. This time, Bernie's own mother said nothing about his moving out. He thought it was time to move on with his adult life, and she had finally accepted that.

Dave's mother was very kind, loving, and nurturing. Dave had chosen to live with his mother, since the pooled finances helped them both. They had their conflicts but resolved them in healthy ways. She made dinners for both "boys," as she called them, and didn't interfere in their relationship. Bernie was struck to see a loving, supportive mother. "I had never seen a mother like that," Bernie told me.

Since childhood, Bernie had heard his mother say to her friends and other siblings that he was the result of an accidental pregnancy. She'd been very open about how difficult her pregnancy with Bernie was, with nine other children to care for. One Christmas, the children decided to peek in the attic to see their gifts and carefully unwrapped some of the packages to see what was inside. The next morning, they found the gifts all under the tree—but minus the wrapping. When they asked their mother why the presents were not wrapped, she said, "Since you all decided to look at your gifts beforehand, it didn't look like wrapping was necessary!"

The kids felt responsible and ashamed that Christmas was ruined. "We were just kids," Bernie said as he related the story.

Bernie and his siblings would be having fun with their father, but when his mother came home, all play stopped and the house became quiet. His father apparently deferred to his wife, who was dominant and in charge. At night, before the children went to bed, she would not tuck them in or read to them. They were to come to her and give her a kiss.

When Bernie told his mother about other boys bullying and abusing him in school, she looked at him with disgust and silently walked away. He recalled feeling humiliated, that he had done something wrong in telling her. Worse, he continued to be bullied at school, and nothing was done. In Bernie's memories of his mother, neglect and abandonment loomed large. But he didn't label them as such. Instead, he said that he tried to be a "good son." As a child he always felt responsible for her unhappiness and tried to cheer her up. As an adult, after his father died and he moved back in, he made her a priority, taking her shopping for groceries and clothes, and driving her to all her doctors' appointments. He recalls his siblings doing hardly anything to help her. Once he wanted to send his mother to vacation with some of his siblings in California, but they said no. He recalled feeling bad for her and confused over why his siblings wouldn't want their mother with them.

Granted, she had her quirks, he told me, but he always enjoyed her company. Even though he asked her several times to call him Bernie, she insisted on calling him by his full name, saying "I named you Bernard."

After Bernie moved out, when he and Dave went to visit her, his mother would talk to Dave and ask about his work but ask little or nothing at all about Bernie's life. Bernie would feel like a "bad son." If Dave tried to talk to him about his mother's "bad behavior," Bernie would defend her and argue that she hadn't *done* anything wrong and that it *had* to be him. He would ask her directly, "Is everything okay between you and me?" to which she would flatly reply, "Yes, Bernard." Her covert narcissism in this instance wasn't so much what she *was* doing as what she *wasn't* doing by not taking an interest in Bernie's life or calling him by the name that *he* wanted to be called. Bernie told me, "I never leave her with a sense of peace or well-being that she will be okay and that moving out was okay, or that we are close in any way anymore."

Now that his mother was moving and his siblings were involved, her covert narcissism and punitive emotional neglect toward Bernie were becoming more overt. For example, he discovered that she added his elder brother's name to her joint checking account with Bernie as well as to the deed to the house. When Bernie asked his mother about this, she said it was easier, since his brother was a financial advisor. But his older brother was never very close to their mother and treated her with disdain. Bernie also discovered that after selling the house, she had given the daughter in California— who didn't want her coming to visit—money to buy a home of her own!

The last straw came in the form of his father's class ring, which his mother had promised to give to Bernie. When he asked his mother if he could have it, she said she'd already given it to another sibling. Finally, Bernie began to exhibit some anger. But it was short-lived and turned to self-hate and depression, which is what first brought him to therapy.

Recovering from the NPD Parent

In therapy, once individuals discover their mothers or fathers have NPD, they often worry excessively that they have it too. They constantly give reasons why and how they're just like their NPD caregiver. Often, they describe times where they imitated a parent or displayed "selfish" behavior. There's a difference, however, between someone with a narcissistic personality disorder and a person who has a narcissistic defense. In other words, NPDs never enter therapy to discover what's wrong with *them,* they wonder what is wrong with *others.* We therapists refer to people as *characterological* when their character is damaged or flawed to the point that they cannot self-reflect. The more neurotic and defensive individuals who only *behave* narcissistically will wonder what's wrong with them and not even consider something might be wrong with others.

Bernie did all of that and more. Each time he said he felt "bad" for his mother, I explained that I thought he was very angry with her but couldn't let himself tolerate his anger consciously. Bringing forward what he possibly did as a child to adapt to this NPD mother, he made himself the "bad one." I urged him to watch what his mother *did,* not what she said—in her case, what she *didn't* do and *didn't* say. What made this so hard for him was that his mother's narcissism and meanness were subtle and indirect. A covert, silent force!

He strongly resisted the idea that he was angry at his mother: "I cannot be angry with her. I love her. I'd never do anything to hurt her." After she moved from her home to her apartment, Bernie continued to help her, despite the negative feelings he got back from her and his siblings. At first he thought it was his fault, even though his partner Dave said the problem was clearly theirs. Then at Christmas, Bernie stumbled across the information that he wasn't invited to a gathering with all the family members from out of town. When he asked his mother why, she said, "I thought you were called and couldn't attend." His siblings said the same thing. The truth was, he wasn't invited. No one wanted him there.

I helped Bernie see that in fact he did *not* feel bad for his mother; this was his defense against his real feelings. Over time, he realized how angry he felt. He had known all along that she hadn't wanted him. "How could a mother treat her son like this?" he asked. "This happens to other families, not mine," he would protest. But over time, he had to acknowledge that in his family it had.

Bernie decided to distance himself from his mother gradually. He initially considered total cessation of contact but decided that was not what he wanted—just calling less frequently and seeing her less often. He noticed that if he didn't call her, she didn't call him. He called to see how she was doing one day, and when there was no answer for two days, he telephoned his brother, who casually mentioned that their mother had been hospitalized. She'd been in and out of the hospital for chest pain, but no one had called Bernie.

Stealing the Key from Under Your Mother's Pillow

As he gained more confidence and self-esteem, Bernie realized that there was nothing wrong with him;he had been a good son. The problem was how his mother had treated him over the years. I urged him to talk openly with her.

I strongly believe that as long as our parents are alive, we need to go to them for healing our issues with them. Whether they're willing to change or even participate isn't the point, but rather that we "take the key from under their pillow," as Bly urges to do in *Iron John*.

After a year of distance from his mother, Bernie decided to begin surprise visits to her new apartment, catching her off-guard, which he said he liked. He wasn't mean, nor did he confront her at first. Sometimes he asked Dave to come along, and other times he went alone, to reestablish power in their relationship, with him being stronger.

Each visit, he began to talk to her more about her behavior, about her breaking promises to him and leaving him out of family matters, particularly those related to her health. She acted confused, denied that there was a problem, and at times outright lied. Ultimately, however, she never conceded the truth:that she'd never wanted Bernie and was punishing him for not being the son she wanted him to be.

Bernie had stolen his mother's key from under her pillow, since she clearly wasn't going to give it to him. Even when he asked for it directly by confronting her, she refused. Bernie continued to confront her until he felt he was done. At one point I asked him why he kept going back, when it was clear each time that she wasn't going to come forward. "Joe," he said, "I agree with what you've taught me: 'Do this while she is alive and leave her with her own baggage,' so I don't have to carry it any longer. Better speak to living ears that won't hear than to ears that are dead and deaf."

It's as though your parents loaded your backpack with very heavy objects for which you had no use. Say to your parents, albeit silently, "You gave this to me a long time ago, and I've been carrying it ever since. I no longer want it and want to give it back to you." If they can deal with that baggage and are accountable for having passed it on to you, that is a bonus. If not, you can let it go, as long as you no longer have to carry something that isn't yours to begin with.

As Bernie progressed in his work with his mother, his relationship with his partner improved. When things bothered him, he began speaking up to Dave and could hear Dave's concerns without taking them personally and degrading himself, as he had done in the past.

Having a narcissistic mother is annihilating emotionally. It is as if your existence depends on her interaction with you, and nothing more. Recovery is about letting others bump into you, experience your boundaries, and work with and around you, not *through* you. Bernie's progress involved his being able to do just that.He found his inner King.

Overt NPD Mothers

An overtly narcissistic mother on the face of it may seem obvious, yet clients still come into my office not realizing they have one. Children have a great way of editing out things they don't want to face. A child can suppress all the negatives—even entire episodes of abuse—to ensure that a parent remains "good." Growing up, you need to depend on the parental figure that ensures your safety. The biggest problem in having a narcissistic parent, overt or covert, is that while you attach to them, they don't attach back. Therefore, when their adult children go into the world, they commonly find those they can attach to but who don't attach back in return.

This was the case with Simon, who came to me after a DUI he received after leaving a gay bar. He knew he deserved the ticket, since oftentimes he drank too much. He said it was to deal with his partner Alan, who "treats me like shit." Alan had been complaining that Simon didn't make enough money for them and that he spent his paycheck on things he shouldn't. They were constantly arguing over material things.

He and Alan had been together for twenty years. Both in their forties and Catholic, they lived together as out and open gay men. Their families knew about them, supported them, and loved them both. Still, both of their mothers continually requested that they not talk about it in church or other places they went. "You know how Catholics talk and gossip," Simon's mother told him. She would say, "I prefer you not do it. I have to live in this town too, you know."

Simon believed he deserved Alan's nagging but didn't want to have to take it all the time. While they did have outstanding bills and couldn't pay off loans, Simon reported that everything was fine and he had his debts under control. Alan was never satisfied that this was true. No longer able to take his complaining, Simon found himself working more hours, staying out at gay bars, and drinking more and more.

Simon was a podiatrist and had his own practice. He had wanted to be a psychologist, but his parents talked him out of it, wanting him to be a doctor or lawyer. When he applied to psychology classes, his mother told him, "No son of mine is going to be a low-life psychologist. I could see a psychiatrist, perhaps, but not a psychologist. What kind of doctor is that? What will I tell my friends? If you do this we will not pay for your schooling!" Simon became a podiatrist, even though this compromise wasn't what he really wanted. He said he felt like a disappointment to his parents, but more to his mother, who had urged him to be a doctor.

When he was little, Simon recalled, his mother often had a phone in each hand, talking to her friends all the time. When not on the phone, she was out with her lady friends at various events. "She goes to see everyone who is in the hospital," he told me, laughing hysterically, "even if it's someone she doesn't know all that well." He believed she did it to appear compassionate to her friends. "Her friends boast about what a wonderful woman she is, that even if their family goes in for something minor, she is there." But she never once went to any of Simon's school functions or sporting events. When they moved to a new neighbourhood where Simon, the outsider, was teased and beaten, his mother evinced little sympathy.

Over the months, I saw that Simon's problems with Alan mirrored his problems with his mother. Even though Alan worked as a teacher's assistant, he never felt satisfied with Simon's professional achievements, though he got along very well with Simon's mother, with whom his own mother was good friends.

Simon talked about how his mother had a strong interest in being friends with Alan's mother. "She's one of the wealthiest and best-known women in the church, and knowing her means you get to meet a lot of her friends."

After a year of therapy, Simon told me he'd been raised by an older African-American woman named Mabel. He hadn't told me about her in the beginning of our work together. It turns out that she was the "nanny" Simon ran home to when he was bullied in school. She came to his school events and was even there for lunches and dinners, while his mother was out socializing with others. Whenever Simon tried to talk about Mabel with his brother, the latter became defensive and asked, "Why are you talking about her? Mom raised us. That would just hurt her to bring up Mabel as anything other than our maid."

The truth at last! His mother would be hurt to hear taboo talk about the "nanny" as a surrogate mother, which she was. In Simon's family, the fabricated story was that their mother was always there and raised her two boys. In burying the fact that she was gone more than she was around and not available to him emotionally or physically, Simon buried his mother's negative aspects. In truth, his nanny, Mabel, who truly raised him, was his *only* mother.

Simon's Journey

In therapy, Simon's work went back and forth between Alan and his mother, and he could see that there were many similarities between the two. Whenever possible, I try to involve one's partner in the healing work, and so urged Alan to attend one of my couples workshops. Keeping one's partner or boyfriend in the therapy loop reinforces and strengthens the couple's connection during the individual's therapy work. So to improve their relationship, Simon and Alan attended an IRT couples workshop.

After the workshop, Simon told me that Alan was very upset that my workshop asked participants to look at themselves and their accountability toward the problems in their relationship, since he felt that Simon's drinking and fiscal irresponsibility were the problem. Simon was crushed, having hoped the workshop would impact him and Alan in a positive way. Simon stopped drinking and went to AA. He started losing weight and feeling better about himself.

Soon he realized he needed to leave Alan. But when he told his mother, she was furious. "You can't leave him!" she screamed. "You need to work things out!" He tried to tell her that he was not open to that, but his mother wouldn't listen. He knew the real issue was that she did not want to lose her "in" with Alan's mother. She was concerned about how Simon's breakup affected *her,* not him.

When he did leave Alan, it was very turbulent and conflicted: Alan hired a lawyer to sue Simon and tried to take everything from him. He kept calling Simon's mother to complain of being "victimized" by Simon's leaving. When Simon learned of Alan's confiding in his mother, he confronted her with it. Her response was, "What can I do? He calls and catches me off guard."

Simon came into my office enraged. "Can you believe my mother is talking with him? Where is her allegiance?" "That's right," I said, "where *is* your mother's loyalty?" We talked about what he could say to her and ask of her. He knew she might not cooperate, but for him, asking her was itself more important than getting what he wanted.

He told his mother to stop speaking to Alan altogether, particularly now that they were engaged in a messy lawsuit and since all Alan did was call to complain. He told her he believed she was more interested in keeping Alan's mother as a friend than in supporting him, her son. She denied this vehemently and expressed her hurt and agreed not to speak to Alan any longer.

When confronted with their bad behavior, overt NPDs like Simon's mother don't want to—and cannot—see themselves in this light. If exposed, they'll do all they can to excuse and cover up their bad behavior. In addition, Simon began distancing himself from his mother, which was unacceptable to her. NPDs may not be able to change their personalities or become accountable, but one thing is for sure: if they want a relationship with someone they're attached to, they will change their *behavior* at that person's request to stay connected to them. In other words, if Simon's mother wanted to remain on close speaking terms with her son, she would have to stop talking to Alan, even if that meant that she could no longer count his parents as friends. Simon's therapy wasn't only about leaving an unaccountable partner but also about dealing with a self-absorbed mother.

Diva Worship

I joke that if you are what I call "Gay Orthodox," you can consider it a Gay High Holy Day when a diva comes to town. If Gay Orthodox, you must commit to closing your business or taking the day off. Treat the day as a Sabbath or consider yourself a sinner. Gay neighborhoods will be ghost towns as we flock to stadiums—our places of worship—for any Diana Ross, Cher, Barbra Streisand, Bette Midler, Madonna, Janet Jackson, or Dolly Parton concert. Today's younger gay men flock to Britney Spears, Jennifer Lopez, Jessica Simpson, Beyoncé, and Christina Aguilera.

I, of course, am Gay Orthodox and must follow the Gay Bible, which is to close shop at sunset on these days to pay respects to these beautiful gay icons! We even saw Jack from *Will & Grace* briefly die and go to heaven, where he found that Cher was a goddess. "It all makes sense," Jack said on meeting Goddess Cher. "*Elijah* and *Chastity* are the names of your children; it's true you are!"

One can never forget, of course, dearly departed divas such as the late, great Bette Davis, Joan Crawford, and the original grande dame of divas—Judy Garland. While not every gay boy or man worships divas, a good many do. Why is that? There are many theories. In *The Rise and Fall of Gay Culture,* Daniel Harris suggests that "at the very heart of gay diva worship is not the diva herself but the almost universal homosexual experience of ostracism and insecurity." Harris feels that we gay men live vicariously through divas who snare the handsome heterosexual men and that we like to imagine ourselves in their place. He equates diva worship to watching football and says that it's actually just as unfeminine as football: "it is a bone-crushing spectator sport in which one watches the triumph of feminine wiles over masculine walls of a voluptuous and presumably helpless damsel in distress single-handedly moving down a lineup of hulking quarterbacks who fall dead at her feet."[13]

Time magazine even addressed diva worship in a review of Judy Garland's final concert on August 18, 1967, at New York's Palace Theatre. The article read, "A disproportionate part of her nightly claque seems to be homosexual. The boys in the tight trousers roll their eyes, tear at their hair and practically levitate from their seats, particularly when Judy sings ['Over the Rainbow']...Judy was beaten up by life, embattled and ultimately had to become more masculine. She has the power that homosexuals would like to have, and they attempt to attain it by idolizing her."[4]

On closer examination, we can see there is something decidedly masculine about these divas. They have a hardened, sometimes aggressively feminine side. In their performance mode, they are almost as hyperfeminine as drag queens: Diana Ross's big exaggerated hair, for example, and Cher's heavily beaded gowns and overly glittering eye shadow.

Mommy Queerest

Another theory I hold strongly is that these divas are our stand-in mothers. Jewish clients and friends of mine have told me that Barbra Streisand saved their lives! Without her movies and songs, they couldn't have survived their childhoods. Many of these men had self-absorbed mothers who were unavailable emotionally, so what better surrogate Jewish mother than Streisand? She is already unavailable in many ways, so clients can worship her and fulfill some needs that their mothers cannot. These diva mommies will never let us down—they are whoever we want them to be. They're our mother shadows.

I am not putting down these divas! I adore and love most of them. My home and office are filled with dolls that celebrate these divas from Cher to Lucille Ball. While growing up, my divas were Diana Ross and Cher, which, if you believe my Mommy Queerest theories, tells you a lot about me and my maternal figures. Perhaps these divas' narcissism is a way to celebrate the narcissistic mothers and female caregivers in our lives.

In our early lives, our inability to attach and identify with men may prompt us to try to escape into the feminine realm to avoid the shame and fear of being compared unfavorably with other males. Although this is true of both gay and straight men, straight men bring these issues to their female partners. Not having women as partners, we turn to our divas.

Dark Feminine Shadow

A gay comedian once quipped, "I like my women like I like my coffee. I don't like coffee." His audience laughed uncomfortably. Did he mean he just wasn't interested in women sexually or romantically, or that he hated them? Some gay men do indeed hate women.

There are many discussions about why some gay men refer to each other as *she* or *her* or *Mary*. When I first saw the movie of Mart Crowley's *The Boys in the Band*, I was shocked that even back in the early 1970s gay men called themselves by female names and pronouns; I have since learned it goes back even fuarther. While this can be in jest—a way of "owning" our feminine side through humor— there are times I think it goes too far and becomes a way to channel hostility, sexism, and misogyny.

Personally, I never liked to be referred to as *she* or *her*. Early in my coming out, I had friends who wanted to call me "Josephine," and I forbade it. As a boy, I was shamed so much by family and friends for having a feminine side that this is nothing I can joke about. I have seen *her* and she used to attack and humiliate other gay men, just as characters in *The Boys in the Band* use these pronouns during an argument. As a mean-spirited insult, it is meant to put women down.

A mother's problematic personality disorder or smothering doesn't cause an aversion to women and thereby contribute to a homosexual identity. If this were true, then more straight men would have become gay, inasmuch as most of the aversion to women and misogyny comes from them. Aversion to women does not create orientation, though it can contribute to anger toward women and anything feminine.

Femininity is not generally acceptable among gay men. Countless times I have heard gay men say of their more effeminate counterparts "if I wanted a woman, I would be straight" in a negative and hostile way. Many gay men accept and tolerate drag and feminine talk and behaviors among friends in the culture but declare this taboo in relationships. Just read the many personal ads seeking out "straight acting" guys, "masculine, no fems."

Homo-Work on Mother Issues

Write down your mother's positive and negative personality traits as *you* perceived her when you were a young child.

1. Identify the worst memories you have of her.
2. Identify the best ones.
3. When you were growing up, what was your mother's view of the world? Did it change as you grew older, or did it stay the same?
4. What did you want most from your mother but never received?
5. How old do you feel when you are around your mother?
6. Do you act like your mother and treat your partner like your mother treated you?
7. What traits in your partner are the same as those in your mother?
8. How were females treated in your family?

References

1. Judith Viorst, *Necessary Losses* (New York: Fireside, 1998).
2. Melody Beattie, *Codependent No More,* 2d ed. (Center City, MN: Hazelden Press, 1986); and Pia Mellody, *Facing Codependency: What It Is, Where It Comes From, How It Sabotages Our Lives* (San Francisco: HarperSanFrancisco, 1989).
3. Robert Karen, *Becoming Attached: First Relationships and How They Shape Our Capacity to Love* (New York: Oxford University Press, 1994).
4. John Bowlby, *A Secure Base: Parent-Child Attachment and Healthy Human Development* (London: Routledge, 1988).
5. Christine Ann Lawson, *Understanding the Borderline Mother* (Northvale, NJ: Jason Aronson, 2002).
6. Kenneth M. Adams, *Silently Seduced: When Parents Make Their Children Partners—Understanding Covert Incest* (Deerfield, FL: HCI, 1991).
7. F. Jim Fickey and Gary S. Grimm, *Gay Warrior: Transforming Betrayal into Wisdom* (San Francisco: GLB, 2002).
8. Michelle Elliott, ed., *Female Sexual Abuse of Children* (New York: The Guilford Press, 1994).
9. Hani Miletski, *Mother-Son Incest: The Unthinkable Broken Taboo,* 2d ed. (Brandon, VT: Safer Society Press, 1995).
10. Kali Munro, *Male Sexual Abuse Victims of Female Perpetrators: Society's Betrayal of Boys* (www.kalimunro.com), 2002.
11. Jerold J. Kreisman and Hal Straus, *I Hate You, Don't Leave Me: Understanding the Borderline Personality* (New York: HarperCollins, 1989).
12. Eleanor D. Payson, *The Wizard of Oz and Other Narcissists* (Royal Oak, MI: Julian Day, 2002).
13. Daniel Harris, *The Rise and Fall of Gay Culture* (New York: Hyperion, 1997).

Chapter 6
Learn How to Disarm—Not Strong-arm—Your Partner in Communication

It's hard to kiss the lips at night that chew your ass out all day long.

—Vince Gill, The Notorious Cherry Bombs

By the time couples come into therapy together, they've lost a feeling of trust and safety in their relationship—usually because communication has broken down. Once this happens, repair attempts are unsuccessful. Moreover, as we saw in chapter 3, most couples are not fighting about the real issue, so they keep hitting a dead end. Their arguments recycle themselves and never reach a resolution because the partners really need to address what's under the surface.

As a couples therapist, I know that what the couple tells me their issue is and what they complain about in our first few sessions aren't really the problem at all; an undertow keeps taking them under a surface that they cannot readily see. If the couple is willing to let me coach them, I can help them understand their real issue by helping them lose their defensiveness and practice the skills of intentional listening as well as intentional speaking—the first step to communication. In Imago Relationship Therapy we call it an Intentional Dialogue.

Once the couple can communicate safely, I help them explain their frustration, hurt, fears, and the associated childhood wound. In IRT, we say that behind every frustration there is a hurt, and behind every hurt there is a childhood wound. To be sure, not everything is attached to childhood, but you want to recognize why you're having such a big reaction to your partner and what part your shadow plays in that. Otherwise, reacting from shadow, you will not be reasonable.

Once your partner can hear the part of your frustration that's really about *you* and what *you* need and want, he'll be more likely to listen and even *want* to change. But you both must know how to actively listen and speak to one another, or else change cannot take place.

The communication technique I teach I also call *clearings*, that is, things you need to clear out between you and your partner so that you can move forward and still stay connected. Otherwise these things will remain in your way, preventing contact from being loving and intimate.

You'll need the help of your Warrior and Magician archetypes to get through the exercise. Sometimes, when you want to talk but your partner doesn't, you must wait until he is ready—within a twenty-four-hour period. Other times, you won't want to talk at all but your partner will, so you're going to have to stretch and talk about things you don't want to discuss.

As the saying goes, *People won't remember what you said. They won't remember what you did. But they will always remember how you made them feel.* Nineteen-fifties culture taught us to keep everything inside and not speak our minds. The 1970s were about letting it all hang out, letting people hear it as long as you need to get if off your chest. Now, in the new millennium, we recognize that we need a balance between those two attitudes. Many people wish they could simply say what's on their minds, not worrying about how they say it. But that only serves to create more trouble in any relationship.

It is very difficult over time to remain in emotional contact and connection unless you operate intentionally, making efforts with your partner. If you and your partner protest that you're not feeling very close to each other, you must be willing to do the work involved to get closer. It is a real chore to feel connected to a partner who's critical and judgmental, who's been talking *at* you all day, instead of *to* you and *with* you. Communication is perhaps the biggest factor that causes trouble for couples and brings them into psychotherapy. They lose their sense of safety, and when psychological and emotional safety evaporates from the relationship, both partners experience distance. Their dialogues become monologues, and contact and connection dwindle.

Danny and Alex had been together for three years. When they came to me, Danny was threatening to call it quits if Alex didn't get control of his explosively angry outbursts. Alex, for his part, stated that Danny was being unfair. Although he admitted that he got angry, Alex felt that Danny was equally responsible by being provocative and that he showed his anger through passive aggression.

Alex was the more verbal of the two, although Danny's nonverbal cues were quite expressive. As Alex reported the history of their relationship, Danny began rolling his eyes, looking away, and shaking his head. At this, Alex angrily told Danny to look at him and pay attention. Danny looked at him blankly, like an unwilling but outwardly compliant child doing what his parent asked. The more Alex demanded that Danny engage himself, the more Danny disengaged.

I watched how each expressed his anger toward the other. Both were caught in the power struggle, the Call of the Child. They told me that they'd started arguing a little under two years into their relationship, right on schedule for the power struggle to begin.

People have many different styles of communicating, often developed during childhood in their families and culture of origin. Later, if they find others who were raised in a similar environment, communication usually isn't a problem. But when they find themselves with others whose style of relating to people may be completely different—as most partners do—trouble can soon begin. It's important to learn what your partner's style is and not personalize it. Most people *do* personalize it, however, and assume that their partner is purposefully acting in a certain manner to hurt them. They don't see that he's behaving in the best way he knows how from his *own* experience.

Alex complained that Danny seldom shared much about himself or his feelings. Time and again, Alex asked him how he felt and what he wanted out of their relationship. At first, Alex thought it "sweet" that Danny seemed so shy and inward and saw it as a "challenge" to get Danny to open up. Now, however, he felt that Danny was withholding his inner world on purpose. For his part, Danny said he'd enjoyed Alex's "gregarious nature" and outgoing spontaneity, but now found Alex to be aggressively pushy and overbearing.

Neither yet understood that as a couple, they were very similar to most other couples, gay and straight alike.

Different Styles of Communication

In most relationships, one partner plays the Turtle and the other, the Hailstorm—terms coined by Harville Hendrix to describe the protagonists in the power struggle. One pulls inward, in the face of the other's explosions. And depending on the issue, quite often the two partners can switch roles. Hailstorms can seem scarier because they're loud and energetic. But to a Hailstorm, a Turtle's retreat can be just as scary—making the Hailstorm feel abandoned and threatened. I use this analogy at workshops, where it usually helps people recognize this common version of the power struggle.

There's no cookie-cutter approach to psychology, and these roles aren't set in stone. You might be more of a Turtle in some of your relationships, a Hailstorm in others, and everywhere in between. A partner in a relationship might start out a Hailstorm and over time retreat into becoming more of a Turtle. You may find that you can immediately recognize these styles in your current life, or as you reflect on your past with a former partner.

Turtles

Turtles use minimizing as an emotional defense against extremely uncomfortable feelings. The goal of their Turtling is not to hurt others but rather to keep themselves emotionally protected and safe. They hope to stay connected to the Hailstorm, and imploding and going inward is the best way they know how. Uncomfortable with long conversations, they want to keep things short and sweet—which is how they stay attached to themselves and their partners. Turtles are not necessarily introverted, shy, and meek; that's more of a social style. They simply minimize their emotional world.

Turtles typically deny their emotional needs and dependency. Seldom voicing their feelings and thoughts, they're inner-directed, seek, and follow, their own council, think and behave compulsively, and exhibit passive-aggressive traits. Usually, they can go off to bed in the middle of an argument and still enjoy a good night's sleep. They do care, but often their partner doesn't feel they do. They do feel deeply, but can constrict their emotions, bury them, and put them aside—and often do so too much.

Hailstorms

Hailstorms are the maximizing partners who paradoxically are also uncomfortable with their feelings, but their defense is to express them immediately. Maximizers fear that their partners (usually Turtles) are abandoning them. As a means of protesting overwhelming feelings of rejection and hurt, they become louder, more verbal, and at times bigger than life to get the Turtle's attention. They explode with emotions and talk incessantly, using their moods and threatening to leave the relationship in an effort to be heard and make contact with their Turtle partners. Being maximizers doesn't mean they're life-of-the-party extroverts who socialize with ease; that's a social style, not an emotional one.

Hailstorms exaggerate their feelings and needs. They're constantly shifting boundaries. They can be clinging, overgenerous, and act and think impulsively, bringing others into private matters and seeking advice from them. They can be manipulative, alternating between aggressive and passive. Rarely, if ever, can Hailstorms go to bed in the middle of an argument or put it on hold. Their motto might well be "Don't go to bed angry—stay up and fight until dawn!" And they do. It's not that Hailstorms are emotional 24/7; rather, they connect with others, particularly their partners, through expressing deep emotions.

Rapture or Rupture? Your Choice

Rapture

When the two first fall in romantic love with one another through the Call of the Wild, Turtle tells Hailstorm, "You are so alive, passionate, vibrant, and compassionate," referring to the outward emotions he observes in the Hailstorm. Hailstorm tells Turtle, "You are so calming, thoughtful, introspective, and relaxing to be around," referring to the way the Turtle handles his emotions inwardly.

At first, this is seen in a positive light. But over time, after the romance ends and the power struggle begins, neither the Turtle nor the Hailstorm finds these traits likable or attractive any longer.

The fact is, both Turtle and Hailstorm have found in each other their own lost and buried selves. Most Turtles long to emote more and be more verbal. Most Hailstorms want to be calmer, to handle situations without exploding. But neither is conscious of this, nor do they know how to accomplish it. The Turtle lost his ability to be more emotional in childhood when his family or culture did not honor or reward strong emotions; his family's message was: "Don't feel." Hailstorms, raised in families and cultures that emphasize strong emotions and discourage passivity and peace, often lose their ability to be calm and emotionally contained. So each arrives in the other's life to unearth his own lost traits and buried self.

Rupture

Turtles and Hailstorms who come to my office or my workshops believe they are mismatched. Each feels superior to the other. Turtles often strut in, enjoying the knowledge that their Hailstorm will eventually show up and hail. Then they can point and say, "See what an abusive, mean, angry person I'm with!" Meanwhile, Hailstorms hope their partners will sit there quietly and let me see what a frustratingly "passive-aggressive" person they're with. Each arrives eager to shine a spotlight on the other.

Until they begin their couples work, they don't yet realize that each is a different side of the same coin. Both partners desire contact and connection with each other. Both are trying to preserve their emotional selves and defend themselves. Both are trying to recapture their lost selves.

And yet, both are scaring each other to death! The Turtle is frightening the Hailstorm by appearing to be disinterested. The Hailstorm is scaring the Turtle by showering him with more emotion than he can handle.

In the couple just described, Danny was the Turtle—the minimizer who would implode rather than explode. By internalizing and diminishing his feelings, he would infuriate Hailstorm Alex, who would often protest, feeling abandoned and ignored, getting angrier and louder (maximizing). The more emotional Alex became, the more Danny shut down, afraid of the strong emotions coming his way. Naturally, Danny felt that *Alex* had the problem and frequently pointed out how inappropriate it was for him to yell and scream and carry on emotionally. What most Turtles like Danny don't see, however, is that to other Hailstorms like Alex, they are just as threatening.

Many feel that this type of conflict is the kiss of death for a relationship. But few of us—least of all, gay men—realize that this dynamic is in fact normal. What *isn't* normal is how most people deal with Turtle and Hailstorm relationships. This is when they can most use some help, through education and coaching. Dialogue is key to getting through the power struggle.

Yes, getting through the power struggle is difficult. But it's purposeful and the gateway to real love. It is supposed to happen, just as it's supposed to end. It may seem easier to break off the relationship, have an affair, or engage in addictions and distractions rather than face your deepest conflicts and fears. But counterintuitively, the good news is that power struggles you face with your partner are actually a positive indicator that you're with the right person for your maximum growth. You've met someone who'll challenge you to make necessary changes in yourself, which can only benefit you both. It's an opportunity to achieve closeness and intimacy, while still maintaining your own individuality.

Reactivity

Reactivity is the single biggest problem in relationships of all kinds: familial, romantic, parental, collegial, and social. Once you begin reacting, all forms of logic go out the window. Early in the dating period, you misinterpret what your boyfriend does and says, personalizing things as if something's wrong with you. You think, *He doesn't like me,* for whatever reason.

Once you commit to a partner and move from dating to a full relationship, you externalize when you misinterpret—believing there's something wrong with *him.* You start wondering if you like him anymore. No longer are you able to communicate effectively. As you become defensive, projections and judgments fly, and misunderstandings occur. It's common to rush into an argument, based on your erroneous belief about what you think your partner did or said.

Along with the psychological and emotional reasons behind our reactions, there are physiological reasons that help explain them. The truth is that we have three parts to our brain. Unless you know or understand this, you cannot use all three parts of your brain effectively.

Is It Safe or Is It Dangerous?

In Imago Relationship Therapy training, I learned that each of us has *three* brains. This concept was borrowed from neuroscientist Paul McLean's model, dividing the brain into successive layers: the "old" reptilian brain, the mammalian brain, and finally the cerebral cortex. You might think I'm becoming yawningly academic here, but hang on. I'll explain this in the simple way that I learned it, making it useful for you in your relationships.

The instinctive reptilian base of your brain is constantly scanning the environment to assess whether it's safe or dangerous. Your survival depends on it. We share this most primitive, least evolved part of our brain with all animals, including alligators and lizards. If you're in a dark parking lot or the last one at work in an empty building, this part of your brain helps you recognize whether you're safe or if danger is looming.

Unfortunately, it only senses safety or danger. It does not know the difference between the year 1966 or 2006. It takes care of all the things concerned with survival that we seldom think about, such as heartbeat, digestion, sleeping, and breathing.

If indeed we are in danger, our old brains kick in and help us get to safety. Our five instinctual responses to danger are to fight, flee, freeze, hide, or submit. This is what you do when you are reactive (and especially overreactive) to a situation—particularly one concerning a partner. Couples tend to fight, flee (leave one's partner or situation), freeze (just stare at each other and do nothing), hide (go to another room or stop talking), or submit. ("I give in. Whatever you want! Just leave me alone.")

Your instinctual response signals to you whether or not you feel endangered. As gay little boys, we felt in danger all the time—and for good reason. Unless you understand how the brain works and how trauma affects you, however, going to gay social functions could well feel very dangerous when in fact it is not.

The mammalian brain is the next most evolved section, where emotion and feelings are stored. So when the reptilian brain feels danger, it sends a message to the mammalian brain to be afraid. If the reptilian brain feels safe, it signals the mammalian brain to relax.

In Imago, we call the reptilian and mammalian brain the *old brain,* which "determines most of our automatic responses," according to Hendrix's *Getting the Love You Want.*[1] Since the old brain is hard-wired from childhood, it is essential to understand how you were socialized and imprinted to ensure you do not recreate this same instinctual reactive pattern as an adult.

Our brains have a third part: the cerebral cortex, or frontal lobe. We call this part of the brain *new* because it appeared most recently in evolutionary history. This is the part of the brain that can reason, make decisions, think, and observe our surroundings. Being logical, it can override the old brain. If you suddenly feel in danger, your automatic response kicks in because you are scared. If the danger is real, the old brain sends a message to the mammalian brain to be afraid, which sends a message to the new brain to do something to remove the danger. When there's really no danger and your immediate environment is safe, your new brain can relax.

Old Brain—New Brain

When your old brain feels itself in danger, you are "emotionally hijacked," to use a phrase of Daniel Goleman's in his 1995 book *Emotional Intelligence.*[2] To override your old brain, you must be able to recognize which instinctual responses are typically yours. Knowing the signs and symptoms of your own reactivity can help you stay in integrity with yourself and others.

Emotional intelligence is a blanket term that includes, in Goleman's words, "self-awareness, managing your emotions effectively, motivation, empathy, reading other people's feelings accurately, social skills like teamwork, persuasion, leadership, and managing relationships." It's a vitally important attribute, particularly in relating with those with whom we feel closest.

But what if things are safe and your old brain senses danger? That is where relational problems occur. If your partner, friend, or family member does or says something and your old brain feels threatened, it automatically sends a message to the new brain to engage one of the five responses to get to safety. The problem is that when danger is nonexistent, you might be making the wrong decision. There may be no need to behave in a threatened way, and yet, if you respond to the directive of the old brain, you might negatively influence a situation and your own peace of mind.

Consider, for example, the person who stays closeted even when it is safe to come out: relationships with gays and lesbians and their families and friends stay distanced and ruptured. Often, the family and friends are waiting for the gay or lesbian person to talk about it and do not want to make that person uncomfortable. The closeted individual is trying not to make the family or friends uncomfortable and feels in danger when danger is not even present.

This is why we must rely on what our new brain tells us in every situation. We must be in check on what is really going on around us or we will behave in ways that may be appropriate to our environments and in our relationships. Reacting exclusively with our old brain is not always in our best interest.

"Response-Ability"

To work on controlling your old brain, I recommend Rick Carson's *Taming Your Gremlin,* which he defines as "your ability to respond to your life....But it's not always easy to respond to this life gracefully, in great part because of a vile, vicious, villainous, insufferable bully lurking in the shadows of your very own mind: your gremlin."[3]

By being reactive, you're more likely to lose your original focus and respond to things that aren't part of the argument. Operating out of your old brain, you might say what you don't mean or do things you'd normally never do, to avoid offending your partner. But you wind up being hurtful to him and relieve your own pain, thereby losing your sense of integrity for yourself and for the relationship.

The book *King, Warrior, Magician and Lover* contains this instructive story:

> The samurai was sworn to avenge his lord's death. After tracking the assassin for some time...and after braving many dangers, the samurai found the murderer. He drew his sword to kill the man. But in that instant the assassin spit in his face. The samurai stepped back, sheathed his sword, and turned and walked away. Why?...because he was angry that he'd been spat on. He would have killed the assassin, in that moment, out of his own personal anger, not out his commitment...out of his Ego and his own feelings, not out of the Warrior within. So in order to be true to his warrior's calling, he had to walk away and let the murderer live.[4]

For relationships, this story has so many lessons. It speaks about integrity, staying aligned with your vision of where you are going in life. It also shows how we can get offtrack when we respond out of reactivity, defensiveness, or erroneous judgments about another person.

Here are a few ways to use your new brain to calm the old brain's reactivity:

1. *Whenever you feel endangered, become aware of your physical reactions.* This requires that you know what happens to your bodily sensations when you sense a threat. Various clients tell me they feel an adrenaline rush or blood rushing to their heads; they lose their breath, breathe more heavily, talk more rapidly, or can't think of what to say; they feel themselves wanting to make fists, and more. Anticipating such physiological reactions can help you override the old brain.

2. *Focus on your breathing.* This is a great way to calm yourself. During the mediations I teach, I usually recommend that clients breathe in through the nose, hold it for the count of two while tightening their bodies, then breathe out through the mouth three times.

Intentional breathing helps you focus on the here and now and prevents your old brain from taking charge.

3. *Take time out, or count to ten.* Do this intentionally and/or out loud. Tell the other person that you're finding yourself reacting to the situation and need to get hold of yourself and not become unreasonable about the situation.

4. *Remind yourself of your shadow and childhood wound.* It is vital that you know yourself from the inside out, as best you can. As long as you've been doing your own personal work, you will be able to avoid acting out by successfully identifying the sources of any strong reactivity that prompt this urge.

5. *Talk to yourself.* Being able to talk yourself down from your reactivity and maintain a sense of personal integrity requires intentionality and self-awareness.

6. *Remain aware of others' judgments and projections.* Whenever someone is getting reactive, most likely he's touched something inside himself, provoking his shadow. The longer you know someone and the more you continue to remain aware, the easier it becomes to remember that person's issues and remind yourself that his reactivity is not about you.

You might be thinking, *Sure, this sounds good on paper, but it's not realistic in an imperfect world.* Many clients tell me that when they have a reaction, they need to be able to express it immediately or else they feel silenced and codependent. I teach them about *containment,* a term we frequently use in Imago Relationship Therapy, which means to contain your reactivity. Once again, the more you practice this, the easier it becomes.

Contain Yourself

Containment doesn't mean suppressing your feelings or shoving them aside. It's the mature, conscious way to manage your old brain and be intentional in how you act on your feelings.

Containing yourself is a form of self-soothing. It means noticing your mammalian brain's emotions and, without getting rid of them, just sitting and holding on to them, letting yourself calm down. You don't wait for your environment or your partner to change, but rather *you* decide to do something. Even in the face of strong emotions, when your old brain feels endangered and urges your new brain to lash out or act out, you contain yourself instead and let your new brain realize that there's no danger in the conflicts with your partner. You can hold on and wait, which is what containing is all about.

Without *response-ability*, your old brain will react instinctually, creating distance, rupture, and disconnection from your partner. With too strong an emotional charge, we "know better than" our partner and ultimately become righteous, responding emotionally and inappropriately. Says relationship expert John Gottman, "We are up on our high and windy mountain looking down on our partner and passing judgment. So because of our egos we stray from ourselves and our original intentionality causing more rupture in the relationship."

Blocks to Communication

When you're being reactive, communication breaks down. During the initial dating period, you don't admit to the guy that you're worried about anything; you try to anticipate his desires and put your best foot forward. During the Call of the Child stage of the relationship, you try to get your partner to change and be the way you want him to be by criticizing, blaming, shaming, and being contemptuous—in short, by putting your worst foot forward. None of this works or is any good for yourself or your partner.

Couples therapist John Gottman refers to the "Four Horsemen of the Apocalypse...four disastrous ways of interacting that sabotage your attempts to communicate with your partner." In his book *The Seven Principles for Making Marriage Work,* he lists the Four Horsemen in increasing order of danger: criticism, contempt, defensiveness, and stonewalling.[5] Over time, he says, a couple using these strategies to communicate becomes more and more entrenched in negativity, leading to a breakup or divorce.

Criticism

There's no room for criticism in a relationship; it's like trying to smoke and jog at the same time: you can't do one while doing the other. It's vital to distinguish a criticism from a complaint. Telling a partner your frustrations about his behaviors or statements is appropriate; criticism is destructive.

In Alex's case, he *criticized* Danny by saying "You don't feel anything and you purposely withhold yourself to hurt me." This is an attack on his personality and basically delivers the judgment that "something's wrong with you, Danny." To voice a *complaint,* Alex might tell him, "When I don't get responses from you, I get frustrated and scared and I really want to hear what you have to say."

This second statement is more about Alex's own emotions, how he feels about a behavior of Danny's that he wants to see more often. Complaints about a behavior that's excessive or absent are totally acceptable in any relationship.

Too often, criticism is projection: throwing your dark shadow onto your partner and accusing him of something you yourself are guilty of. In short, it can be a form of self-abuse: being critical of the very thing that lives inside of you, you take it out on your partner instead.

But we're all human, and when we are hurt and feel pain, often we lash out at those we love most. So it may not be realistic to completely avoid criticizing 100 percent of the time in your relationship. Your goal is to greatly reduce it. Be as intentional as you can. At least express an apology after voicing any criticism. Be accountable for *your* error and don't blame your partner for it, as many do: "Well, if you stop acting that way, I wouldn't have to lose my temper."

Contempt

Contempt is when you express the disrespectful attitude that your partner is inferior or worthless, purposely insulting and psychologically abusing him. Danny was being contemptuous, shaking his head and rolling his eyes while Alex spoke to him in my office. Danny was sending a nonverbal message: "I discount what you're saying, because you're ridiculous and a fool."

During the Call of the Child, a relationship can get so choked with lost hopes and dreams that negativity can seem one sure way of staying connected and "getting through." Partners will say things like "Don't you know that?" or "What's wrong with you?" or "I can't believe I have to tell you things like this!"usually with an aggrieved expression and patronizing tone, as if the speaker were superior in some way.

Symbiosis, you'll recall, is the righteous but mistaken idea that your partner should think, act, and feel about your relationship almost exactly as you do. One partner will begin a sentence with, "In a relationship, two people should . . ." or "Most people who want to be together are . . ." There are hundreds of other examples. I help clients remember that once they begin to preach about how they think things "should be," they've assumed a contemptuous stance and are trying to impose their righteousness on others. Obviously, this does not work in relationships of any kind.

The poet Maya Angelou says that using sarcasm and being critical is like committing "little murders" to the soul and the humanity of whomever you're treating this way. Over time, with enough criticism and contempt, you will "kill" the relationship with your partner.

If you've just begun a new relationship, you might find it hard to foresee ever reaching this point with anyone you love so much. You might think: "I could never treat him like that, and if he ever treated me that way, I would leave." But by the time you two get into the power struggle, you'll be so attached that you'll find yourself unconsciously (and often consciously) acting out your anger in mean and hurtful ways.

Defensiveness

The more critical and contemptuous you act, the more defensive your partner will become. Unleashing your anger in a reactive way makes you seem frightening, and the more scared someone gets in a relationship, the more defensive he'll become. The more you scare your partner, the more threatening he'll get in return.

Being defensive denies *your* accountability and responsibility for the problem. Yes, it arises from a positive intent, in that you're seeking to protect yourself. But by doing so, you're denying your contribution to the problem between you two.

Another form of defensiveness is saying "I didn't mean it" or "That wasn't my intention." Statements like this relieve you of being responsible for your own words and behavior. It blocks any introspection on your part. You may not have consciously meant to impact your partner negatively, but may have intended it unconsciously. You could have shadows of which you're not yet aware.

Another way to be defensive is changing the subject, as, for example, bringing up what someone has done in the past: "What about the time you did that to me?" or by choosing style over content: "I don't like your tone of voice." Begin talking about yourself instead of first acknowledging what the other person's saying. If you still feel the need to discuss these topics, do to so *after* you've honestly listened to what your partner has to say.

Stonewalling

I'm not talking about the 1969 gay riot at New York City's Stonewall Inn. This term reflects a style of responding that sabotages communication. The stonewaller doesn't react to the speaking partner. Whereas committed listeners will give encouraging signals such as "Uh-huh" or "Hmmm," the stonewaller just sits in unresponsive silence. As Gottman writes, "they are trying to be 'neutral' and not make things worse. They do not seem to realize that stonewalling itself is a very powerful act: it conveys disapproval, icy distance, and smugness. It is very upsetting to speak to a stonewalling listener."

The main message any stonewaller is sending is that he's disengaged and not listening. This is very similar to how a Turtle sometimes behaves with a Hailstorm, perhaps in a more extreme way.

Couples Dialogue: Breaking Symbiosis

I advise couples never to begin a sentence with "You *always* say that..." or "You *never* do this..." That's making a blanket statement that excludes even the one exception to the rule you're trying to lay down. When you're angry, it feels good to utter these sweeping judgments, but they do nothing for your relationship. The ideal thing to do is to qualify and leave your partner an escape hatch: Say "mostly," or "for the most part," or "more than I like." Then you're giving credit where it's due. You're acknowledging the (admittedly few) times your partner might have said or done what you're accusing him of doing.

You mustn't say "I shouldn't have to ask." Yes, you *should*— in any relationship, you must ask for what you want. It's naïve to think that your partner should "just know." He may have been that intuitive during the romance stage, but that is because of the love drugs and because you were closely tracking each other. Remember, the purpose of all that was to bond the two of you together. That shouldn't set the tone for your relationship. If you expect it to, you'll be disappointed.

I have seen clients whose parents didn't watch them closely when they were children. Their parents didn't track them well or at all, not anticipating their children's needs, as parents should do. Now as adults in relationships, these clients unconsciously expect their partner to make up for the attentiveness they didn't receive as children. This is completely inappropriate, and I quickly point out that they're bringing their little Inner Child to their adult partner. Unconsciously, they're trying to reclaim what they didn't receive, having come from a family where the parents weren't there enough for them. Their work is then about grieving the loss of what they should have gotten but didn't.

Together, the communication models of Cliff Barry's Shadow Work Seminars and Hendrix's IRT model create a safe container for effective communication.[6] They break down symbiosis and the idea that your partner should see the world the way you want him to and vice versa.

I use Imago's Intentional Couples Dialogue with almost every set of partners. It offers couples a process that includes mirroring, validation, and empathy. Since most couples engage in monologues, not dialogues, this offers a realistic, valid way to communicate.

While our partners are trying to convey a message during a conflict, most often we're not really listening, just waiting our turn and sitting in our own reactivity, without truly hearing our partners from *their* point of view.

The first part of the Intentional Dialogue communication skill is *mirroring:* one partner sends information, and the other receives it. The Sender delivers all the information relating to one topic until he's entirely finished, using short declarative sentences that start with the word *I*. The Receiver doesn't interpret, diminish, or magnify what was said but simply repeats it like a parrot. He reflects back, asking, "Did I get it?" and asks, "Is there more?" until the Sender says, "There is no more." (Reflecting or mirroring back can also be done in paraphrasing.)

After your partner sends some information, you reflect back what you heard him say. For example, he might say, "I'm upset that you did not clean up after the dog after we agreed you would." You—the Receiver—would say, "I heard you say that you're upset that I did not clean up after the dog after we agreed I would." Then you add, "Did I get it?" and "Is there more?"

This process blocks any misunderstanding and continues until the Sender feels heard and understood. Asking "Did I get it?" sends your partner the message that you're really trying to understand what he's saying. "Is there more?" tells him that your ears are open and you're eager to listen.

Adults do this with children who are learning to speak. We anticipate that at ages two to five, they may have difficulty, so we often listen more carefully and show close interest in what they're trying to say. When I can't understand my younger nephews, even though they're talking to me as best they can, I get down on the floor and ask, "Are you saying that _____?" Then they either correct me or smile and say "Yeth!"

Intentional Dialogue counteracts common intimacy—blocking behaviors such as dominating the conversation, interrupting and finishing each other's sentences, being overly critical or too close-mouthed, failing to pay close attention, and being judgmental by interpreting what *you* think he's really saying, or walking away. The couple's dialogue prevents all that and creates intentionality in their communicating with each other.

The second part of the Intentional Dialogue is *validation*. After your partner finishes what he's saying, you validate what you heard him say—not from your point of view but *his*. The Receiver says, "What you are saying makes sense to me. From your point of view I can see why you'd think this way." You are not agreeing, simply validating *his* point of view. For a moment, you are looking through *his* eyes, not yours, and validating the way he views the world. You're acknowledging that yours is not the only way to view the conflicts in your relationship.

For most people, such validating can be very hard, but especially so for gays and lesbians. Over and over, we've been told that what we think and what we feel are wrong, so in this area, we're hypersensitive. Telling someone "What you say makes sense" can suggest that you think it *doesn't*. We live in a world where what makes someone right makes another wrong. Wars break out because of this mentality. IRT suggests simply suspending your point of view temporarily and letting your partner's reality surface. It's good practice to keep your reality while validating the reality of another person too.

During my master's program, I received word that my first internship would be at a Catholic organization. When I told my Jewish grandmother, she said, "Oy, those *goyshe coupes*! Those Catholics really have problems, don't they? Thank goodness you can help them!"

Goyshe coup is Yiddish for "Gentile head," an expression that implies that Gentiles' thinking is inferior, illogical, and wrong. I told her that similar agencies exist for Jewish people with a *goyshe coup* who think dysfunctionally. "Well," she responded, "I don't know about all of that." By which she meant she didn't want to hear that, since it didn't fit with her worldview.

Most cultures, religions, neighborhoods, and families all believe that their worldviews are superior and correct. Even we therapists become arrogant about how we serve our clients. In fact, everyone has a point of view that deserves to be honored.

The final part of the Intentional Dialogue is *empathy*—trying to imagine what your partner might be feeling, given what he is saying. Here again, you put aside whatever your feeling is, contain it, and try to imagine his point of view. What is *he* feeling? But for men, even gay men, imagining another's emotions is very hard. Unlike women, we men are not taught to empathize with others.

After the Sender is finished and the Receiver has mirrored back, validated, and empathized, the couple then switches roles: the Sender becomes the Receiver and vice versa. But they stick to the same topic, so as not to stack up issues, which allows both partners' realities to coexist. Afterward, if this doesn't settle their conflict, IRT implements many other communication techniques. I suggest picking up Harville Hendrix's books to learn more.

Clearings

Cliff Barry's communication model, which complements the Imago model, has four parts: data, judgment, feelings, and "what I want." Barry calls these communication strategies *clearings,* in that you clear up the misunderstandings that stand in the way of you and your partner's having good feelings toward each other and staying connected.

Data

As Sender, you say to your partner, "I want to do a clearing with you regarding my frustration about _____," then tell him what your frustration is. You state the data by talking about only the facts. You report what you heard him say and saw him do, word for word, and action for action. As Sender, you do not interpret, judge, or try to change anything you perceived. Describe his behavior dispassionately, as if you were explaining it to a third party who wasn't there and wanted "just the facts."

Talking to someone with whom you're in a relationship, you would say "I heard you say, '_____'" or "I saw you _____," keeping your own feelings and judgments totally out of this part of the exchange. Other behaviors you can mention include "When you rolled your eyes..." or "When you looked away while I was talking."

Using the Imago communication method, the other person simply mirrors the data of what he hears. All that the listener—or Receiver—is to do is reflect back what he hears you saying, nothing more. Otherwise, he breaks the mirror. Your tone of voice should be the same as if you were in a restaurant, asking "Please pass the salt and pepper."

Judgment

In any significant situation, we can't help judging what happened, and the closer we are to the person involved, the more reactive we are and the more judgments we have. But in the judgment phase, you have the opportunity to verbalize your beliefs and explain your opinions about what you saw and heard, and the listener should mirror your judgment. We can't help judging what happened in any significant situation, and the closer we are to the person involved, the more reactive we are and the more judgments we have. Here you are free to go into details of what you *assume* is going on. Remember that it's *your* truth, not *the* truth. Here, you can say things like "My guess about why you did that or said that is _____."

A cautionary note: one can go too far with judgment by becoming critical or contemptuous, turning into one of Gottman's Four Horsemen. That's not what this process is for. Understand that it offers a safe way for you to purge your judgments so they're no longer in your way. Doing so, you may discover some information about yourself; indeed, most of your judgments are really reflections on yourself. Removing your judgments lets you hear your partner more clearly.

This process lets the Sender discover what his own judgments say about him as well. In other words, your judgments are almost always more about you than about whomever you're judging. This helps you discover your shadow. Listening to your partner's judgments, it's crucial to keep this in mind. Otherwise, you'll take things too personally and not be able to listen. But there's almost always some truth to what your partner is telling you. Staying curious about whether there's any truth to his judgments helps you, as the listener, examine your own shadow.

We often fear judgment because it is wielded in such negative, punitive ways. In my groups and workshops, I invite participants to voice their judgments in a safe and contained way. Through hearing others' judgments—as well as their own—group members can learn a great deal about themselves and how they're perceived by others. If expressed and explored constructively, these oft-distorted reflections get corrected, helping people identify and work through each of their shadows.

Feelings

To accomplish this next stage, you need to be in touch with your *feelings* as the Sender and know how to express all of them, both positive and negative. Typical emotions to use as baselines are *mad, sad, glad, afraid, ashamed,* and even sexual. Most other feelings are spin-offs from those. As the Sender, you would begin sentences like "What hurts me about this frustration with you is _____" and "What scares and worries me about that frustration is _____."

The next important technique comes from IRT. The Sender begins by saying "This reminds me of my childhood when _____." This helps both you and your partner remember you're often being triggered by something that happened in your past. The event in question needn't be about your childhood (though it often is), but also about your past relationships. It's to your advantage to determine how your shadow is interfering in your current life. If you don't clear up unresolved issues from those past relationships, they'll likely follow you into the next one.

All of these feelings, judgments, and what you are reminded of in your past helps you move away from the surface problem (which is usually not the real problem anyway) and helps both the Sender and the Receiver understand that more is at play here than the specific, superficial argument they're having. Feelings and histories also play their part in the conflict.

But when you share your feelings, it's not fair to say things like, "*You* make me feel _____" or "I wouldn't feel this way if you wouldn't _____." This puts the cause of your emotions on your partner, where it doesn't belong. Better to say things like "*When* you tell me_____, I feel _____" or "I feel this way when you _____." That keeps the responsibility and accountability on you.

Before progressing to the final "what I want" quarter, I suggest that the Receiver validate what his partner is saying. Remember: this is *not* agreement—rather, it's simply letting him know that you've listened to him and that what he says makes sense from his point of view. Again, you keep on breaking through the "belief symbiosis" trap that suggests that your partner thinks as you do and sees things exactly the same way (or damn well ought to).

"What I Want"

What do you want that would relieve the frustration you're having with your partner? Imago employs a technique called Behavior

Change Requests (BCR), in which one partner tells the other partner what he wants in a specifically outlined way. These requests should be positive, measurable, specific, and time-limited (PMST). As you can see, BCR works perfectly together with the "what I want" phase of communication.

"What I want" means saying what you *do* want, not what you *don't* want. Be specific: say exactly what you want, so there's no guessing and your partner knows exactly what to do. Make it measurable, as in "I want ___ every day" and time-limited: "for the next two weeks" or "over the next month." The trick here is to keep the time duration short enough that it can be measured and thereby not easily forgotten.

Usually, the Sending partner suggests three BCRs. That gives the Receiving partner choices and lets him choose which one he can fulfill. The Receiver, however, might hear all three and not be able or willing to do any of them. As the Sender, you need to be flexible, remembering that if your partner says no, it simply means that right now, he cannot make that kind of commitment to any of the three. You want him to commit only to what he can do.

For his part, the Receiver can modify one request and ask, "Is that okay with you?" Also, he needs to understand that the Sender may not be okay with that at all—and be willing to come up with three more things.

As the Sender offering three BCRs, you might secretly hope that your partner will pick a certain one and feel angry, sad, or hurt when he doesn't. You have to remind yourself that you will get whatever he can give at this time. Later, you'll have other opportunities to return to whichever BCR you want to give.

The secret here is keeping the same goodwill toward each other that you shared at the beginning. In these moments of communication, suspend judgments or at least don't act on them, and remember that each of you is doing the best he can and committing to the things he knows he can do best.

Your Partner Holds the Blueprints to Your Personal Growth

What you most need from your partner is usually the hardest for him to give; and what he needs most is hardest for you to give. This is because these are the very things you each need to do for yourselves. This is the custom-made part of real love. By giving to him, you are giving to yourself.

Any relationship challenges you to learn more about yourself, to stretch into undeveloped aspects of yourself, and to deal with things differently than you were taught in childhood. In Imago therapy, when one partner requests a behavior change of the other, the request itself can trigger old childhood memories of feeling "forced" to conform to someone else's ideals, which may in turn trigger fears of losing a part of one's identity. For some gay and lesbian couples, this is a stumbling block.

By giving your partner what he wants, you are performing your own healing. So for lesbians and gays, giving partners whatever they ask for is an opportunity to discover that we won't lose ourselves by doing so—the way we did for heterosexism. By giving to your partner, you'll learn that nothing psychically dangerous will occur and that your relationship will only deepen.

To get to real love, you need to recognize who your partner really is, separate from you. Symbiosis ends and you recognize that the person you have partnered with is different from you—and that that's okay.

When you engage in these clearings, your tone of voice is very important. I suggest you use the same even, everyday tone that you would at a dinner table when asking for the salt and pepper. Raising your voice or getting sassy will create defensiveness and reactivity in your partner.

When couples at my workshops learn this communication process, often they complain that it's time-consuming and unrealistic, also that it feels contrived and mechanical. They shouldn't have to talk to one another this way. I don't disagree, but it's also usually true that by the time they get to therapy or a workshop, their communication has broken down almost completely. Safety has diminished to almost nil, and each has lost trust in the other. So I always recommend that no matter how they feel in the beginning about this communication process, to do it the orthodox way when conflict arises.

It's like any exercise program, diet, or new regimen to learn.

Follow it the way it's set up—the orthodox way—and later tailor it to your particular style as a couple so that it works better for you. This communication process teaches some highly important skills, including how to actively listen, actively speak, suspend your judgment, stop interrupting and interpreting, remain in dialogue and not move into a monologue, and, throughout, how to contain your old brain in the heat of any conflict.

Here are ten tips to help you and your partner communicate:

1. *Ask for an appointment to discuss conflicted conversations.* It is very important not to begin talking to your partner about a frustration or angry matter unless you've both agreed to the right time to do so. Hailstorms typically force a conversation with their Turtle partners without their consent. Many Turtles have difficulty even asking for appointments, as they often stifle their feelings.

2. *Informed consent.* Even if your partner has agreed, never begin talking about your frustration without first informing him what that frustration *is.* You should provide a one- or two-sentence overview of what you want to discuss. Both of you should be on the same page, knowing what the topic is and when you'll discuss it.

3. *Don't wait more than twenty-four hours to discuss a frustration.* Usually the Turtle isn't prepared or ready to talk about what the Hailstorm wants to address. Usually the Turtle will say no to the Hailstorm's request to talk. Often, the Hailstorms feel they are being pushed away, rejected, and take this personally. It is not personal at all. Remember it is the Turtle's protective shell trying to manage strong feelings and emotions. If it were up to the Turtle, often it could take days or weeks (or maybe even never) to discuss the conflict. So the rule is to not wait more than twenty-four hours.

4. *If you're the one who declined the appointment, be the one to suggest when a good time would be.* Both personally and professionally, I've found that regardless of whether the Turtle or the Hailstorm partner rejects the overture for an appointment, he leaves the initiator to keep asking "Is now a good time?" or "How about now?" If you're the one who declined, it's up to you to say "Okay, I'm ready now" or "I'm still not ready. Can we do this tomorrow?"

SENDER	RECEIVER
Asks for an Appointment for Dialogue or Clearing and tells partner what his frustration is	
"I feel frustrated about ____. Is now a good time?"	*Mirrors back frustration and grants request to speak now or later.* ("What I hear you saying is 'Did I get it? Is there more?'")
Expresses frustration	*Mirrors each sentence stem and then asks sender* "'Did I get it? Is there more?'"
"The data is _____."	
"My judgment is _____."	
"What hurts me about this is _____."	
"What scares me about this is _____."	
"Other feelings I have about this are _____."	
"This reminds me of my childhood when _____."	
	Validation: ("You make sense to me." *And what makes sense and why it makes sense.*)

BEHAVIOR CHANGE REQUEST

"The first thing I want   *Mirror*
is_____."
(*Positive, Measurable,*
Specific, Time-Limited)

"The second thing I want   *Mirror*
is_____."

"The third thing I want   *Mirror*
is_____."

                                           "I am choosing Number
                                           _____."

---

5. *Both partners should keep stretching.* This is different from changing. By stretching, you become willing to give more of what your partner wants. In so doing, you're giving yourself something too. The Turtles need less reactivity, and the Hailstorms need to learn to "chill out," to contain their bigger, stronger emotions. They can trust that the calm approach will be effective and don't need to become loud, volatile, and overly angry over every conflict. Likewise, the Turtle needs to learn that he doesn't have to protect himself by always remaining inward and detached. The Hailstorm is teaching him about connectedness when strong emotions are part of the conflict—and letting him know that he's safe to venture out of his protective shell.

6. *Use safe and effective dialogue.* Imago Relationship Therapy offers several effective ways to talk with a partner, particularly when the conflict or frustration is emotionally charged. I recommend that couples pick up Harville Hendrix's books *Getting the Love You Want* and *Keeping the Love You Find.*[7] You'll learn more about Intentional Dialogue and how to use it.

7. *Reduce reactivity.* Most conflicts don't go well because of both partners' reactivity. It is important that you both wait until your tempers have cooled (or at least subsided considerably). This doesn't mean that the underlying frustration or conflict will be gone, but if you remain defensive and overreactive, you won't be able to hear each other.

8. *Avoid criticizing.* Criticism kills love. When you feel angry at your partner, it's easy to be critical, thinking—wrongly—that if you point out your partner's faults, you'll get what you need. But in fact this ensures that you will not get what you want and need.

9. *Stick to one subject.* Most couples usually start arguing over one topic and then drag in other grievances. It's vital that you stay on one frustration for your entire dialogue. If you have another issue to clear up, make another appointment for another time.

10. *Avoid staying in judgment.* It's so easy to tell your partner— objectively, and for his own good (of course!)—who you think he is and where he's going wrong. Being and remaining judgmental is not relevant or helpful to rapture.

What if you follow all these suggestions and still find you can't communicate? Then it might be time for therapy, a couples workshop, or a talk with a couple who have been together and have done this work. Look for "been there, done that" friends who can mentor you and your partner to help make things work. But if neither of you has the interest or the motivation, then it might be time to think about breaking it off and moving on.

Monogamous Ever After?

If you and your partner choose to have responsible monogamy (or responsible nonmonogamy), it's imperative that you have effective communication. Without it, you risk ruining your relationship. Healthy, open, and effective communication is like an antivirus program on a computer.

The trouble is, no matter how healthy your relationship, opening it up to others is never fully free from opening it to problems. If you decide to have an open relationship, that's the risk you take. But doing so doesn't necessarily mean there is anything inherently wrong in your relationship.

I used to believe that if I saw a couple—socially or in therapy, straight or gay—who were open and swingers, automatically I assumed they had some kind of attachment disorder or other problem that prevented them from enjoying full intimacy. Now, after more than twenty years as a therapist, I have seen all sorts of couples able to make it work without creating problems in their relationships. I have seen many even get better as a result of opening the relationship! It is about what works for the couple, not what someone else believes should or shouldn't work. The couple themselves should decide, not friends or therapists.

I began working with a gay male couple who told me that they were monogamous. After several months, however, they informed me they had had a three-way. When I asked if they had changed from monogamy, they said, "No."

I was confused. Maybe I hadn't gotten the correct information in our initial consultation? I told them, "I thought you told me you were monogamous," and they said, "We are." Now I was really confused! I said, "But you just told me that you have had a three-way."

They replied, "We are monogamous. We only have three-ways together, and are never sexual with others apart from each other." Okay, now I was slowly getting it.

I quickly learned to ask what a couple means when they say they're monogamous. Now, in fact, I routinely ask each couple, gay or straight, what their contract is around sex and commitment. Do they have an assumed or an explicit contract, verbal or otherwise? I don't assume that every couple or individual who comes in for therapy is in an open or closed relationship. Nor do I assume that they have—or haven't—talked about it.

Books on affairs have been exploding in the self-help market over the past ten years. This seems to acknowledge the lack of conversation and openness among couples, gay or straight, that leads to ruptures in relationships and exits from intimacy.

Open relationships are controversial, to be sure. Claiming that gay male couples can show how to manage them successfully is even more controversial, at a time when the issue of gay marriage is making headlines. Yet many heterosexual couples' lives are torn apart because of affairs and cheating and only rarely do these couples talk openly about their sex lives. This is far worse than a couple talking openly and honestly with each other about a sensitive topic like sexuality.

Monogamy Versus Nonmonogamy

Gay men hold a lot of judgments about monogamy and nonmonogamy. Over the years, I've found that gay men who are not partnered or find themselves in new relationships are the most judgmental of their nonmonogamous peers. They strive to maintain the value of monogamy, because that's what they have learned they should want. But after they've been together for a while, particularly around the fifth to seventh year, many couples decide and agree to open their relationship to include others.

In fact, studies show that 75 percent of gay male couples are nonmonogamous after passing their five-year mark. You can read more about this in David Nimmons's book, *The Soul Beneath the Skin*.[8] Overall, the research into nonmonogamy among gay couples is positive, because a sharp distinction exists between emotional and sexual fidelity. Some couples decide to have three-ways only; some decide to play separately from each other, while others mix it up.

All in all, problems arise for couples if secrecy is involved. If any couple wants to be nonmonogamous, making it work within their relationship requires a lot of dialogue, communication, and trust. Trust is broken if an agreed-upon contract changes and neither partner tells the other. That is cheating.

I've also found that many gay male couples go back and forth between monogamy and nonmonogamy. There's really no hard and fast rule about when, how often, and for how long they do so. I've also seen many couples make it work. But there are times when I think that gay couples (or any couple, for that matter) should be monogamous:

If they enter therapy as a couple. Deciding to do so usually means that their connection has suffered some rupture. Nonmonogamy may not be the problem. Therapy, though, is about closing all exits and energy leaks, so for the duration of therapy I recommend being monogamous until the relationship issue can be resolved.

If sexual addiction is a problem. Usually, both the partner who's acting out and the coaddicted partner are struggling over what constitutes sexual acting out and what doesn't. Until they figure this out, I usually recommend that they maintain monogamy throughout their therapy and until the sexual addiction is healed.

For the first three to five years, I recommend monogamy. It takes that long for partners to bond and establish a sense of safety, trust, and attachment to each other. If, after the fifth year, you still want to have a nonmonogamous relationship, I recommend that you discuss it then.

Intimacy with your partner—and yourself—requires honesty, communication, self-awareness, and integrity. It demands that you say and be who you authentically are, to yourself and potential partners. It means being up-front, aware, conscious, open, and communicative—all of which takes a lot of work. Most people are not up for it, because it's often painful, rife with conflict, and, overall, basically not a lot of fun. But the truth is, doing the painful work can be extremely satisfying, even fun.

Responsible Nonmonogamy

If you and your partner choose to have an open relationship, here are guidelines to consider:

Both partners consent to a mutually open relationship. Here, each agrees to open the relationship in ways satisfactory to both. Some partners prefer not to know about their partner's sexual behavior outside the relationship; others want to know; and many insist on knowing. Rules are important here. I've heard gay male couples say, "We only do it on vacation" or "only with people we don't know." Working this out is imperative.

Playing safely. When sexually playing outside their relationships, gay men should be very cautious about STDs, and they should use condoms. Assume that everyone else is HIV-positive and act accordingly. It's neither appropriate nor realistic to hope the person you're with is telling you the truth—or how recently he's been tested. Play safe, no matter what.

Fidelity without sexual exclusivity. Gay couples often report that what works best for them is to engage in sexual encounters based on sexual attraction only and not emotions or affection. It's about sex and nothing more. They avoid getting to know temporary partners at any deep level, to avoid turning the encounter into something emotional that might develop into a full-blown relationship. In other words, any sexual inclusion is simply behavioral in nature, not relational.

Maintain an open dialogue for regular clearings. Effective dialogue is the best thing couples can do to ensure safety and trust. This kind of respect and communication is essential for any open relationship.

Know—in advance—what problems can occur with nonmonogamy. When couples open their relationships, jealousy is also bound to get aroused. I've heard couples, gay and straight, voice their anxiety that their partner liked the other person more, preferred some sexual behavior from the other person, and so on. Again, resolving this requires dialogue and safety between the partners. Knowing in advance the kinds of issues that an open relationship may present can help prevent some of these conflicts in the first place.

I believe that when gay couples are maintaining an open relationship, it's most important that they distinguish between emotional and sexual affairs. In general, men can have sex without being intimate or emotional with their partners. This is why, I think, gay men can do this effectively, not because we're gay but more because we're men.

Some say that relationships are hard enough, so why add another element such as nonmonogamy? If this is what you choose to do as a couple, make sure you take precautions and keep a dialogue going. Do this, and you can keep heading in a positive direction.

And remember most of all, safety and trust are imperative to all relationships. This is why contracts and dialogue are essential, no matter what the topic. It's not up to me, any other therapist, or anyone else to judge whether you should be in a monogamous or non-monogamous relationship, or say how you "should" be in any kind of relationship. The type of relationship you want and should have are what you and your partner decide it to be as long as it works for the two of you.

Homo-Work on Communication
1. Are you the Turtle or the Hailstorm?
2. What is your instinctive reaction or response? Do you fight, flee, freeze, hide, or submit?
3. When your reactive old brain is in control, what happens to you physically?
4. How are you critical of your partner?
5. What are your judgments about him?
6. What are your Behavior Change Requests of your partner? What behaviors does he want *you* to change? How can that benefit you?
7. Are you monogamous with your partner? Why or why not?

References
1. Harville Hendrix, *Getting the Love You Want: A Guide for Couples* (New York: Owl Books, 2001).
2. Daniel Goleman, *Emotional Intelligence: Why It Can Matter More Than IQ* (New York: Bantam Books, 1995).
3. Rick Carson, *Taming Your Gremlin: A Surprisingly Simple Method for Getting Out of Your Own Way,* rev. ed. (New York: Perennial Currents, 2003).
4. Robert Moore and Douglas Gillette, *King, Warrior, Magician and Lover: Rediscovering the Archetypes of the Mature Masculine* (New York: HarperCollins, 1990; reprint, HarperSanFrancisco, 1991).
5. John Gottman, *The Seven Principles for Making Marriage Work* (New York: Rivers Press, 1999).
6. Cliff Barry, *Shadow Work Seminars* (www.shadowwork.com).

7. Harville Hendrix, *Keeping the Love You Find: A Guide for Singles* (New York: Atria Books, 1993).
8. David Nimmons, *The Soul Beneath the Skin: The Unseen Hearts and Habits of Gay Men* (New York: St. Martin's Press, 2002).

Chapter 7
Know Your Sexual Shadow

My mother just doesn't get it! For my birthday she gave
me a buckskin jacket, with fringe...When I complained,
she said, "Wait a minute. I heard you tell your friends how
hard it is to find a leather top!"

—Eddie Sarfaty, gay comedian

Overall, we live in a sexually illiterate society. Jokes like the one about Eddie's mother symbolize our ignorance as to what to call many sexual interests, let alone what they mean. Gays and straights are given little permission to explore all of their sexuality, including fantasies and behaviors that some may consider out of the norm. Your sexual behavior should *not* be ruling you, particularly if it is taking you to unhealthy places. Most people, gay and straight alike, don't know if their fantasies and behavior are healthy or not. While gay men are more inclined to act out their desires and fantasies more candidly than their heterosexual counterparts, still they remain confused as to what's truly positive and self-affirming.

Therapists are typically uncomfortable talking to their clients about sexuality, mostly because they haven't worked on exploring their own sexuality issues. In J. C. Duffy's comic *Go Fish,* a client and therapist are talking with each other. "There are things I keep hidden from you, Dr. Floyd," the client admits. To which Dr. Floyd responds, "And I want you to know how much I appreciate that, Mr. Pendleton."

Believe it or not, better than 50 percent of all therapists feel like Dr. Floyd when it comes to their clients' sexual confessions. We are *all* still pioneering this path, and all too many psychotherapists still have a low comfort level. If sexuality has been explored much at all, it's from a negative perspective. An increasing amount of literature is coming from a sex-positive place, describing the benefits of understanding your erotic map.

We all have a sexual shadow. What is *your* sexual shadow? How can you learn about and from your sexual shadow? Is it standing in the way of finding real love? Can knowing it help you find a partner? Yes, it can help and hinder relationships. Again, the easiest way to know if you're in shadow is to consider what you most admire or dislike in others. So in sexual terms, that would equate to your peak erotic sexual interest. What sexual desires and fantasies do you *most* admire *or* dislike? Your peak erotic experiences and fantasies have coded information about you that can help you understand yourself better. It can even help you find the right partner for you, if you can decode the erotica of your desires.

There's a saying that you can tell a lot about a person by knowing who his friends are. Well, if you understand your sexual fantasies and desires, you'll learn a lot about yourself as a person. Sexual fantasies are not separate but a result of your psychological makeup—a part of you, an extension of your psyche.

Sexual behaviors and fantasies are an extension of our inner core, windows into another facet of who we are. Whatever gives you the greatest pleasure sexually is information about you. It's telling a story, not necessarily on a conscious level. Regardless of what type of fantasies you enjoy, it's helpful to translate fantasies into reality, albeit in nonsexual ways. You'll find aspects of yourself that you've been seeking all along.

For example, if a client enjoys fantasies about straight men, I suggest that he explore his relationships with the important, influential straight men in his life, starting with his father. His answers may encourage him to find ways to make friends with straight men and accomplish some personal healing. Why do people get into topping, bottoming, rimming, fisting, oral and anal sex, and all the other variations? Why do people have sexual fantasies and role-playing like daddy-boy fantasies, converting straight men to gay or convincing them to be sexual with you, dominance-submission fantasies, humiliation, and fetishes, to name just a few? Sometimes, it's simply because their body responds erotically to those behaviors. But other times, a psychological meaning is trying to express itself. Often it's a little of both, but in any case, knowing your sexual shadow can help you understand yourself more.

Otherwise, this information goes into the darkness, where it sees the light of day rarely, if ever. In helping those with troubled and dysfunctional desires—from sexual addiction, compulsivity, sexual abuse—we learn a great deal about them and their recovery from their sexual desires. And those without these problems still can—and should—examine their sexual shadow in order to enrich their relationships with partners and themselves. Without bringing your erotic moments out of the darkness, you will not be experiencing much sexual freedom or choice about what you are doing and want to be doing erotically.

Here, in the sexual realm, is where individuals and couples can get stuck. Those who contact me for help with their sex lives—couples, particularly—inevitably learn that before they can improve themselves through therapy, they have to learn the nonsexual meanings of their sexual problems.

Some enter relationships with an existing sexual dysfunction—abuse, addiction, physiological dysfunctions, and other problems—that cause the relationship to suffer. Or the couple's relationship itself can create sexual conflicts for the individuals involved, which express themselves through their sexual interactions. Whatever the case, this chapter will help you explore your own shadow more skillfully and thoroughly.

In archetypal terms, this chapter addresses your Lover energy: that aspect of you that carries and releases your passion, sexuality, sexual urges, and fantasies; your emotions, sensuality, and erotic energy; and unconditional love for yourself and others. For us gay men, this is the source of perhaps our biggest wounding. As *men,* we are squelched by patriarchy to act like an unemotional and unaffectionate male. On top of that, the covert cultural sexual abuse we suffer as *gay men* squelches our Lover archetype. Perhaps we gay men get punished so severely because we're more emotive and lead with our Lover energy, right from childhood. Parents, anecdotally reflecting on their gay little boys' childhood, often describe their sons as more sensitive, emotional, and thin-skinned. All of this gets buried under shame, internalized homophobia, and self-hate. Our psyches and souls become a burial ground.

Most buried and suppressed parts of yourself don't stay that way. Your unconscious is going to knock on the door of your consciousness repeatedly until it gets let out. Until then, it will communicate in code, and your work to discover yourself and your shadow is to decipher the message. Sexual fantasies usually have some unconscious intent that isn't even sexual at all! I learned this over time through treating sex addicts and sexual abuse survivors whose best recovery was based on their understanding the secret logic underneath their sexual fantasies, behaviors, and preferences.

What is healthy sexuality and what isn't? In various ways, nonsexual material gets coded into sexual fantasies, desires, preferences, and behaviors. Many of my clients have unlocked their Lover energy, discovered more about themselves, and integrated it into their whole person. This chapter, I hope, will help you understand your erotic landscape and how your erotic mapping directs you to the right partner for you, as well as how you relate sexually with a partner, and how you and he negotiate sex within your relationship.

This chapter is about getting the gold from our sexual shadows.

"Fairy tales don't teach children that monsters exist. Children already know that monsters exist. Fairy tales teach children that monsters can be killed." This quote from G. K. Chesterton explains the positive intention of fairy tales, which are to help children create a world that's safe and empowering. Paradoxically, sexual shadows do the same. The secret logic of your sexual preferences and fantasies is to kill off the perceived monsters from your childhood. In other words, sexual fantasies and arousal templates are formed with a positive intent. In his book *Arousal: The Secret Logic of Sexual Fantasies*, Michael Bader writes, "my theoretical and clinical approach to sexuality is an affirmative one, viewing sexual fantasy and arousal as resulting from an unconscious attempt to *solve* problems and not, as many psychoanalysts would have it, recreate them."[1]

Sexual Fantasies and Integrity

Sexual fantasies allow us to be out of integrity. Things we would never do or say in reality we get to do in our fantasies. Pay careful attention to your sexual desires, erotic needs, and sexual fantasies, and you can learn a great deal about what you're looking for in a partner and want to receive in a relationship. The details of your sexual fantasies don't matter as much as their themes, an important distinction, lest you get lost looking at the details and not be able to see the forest for the trees. Following the themes is like interpreting a dream. The details seem silly, but the symbolism is full of information about you. Whether you have healthy or unhealthy sexual desires, fantasies, or behaviors, it is to your benefit to understand what they represent for you. Believe it or not, you can improve your romantic relationships by making logical sense from them.

As Guy Kettelhack writes in *Dancing Around the Volcano,* "sexual symptoms and fixations are the psyche's energetic and ingenious attempts to cure itself—to give itself what it craves." That is, sexual fantasies and erotic desires are not pathological but a form of self-help,erotic blueprints that can help you discover yourself, along with the right partner for you.[2]

Our sexual fantasies and erotic templates are like fairy tales: unconscious attempts to adapt and resolve unpleasant and unwanted childhood memories. Bader goes on to say that "we construct particular sexual fantasies and sexual preferences that negate self-denigrating beliefs and feelings, thus allowing sexual excitement to emerge. In order to feel aroused, we temporarily transform ourselves from frogs to princes and princesses. Sexual fantasies undo rejections, turn helplessness into power, redeem feelings of unworthiness, and stamp out even the slimmest vestiges of depression. For just a few moments, just long enough to have an orgasm...the ordinary person with dreams of grandeur imagines him- or herself to be sexually powerful."

The guy seeking out Leather Daddies might be looking for a father figure. There's nothing intrinsically wrong with that, unless he's looking for someone to take care of him so that he needn't be accountable for his own life. As a child, he may not have had a father in his life, or the father he had was weak, passive, or abusive. A partner cannot make up for what he didn't get as a child; seeking this out in the nonsexual realm could therefore lead to relational problems. In sexual fantasy and play, however, this desire can be satisfied on a temporary basis. That is the cleverness of erotic moments.

Another guy may get aroused by twinks because he came out late and longs to recapture his own youth. His driver's license says he's in his late thirties or older, but in "gay years," he's still in his early twenties. And he may find that while sexually erotic, a true relationship with a guy that young is not effective or even possible. (There's nothing wrong with dating someone that young except if it's only about erotica and nothing more.) The answer might then be to recapture his youth with a younger partner but without the enormous age difference. He might find other ways to recapture his youth outside the relationship as well. His self-help work in this case is to find ways to recapture his youth and mourn for those lost younger years.

If you asked a hundred different men about their sexual fantasies and preferences, you'd get a hundred different answers—many *quite* different. Certain things—even trivial ones—may be important to arousing one man, whereas the same fantasy might turn off the next guy. That is because everyone's history, childhood, and socialized imprints are different. Each of us has his own erotic thumbprint. Later, they become the erotic blueprints for arousal, cleverly reenacting the original disturbing event, this time with a happy ending. Unfortunately, fantasy does not translate into reality. Therefore, the more bonded you are to your fantasy, the harder it is to learn from it and bring it into actuality. In other words, if you let yourself be ruled by sexual arousal instead of being in control of it, it can interfere with finding a partner and entering a relationship.

A good example is a heterosexual male I saw who was about to be married when he came into some legal trouble. Aaron was arrested for approaching adult women in mall parking lots, flashing them with his erect penis, making gestures with his tongue, then getting in his car and speeding away. One upset woman took down his license plate and quickly called the police. Arrested, he admitted to this sexual behavior. He was puzzled as well as ashamed of it and couldn't figure out why he was doing this. To me, he admitted to having done it for some time—and increasingly more often since his engagement and upcoming wedding. Now he faced the shame of telling his fiancée what he had done and the risk of losing her.

Aaron continued in therapy. In looking into his past, we discovered that his mother had been very dominant and controlling, and his father, passive and distant. There were older sisters, and he was the youngest child and only son. His mother acknowledged and validated his sisters, but silenced both my client and his father. If Aaron made any attempts to voice his thoughts, the females would tell him to be quiet. He felt stifled and emasculated.

His sexual fantasies and desires had resolved these feelings by showing these anonymous women what a "man" he was. His tongue gestures let her know he could use his mouth and could pleasure her with it, whereas his family hadn't wanted him to open his mouth to talk and basically gagged him. The women he flashed were stand-ins for his mother and sisters.

His work now, determined by the erotic impulses that we uncovered, was to assert himself more with the women in his life. It turned out (not surprisingly) that his fiancée was opinionated and had a dominant side. Aaron had given her what she wanted and subordinated his own needs but resented it. Many times he silenced himself and blamed her for it. At work, with female superiors and coworkers, he did the same thing, returning to the scene of the crime by recreating his family dynamics. His sexuality was telling him, "You need to express yourself and your masculinity to women" and channeled it through his sexual behavior by flashing.

Aaron did in fact assert himself more to his wife, and their relationship improved. He read men's studies books and healed his masculinity by embracing it more. His wife had difficulty with this at first but did adjust. His mother and sisters, however, were not receptive when he made the same attempts with them. So Aaron distanced himself from them and built a stronger relationship with his father. Ultimately, although the thought of flashing women still aroused him, he no longer did so. His erotic fantasies no longer ruled him; he had mastered them.

Not surprisingly, Aaron's sexual behavior increased since his becoming engaged. His unconscious was reaching backward in time to when his dependency needs were highest and he was attached to women who humiliated and emasculated him. His sexual behavior was trying to give him long-delayed resolution for his childhood resentment of the women. Luckily, he found the help to do it, otherwise his sexual acting-out would have caused further problems, especially in his marriage.

All sexual fantasies are healthy, though some—like Aaron's—should never be acted on because they might put the one who has them (or someone else) at risk. Some men discover, for example, that sex with escorts is a form of "paying for love." As children, they weren't loved or loved enough by their caregivers. Other men feel compelled to take orders, to be dominated and spanked in an effort to be disciplined in ways they never were as children. Others want to dominate and be in charge, since they often feel helpless and powerless in life. Some like to be humiliated by golden showers, being spit on, and verbally abused, possibly because they struggle with maintaining a sense of pride in themselves. This doesn't mean that you have to stop your fantasies or change the desires or behaviors they play out. It does mean that if you want to feel more powerful and take more pride in your life, find a way to be loved without paying for it, and make an impact on others in your relationships; this can then provide a map for how to improve the nonsexual parts of your life.

So much of porn—gay and straight—centers on rape fantasies: the hot military/police/boss/coach/teacher or other straight guy in authority who forces himself on the gay man, with both ultimately enjoying it. This allows gay men to feel accepted by a dominant straight man (see chapter 2) and provides them with a way to feel good about what's happening to them. Studies show that a high percentage of heterosexual women have rape fantasies, but this doesn't mean they *want* to be raped. For them, I suspect, it's a way of sexualizing the male dominance and patriarchy in their lives.

Gay porn abounds with fraternity fantasies. During initiation, the fraternity guys humiliate the pledges, notice the gay guy enjoying himself, and ultimately overpower him—to everyone's sexual and erotic pleasure. Everyone wins. The frat brothers get to stay in charge and dominate, while the gay initiate gets his fraternity brothers' acceptance and the sense of belonging that he's longed for.

There's nothing wrong with that fantasy and nothing wrong with play-acting it out. But I want to help clients explore—in a positive, not a negative way—*why* they've developed that particular fantasy. And what about incest stories—which can be found in both gay and straight porn? Sexual fantasies about family members ensure that attention is paid and connections are made. For example, if a parent was depressed, disengaged, and unavailable during a boy's formative years, then an incest fantasy of a parent being sexual with the adult son fixes this. The sexual connection of the fantasy lets both parent and adult child experience a tight-knit bond. Also, as Bader points out, you can't be sexually aroused and unhappy at the same time. So again, in this parent-adult child fantasy, everyone is happily turned on. Sadness and longings are banished.

This is a far better explanation for sexual fantasies and arousal than attributing them to pathology and sickness. The human psyche is always looking to repair itself and return to wholeness, so it's not surprising that it would use erotica and the sexual realm as corrective tools.

Emotional Landscape

As discussed earlier, early attachment and bonding experiences shape your later ability to attach and bond to others. We sex therapists understand that these same attachments and experiences help develop and shape sexual fantasies and preferences in adulthood.

This is not to be confused with sexual orientation—how you identify yourself as gay, lesbian, straight, bisexual, or otherwise. Sexual and romantic orientation is who you are inherently at your core. Sexual preferences are learned and shaped more by how you were raised and the types of relationships you witnessed in childhood.

Sexual arousal is imprinted, beginning in childhood, when your sexual map is determined. We observe and absorb how others love, neglect, or abuse us—and that becomes our "love map," or template for what we seek out for pleasure as adults.

In *Arousal: The Secret Logic of Sexual Fantasies,* Bader writes,

> The unconscious management of psychological safety does not begin with the onset of mature sexual desires. It begins in childhood, almost from the moment of birth. As research now tells us, the newborn baby is wired to form an attachment to its mother. The baby can recognize the mother's particular voice and face and prefers them over all other voices and faces. Evolution has guaranteed that the baby has the ability and desire to connect to the human being most able to help it survive. Furthermore, our brains and psychological natures are primed to make us love those people who are responsible for our well-being. We become attached, and we fall in love. Without such attachment, psychological research has shown that babies become frantic, disorganized, and depressed. A secure attachment is crucial to healthy psychological development.[3]

Attachment is the first crucial stage of development. How you learn to attach and bond sets the stage for your later relationships, as we talked about in chapter 3. It also sets the stage for your later sexual content and fantasies. You must learn who your attachment figures were and how they were with you during this developmental time when you were learning to attach.

Were your attachment figures smothering, or distant and disengaged? Did you feel like you were a burden on your parents? Did they grant your wishes, or did you have to grant their wishes? Did they allow you your independence growing up, or was that discouraged?

If your parents were unhappy, depressed, and unavailable, and you responded by trying not to upset them or demand too much, then you may be working out these conflicts within your erotic landscape. In *Arousal,* Bader writes about people in sexual fantasies being happy; in the sexual sphere, everyone is pleased—no depressed mother, a "giving" parent, a sense of belonging unlike that which you might have had in your family.

In addition, the needs of gay children are less likely to get met.

We gay men have not been allowed to explore our sexuality openly and consciously from the beginning.

Erotic Intelligence

Sex therapists, rather than pathologizing and diagnosing someone as having disturbed sexual thoughts or troubled fantasies, are reframing this imagery as self-healing and corrective—the client's attempts to resolve and understand his own psychic issues. Line up ten people and ask each one to be honest about what turns him on the most; you're likely to hear ten different answers. And each response will tell you about that man and his history.

It may be difficult for clients to reveal their sexual fantasies and interests in therapy, but once they do, we find plenty of information about them. From sex addicts, I've learned that if we can uncover the nonsexual aspects of disguised material or "story," then I can help them a great deal more. Using this lens on even healthy sexual fantasies provides a wealth of information about them.

Healthy Sexuality

Before we can explore sex and sexual preferences, we need to understand healthy versus unhealthy sexuality. In his book *Sexual Anorexia,* Patrick Carnes has written the best description I've encountered on what is involved in the dimensions of healthy sexuality.[4] Carnes describes these twelve dimensions as follows.

1. *Nurturing*—capacity to receive care from others and care for oneself.
2. Sensuality—awareness of physical senses that creates emotional, spiritual, and physical presence.
3. Self-image—positive self-perception that includes embracing your sexual self.
4. Self-definition—clear knowledge of both your positives and negatives, and the ability to express boundaries as well as needs.
5. Comfort—capacity to feel at ease with yourself and others about sexual matters.

6. Knowledge—about sex in general and your own unique sexual patterns.
7. Relationship—capacity to enjoy intimacy and friendship with friends of both genders.
8. Partnership-ability to maintain a relationship that's intimate and erotic, and interdependent but equal.
9. Nongenital sex—ability to express erotic desire emotionally and physically, without using your genitals.
10. Genital sex—ability to express erotic feelings freely.
11. Spirituality—ability to connect sexual desire and expression to the meaning of life.
12. Passion—capacity to express deeply held, meaningful feelings of desire about one's sexual self and intimate relationships.

As you read on, consider whether your sexual desires, fantasies, and behaviors have these healthy dimensions. If not, that simply means you might want to seek out a therapist who understands how to help you understand them. But if you're acting out any fantasy that puts you or others at risk in any way, you should seek help immediately.

Sexual Intimacy

Men—gay, bisexual, and straight—often say they can separate sex from love. They can have sex with one person without attaching or wanting anything else, and can also have sex with those with whom they fall in love. I once worked with a couple who said that they would either make love or have "throw-me-down" sex—simply gratifying raw sexual needs without affection being a part of it. While not all men are this way, many are quite capable of making this sort of division.

But sexual contact with another guy can get confused with a genuine emotional connection. Many people use sex to fill a void in their lives and to feel wanted, but sexual contact alone is *not* love. While it can help couples stay close to each other and let individuals release their libido, the rest of their relational work needs to happen outside the sexual realm. In other words, even though sexual contact might fulfill your psyche somehow, it's no replacement for the work necessary to attach to a partner and have real love—which isn't easy. Sex offers instant pleasure, but true sexual and romantic intimacy takes work. If you're not doing that work, the relational intimacy is often shallow and superficial.

I often meet clients who were raised in families where affection was not shown outwardly. Often they'll explain away this lack of expression as the "WASP way" or "a German thing" or "the way of the English folk." They'll tell me they never doubted they were—and are—loved by their parents but were never shown its outward expressions. I begin to teach them that while they logically understand that they're loved, the old brain doesn't understand. Lack of demonstrative affection can often make children feel emotionally neglected. These children are starving for direct affection, and act out in ways to get it somewhere else. Frequently, there is incest between siblings, or sex between cousins and neighborhood kids, as a means of attaining physical affection.

A Couple's Sexual Shadow

Todd called me for couples therapy. He and his partner, Gary, had been together eight years, and Todd was feeling unloved. Gary stated he loved Todd very much. But the frequency of sex between them had diminished from twice a week to once a month. Todd saw this as a sign that Gary was falling out of love with him.

When they came in, Gary reported feeling happy with the frequency and amount of sexual activity they had together. Todd felt frustrated with Gary's unwillingness to top for him. Todd was a top himself and mostly enjoyed that but wanted to bottom at times, but Gary wouldn't do it. Gary said that in the beginning of their relationship, he was open to it and actually did top for Gary. But after three years together, when Gary did try to top Todd, he would go limp. So with Gary's permission, Todd found a "fuck buddy" on the side whom he would see monthly. Gary seemed truly okay with Todd's activity outside the relationship—in fact, he seemed *too okay* with it. Yet Gary didn't want to be sexual with others outside the relationship: he reported having a much lower libido and less inter-

est in sexual contact. Todd often felt unloved because of Gary's lack
of sexual interest in him. One way they negotiated this was for the
two of them to have sex with other male couples, igniting sexual
energy in Gary and restoring some of the passion between them.

Gary was beginning to feel uncomfortable having sex with these
other couples. He wanted to keep what they had just between them
and was fine if Todd wanted to keep his fuck buddy. But this made
Todd feel even more unloved. Gary said that in general he just didn't
have as much interest in sex as Todd did, and his desire was lacking.
But Todd found this hard to believe as he found cum rags and
Kleenexes on Gary's side of the bed and also found Internet sites that
Gary was visiting online. Gary admitted that yes, he masturbated but
said that was easy and faster than making time for them to have sex.
This hurt Todd even more. When they did have sex together, Todd felt
that Gary was forcing himself, that he was not really into it as much
as he could be. Gary said that when they were sexual, he *was* into it,
but Todd didn't believe him.

Todd was okay with having his fuck buddy outside the relationship.
He said he wished Gary were into it, because he preferred to keep sex
within the relationship. But he understood that Gary wasn't, so he said
having a fuck buddy fulfilled his appetite.

Looking into each other's pasts made things clearer. Todd was from
a family he described as "WASPy," where not much affection was
shown, but he knew he was loved. His father worked quite a bit out of
the house, and his stay-at-home mother mostly cared for the house,
provided meals, and always attended his school and sporting events and
drove him wherever he needed to go. He didn't recall many instances of
his mother telling him she loved him, and she gave him few kisses and
hugs. She provided custodial care at best.

When Todd was twelve, a sixteen-year-old cousin fondled him
and then had Todd give him oral sex. Todd recalls very much enjoying his first sexual experience with another guy. Later, he became
very sexual with other boys his age on his street, inviting them to
sleep over at his house and then engaging in mutual masturbation
and oral sex.

Todd learned early on that being sexual with his older cousin felt good, but the truth was that his cousin sexually abused him. Instead, Todd saw it as love, because of the emotional neglect he'd experienced within his family. Sexual abuse and incest is not uncommon in families that don't show emotion and affection. In fact, most sexual predators can spot children from this type of home and use their craving for love and acceptance to their advantage. Now, as an adult, he was reenacting his childhood in his relationship with Gary. To get the love he craved, he was going out of the relationship to have sex with other men. It was no accident that he was partnered with Gary. Theirs was a true imago match.

Now their *real* couples work could begin. I told Todd he'd "hired" Gary to rewound him the same way his parents had by not showing love the way that would have felt familiar and fulfilling. Gary was doing so by not showing sexual interest the way Todd wanted it—how he'd learned to feel loved as a boy. But Todd was letting Gary off the hook as he had his parents, by seeking "love" outside the family—which was why he sought sex outside his relationship.

Most couples would feel hopeless, not understanding what to do once they'd figured out this dynamic in their relationship. I recommended that both Gary and Todd stop all outside sexual activity. While couples do manage to have successful open relationships, I usually recommend they discontinue all outside sexual activity when they enter therapy so that they can sort out the rupture that has occurred between them. Once that's fixed, then they can return to their outside activity.

It was to Todd's benefit to stay and fight for the monogamous relationship he wanted and to negotiate more for Gary to comply with topping him. This brought up Gary's issues, as I knew it would. This all needed to happen, since both Gary and Todd were reenacting issues from their pasts.

Gary's mother and father had a distant relationship, and his smothering, engulfing mother turned to Gary for her emotional needs. Gary was a good student with polite friends, but his mother distrusted him. During high school, she made him come home earlier than all of his friends and would smell his breath, not trusting that he hadn't done drugs, even though there were no signs of any chemical use.

So in Gary's unconscious effort to keep Todd from smothering and engulfing him, it made sense that he would keep him at an emotional and sexual distance. IRT work has a saying: "What you want most from your partner is hardest for them to give, because it's the very thing they need to do for themselves." So it was in Todd's favor to ask Gary for what he wanted and continue his attempts to get his needs met *inside* the relationship (and thus, symbolically, without leaving his "family").

He let Gary off the hook of having to face his issues with his mother. Gary needed someone to demand more closeness so that he could work through learning that intimacy doesn't have to mean being engulfed.

Ultimately, Gary was able to top more for Todd, who no longer felt compelled to go outside their relationship. They left therapy with the understanding that if they did choose to bring in others for sexual play, they would do so knowing it was a choice, not an acting—out of some issue within their relationship.

Jack Morin, author of *The Erotic Mind: Unlocking the Inner Sources of Sexual Passion and Fulfillment,* invites people to explore their peak sexual experiences, favorite masturbation fantasies, and the pornography they choose to read and watch. He argues that examining these things helps you to discern your core erotic theme (CET).[5] This internal blueprint for arousal, says Morin, "transforms old wounds and conflicts into excitation." He goes on to say that "hidden within your CET is a formula for transforming unfinished emotional business from childhood and adolescence into excitation and pleasure."

Morin believes, as do I, that these internal blueprints are about more than just love: they enter our erotic minds as well. But most people—male and female, gay and straight—don't need to examine their sexual behaviors and fantasies if they aren't interfering with their lives. As a result, they have healthy sexual behavior and can relate well with sexual partners. There's no *call*, as Joseph Campbell would say, to examine their sexuality very closely. Thus, the examples I use in this chapter are from those suffering from behaviors and desires they wish they did not have and that they don't like. This doesn't mean, however, that you could not learn more about yourself from the sexual behaviors that you enjoy and like. You can—and will—as you read on.

Cultural Scripts

Culturally, we lack nonsexual rituals and initiations into gay manhood. Our society lacks images of men—particularly gay men— touching and expressing affection; gay porn reconciles this lack, if only through sexuality. Heterosexually married gay men who lack the courage to go to a gay bar or support group find porn and the Internet the easiest, safest way to explore their homosexuality. The closeted man fears being stigmatized and marginalized if he comes out publicly, but can find some comfort knowing that no one will judge him in a bookstore, X-rated movie theater, or the privacy of his own home on the Internet. Pornography can be a source of recreational pleasure and a rite of passage into gay manhood, but also a source of pain that interferes with your life.[6]

Having pornography serve as one's initiation into gay manhood can feed a man's impression that being gay is forbidden and underground. Sneaking around to a "dirty" bookstore can make him feel shameful but also add to the excitement. Recall that during sexual arousal, phenylethalimine (PEA) is released into our system, causing us to feel excitement, ecstasy, and euphoria. The higher the risk and danger involved, the stronger the fear and consequent "hit" of PEA, which would logically increase the sexiness of porn and potentially hook gay men, all of which can lead to sexual addiction.

Recall too how covert cultural sexual abuse has contributed to our internalized homophobia and how we relate to one another as gay men romantically and otherwise. I strongly believe that we gay men are sexually scripted and shaped by cultural, societal, and religious messages. I felt sure the chapter on sexual addiction in my first book would get some attention, whether it was positive or negative feedback. But in fact it received little or no acknowledgment—a strong indication of the gay male culture's sexual shadow that sexual addiction doesn't exit, when in truth it does.

I discovered some positives occurred when gay men told me that it helped them identify whether or not they were in fact sexually addicted. Many let me know that it confirmed what they feared: that they did have a sexual addiction. Like any addictive activity, a sexual addiction can lead to negative and dysfunctional behavior. Despite what critics may say, refusing to identify it as such would create more problems than ignoring it.

Bathhouses

In my opinion, anonymous sex at the baths is just a higher form of masturbation. You can dramatize what is going on in your head by acting it out with men at the baths, but no true intimacy is transpiring, and all the men are in a very self-absorbed state of mind. Even those who go there to "please" or "serve" other men are really there to meet their own sexual needs.

Recreationally, there's nothing wrong with going to the baths if you see it for what it is—a sexual thrill, a quickie, and release. No relational or social connection is happening there. For someone not interested in having a partner, the baths may provide touch, sexual release, quick and immediate contact, and pseudoconnection—as well as an area for play and fantasy fulfillment. If that's all you want, then the baths provide an excellent forum for that, as long as you practice safe sex.

Going to the baths requires few social skills. The baths and other areas where cruising is common have rituals that are predictable and expected. But as you will see in chapter 10, the difference between flirting and cruising is that flirting requires the social skills necessary to form attached relationships.

Most interestingly from a cultural perspective, bathhouses are acknowledged and frequented in our gay culture, yet stigma is attached to admitting that one frequents them. As out and open as going to bathhouses seems to be—even to straights (Bette Midler admits to having performed at bathhouses with Barry Manilow before they got their big starts)—it's impolite to talk about it at parties and when dating; and many (if not most) gay men will never admit to going. I've heard both clients and friends tell me that they'd never date a man who goes to the baths, even though they may have gone themselves.

Baths aren't the place to find Mr. Right. Odds are against you, although of course anything is possible. The problem arises when someone who reeally *wants* a relationship prefers going to the baths to seeking a serious partner. For men who want a partner, making the baths a regular and preferred place to be will prolong the search and even interfere with it. Getting sexual and emotional needs met on some level, superficial as it might be, deflates the motivation you need to get out and find a partner and get a relationship going.

Sexual connections remind us that we exist. As gay men, we're taught not only that we don't belong but that we practically don't exist—by not seeing ourselves portrayed in the media or in print. From childhood on, we're not mirrored or acknowledged for being gay little boys. The bathhouse is a way to remind ourselves that we're still "there," hardly having to exert any emotional or mental work.

Sexual relationships with partners also remind us that we exist, but they come with emotional pain in the power struggle, which is removed by going to baths. Given the emotional angst of dealing with a partner, it makes sense that men would be drawn to the baths instead. Yet ironically, in that very emotional angst lies your potential for healing and growth.

Attempts to Solve the Scene of the Crime

Baths fulfill our sense of belonging. Finally, there's a shower room where we can look, be ogled, touched, and not worry about being harassed or humiliated for staring too long or too much. What a great way to undo the trauma we suffered as gay boys. I had my own sixth-grade shower experience, as you may recall; others, like Carter, are there to solve other childhood crimes as well.

Carter came into therapy troubled that he was almost forty and had never had a healthy relationship with another man. He had come out in his early twenties and in a short time had fully accepted himself as a gay man. He told me he was well read on gay topics and attended gay events either with friends or alone without anxiety. He was a handsome man with a nice build and everything that most gay men would find attractive. Then why was he having trouble attracting them? He couldn't see it at all.

Carter had a nice personality and healthy outlook on life. On the outside everything seemed normal. His childhood, however, was anything but. In my initial assessment of him, I asked about his sexual behavior. He told me he liked attending the gay baths, locally and when he traveled. He saw nothing wrong with this, and, when I asked more about it, Carter immediately became defensive: "Don't you dare tell me there's something wrong with going to the baths" he snarled. "I can go to a straight therapist and get that feedback."

Once he realized that I wasn't going to pathologize the gay culture in general for going to the baths, he was more receptive to hearing me out. I explained that the more he was willing to share with me about his sexual acting out, the more I could help him.

He began opening up to me about his sexual behavior, and over several sessions, told me bits and pieces of what he did sexually. As Carter grew more comfortable, he was able to fully express his experiences:

> I like to go to the tubs and take my clothes off while people are watching. I like to flash my cock around so others can see how big I am. Even soft I have a nice-sized cock that hangs well. I put on a towel and start walking around. I go to the video rooms, the showers and hot tubs, where I can take off the towel and show off my cock. I enjoy watching the looks on the other men's faces when they see it both hard and soft. That's very exciting to me when I see their surprise that I'm as big and round as I am.
>
> Then I get a room, and while the door is open, guys walk by and see my cock. I nod to the guy I'm finally interested in, and he walks in and shuts the door. We never say a word to each other. I stand up, and he puts my hard cock in his mouth. If he looks up at me, I look away. I don't like eye contact. Then I start to face-fuck him. I grab his hair and his ears sometimes. I literally like to rape his mouth. What I like most is to shove my cock down his throat so far that momentarily he can't

breathe. If he chokes, I don't care. Then I pull back, and he gasps for air sometimes. That arouses me even more. I'll let him catch his breath and then go right back to face-fucking him. I like it best when they're in this position and let me do that to them without protest.

Then I turn around and shove my ass in their face and have them rim me. I position us so that I can literally sit on the guy's face and force my ass over his nose and mouth, and I sit there knowing he momentarily cannot breathe or make a sound. Then I decide to let him up, and again he gasps for air. Then I turn around and come on his face or body and leave him there.

Direct and raw as this story is, it took Carter an entire year to tell it all to me. He was very embarrassed and often wept while recounting it. He admitted how very out of character it was for him to be so cold and aggressive with the men at the baths, because otherwise, he never dominated or was this harsh with people. In fact, one thing that frustrated him most about others was when they acted dominant and aggressive with him.

Together we started to decipher the coded message—the theme of his sexual script—to understand what he was acting out. As in the expression "you take my breath away," I told him that sexually he had found a way of literally "taking a guy's breath away." Carter's ultimate fantasy was the moment when the guy couldn't breathe. Not that he wanted the man to show discomfort or protest, or even be humiliated; he simply wanted the guy to be willingly suffocated and smothered by his erect penis and buttocks. At these moments, he realized, he became the other guy's *whole world*. When the man couldn't breathe, he could think of nothing else except when Carter was ready to give him air. Later, in talking about Carter's childhood, we would learn how he never felt precious to his parents or anything close to "taking their breath away" as a revered and honored son.

Carter had no idea why this should excite him, nor had he ever thought about figuring it out. He just knew he liked it and didn't think much about it after leaving the baths. Nor did he like to do this with guys he dated. Only with anonymous men was this a turn-on for him.

Carter was the third of five children, in the middle of two brothers and two sisters. His father was passive and introverted, his mother self-absorbed and narcissistic. She warned her daughters about how men "only think with their penis-heads, not with their cerebral heads." She warned her boys *never* to urinate outside or at a bathroom latrine—to always use a stall. She told them all this while they were still under the age of ten.

When Carter was fourteen, his mother found his older sister's diary in which she wrote about having sex with her boyfriend. He recalls his sister being scolded and their mother using this as proof that males can't keep their penises to themselves. That year, the family moved away from their neighborhood to a whole new community to have a "fresh start" from the embarrassment this sister caused her.

For some reason of her own, his mother was obviously preoccupied with men's penises, and she took out her unfinished business on her children, with language and warnings that were shaming. Her inappropriate comments about males' penises sent Carter the message that boys can't control their sexual urges. As a little boy, how was he supposed to respond to that?

This background shed light on why it was so important for Carter to show off his penis to men as a rebellious way of going against his mother. His unspoken message was "See? I can show off my penis, and people will like it just fine!" It would have been too simplistic for us to attribute all this to the gay male community's emphasis on size. It just coincidentally worked in Carter's favor that he had a larger penis.

The next factor we uncovered was his never-ending attempts to please his mother. Even when he felt he'd done exactly as she wished, she was never satisfied. Parents should have a certain amount of awe for their children, hold them in reverence and see them as precious. This was not the case in Carter's family. Like the NPD or BDP mothers we read about in chapter 5, Carter's mother used her children to please *her* and didn't see that it was her duty to please *them*. His introverted father didn't stand up for males when his mother talked about them in derogatory ways, so Carter was imprinted with the idea that men were no good and ineffectual like his father—and the men his mother complained of. So he had become her "bad boy" at the baths, showing off to everyone and defying his mother's wishes, while also being the center of many men's attention.

It made sense that Carter's erotic mapping, in its corrective efforts, sought out men who saw him as virile and able to provide them pleasure. The sexual contact provided a pseudoconnection, and through sexual pleasure, Carter was able to satisfy these men. He wasn't successful in pleasing his parents, so in his sexual conquests, he returned to the scene of the crime—and solved it. Yet his parents' original neglect and invisibility wasn't corrected by this momentary sexual acting—out; thus, Carter created a cycle of going to the baths repeatedly. In the long run, Carter continued to perpetrate the crime on himself.

In his search for boyfriends, Carter kept meeting men whom he described as self-absorbed. Clearly, his relational mapping was affected as well. These men wanted him to attach to them but wouldn't attach back to him. Guys like this rarely asked about Carter himself, and this would enrage him—which made sense, since this was a close imitation of his parents. His anger was really at his parents, not so much at these men. Other guys might date these men once and never see them again, but Carter would keep seeing them over a period of months. Once we decoded the themes of his sexual script, Carter was able to deal with the covert sexual abuse he suffered as a child by his mother's inappropriate preoccupation with males' genitalia and their "bad intentions." He also started to face the emotional neglect he'd felt in his family. Now his work was about finding a sense of belonging around others, particularly gay men, instead of trying to find it at a bathhouse.

Lost Tweakends

Crystal meth and sexual behavior often go together. In his book *Tweakers,* Frank Sanello reports that crystal meth is the drug of choice for sex addicts because it "artificially rewards the user's brain by releasing torrents of dopamine and other neurotransmitters."[7]

Elevated levels of dopamine, as mentioned in chapter 3, provides craving for sex; what better way to be reassured that you exist, with high levels of dopamine causing exhilaration, increased energy, and sexual desire? You have only to take the drug, and you are there! But like NutraSweet, "Tina" only tastes and looks like the real thing.

In Andrew Miller's article "Lost Tweakends," about crystal meth use, he writes about his family's reaction to his addiction:

> My parents have been a little cold through the whole ordeal. And they go to a support group at their church for parents of gay people where they sit around and pray that we all become straight. Eventually I have to accept that they are simple, intolerant, bigoted, selfish people; that they'll never give me the kind of support I need. But I'm not there yet. Why can't I have parents who love me as I am? I'm still so angry with them.[8]

His own parents treat him like he doesn't exist—or at least do not want him to exist as the gay man he is. I see this perception so often in the therapy room. Gay men get the messages that we don't belong. We have no mirrors of ourselves in view, so early on we learn that "officially" we don't exist. Is it any wonder that drugs and sex can become a way of feeling alive, of achieving a sense of belonging? In violence toward the self, the shadow provides a pseudosense of belonging, much as it does in people suffering from post-traumatic stress disorder. Our trauma is that we are invisible, even to each other, and we use sex and drugs to perpetuate our invisibility.

How many "lost tweakends" will you suffer before you stop, find yourself, and direct your dependency needs into good romantic or friendly heart-to-heart relationships? You deserve what you were seeking to begin with—real live connection, attention, and affection.

Bodily Harm

The gym is yet another place where we felt rejection and trauma around changing and showering with other men, without permission to stare. While some sexuality and cruising does go on in health clubs, the gyms have become a serious place for gay men to get their bodies into shape—but not always for the right reasons. Gay men build their bodies to look like Warriors, but again, integrity is an issue. How they look on the outside doesn't reflect who they are on the inside.

In *Dancing Around the Volcano,* Kettelhack writes: "There's an odd disjunction in much of gay male experience: while the gym has become as sacred and important an experience to gay men as church is to nuns, few gay men I've talked to have much physical self-acceptance. The Body, as purveyed by The Gym, is like an Armani suit that takes money and untold hours of discipline to earn. It is something acquired—something almost external to the being acquiring it." I couldn't agree more.

Often when I see these gay men—ripped, buff, and hunky—I have to remind myself that these are my gay brothers, not the bullies who intimidated and humiliated me in school. Yet that's how these gay men present themselves. Many of them have "stay away from me" attitudes and look as though they'll shun me or look down on me if I speak to them. On a recent gay cruise I was on, one man said that he purposely stayed away from those "Armani suits" around the pool, out of fear they would reject him. Finally, he decided not to let this intimidate him and he took his imperfect body to sit by the pool anyway.

In many ways, gay men who are into building their bodies are finding *their* sense of belonging. As teenagers, we often were not part of the club of those other aggressive boys who intimidated us. Bodybuilding at the gym is a way to recapture those lost years searching for the masculine archetypes we weren't allowed to claim; but becoming *supermales* is only a continuation of what we've always done to compensate: to overachieve. How about letting ourselves own our masculinity and blend the Warrior and Lover energy in the mature masculine? The other way seems to have internalized the patriarchal male.

Being preoccupied with looks and body—your own or someone else's—can be another exit and distraction from finding real love and being in intimacy. As two men, we have the luxury of being able to say to our partners, "Wow! Look at that guy over there! What nice pecs!", or whatever else we see that we want to comment on.

Heterosexuals do not have this freedom in relationship to their opposite gender partners, since they often feel threatened, as though complimenting someone else's attractiveness were a personal slight. Yes, some gay men feel this way too, but overall, it's understood that we're just admiring, not contemplating infidelity.

But if you're looking too much or comparing too much, it can lead to your growing dissatisfied with your partner or your own body. The shadow takes over when you cannot be satisfied with your body in whatever state it's in. It is fine to want to get in shape, to look and feel good; it's another matter to be doing it at the risk of your health and self-esteem.

As a culture of men, we are more visual. Appearance attracts us to a partner, while women are more forgiving of their partners' looks. *Looking Queer,* edited by Dawn Atkins, cites a study that "found that lesbians, heterosexual women, and gay men expressed similar degrees of body dissatisfaction, significantly more than heterosexual men. This study suggests that perhaps *both* sexual orientation and gender are implicated in negative body image."[9]

This information suggests that heterosexual women and gay men, measured by heterosexual men's standards, are more conscious of how they have to look. Much too often, however, I notice that gay men tend to go into shadow and rate a person's body and appearance as more important than the person himself. This can be a recipe for problems with your self-esteem, intimacy with others, and sexual addiction as well as blocking the road to real love.

It wouldn't be fair to say that all of those who go to the gym to perfect their bodies have attitude and separate themselves from other gay men. But so many do, and the shame of it is that we're doing to ourselves what was done to us. As we saw in chapter 1, this is a common response to being victimized. If you are bullied, intimidated, and humiliated and put in a subservient role, one way to overcome it in shadow form is to *become* the bully. Still, you are not in a position of power but rather powerlessness.

But what about those who choose not to or cannot have bodies like these men?

Unhung Heroes

One of the worst shadows we men—both gay and straight—have is how we feel about our penis sizes. And I have heard gay men say that this matters in terms of partner selection and sexual satisfaction.

The March 2005 issue of *OUT* includes Erik Piepenburg's article "Is Small Beautiful?" which focuses on gay men with small penises. The journalist interviewed Robert Woodworth, a fifty-nine-year-old gay man and director of Institutional Services at New York's Lesbian, Gay, Bisexual and Transgender Community Center. Woodworth began an ongoing series of discussions about gay men and their penises, which led to a four-week support group for gay men who felt that theirs are small.

Bravo to these men! They are truly unhung heroes, willing to disclose their genital size and come out of their fly as well as the closet. What pressure they must feel as men—particularly in the gay community—where penis size is talked about so relentlessly and so judgmentally, as if it were a measure of the whole man.

I'm sure there are many, many jokes about this support group. When I was researching this topic, one colleague asked me, "Is it a small support group?" Another colleague inquired, "How long will your article be?" Snicker all you want, but the real joke is on all of us men—gay and straight alike—since such remarks make many of us feel self-conscious about our size. When I hear any gay man make a small penis comment—particularly in front of others in my gay men's groups or workshops—I cringe to think of those insecure men who might feel badly or those who just worry about their size in general.

What Is Too Small—Really?

The standard for penis size was set by the Kinsey Institute in the 1960s. Alfred Kinsey and his merry men studied American college-age men and found that 80 percent of fully erect penises measured between five and seven inches long, with most falling in the six- to six-and-a-half-inch range. But size queens beware! Despite what you might surmise from gay personal ads, less than 1 percent of those erections Kinsey witnessed in the flesh exceeded eight inches. The odds against finding a true nine-incher are a thousand to one, but still considerably better than winning at Lotto. The difference between Internet inches and real-life inches is in the eye of the owner, not the beholder.

But does the rarity of those knitting needles in the haystack make any one of us men feel any better? No! Men are hung in different sizes, widths, directions, and shapes, and each of us is different, whether hard or soft. Some men are showers and some men are growers. Still, at a nude beach or locker room, men with bigger and longer flaccid endowment are more fortunate. They have less to worry about in terms of being judged and found wanting, or hearing snide remarks made about them. Even if their four-inch softie doesn't grow when erect, straight guys in a locker room, bathhouse, or nude beach won't know that. The guy who might boast only one to two inches soft and grow to eight inches hard still feels self-conscious, thinking that when at ease, everyone sees him as too small, even though at attention, he knows he's not!

What we're really talking about here is how much of a man someone is. And we tend to measure masculinity by various standards—how tall or short he is, how successful or wealthy or athletic or stoic, and so on—all measurements of outward qualities; how sad that is. We need to look more at the inside, evaluating a man on the basis of his integrity, responsibility, talents, eloquence, and accountability. Why not measure a man by the size of his heart? That is what real love is all about. That way, you'll wind up with more satisfaction than you've ever dreamed of.

Queer Eye for the Straight Guy

I've identified the cultural phenomenon of gay males seeking "straight-acting" gay men because of internalized homophobia and how they're more often looking for *masculine*-acting men. But what about gay men's sexual obsessions with real straight men? I've heard countless clients tell me of their interest in "getting sexual with a straight man" for one night. Some clients talk about wanting the man to remain straight all the way through the fantasy while they "service" him without reciprocation. Others want him to participate by talking or telling him what to do, while still others want him to lay back and be worshiped. Others want the straight man to humiliate them, while still others want the straight man to reciprocate by suddenly becoming sexually interested in him. Whatever the case, it gives you more information about yourself.

I see sexual fantasies about straight men as longings for being accepted by your father or straight men in general. Straight men can be stand-ins for your fathering figures—a dynamic very similar to that of the fag hag who flirts heavily with gay men, knowing nothing will come of it.

In *Arousal*, Bader describes the situation of straight women sexually attracted to gay men because they're "safe." He writes that these women can become "sexually expressive...in a more confident and spontaneous way than they can with straight men...because their overtures will not be reciprocated. These are women who have anxieties about being sexual with straight men because they're afraid of being overpowered or rejected." A gay man won't cross the line toward her, making it safe for women to flirt and be sexually aggressive with him without risking rejection, since he is gay anyway. If she convinces the gay guy to be sexual with her, Bader states that this is "reassurance that she is *especially* attractive."

Gay men have been wounded, bruised, beaten down, and humiliated by straight men, which has resulted in straight men, particularly those in a position of authority, being recipients of both positive and negative transferences from gay men. We hear over and over that these men would never accept a sissy boy, which we have accepted that we are. Because of this, gay men often fear straight men. As children, we do love these paternal figures and we want their acceptance; as adults, we sexualize these straight men because it unconsciously offers a way to feel safely and pleasantly attached to them. In the sexual fantasy of pleasing a straight guy, you finally get a chance to make contact with him and get the approval you have always wanted.

Some gay men have fantasies of overpowering straight men—seducing or forcing gay sex onto them. Again, while these fantasies can make for exciting fun, preoccupation with them or acting on them—even with a willing straight male—won't help you find Mr. Right in the long run, if that is in fact what you are looking for. It can also be a distraction from examining your own issues around straight males.

Recall from chapter 2 how my family tried to make a "man" out of me. I harbored a lot of resentment toward the straight men who were either abusive or simply not there for me. Straight boys bullied me quite a bit throughout elementary and middle school, so as you might guess, I have my own issues around straight men.

I'm not immune to having sexual shadows, and one of mine came up at the ManKind Project's New Warrior Workshop mentioned earlier. I was assigned to sleep in a room with three other men—all straight. One was a landscaper in his early twenties (now one of my best friends) and the other two were twenty and twenty-two, basically good ole straight boys. I'll call them Nick and Jeff.

When we all met to go to sleep the first night, I hadn't yet disclosed my being gay. I wanted to at some point, but wanted to know how safe—really safe—it would be. Sure enough, the two younger guys started talking about the "fags" at this workshop. Their friends had teased them that attending an all-male workshop might "turn them gay." Nick and Jeff then started talking very graphically about being sexual with their girlfriends—probably their way of distancing themselves from any "fags" attending the weekend and to reassure each other that they weren't "fags" themselves. Laughing, they told stories about shoving their fingers in their girlfriend's anuses and making them bleed. One talked about how he received oral sex and promised his girlfriend he would tell her when he was about to orgasm, but when the moment arrived, he wouldn't and ejaculated right into her eyes. She would be angry and weep about his inconsideration. Nick and Jeff laughed uncontrollably together about this.

I was horrified and mortified. How did I end up stuck with two redneck yahoos? If this was how things were going to go, the weekend workshop was ruined. This experience was not reflective of the weekend at all but certainly contributed to the work I did at it. I stayed quiet, pretending to sleep, even though I wanted to get up and yell at them for being so sexist, cruel to their girlfriends, and homophobic about gays.

The next day we all showered and dressed in groups, since that was how the open bathrooms were set up. These two guys happened to have great physiques, extremely good-looking, with handsome faces—very aesthetically pleasing to the eye. They still did not know about me being gay as we showered next to one another, talking and getting ready for the day. Later, during the the workshop it came out that I was gay. That night, back in our room, Nick and Jeff approached me halfheartedly apologetic. "Dude, sorry for saying 'faggot' all night long. We hope we didn't hurt your feelings or make you feel bad about being gay."

I looked them in the eyes and realized I had two straight guys groveling to me—a gay man! I felt so uncomfortable that I turned it into a joke. "Look, that part was easier to handle than what you said you did to your girlfriends. You need to know that when sperm gets in your eyes, it BUUUUURNS!!! Just like Miss Coco Peru in the movie *Trick!*"

There was a thirty-second pause (no doubt for the visual image to sink in), and then both of them looked horrified. They looked away half smiling, half taken off guard. "Dude, don't talk like that. Man that is gross!" But I told them that I absolutely *would* talk to them like that, as long as they talked about what they did with girls.

They didn't believe me. So when they continued talking and brought up female genitalia and sex acts with women, I talked about my experiences and fantasies with other guys. They told me to stop, and I wouldn't.

At this point, I didn't feel I was in sexual shadow. I felt free to articulate my experiences if they were free to talk about theirs. My shadow was that I became more sexually aggressive, telling them how hot I thought they both were and that in the showers, it was nice to take a peek at the "goods." Now I *was* in sexual shadow, wanting to overpower them with my sexual attractiveness to them. It was like having power over them in the sexual realm. I felt empowered. In truth I wasn't, but it felt like I was.

They were twice mortified. "Dude, you were not looking at us there, were you? Come on, that's where we shower!" At this point I was mad at them for trying to silence me; I was on a mission to punish and humiliate them. This was my sexual shadow. Instead of owning my anger in a clean and direct way, instead I made them uncomfortable by telling them how attractive they were.

The next day in the showers, they wore their underwear from the night before. I felt empowered, having "scored" one over these two straight men.

In fact, though, this wasn't a mature stance of empowerment. I was taking on the role of the perpetrator, dishing out the humiliation and sexual manipulation that had been done to me by all the straight males from my past. I spent the next few months doing things like this with straight guys, feeling entitled and empowered by telling them my sexual interests in them. Later, as I realized what I was doing, I apologized to as many men as I could for my behavior toward them.

Now you see why knowing your sexual shadow is so important. If you remain unaware of your intentions, you can do a lot of damage to yourself and others.

Forbidden Fruit

Straight men are also forbidden. Since we know we cannot have them, this might enhance our desire to want them. The danger involved in hitting on a straight man, at the risk of humiliation and verbal and physical harassment, can actually add to the sexual arousal. Abe is a good example.

Interpersonal Scripts:
Paying for Love

Although an extreme example, Abe's story is worth telling if your attraction to straight men stands in your way of healthy relationships with men, both gay and straight.

Abe came to me for depression, worried that he was over thirty-five and never had had a significant relationship. He wanted one, but could never make them work. He even knew what the problem was: he was sexually attracted to straight men. In fact, if he thought a man was straight who later turned out to be gay, he'd get turned off. This he identified as internalized homophobia, which in part it was, but it was also a symptom of something more. He was returning to the scene of some crime with a straight man, as the sexual details of his story would make clear.

Abe always had had fantasies of straight guys wrestling. He'd spend a lot of time watching wrestling on television, then go into his room and masturbate. In middle school, however, he hadn't been interested in wrestling. Outside of the sexual fantasies, it would provoke anxiety and low self-esteem, since he had a smaller build and wasn't very strong or athletic. Abe always masturbated to fantasies of meeting these straight guys, who overpowered him through various wrestling holds. The bigger and more muscular the guys, the better; this was his ultimate fantasy. When he was with gay men, he would use this fantasy to ultimately get himself off. Thus, his fantasy was so strong that it prevented him from truly connecting, which is why he was unable to have healthy relationships with other gay men.

Abe found a Web site where there were male models—escorts—specifically, those who wrestled and pumped up their bodies. These guys were straight and only interested in letting guys pay them to show off their muscles. Abe would meet them, but they would *not* allow him to undress or masturbate; they only modeled their bodies while Abe watched. They would strip down to briefs, but never get naked, and perform wrestling holds on him. For Abe, this ensured their heterosexuality and turned him on even more. If they even hinted that sex or nudity might be involved, he'd lose interest. His favorite erotic scenarios were of nonsexual contact with a straight male wrestler. He loved the feeling of one being on top of him.

One time, one of the models got him in a wrestling hold and told him, "You're a good boy. You paid me well. You behave well. You deserve the honor of being in my wrestling holds and in my presence. This is your gift for being a good boy." These words came out of the blue, but after the model left, Abe had an orgasm like he had never remembered.

Afterward, these words haunted him. Why had they aroused him so? Not fully understanding, he would ask future wrestling escorts to say this to him, but it was never the same as when this particular man said it spontaneously. He compulsively returned for more contact with that escort and the more he was told he was a "good boy" the more he paid him.

What was this shadow in Abe's sexual acting out? Why did the guys have to be straight? Why was paying them a part of what aroused him?

Abe had never been able to please his alcoholic father. His parents divorced when he was ten, and when he visited his father, the man would be watching sports on television and couldn't be easily pulled away. He constantly asked Abe to get him things, which Abe would do to please him. Abe recalls being frustrated with his father's greater allegiance to television and alcohol than to Abe himself.

When Abe's mother remarried, his stepfather ordered Abe around, making him do house chores. He asked for allowance and payment for the chores, but his stepfather gave him nothing, not even thanks or recognition. He recalls feeling much anger about this, but dared not to say anything for fear of his mother and stepfather's disapproval.

Whenever someone pays for sex, the metaphor "paying for love" is the first thing I think of. Abe had to please his father by performing acts of servitude. He had longed for both his father and stepfather to express appreciation for the acts of service Abe provided but never received it. So in Abe's sexual fantasy, he was able to please his stand-in father, the bodybuilder, with servitude all over again—only this time, receiving recognition by the guy's willingness to recognize Abe for his work. In his fantasy, Abe won his father over and everyone was satisfied—dad and son. This is why the men had to be straight, like his father and stepfather. This fantasy allowed resolution from earlier pain in his life.

There was one other factor—the guys had to be big and strong. Why was this so important and the biggest turn—on for Abe? Abe had never been able to show his strength to his father or his stepfather. He had to comply, take orders, and be subordinate and submissive. In his fantasy, he could sexualize his feelings of weakness and helplessness, when in reality, he was afraid of showing his strength and talking back. In fantasy, he could let himself feel powerless and remove the childhood pain that he'd felt at being forced into servitude. His obsession with muscular wrestlers was his unconscious attempt to seek out a stronger father figure.

Abe could feel the truth in this interpretation, though it's no cookie-cutter explanation for all who engage in this behavior. Everyone will be different in what the interpretation is for them. Once it *fits* for you—and you will know if it does—you're ready to do the work that's waiting for you. For Abe, decoding his fantasy about pleasing straight men brought up unfinished business with his father and stepfather. His therapy work was now about focusing on his relationships with those father figures and reclaiming his buried feelings about how they treated him.

Abe began to consider talking to his father and his stepfather about his feelings from childhood. I encouraged this, as I saw it would benefit his healing. This helped Abe's search for a partner, since he now understood the importance of a strong man. It opened up a whole new avenue for Abe to let himself attach romantically and sexually to gay men and feel real love for men who could return it. Talking to these paternal figures allowed him to reclaim his own strength as a gay man.

Many people have problems attaching deeply and romantically because in their childhoods, one or both parents might have been depressed or portrayed themselves as sick, weak, or incompetent. Children are very sensitive to their parents' needs and in attempting to please them, will adapt to being less of a burden. In adulthood, this can lead to difficulties in being a "burden" to a potential partner, and can be sexualized in a number of ways.

Objects of Passion

When they're compulsive, objectification fantasies also can get in the way of getting real love with a partner. These include fetishes and fantasies where body parts and objects, *rather* than a whole person are desired. I've heard clients fantasize about being a guy's footstool, table, chair, ashtray, or toilet; doing his chores, cleaning his house and car, and being totally humiliated and submissive to him. This can signify that while growing up, the gay male was treated poorly, like an object, as we saw at length in chapter 2.

Again, as sexual fantasy and sexual play, there's nothing wrong with this if you enjoy it safely and sanely with those willing to participate. But if you want a relationship, then you need to somehow incorporate this sexual fantasy with a partner.

Bader writes: "People often use fetishes to become aroused. In these cases, the function of fetishes is to eliminate any guilt and worry that might interfere with sexual excitement by eliminating the human dimension of the other person." Doing so can remove any anxieties or concerns about truly connecting to another person and letting oneself have relational experiences.

The Internet

The Internet makes it easy to find men interested in dating and sexual hookups or to just contact others for chat and sharing pictures and images of particular fetishes. For gay men and others with sexual interests outside the mainstream, the Internet has become the preferred method of meeting potential partners. This forum alleviates the stigma of meeting others in such known "cruising areas" as parks, gay bars, and bookstores. It makes meeting other men much easier and opens the door to a much larger population of potential partners. Personal profiles and often a digital photo convey potential partners' attributes and interests, providing considerable information before even interacting with them in person.

The Internet can be an outlet for our Magician and our Lover archetypes. But problems can arise if one overrides the other. If you prefer to be a Trickster online—if you're more comfortable pretending to be someone you're not—then the Internet can be a problem for you. There is nothing wrong with experimenting with the Internet, pretending to be someone you are not if you are exploring other sexual parts of yourself. If your sexual self is *mainly* or *only* satisfied through porn and fantasy, however, then real flesh-and-blood relationships will never come your way. To use the Internet responsibly, your Magician and Lover must be integrated and talking to one another.

If you're interested only in a particular sexual scene or fetish and aroused by certain images, the Internet means you never have to leave home to explore and potentially embarrass yourself. You can experiment safely by browsing online and chatting anonymously with strangers all over the world about what they are into.

The Internet has made coming out more possible for those who might otherwise have lived a closeted life. Historically, men and women have had nowhere to go, with no one to speak to honestly and openly about their sexual and romantic orientation. The downside to this ease in meeting more potential partners is an increase in sexually transmitted diseases, adverse effects on self-image and the images of potential partners, and cybersex addiction. The Internet has made it easier for many people to lose their integrity. Online, you can lie and be anyone and anything you want. I once saw a cartoon showing a dog typing on the keyboard and saying to another dog sitting beside him, "No one on the Internet knows you are really a dog." Anonymity has always been an invitation for those interested in testing out being someone different and acting differently. Chat rooms are full of gay men pretending to be women so that they can talk to straight men. Other straight men pretend to be women and go into lesbian chat rooms to cybertalk with lesbians! The scenarios are endless.

The Internet Highway's Exit Ramps

Another downside is that it's too easy to harbor negative feelings toward your partner, retreat into the computer and find a quick cyber hookup, or masturbate to an image instead of resolving your needs with your partner. Chapter 9 discusses how exits can lead to the downfall and breakup of your relationship, because they enable you to act out your feelings be acted out *outside* the relationship. Doing this occasionally doesn't necessarily reflect a problem, but when it becomes regular and normal—and even worse, preferable—your relationship is in trouble.

I have heard clients in my office say that to them, having their partners look at porn is "cheating." I am in no position to argue for them if it is or isn't. I do suggest, however, that it doesn't have to constitute cheating, if it works for the couple and the individual involved. I've seen many couples and individuals use porn and the

Internet for sexual release with both partners' knowledge and agreement. They don't consider it cheating, and it causes no problems in their relationship. It's pretentious of anyone to define what it is for any one couple or individual. It's up to them, but they should be armed with information to rule out whether it's a problem for them.

Type Dirty to Me

For the most part, cybersex can be a harmless, safe way to be sexual with another person and engage in interactive virtual sex. Studies have always shown that erotica is more about what is between the ears than between the legs. Our brains contribute more to sexual excitement and creativity. Cybersex is a great way to introduce new concepts and ideas and try out various sexual scenes without having to actually meet people and put yourself in any emotional or physical risk. Cybersex has also helped closeted gay men who would never have gone to a gay bar, bathhouse, or anywhere else come out. Since sex is still often the first motive for gay men to meet, given the stigma attached to being gay, cybersex offers an easy outlet.

Safe as cybersex can be, however, it can also become dangerous. In their essay, "Compulsive Cybersex: The New Tea Room," Mark F. Schwartz and Stephen Southern of the Masters and Johnson Clinic call the Internet the new place "for meeting anonymous partners for impersonal sex and enacting many of the rituals of bathhouse or public restroom sex. Compulsive cybersex represents a courtship of disorder in which the 'high' of being wanted by someone for sex regulates affect and bolsters a fragile self. The fantasy world of cybersex is a dissociative experience in which a person escapes the demand of daily life as well as the pain and shame of past trauma."[10] Additionally, it lets those who find relationships difficult become distracted from the work necessary to be more intimate with a partner.

I have to admit that while I'd heard the word *tearoom* and knew that was where the expression tea dances came from, I knew very little about the actual dynamics of how it all worked, particularly in the early 1950s and 1960s. I remember picking up my mother's book *What You Always Wanted to Know About Sex but Were Afraid to Ask* and reading that "homosexuals" would sit in public toilets and tap their feet to show interest. This is what constituted tearoom behavior. Schwartz and Southern's article mentions Laud Humphrey, who in the 1970s completed research on how men behaved in public restrooms. After reading this, I bought Humphrey's book, *Tearoom Trade: Impersonal Sex in Public Places*—fascinating to read, because cybersex and tearooms have so much in common.[11] Cybersex truly is the new tearoom!

Is the Internet the New Cocaine

The late Al Cooper, one of the leading researchers of the Internet, wrote that its "'Triple A Engine' of Access, Affordability, and Anonymity" combine to turbocharge (that is, accelerate and intensify) online sexual interactions.[12] In the 1980s, cocaine had increasingly used and abused. If it took an alcoholic thirty years to ruin his health, it took a cocaine addict only one year. For sex addicts, the Internet became the cocaine of the 1990s. It used to take months, even years to find various esoteric types of porn, and it was too time-consuming to go out and find a willing sex partner. If caught, the risk of social stigma was high. The Internet offered straight A's in every standard that Cooper cited—access, affordability, and anonymity.

Cam You See Me?

It's been said that the word *intimacy* breaks down as *into me you see*. While you can let some of yourself show over the Internet with a Webcam, it's not the same form of intimacy that being face to face demands. Watching our culture—gay and straight—become more computer-dependent and using the Internet for contact more and more, I fear that our skills for attachment and intimacy are starting to atrophy. Gay men from all over the country have told me how hard it is to socialize with other men to find Mr. Right. In many places, gay men are no longer even going to bars to find dating partners—they're logging on to the Internet.

Most men willing to show themselves on cams are going to be more confident about their looks and their bodies. For the most part, they have bigger penises, gym bodies, and average to better-than-average looks. This gives many gay men the impression that their partners should look something like this. Thanks to the display of men on the Internet, sexual attraction has become more narrowly defined.

Some gay men in my office and workshops seem very picky about the type of men they're looking for. Like women who see only photographs of slender Barbie-like models, gay males are moving in that direction too, and it's largely due to the Internet. Gay men are comparing themselves to the guys they see in still photos or on Webcams and saying "What's wrong with me? I don't look like that! I'll never find a partner!" I tell them that men willing to display themselves in the buff are those who have larger endowments overall and feel better about their bodies. They're not necessarily men to measure yourself against.

Does HIV Really Have to Be the Price to Pay to Belong?

Jonathan came to me after struggling with sexual fidelity with his partner. He had been cheating for the past several years and finally had to admit it after becoming HIV-positive. He knew he was out of integrity but also knew that cheating on his partner was compelling and exciting. We explored his sexual behavior to decode what he was seeking through his compulsiveness.

Jonathan had never felt that he fit in anywhere and always had a desire to belong. Effeminate and overweight, he said that "gay men look right through me." For sex, he went to bathhouses and bottomed at sex parties, where gay men took turns penetrating him without condoms. His one rule was not to let anyone ejaculate inside him.

I asked what his peak erotic fantasy was and it was of men using him for *their* enjoyment by having anal sex with no protection. He wasn't concerned about getting any sexual pleasure back from them. His desire for acceptance and pleasing these men overshadowed his worries about HIV infection. In fact, it turned him on more that he was there for *them*—completely.

One time, a man was just about to orgasm, and Jonathan knew the man should pull out, but he didn't. At the moment, Jonathan didn't care. He knew it was wrong, but his urge to please this man was stronger than the urge to protect himself.

The man ejaculated inside him, and Jonathan recalls being sick several weeks after the incident. Later, he tested positive for HIV. Why would he have put himself at risk like this?

In his therapy, we uncovered his strong need to be accepted by his peers and to belong. Jonathan grew up in an upper-middle-class neighborhood even though his parents could barely afford it. His status-conscious peers dressed better and he always stood out because his family could not buy for him the things his friends had and wore. He'd never felt accepted in his family, who praised his older brother for his proficiency in sports and his sister for her excellent academic record. In school, he was excluded from the various cliques. Unable to achieve acceptance and community for himself, he found that being everyone's bottom at the baths and sex parties made him feel like he belonged.

Jonathan's therapy now centered around his finding a sense of acceptance and belonging in nonrisky, nonsexual ways, such as volunteering at organizations to help other gay men, even those living with HIV. HIV was his wake-up call, but he wished he had gotten help sooner. Jonathan's story is important for anyone who can get help sooner rather than later, regardless of one's state of health.

Recall from chapter 1 the discussion of sexual abuse survivors engaging in self-abusive behavior. Many theories seek to explain why sexual abuse survivors so often cut themselves with razors and other sharp objects. Research indicates that, among other things, they're trying to bring what feels so inwardly awful into outside pain. Also, they prefer to feel present-tense pain related to a new injury rather than the lingering emotional injury from past sexual abuse.

Again, our gay male culture is forced to experience covert sexual abuse in the quantity of hate and homophobia in the media and we gay men experience it personally on a daily basis. We can't serve openly in the military. Religions condemn us. In the United States, legal marriage is still a long way away. The patriarchal male fraternity determined to keep us out, we can still be excluded from housing and jobs with no legal recourse. The result is that we become our own oppressors, via the self-abuse and self-injury that I see manifesting in barebackers and so-called bug-chasers.

I've listened to men involved in both these dangerous practices, and always see them as forms of self-cutting and abuse. It is like the childhood abuse survivor unconsciously saying "See how damaged I am? You don't believe me? I'll show you" and revealing his scars for everyone to see. Those seeking to contract HIV are looking for a sense of belonging—a sort of brotherhood or community that they can't find in other ways. Sadly, they're looking for it in the sexual shadows. Like the Wild Man at the bottom of the pond, these men have been humiliated like the rest of us, scorned, and told they are unwanted. So they hide at the bottom of the pond, killing everyone who gets near them, as did the Wild Man in the Iron John story.

But of course they don't frame it that way. Some men say, "I want to get the virus. It relieves me of the anxiety of worrying about getting it." Others say, "I should be able to bareback. Sex was taken away from me once by those against my homosexuality, and they're not going to take it from me now. I'm not going to deaden my pleasure with latex." Statements like this are cries for help. Wanting to belong at the cost of something that can kill us is a trauma response from the abuse we gay men endure.

The Gift That Keeps On Giving

Terry was always paying for sex when he would travel for his job, which he did on a regular basis. One time, he was receiving anal sex from an escort who purposely removed his condom right before ejaculating. Terry knew it happened, since he felt the wetness running down his thighs. He was frozen in shock, as the escort put his clothes back on and left in silence. Neither said a word.

Terry had been living with this for one year now. For therapeutic reasons I asked Terry to write the escort an angry letter, but not mail it. (He wouldn't be able to find the guy's address anyway.) I wanted him to read the letter aloud, but he wanted me to read it instead. He said he did not want to cry and wanted to distance himself from his feelings because this was so hard for him. So I read it aloud.

> *You won't remember me.*
> *We had a brief encounter in my hotel room last summer.*

Know Your Sexual Shadow

Our meeting was probably nothing out of the ordinary for you—you must have many such encounters in your line of work—but it changed my life.

You infected me with HIV, and I have to believe you meant to. Our encounter had been safe right up to the point when you deliberately removed our protection. After six weeks, I had the symptoms of acute HIV infection and was diagnosed as positive.

Since then, I've been holding myself to blame: I was a consenting partner, aware of the risks with someone I'd met on the Internet, and had taken such risks for some time. Maybe my luck was bound to run out.

On reflection, though, that's too easy. The fact is, on my other encounters, the play was always safe. So why did you remove our protection? Was it just recklessness on your part, a wish to play dangerously? I think you knew you were positive and had every intention of passing on the virus. But either way, what you did was wrong, and had the same consequences I now have to live with.

I can't change what happened, but believe me, I agonize over how it did. For a brief physical pleasure that would otherwise be soon forgotten, I must suffer the memory of how easily and cheaply you cut my life expectancy. For the time I have left (hopefully years, not months) I will suffer a reduced quality of life to protect my health. I may never find a life partner. Perhaps worst of all, what will this do to my family and friends?

Were these thoughts going through your head when you went out of your way to infect me? Did someone pass the virus to you in a similar way, and therefore, drive you to seek revenge on others? I can only imagine this is the retribution you sought.

How easy it must be to become a victim, blaming everyone but yourself and making a career (literally) out of passing on the infection. But you have to stop. You have to get the anger out of you and stop the chain of suffering. I am

*trying to find room in my heart for forgiveness, trying hard
to control my anger and act responsibly toward others and
not become a risk to them in the way you were to me.*

*I guess I'll never know your reasons or what became of
you. It's ironic that you won't remember me, and I will
never be able to forget you.*

After I read this—with tears in my eyes—Terry said it was actually worse having me read it and him having to hear it. But it did put him in touch with feelings that he wasn't able to access before the session.

Homo-Work on Your Sexual Shadow

1. What is your peak erotic fantasy?
2. What sexual fantasies do you dislike the most?
3. Which of your sexual fantasies have you never told a soul about, not even your partner—and which might you not have admitted even to yourself?
4. What physical type of men are you attracted to sexually?
5. What type of porn do you look at most? Vanilla, kink, role-playing, solo, threesomes, or orgies?
6. Are you the sexual pursuer or the pursued—in fantasy and on the Internet?
7. What are your most enjoyable sexual positions?
8. How do you feel about your body, particularly your penis size?
9. Can you enjoy sex—both receiving and giving—with your partner?

References

1. Michael Bader, *Arousal: The Secret Logic of Sexual Fantasies* (New York: St. Martin's Press, 2002).
2. Guy Kettelhack, *Dancing Around the Volcano* (New York: Crown, 1996).
3. Bader, *Arousal.*
4. Patrick Carnes, *Sexual Anorexia: Overcoming Sexual Self-Hatred* (Center City, MN: Hazelden Press, 1997).
5. Jack Morin, *The Erotic Mind: Unlocking the Inner Sources of Sexual Passion and Fulfillment* (New York: HarperPerennial, 1996).

6. Joe Kort, "Gay Men and Their Porn," *In the Family* (Summer 2002).
7. Frank Sanello, *Tweakers: How Crystal Meth Is Ravaging Gay America* (Los Angeles: Alyson Books, 2005).
8. Andrew Miller, "Lost Tweakends," *Out* (October 2004).
9. Dawn Atkins, ed., *Looking Queer* (New York: Harrington Park Press, 1998).
10. Mark F. Schwartz and Stephen Southern, "Compulsive Cybersex: The New Tea Room," in Al Cooper, ed., *Cybersex: The Dark Side of the Force* (Philadelphia: Taylor and Francis, 2000).
11. Laud Humphrey, *Tearoom Trade: Impersonal Sex in Public Places* (New York: Aldine de Gruyter, 1970).
12. Al Cooper, "Cybersex and Sexual Compusivity: The Dark Side of the Force," in *Cybersex*.

Chapter 8
Understand the New Mixed Marriage:
When Three's a Crowd

Don't marry the person you can live with.
Marry the one you can't live without.

In looking for a partner, some gay men face the hurdles of dating a heterosexually married man, or of being heterosexually married husbands themselves. To establish a full relationship with another guy, both routes are potentially dead ends. But too many married gay men try to make do by cheating on their wives, going on the "down low," or just enjoying sexual hookups, assuming that nothing romantic will develop. And many gay men will date them and enter into an underground affair, believing that eventually, they will leave their wives for them. Both situations are out of integrity and can only cause problems for everyone involved.

For the heterosexually married gay man (hereafter, HMGM) telling his wife he's gay and deciding to divorce is analogous to "stealing your mother's key from under her pillow" in the story of Iron John. I've seen many gay men who married "mother figures"—in essence, marrying the "good" mother and thereby deciding not to steal the key from under her pillow. But in telling her he's gay, he allows himself to take the key and find his Wild Man.

Gay men emerging from their heterosexual marriages can be the best candidates for dating and even a long-term relationship (LTR). From females in our society, they've learned to value relationships and gained skills generally lacking in gay men who've never enjoyed close relationships with women. They know how to deal with their emotions and express them, when and how to sacrifice their needs deal with their emotions and express them, when and how to sacrifice their needs for a relationship, and how to keep connectedness and commitment alive. Unless we gay men are in some form of positive and healthy relationship with women, straight or lesbian, many of us will miss these lessons. I notice that well-mothered men—both gay and straight—share these abilities as well.

As mentioned earlier, single gay men often believe that their married boyfriend will eventually leave his wife for them. While this does happen, it often signifies—ironically—that they themselves aren't fully available for a relationship. If you're attracted to someone who's married and thus unavailable, whether a man or woman, that means you're unavailable as well. So once the heterosexual husband does become available, often his boyfriend will become distant and unavailable. Your inner saboteur might emerge and throw up roadblocks to establishing more intimacy—as we'll see in this chapter.

If you're in a relationship with a heterosexually married man, there are a number of factors to understand if you choose to continue on that route. First, it's dishonest for you—and for his relations with his wife and family—to do this secretly. If he has children, you're not involving yourself just with him but also with his wife (whether they're going to divorce or stay married) and his children. This isn't just a romantic affair; it's a family affair, for the guy you're getting involved with, they are in a lifetime commitment, emotionally and financially. Not a negative, necessarily, but a vital consideration to remain aware of while dating him. If all is out in the open, and she has an agreement or is in the process of divorcing, that's more appropriate. Always remember, being out of integrity brings on still more dysfunctional problems, so your goal in any situation is to strive for integrity as much as possible.

Who are these heterosexually married gay men? Why do they choose that route? Who are the women who fall in love with these men and marry them? Who are the gay men who date these HMGM? This chapter will help you understand these HMGM are and those who get involved with them.

Gay Men Who Date HMGM

Who are the gay men attracted to gay husbands, and why? Why would they put themselves in a position to be on the outside of a triangle? Is it healthy or not? And what about the gay men who heterosexually marry? When and how do they tell their wives, "I'm gay"? How do they determine whether to stay married or leave? And who are the women that marry gay men?

For every one of these situations, the path is extremely personal and varied. You must do what's right for you individually, and not what any therapist, friend, relative, or anyone else says you should. But for your mental and physical health and the welfare of your wife and any children involved, go forward with integrity, honesty, and informed consent on everyone's part. Whether or not they stay together, I think that HMGM and their spouses are very brave individuals exploring how to proceed with their mixed marriage. The following is a classic example of what I see repeatedly in my office.

After being together five years, Anthony and Rick came to me for couples therapy. Rick wanted to settle down and move in with Anthony and was angry that he was stalling on this issue. Anthony, for his part, was avoiding dealing with his difficulty over making this commitment to Rick—who was threatening to leave him unless Anthony was willing to go to the next level with him and become a committed couple by living with him. Not that Anthony didn't love Rick or want to go further and create a life with him—it was that Anthony was still legally married to his wife.

She and Anthony had three children, the last of whom was going to college in a year. Anthony had separated from his wife four years earlier, when he met Rick online and fell in love. After six months of romantic love with Rick, Anthony moved out into his own apartment and had lived there ever since.

Anthony didn't want to divorce his wife and asked Rick why it mattered whether he was married or not. He promised Rick that they were likely to divorce after his last child graduated college. Rick stated that was too long a wait and that it did matter. He knew it was over between Anthony and his wife, but still felt that Anthony's insistence on maintaining his marriage to his wife was a sign of his enduring loyalty to his family. Rick stated that going in, he'd known that Anthony would have other obligations. He'd spent their entire relationship watching Anthony devote money, time, and energy to his wife and children. Now Rick felt that his family was interfering in something that should exist between just the two of them, preventing their moving in together and becoming a "married couple." His patience was growing thin, he said, and he was on the verge of leaving.

I started to probe further, asking Anthony to explain more, but he became very defensive. Looking at me, he asked, "Have you ever been married to a woman?" When I replied no, he said, "Given that, I don't believe that you or Rick could ever understand what divorcing my wife means." I asked him, "Tell me, then, from your point of view," adding that I had seen hundreds of heterosexually married gay men in my practice and at the workshops I've led. For ten years, I even ran a gay men's group where most of the men were divorcing, separating, or struggling with their heterosexual marriages. So while I validated his reality—that I could never know what it was like for him—I at least had some idea of the process that men like him went through.

Anthony stated that his wife was "fragile" and that in their relationship, he'd felt always that he had to care for her. On several occasions he'd thought about raising the issue of divorce with her, only to find himself "chickening out," not wanting to hurt her or cause her more distress. He worried that if his kids knew he was gay, they would see him as a weak role model; and the last thing he wanted was to be shut out of their lives.

After several sessions, Anthony began to open up. He admitted he felt threatened and rushed by Rick's insistence that they live together, and that was why he was so defensive. He began talking about his marriage, the life he had with his wife and kids, and described the guilt he felt for leaving them behind to "selfishly" pursue his own happiness as a gay man. Pure guilt drove him to ensure his wife would still have health care throughout his employment and that his children wouldn't have to have both a gay dad and divorced parents. It was difficult for him to separate from his wife but, he told me, it was "better than divorcing her."

I sat with Anthony and Rick as Anthony painfully told his story. What I like most about couples therapy is that I can work with one individual while the partner is present, and their work can then become part of their relationship. Rick listened intently as Anthony spoke about his profound guilt over leaving his family. Anthony began to get tears in his eyes as he described the look on his wife's face when he told her he was gay and then the look in her eyes when he said he had met someone. He recalled his children's painful expressions when he told them he was moving out. For fear of hurting them further, he never did tell them he was gay.

I told him that if he felt such guilt and saw such pain, it made sense that he'd want to lessen any further trauma by not divorcing his wife or coming out to his children. I told him of all the men in his situation whom I'd treated and his bravery in taking the steps he had. I normalized his situation, telling him of other gay men married to women. Their path to healing lay in recognizing that their wives had in fact played a part in marrying a gay man. Anthony looked at me intently as I explained that in any mixed marriage, the straight woman has her own issues, which contribute to why she marries a gay husband to begin with. With Anthony's wife, we explored her issue of not divorcing him on her own and moving on with her life, as he was doing for himself.

I purposely kept repeating that it wasn't his entire fault, and that he didn't have to punish himself for having heterosexually married. I wanted him to get this understanding inside himself. He began to weep, saying "I feel like a bad person. I ruined everyone's lives, and now I am ruining Rick's." I told him Rick was there for his own reasons too, and that Rick must love him very much since he wanted to stay connected.

I explored both Anthony and Rick's childhoods. Rick revealed that in his family, he was always "second rate" to an older sibling who was athletic, excelled academically, and always had girlfriends—the apple of his parents' eye. Now as an adult, his brother had a successful high-paying career, with a beautiful wife and children who excelled in school as well. This contributed to why he had stayed with Anthony, even though Anthony was still married. Unconsciously, Rick had placed himself in the same situation, feeling "second rate" to Rick's wife and children. Anthony was Rick's imago match, in that he had *hired* Anthony to resolve his unresolved childhood issues. Finding himself second rate once again, he now to fight for himself and demand that he be Anthony's number one partner.

As he listened to Rick's story, Anthony was able to feel less responsible for his unhappiness; that this was mostly Rick's issue and that he himself wasn't wholly to blame. The more we talked about his wife, the more he began to recognize her role in this as well. In therapy, Anthony also learned about his imago: he'd grown up feeling he had to take care of his "fragile" mother who, through most of his childhood years, was depressed and unhappy. He was projecting this onto his wife, as if he had to protect her and make her happy too. The time had arrived for Anthony to "steal the key" from under his mother's pillow and pursue his own happiness.

I continued to comfort him by telling him it was okay to move on with his life. His wife and children—the youngest being eighteen—could bear it now. For the rest of the session, he cried uncontrollably. I had Rick hold him, and they both wept together.

This was the beginning of Anthony's emancipation and of his life together with Rick, as a gay couple on their next level of intimacy.

The next few months went by. Anthony promised to talk to his wife about divorce, which he did. His fears of her collapsing and not being able to handle it were unfounded. She agreed that it was time for a divorce, but they both wept over what could have been had he been straight. If their marriage had survived, they could have enjoyed their life together. They agreed that it was time for divorce, and for him to come out to their children.

Triangles Aren't Always About Gay Pride

The Oedipus complex may very well contribute to why gay men are drawn to date HMGM. Freud theorized that any young boy around the age of four—whom he always presumed to be heterosexual—has normal sexual feelings and overvalues his own penis. (It is not uncommon for boys to become aware of their genitals by age four and be awed by them.) Freud also believed that for the boy to want to sleep with his mother and view his father as a rival is normative as well. So the boy's secret unconscious wish is to eliminate his father so that he can have his mother all to himself. But he worries that to do so, he would risk punishment from his father—most likely, castration. This specific fear arises from the boy's awareness that his mother has no penis. So to preserve his own penis, he surrenders his love object—his mother—represses his desire for her, and accepts his father's authority. Homosexuality was long considered as "Oedipal gone wrong," resulting in the boy being attracted to males rather than achieving an alternative "healthy" outcome.

More recent psychotherapists and gay theorists—including Ken Lewes in *Psychoanalysis and Male Homosexuality*, Jack Drescher in his Psychoanalytic Therapy and the Gay Man and Richard Isay in *Becoming Gay*—have added to this Oedipal discussion of how gay boys develop.[1] They all agree that Oedipal feelings exist, but that from them arise other issues that are *not* about homosexuality, but instead about the lack of acknowledgement for normal homosexual development. They surmise that gay boys naturally yearn to get physically close to their fathers and so fall in love with them. This usually leads to rejection and becomes a source of wounding that is never resolved. As talked about in chapter 4, most fathers reject their gay son's yearning for intimacy. Sensing that their son is queer but seeking to "make him get over it," they follow the traditional patriarchal attitude of being tough and distant with boys.

As a therapist who's seen and treated children and as an uncle who now has had opportunities to watch four children closely, there's no question in my mind that Oedipal conflict exists. But I believe that it shapes relational skills, sexual behavior, and personality later in life, not sexual orientation. I know many heterosexual men whose sexual fantasy consists of seducing another man's wife, just as there are heterosexual men who enjoy other men making love to their wives. These fantasies too are Oedipal, no doubt.

A gay man is most likely playing out unresolved Oedipal issues when he dates and enters a relationship with an HMGM who is either closeted or not resolved to work things out with his wife. Following IRT's theory that relationships seek to repair issues unresolved during childhood, it makes sense that for resolution, when these repressed, unresolved issues arise, the HMGM and his wife become stand-ins for Mom and Dad. A gay man (still in the role of son) would be drawn to the HMGM (or surrogate father) and wishes to win him away from his wife (or surrogate mother).

The problem is, this is not true resolution, but instead encourages the gay man to move out of integrity and be willing to disregard the HMGM's wife and children. The little boy he once was is driving the bus, so to speak. He is acting out with these adults his hostility at his parents for withholding what he wanted in those early years.

Remaining in Integrity

How to proceed when you are attracted to an HMGM? The best way is first to determine what stage he and his spouse are in. Are they separated? Are they planning to divorce? Are they going to stay married and have an open relationship? What course are they on, in terms of how they see things resolving? Do they see things ending? Before getting involved, you need to ask these questions and explore the answers.

I don't recommend dating or going forward in a relationship with an HMGM unless he has an open, totally above-board agreement with his wife. If he doesn't, you'll avoid deception and heartache by avoiding him and walking the other way. Otherwise, you'll be stepping out of integrity, which can only cause harm and pain—not just for you and for your HMGM, but his wife and family as well.

If he tells you that his wife *does* know and has arrived at some sort of agreement with him, you still have a lot to consider. Do you want to be with a man with two partners? Even though he may not be involved with his wife emotionally or sexually, his being legally married creates a built-in exit in your relationship. If he does plan to leave her and divorce, you are still going to be with a man whose ex-wife will likely be in the picture for better or worse, especially if children are involved. There is nothing wrong with this but you need to be aware of that.

When you date an HMGM, you have no way of knowing for sure whether he will leave his wife. It's best not to get involved at all until he does leave her and moves on or at least decides what to do. Otherwise, you can end up waiting and waiting, but nothing happens or changes. If this is the case, then you must ask yourself: Are you just as unavailable as he is?

In other words, gay men who pursue closeted HMGM are just as unavailable as their potential partners. It's too easy for the single gay man to state that his heterosexually married gay boyfriend has all the issues, and until *he* is ready to make some decision, they can't have a relationship. Too often, I have seen an HMGM leave his wife only to find that the other man begins to distance himself. This usually happens for a number of reasons, the most common one being that the single gay man is attracted to the HMGM for one simple reason—there's a low possibility of anything more serious. For the single gay man not really interested in pursuing a serious relationship, the HMGM is almost as safe as a straight man, or a gay man involved with a male partner, would be. Unconsciously, the single individual assumes that not much can come from this—but if it does, he will flee the relationship.

I know this is not always true. I have treated many couples—gay and straight—whose relationship began as "just" an affair. While this does happen, it is not optimal and I don't recommend it, if only because it seldom works out for everyone involved—and especially not for the innocent people who *just* get hurt. I've worked with couples who "just" began an affair, then found that more affairs occurred within that relationship. Other couples who began an affair often grow to distrust their relationship and each other and worry their partners will begin cheating on them. (More about how affairs jeopardize relationships in chapter 9.)

If you're dating or in a relationship with a heterosexually married gay man who is *not* out to his wife, it's important to question what this says about *you*. What draws you to a guy who, you know from the start, is not available—yet you go for it anyway? What lets you minimize the hurt you are doing to his wife and children? What factors contribute to your denying the hurt you might be causing to yourself and the others involved?

The New Mixed Marriage

The term *mixed marriage* usually refers to two people of different races or religions who agree to wed. The mixed-orientation marriage, however, is becoming increasingly visible and has been around even longer. Gays and lesbians enter heterosexual marriages for many reasons, one being the hope that (as professionals often tell them) they will outgrow their "sexual perversions" so that they can pass as straight—but more often than not because they hadn't become aware of their true sexual and romantic orientation until they were already married and oftentimes had begun raising children.

Of the many books and articles written for the heterosexual spouses of gays and lesbians, Amity Pierce Buxton's *The Other Side of the Closet: The Coming-Out Crisis for Straight Spouses* has been particularly well received.[2] The discussion widened with *On the Down Low: A Journey into the Lives of "Straight" Black Men Who Sleep with Men* by J. L. King, who went on *Oprah* to discuss his book.[3] Even the *New York Times* jumped on the mixed-orientation marriage story when Governor James E. McGreevey of New Jersey came out as a "gay American" while standing next to his wife. The story by Jane Gross, "When the Computer Opens the Closet," explains how the secrets of gay spouses are being revealed by the computer and that the rise of these revelations is due to the easy online availability of gay porn and gay chat.[4]

In fact, there are over two million mixed-orientation couples, according to the Straight Spouse Network (SSN).[5] Here, a mixed-orientation couple is defined as one spouse being gay, lesbian, bisexual, or transgendered. The SSN also reports that more than 80 percent of these couples end up divorced. Many don't, however, and this chapter will address how one gay man and his heterosexual wife were able to make their marriage work.

Much of the talk about the new mixed marriage focuses on a straight spouse's reactions and on a gay man going underground to a secret sexual life. Many men I've treated belong to clubs where the heterosexually married members want one boyfriend on the side. In other words, they have a wife and a boyfriend who's also heterosexually married, and remain "monogamous" with both. Each man knows of the other's secret life, but their wives don't.

Needless to say, I don't support these arrangements for many reasons; chiefly, my objection centers not so much on matters of morality as *personal* integrity—being congruent with yourself from the inside out. Being on the down low is secretive and, as the Twelve Step maxim has it, secrets keep us sick. I wholeheartedly agree. If a couple decides to have this arrangement with each other, openly and honestly—on the "up high"—I completely support that. Many couples I've worked with do choose to stay married for many reasons and work out a variety of different arrangements. For example, the gay spouse might have someone on the side or pursue sexual hookups outside the marriage with his wife's knowledge and agreement.

Ken and Sharon came to see me as a couple. Sharon made the call, stating her concern over her diminishing sex life with her husband, Ken. She'd known he was bisexual from the time they were high-school sweethearts, ten years earlier. At the time, Ken said his attraction was strictly sexual and that he had no interest in pursuing men for any kind of relationship. During their courtship, he continued to have sex with other men, with Sharon's full awareness. She was open-minded about the whole situation and even accompanied him to gay bars, banking on his true commitment to her. But during their engagement, Sharon became uncomfortable with Ken's continued sexual encounters with men. He agreed that once they married and started a family, he would end his sexual *activities* with men. Ken believed that this wouldn't be an issue, since he knew he loved Sharon and that she satisfied him both emotionally and sexually. As Ken saw it, his attraction to men was strictly sexual.

For the past six years, their sex life had been largely moribund. Following the birth of their first child, they had sex for procreation and otherwise only about once or twice a year. Sharon was growing frustrated and wanted a more active sex life with Ken.

One night two years before, Ken came home to find Sharon on

their computer with images from the Web sites he had visited. "A pop-up ad took me to this site," she said. "I looked at the history and there were all kinds of gay sites up. What's going on?" He admitted that he had been surfing the Internet, masturbating to images of men as well as connecting with men, but only in chat rooms, never in person. He said he wanted to tell her before she found out by surprise; but that over the years, he'd come to understand he was closer to "homosexual" than bisexual: the Internet had helped him see this. But he didn't want to come out as a gay man or live his life that way, believing that his desires were only "sexual" not emotional, and that Net surfing and the occasional cybersex connection would be enough to satisfy his urges.

When a man identifies himself as "homosexual" and not gay, often it's because the word *gay* is affirmative. Being gay is a lifestyle, whereas from a gay-affirmative psychotherapy perspective, *homosexual* is just about sex and often has negative connotations, although sometimes the word is used for a man who's just coming out. Reparative therapies and antigay organizations such as the Family Research Council, for instance, never use the word *gay*, always *homosexual*. Ken and Sharon both needed to understand that just because he was turned on by homoerotic images and homosexual sex did not necessarily mean that he was moving toward a gay identity. We continued to explore whether he was in the beginning stages of coming out, but for Ken, none of that seemed true. He still had no desire to live as a gay man. All of this helped them both come to terms with themselves as individuals and a couple.

Sharon had no reason to question Ken since they were always open and honest with each other. She worried that he might go out and meet men, but he promised not to: if his physical desire for men returned, he would tell her before acting on it. Meanwhile, he said, he would simply masturbate looking at images of men on the Net, and that was all. But Sharon didn't feel comfortable with this, now that their three small children could walk in on him at any time. Ken's computer was the only one in the house. Their two youngest used it too, and Sharon feared—understandably—they would click onto one of the sites he visited.

He agreed to stop going onto the Net, again promising that he could control his sexual urges for men. Both wanted to continue as an intact family and raise their children together. But after Ken's promise to stop going on the Net, their sex life together reduced to complete abstinence. Physical affection was absent, and both felt touch-deprived. The children had begun coming to sleep with them in the middle of the night, and they both allowed it. This let him off the hook from having to be sexual with Sharon, and she didn't have to acknowledge that Ken no longer pursued her. Both could blame it on the kids sleeping in their bed.

I asked if Ken was dissatisfied with being asexual in his marriage. He said he felt "fine with that." It even helped him quell the urge to surf the Internet looking at images of men. He admitted that being sexual with Sharon would stimulate his sexual desire for men; and although she would satisfy his orgasm, he was left with a sexual appetite for male-to-male sex. Hard as it was for Sharon to hear this, she understood.

But she was upset about the lack of sex in their marriage. She particularly missed the affection that seemed to have vanished along with it and protested about living this way. All three of us agreed that if this were to continue, Sharon was likely to enter into an affair. She was dissatisfied with the asexuality in their marriage, not with Ken. He was interested in bringing sex as well as affection back into their marriage, but was afraid it would stimulate too much homoerotic impulses compelling him back on the Internet.

Again I quizzed Ken on his sexuality and wondered aloud why, to avoid the homosexual urges, he had to squelch his entire sexuality. Could it be he was stuck in the early stages of coming out, where a man has yet to reconcile his innate homosexuality? Once past these urges, could he accept that he was in fact gay and needed to come out?

Ken looked at both Sharon and me and said, "This is where I want to be—married to Sharon and enjoying our children. If I'm in the early stages of coming out, I won't let myself evolve. That simply isn't for me."

I suggested that they remove the children from their bedroom at night, if not for their sake, then for the children's. If a child is having a bad night, it makes sense to let him come and sleep with you—once in a while. But to do this on a regular basis violates the boundaries that both parents and children need. There are places in parents' lives, whether physical or emotional, where children need to learn they don't belong, and the parental bedroom overnight is one of them. Children should never be used to resolve or avoid issues in a marriage.

But what were Ken and Sharon to do next? He truly didn't want to live a gay life and, what was most important, didn't want to be without Sharon. Also, he had no interest in the "ex-gay" movement; from what he'd read it was too homophobic for him. Sharon loved Ken very much and didn't want to divorce him. She too wanted to make it work.

Together they started talking about options. Ken said that he would buy a separate laptop computer for his use only; the children would have no access to it. He would look at Internet porn and enter chat rooms without actually meeting men; that would be enough for him. Sharon agreed, but worried that chatting and looking at gay porn might impel him to meet men. Ken was concerned about this too, but they were both happy to take this first step.

Mixed Marriages and Psychotherapy

Plenty of therapists would disapprove of Ken and Sharon's decision. They would call their "arrangement" an intimacy disorder and seek to explore their histories of attachment and intimacy. They might even urge Ken to identify himself as bisexual. As true as that might be, the issue he and Sharon desperately sought to resolve was living together as husband and wife—and negotiating how he could manage his homosexual urges.

Other therapists might rush in and pressure the couple to examine divorce and separation options so as to move on with their lives. Why would Sharon want to stay married to a man who couldn't be fully present for her as a full-time lover? They'd evaluate Ken as a man who needs to come out of the closet fully and lead a gay lifestyle. Or they might advise him to remain in the closet and be the husband and father he promised to be—in short, have him rewrite history. But such therapists ignore society's heterosexism and homophobia and hold him accountable as the only responsible party.

I agree that these therapeutic angles need to be examined and evaluated in terms of what attracted the wife to the husband in the first place and has kept them together. But as a couples therapist, I take the position that it's not for me to decide whether a couple should stay together. The *final* decision is theirs. As therapists, our job is simply to inform our clients and make them aware. The rest is up to them. We support them in what works for them, not us.

At one time, as a therapist I used to take the position that anything except monogamy was a betrayal of a committed relationship. I no longer agree with that position and have opened my mind to the various arrangements that people make in relationships. But whatever the arrangement is, I believe it should be aboveboard and agreed upon by both parties. Neither should feel resentment or that one has no choice but to go along. The dedication needs to be to whatever contract both partners have agreed to, which is an honoring of their relationship.

What's it like for the heterosexual husband who comes both out of the closet and out of his marriage? If you are one or are dating one, you need to know what typically follows for these men so you can have some idea of the road that lies ahead.

The Gay Husband

Many gay men tell me they get married to heterosexual women because "society pressures us." But there is more to it than just that. Many of their contemporaries didn't get married and were able to be out and open and enjoy happy, healthy gay relationships. Every gay man who marries has family of origin and personality factors from his past that led him to stay closeted and get married in the first place. Simply chalking it up to a homophobic, heterosexist society is not enough of an explanation.

For the single man coming out of the closet, the hero's journey is just about him and his family of origin. But for the heterosexually married man, it's very different, since he also has his wife and often children to change the landscape on which he travels. Over the years, I've seen many different variations of this scenario, but one common theme remains—they feel 100 percent responsible for coming out and hurting their wife and children. In therapy, their work is to learn that they are not 100 percent responsible. They do need to acknowledge that their self-denial and incongruity with themselves contributed to their following the wrong path and now involves their wife and children. But the wife has a story too: Why did she consciously or unconsciously marry a gay man?

According to the Imago Relationship Therapy theory and the psychological processes talked about earlier, we are predisposed from childhood to pick the partners we do. We "hire" them to help us with the psychological work we need to accomplish. Thus, women who marry gay men have their own reasons, conscious or not, as to why they need to be married to an unavailable man—in this case, a man who happens to be gay. Their personalities, levels of emotional intelligence and self-awareness, and how evolved they are psychologically all enter into the picture but are neither excuses nor reasons to blame them for their decisions.

I've treated hundreds of heterosexually married gay men. What must it be like for them in midlife, still raising their family and building up equity in property jointly held with a spouse? They had wanted to enjoy the fruits of their efforts but may now they face the prospect of losing it all and starting over. Everything they built for security is now tenuous. And an HMGM may lose his wife, who is usually his best friend, along with the right to see his children.

Compared with these men, my coming out was easy, with no wife, kids, or equity to worry about. Not to minimize my experience or anyone else's, but building your life up to where you want it, only to find everything you know and love changing around you—that has to be difficult.

Sexual Abuse

Childhood sexual abuse is another reason gay men get married to women. Sexual abuse at a young age clouds and confuses an individual's sexual and romantic orientation. In chapter 1 I talked about how sexual abuse, both overt and culturally covert, plays a part in shaping our lives. Overt abuse for anyone—male or female, gay or straight—alters the course of one's true sexual interests and behavior, not orientation. Many have believed that it shapes orientation, but I've never seen any evidence of this. Instead, I see individuals who deny their own sexual identities and bury their authentic sexual selves to the point where they don't even know what's true for them.

I have treated heterosexual men with homosexually imprinted behavior from childhood sexual abuse who act out homosexually. Once their sexual abuse is healed, their innate heterosexuality is clear—but these men were heterosexual to begin with and were not of homosexual orientation. These are the men reparative therapists like to call "healed from homosexuality." In truth, they were straight men acting out homosexually. For gay men, the opposite is true: they "act out" heterosexually because their childhood sexual abuse clouds their true orientation. Once the abuse clears, their innate homosexuality surfaces and the coming-out process begins.

Many HMGM have histories of sexual abuse. Society has denied them permission to explore their homosexuality and, on top of that, the abuse had further buried awareness of their true orientation. As these men grow older and their defenses around denying the abuse break down, what emerges as well from that same closet is their true homosexual orientation. By now, however, they have been married to their wives for some time and often have children; in the wake of dealing with past abuse, they must deal with the present consequences of that abuse having shaped a life they weren't meant to live.

Heterosexual Golden Handcuffs

The heterosexual husband will miss his heterosexual privileges, which allowed him to explore his orientation and romantic desires. He could hold hands, kiss, and openly be affectionate with the object of his affection, skills that he learned from childhood on. He could get legally married without fuss, announce his engagement and wedding without the least resistance, and even be promiscuous, and no one would flinch or give him any grief. In archetypal terms, a gay man gives up his inner King, sacrificing his personal vision for heterosexual privilege. He turns his Lover energy over to heterosexuality when it's naturally meant for being gay.

Loss of Heterosexual Privilege

Coming out as a gay man, the HMGM loses his heterosexual privilege. In the world we live in, most people take heterosexual privilege for granted and never think about it much. But coming out, a husband realizes that he was never even permitted to explore any part of himself other than heterosexuality.

Many people dishonor gay men who leave marriages and kids, and this fuels the men's guilt for marrying in the first place. The cultural mind-set is that the gay man shows more integrity in staying with his spouse and children rather than leaving them, since he "made his choice" and should "live with it." But those who hold to these views forget what brought the gay man to heterosexually marry.

If you do decide to leave the marriage, it's important to stay conscious about how this will affect you and your family. Ease the hurt as much as you can, knowing that pain will inevitably be a part of it. I educate men to understand the anger and misunderstanding that will come their way from wives, children, family, and friends, and how to protect themselves against potential injury as well as be accountable for some—not all—of it.

In addition, the HMGM's family of origin plays a major part. The way in which a gay man was raised would cause him to choose to live as a heterosexual. He may have been conditioned to be conflict avoidant, obedient, people-pleasing, appease mom or dad, and conform. He might have been sexually abused, physically abused, or have suffered other forms of neglect and abuse, causing the trauma to manifest by his conforming to the "authority." In other words, children who are being abused learn to adapt by conforming to what the perpetrator demands through the abuse. Later, as adults, they will reenact their early abuse by conforming to other figures or societal "authorities." Conformity to heterosexist norms is the reenactment of the abuse for the gay man who is living as a heterosexual. Not all gay men who suppress their homosexuality grow up to eventually marry, but the cultural sexual abuse and other covert factors can push him in that direction.

Hetero-Emotional and Homo-Sexual

Why do these men with homosexual tendencies marry women? When I raise this confusing concept, many either dismiss it as unbelievable or can't understand it. Yet many hetero-emotional men are romantically and emotionally attracted to women and can enjoy sex with them because they love them and want to spend their lives with them. But sexually, these men prefer men. Most people would judge them as either gay or at least bisexual. These men would tell you, however, that they're not romantically or lovingly interested in a relationship with a man in any way. These are the type of men described in the book *On the Down Low.* We therapists and sex educators still don't understand many of the reasons for this type of developmental love and sexual mapping.

The reasons for this, many argue, are cultural. If society was more tolerant of homosexuality, these same men might be gay or at the least, bisexual; but patriarchy's taboos and antiemotional stance caused them to suppress their loving and romantic feelings for other men. This might be true, but we don't know. There are cultures in which the men bond, connect, and love one another and view women as useful only for procreation and meeting their needs. We therapists see this same attitude in American culture but don't label it as homosexuality. We might say that a heterosexual man "has issues with women" and, due to whatever ruptured his developing ability to connect with them, can only let himself connect to other men. While all of this is anecdotal and circumspective, we need to respect how the heterosexually married man self-identifies.

Also, some hetero-emotional gay men are married to women but do not have sex with them. Yet they enjoy a life that's full of love and family, and may or may not decide to be sexual with other men outside the marriage. If you are one of these men, then know that you are hardly unique. To be sure, you must ask yourself if this is the life you really wish to live. Are you adapting more to someone else's will than your own? Are you aware of the available literature both for and against this lifestyle? Many people suffer depression as a result of suppressing their sexuality. Over the years, I've met and treated men who do decide to live this way. Having often weighed every consideration, they are healthy and happy hetero-emotional men.

Heterosexual Prison

It's widely acknowledged that heterosexual men in prison often engage in homosexual acts. Most would agree that these men aren't gay, that being imprisoned causes men to be sexual with other men out of necessity. I am not referring here to rape; that's different.

A client of mine once said that for him, married life was like "heterosexual prison." He had sex with his wife to relieve his sexual urges. He wasn't sexually attracted to her, yet he was not repulsed either. Out of love for her, he was able to be sexual and romantic with her. Other gay clients I've heard over the years agree that they live imprisoned within the structures and boundaries of heterosexism and that, like the incarcerated, they do what they must to survive.

Heterosexually married gay men do love their wives—overall. But unlike the prisoner who has no choice about where he'll be incarcerated, the gay male does marry out of choice, usually a woman with whom he's already good friends.

Heterosexually married gay men who come to me feel enormous responsibility and guilt. It takes them years to get through feeling that they've ruined everyone's lives, including their own. "How could I've done this to my wife? She didn't know. This isn't fair to her. It's my entire fault, and I should suffer!" is the mantra I hear in my office. Yes, they need to take responsibility for not having come out sooner and avoided heterosexual marriage. Yes, the wife may not have consciously known. But when I talk with and counsel the wives of gay men, usually there are personal issues on their side as well. It's no accident that they married men who couldn't completely commit or be intimate and available to them, the way a straight man could.

Tall, skinny, and forty-eight years old, Eric was a manager for a major export phone company and married for the past twenty-five years to his wife, Ann, with a fifteen-year-old son and twelve-year-old daughter. Eric phoned me after having some homosexual experiences. He said he wasn't sure if he was gay, or bisexual, or a sex addict. He wanted to talk further about this and scheduled an initial consultation. Eric told me that he'd always had sexual fantasies about men. When he was twenty-one and still in college, a therapist had told Eric that his urges were simply sexual perversions that would pass. He shouldn't act on them, and to go ahead and lead a healthy heterosexual life. He was relieved! This therapist had told him what he wanted to hear. He decided to get married to a woman he'd met in college and to keep his homoerotism to himself.

Eric loved his wife and enjoyed sex with her, but admitted he often used images of men to stay aroused and achieve orgasm. There were times he didn't think about men and was able to be present with his wife and be satisfied by his sexual relationship with her. Over time, however, that reduced and was no longer true. He didn't feel badly about his homosexual urges, since he never acted upon them: "They were just in my mind." Occasionally, he would buy porn and mastur- bate to it, but always threw it out and never kept it in the house. He didn't have romantic feelings for other men, which convinced him that his urges were "simply" sexual and not part of his identity.

Eric told me that he'd been able to keep his urges closeted until seven years ago. After he and his wife bought a computer, he began surfing gay porn on the Internet and entering chat rooms. He pro- gressed to meeting men for anonymous encounters. He believed in monogamy and felt horribly guilty for cheating on his wife, but found his sexual urges increasingly compelling. He wished he could either stop completely or find one man with whom he could main- tain an ongoing, if secret, relationship. That way, he could satisfy his homosexual urges and also maintain his marriage with the wife he loved.

Ultimately, he was stunned and excited to discover an Internet club for married men who wanted monogamy with another man and not to leave their wives. He e-mailed the group, and the moder- ator in charge screened him to verify his authenticity. Once he was in the group, Eric met a man, Harris, with whom he wanted to have a relationship. Harris was also married with a daughter, and both agreed they'd found the perfect arrangement. They met at hotels and went on weekends together, and introduced each other to their wives as "my friend."

But Harris had just come out, and over the period of a year, he wanted to have sex with other men. This bothered Eric quite a bit, since he wanted monogamy for many reasons, both emotional and physical. Harris stated that he did too, but felt he needed to have other experiences—having entered into a relationship with Eric so quickly, he'd missed his "freedom to experiment." This caused Eric much distress, which contributed to the onset of anxiety and depression. His wife noticed his mood change, but when questioned, he lied and said it was work-related stress. Unable to sleep and losing weight, he ruminated for hours about Harris leaving him for someone else he might meet while having sex with other men. No longer able to manage his mood changes and depression, he called me.

After listening for a while, I told Eric he was living out of integrity. Thinking I was being moralistic, he snapped, "This from a gay therapist? For a response like that, I could have called Dr. Laura!"

I assured him that I was talking not about morality so much as secrets, deception, and not being congruent with oneself. I explained to Eric that living out of integrity with himself and others served only to place him at risk for negative psychological consequences, problems in everyday living, and even addictions. Never mind the risks he was inflicting on his wife, who had no idea of his underground life. He was in shadow, defending his dark side by being righteous and defensive with me.

"You don't know what my life is like!" Eric shouted. "You've never had a wife and kids you loved—have to face that for the rest of your life you might never be able to express something as strong and compelling as a love for someone else." He started crying uncontrollably. "Maybe you're not the right therapist for me. I need someone who can support me and help me make this work."

"Make what work?" I asked.

"My relationship with my wife and my boyfriend."

I agreed with Eric. If he wanted someone to support and approve his living a *lie* with his wife and himself, I wasn't the therapist for him. I could help him address what his problems were and why they existed, provide empathy and support for his pain, and refer him to a psychiatrist for medication to stabilize his mood state; but I couldn't align with his belief that it was okay to cheat on his wife. Only if she consented to all of this could I be supportive.

"You're right, Eric," I said. "I can't know what it's like to be heterosexually married with kids, suddenly realize I might be gay, and have to face these issues you do. But I do know what living in integrity is about and the negative consequences people face as a result of living with secrets. I can help you face that and make your own decisions about what you're going to do. I'm not here to tell you what to do, but you hired me to tell you what is causing you trouble. And your secret life is what's interfering with your life as a whole."

Eric disagreed. He remained angry with me for the rest of the session and vowed never to return. "You just think I should come out and never look back," he said.

"No, I don't. I want you to take a look at why you have chosen to live this way and what you can do to clean this up for yourself. You're not a victim of circumstances and if you live from that victim position, you will never solve this effectively."

After the session, Eric said he'd call if he wanted to reschedule. I never thought I'd hear from him again, but the next month he did call me, wanting to return. His depression and anxiety had worsened, and his wife trusted him less and less. "I gotta tell her," he said.

I agreed: it was either that, or decide to no longer act on his homosexual urges in any way. But he didn't want either alternative. "I don't want her to leave me, nor do I want to come out. Being a gay man doesn't interest me. I don't see myself as gay. I might be bi, but I'm not interested in any woman other than my wife. I am in love with *both* Harris and my wife."

Listening, I thought that this could be the early stage of coming out, where a man of homosexual orientation does not want to see himself as gay. I educated him on these stages so that he could decide for himself if he fit the pattern. We also explored whether any sexual abuse occurred in his childhood that might cause homosexual acting out, and there were no signs at all pointing to that. Eric was certain that he didn't want to lose his wife. He wanted to make it work with her and still act on his homosexual urges—if she would agree to it.

When he decided to tell Ann, she was horrified and angry. She exclaimed that she'd had no idea and told Eric she felt betrayed. She screamed out such questions as, "Did you marry me just to have kids?" and "Was I your beard? Was I your cover? You used me!" She blamed him for ruining her life and went through all the normative stages—and more—of what spouses do upon learning their partners are gay.

Stages of Coming Out as a Couple

Couples in a mixed marriage come out in several ways. Just as there are stages for the gay man and for his wife individually, so there are stages for them together as a couple, from the time the husband admits his homosexual orientation to the time that they arrive at resolution. In Aimee Lee Ball's article, "When Gay Men Happen to Straight Women," Dr. William Wedin, director of Bisexual Psychological Services in New York City, identified four stages of the coming out process for couples: humiliation, honeymoon, rage, and resolution.[6] Using these stages as guidelines, I've adapted Wedin's theories to my own work with mixed-orientation couples, adding my own observations here as well. As with the stages of death and dying, grief, and so on, there's no linear, cookie-cutter format for mixed-orientation couples to progess through the stages of coming out. A couple might go from humiliation to anger to honeymoon to resolution, or any other variation of the sequence.

For a gay husband, coming out to his wife is a very painful and courageous step. Coming clean and moving into integrity with himself and his wife, he has much at stake and so much to lose. It's easy for him and others to get distracted by the accusations of betrayal and deception. Others want to label him a coward, manipulative, and selfish for not telling his wife and pretending to be something he's not. For the gay husband to accept living a deceptive life even to himself is a very brave act. I'm not talking about men who purposely marry women for their own selfish, narcissistic ends, so as to have heirs or gain social acceptance; yes, these types of men are out there, but they're rare. The majority of these heterosexually married gay men genuinely wanted to make it work and wholeheartedly believed they could—because it *is* what they wanted. Most will tell you they loved their wives deeply and wanted a life with them.

I've listened to many gay men speak appreciatively of the deep nurturance and love they've received from their wives. Often, they've picked women who are good mothers and have natural, loving, maternal energy. This is why I refer to the mother's pillow detail in the story of Iron John: on an unconscious level, many of these men have married the "good mother" and have never really left home.

To be sure, this isn't true of all gay men who are heterosexually married. I've counseled many gay men whose wives aren't the least nurturing and where the husband has brought maternal energy to the relationship and the children. But those who are married to good women find it very hard deciding what to tell their spouses and whether to leave or stay.

The Humiliation Stage

The humiliation stage is when the gay husband comes out to his wife, and both suffer. Wedin talks about the wife "blaming herself for not being woman enough to keep her husband interested" and states that she "may question whether she ever really had anything in terms of a partner and marriage." I've met these women, and they report feeling that their husbands must be bisexual, since they experienced what they thought was good sex and loving connectedness. "How could he be completely gay and still have been sexual with me?" they ask. I explain the heterosexual prison syndrome (while not using those words, of course, because it would make them feel even more devalued than they do already).

Ann was in shock. Feeling betrayed and misled, she initially threatened to tell their children and their families, go to a divorce lawyer, and fight for custody of their kids. She made him realize that no judge would ever let a "homosexual" have custody of his kids or even visitation rights. I explained to Eric that this made sense: she was trying to shame him because of the humiliation she felt. But now he was worried she might act impulsively and try to hurt him. He asked her if she would be willing to come in and talk to me— which she was. I suggested they come in together, and they made an appointment.

But before they came in, Ann sent me a very long e-mail letting me know everything she could about Eric's childhood, personality traits, fathering traits, work and sleep habits, and more. It was the most elaborate e-mail I ever received from someone about to enter therapy with me. Obviously, she was not very focused on herself, but focused on him, as most spouses are who learn their partner is gay.

When Ann entered my office, her first remarks to me were that since I am gay, she worried I might try to separate her and her husband. She didn't trust that a gay therapist would be interested in helping them work out whether or not to stay together. She said she wanted to go to a therapist to figure out "if we *should* stay married, not just if we *could* stay married."

She wanted answers. What made someone "homosexual"? How could he change back to heterosexuality? What might be wrong with her that she did not see that he was gay all along? "He must be bisexual," she cried. "Otherwise, how could he have had sex with me and fooled me!" I sat and listened and let her express her flood of thoughts and feelings.

Both Eric and Ann wept while talking about how they wanted to stay together, but weren't sure if that was possible. I spent the next several sessions doing couples work so they could communicate with each other without reactivity, hearing what the other wanted and how they each might proceed. As the weeks passed, Ann calmed down and expressed a growing awareness of things that had occurred during their marriage that pointed to his homosexuality, but which she hadn't wanted to see. She had discovered his visits to gay porn Internet sites, she noticed him eyeing other men when they were out. She'd even wondered if Harris was gay when they first met. Meanwhile, Eric had told her his thoughts about staying with both her and Harris. She made it clear she didn't want this and said he'd have to make a choice. This became a source of tension between them until Harris called it off with Eric, claiming he wanted to "play the field" with more than one boyfriend.

Eric was crushed and became deeply depressed. Yet he knew he still wanted to have both his wife and a homosexual outlet. Now that he'd lost Harris, he began thinking that perhaps this wasn't feasible and talked to Ann about staying in the marriage monogamously. Ann welcomed his decision.

The Honeymoon Stage

In the honeymoon stage, Wedin explains that "the gay husband wants to stay in the marriage for good reasons, that he really loves his wife. The more he has genuine heterosexual feelings for her and empathizes with what she is going through, the more she will feel that this is the man she married. And almost every man is blown away by her saying that she wants to stay with him; he feels tremendous acceptance and love."

Here is where I think the gay man has to choose whether or not to go for the key under his mother's pillow. I've seen men come out and change their minds, realizing that a man may never love them the way their wives did. It's true that men love differently than women, but that's not always a good enough reason to return and try to fix the marriage. If that's your main motive for staying married, it won't be enough, and eventually you will return to seeking male partners. (More about this later in this chapter in the section on women who marry gay men.)

Ann experienced exactly what Wedin describes: relief that the man she originally married seemed to return with heterosexual feelings for her and compassion for what she is going through. Said Eric, "She let me come back home, for heaven's sake! This woman is a saint!" He had placed Ann high up on a pedestal, and for good reason. He felt terrible for what he had done.

Still, he was crushed by losing Harris. He began to believe that gay men couldn't love him as his wife did. Ann stopped coming to see me, but I continued to see Eric in individual therapy. After only a short time with Harris, he had risked almost everything. And now, overwhelmed by Ann letting him return home as if nothing had happened, he was vacillating about whether or not he was truly returning to a heterosexual lifestyle. Meeting Harris had changed his life, in that never again could he deny that he wanted relations with men. Without a homosexual outlet, life back home with his wife and children seemed mundane

The Rage Stage

Wedin explains that the rage stage is when the partners "both come to the limits of what's possible." Ann was satisfied with their current situation: having back the husband she married and the father of her children. But Eric felt a loss that was starting to weigh heavily on him.

For several months, Eric continued attending individual therapy with me, but grew increasingly depressed. "My life is boring now. I mean, I love my wife and my kids, but it just isn't enough." As his depression worsened, he found himself up late at night looking at Internet porn after everyone went to bed. Initially, he stayed away from chat rooms, since that was how he'd met Harris. But shortly after he began going to chat rooms again, he was back to telephoning men and meeting them. He tried to reunite with Harris, but Harris wasn't interested.

One night, Ann had a hunch that he was doing more than just working late at night and found him on the computer, masturbating to homosexual imagery. They had an argument. Eric said he couldn't repress these urges in the way he would have liked and if he was not meeting men, he at least wanted to have this option. He assured Ann that he wanted to stay married but needed to express this part of himself, if only in private. But he soon began hooking up with men online and going out with them. This time, he realized he was out of integrity without my having to point it out.

Eric and Ann both came back to my office together. He talked to her about wanting to express his homosexual yearnings and stay married to her too. Ann wasn't happy about this, but agreed to it. She loved him very much and wanted his happiness, but not at the cost of her own.

Our session ended with Ann telling Eric that whatever he chose was fine with her. She preferred that he stay in the marriage, but would support his decision to leave and live as a gay man. They both wept, and throughout the entire session Eric repeated how much he never intended to hurt her. Ann told him she understood. I strongly recommended to Ann that she receive her own individual therapy but she refused. "I can handle this on my own," she said.

Eric kept coming to see me weekly and reluctantly joined my gay men's group, telling them he had decided to explore his gay self, but might decide to stay married to Ann. He worried that the other men in the group wouldn't accept his situation and urge him to come out and not stay with his wife. I assured him that even if they felt that way, it was good for him to hear it but that he wouldn't be under peer pressure to do anything he was totally unwilling to do. Some of the gay men in the group had been heterosexually married as well, so he had a spectrum of men to react to him and his issues.

Eric started meeting guys. But now when he left, he would tell his wife the truth about where he was going—"I met a guy on the Internet and I'm going out on a date." He would sit in their drive-way for long periods talking on the cell phone with guys he met online.

Then one night he returned home to discover that Ann had told the kids that he was gay. Furious, he confronted her. "How dare you tell them before we talked together and didn't involve me in the process!"

"What was I supposed to do?" she countered. "You're out all hours meeting guys off the Internet, and I was worried sick you were going to be killed!" Hearing them, the children woke up and came downstairs. "Dad, are you okay?"

With their family now in a mess, he and Ann came back into therapy as a couple. Ann held her position that she should tell the kids the truth—after all, it was her story too. I asked why she would tell the children that he was out with someone from the Internet. She stated she was worried out of her mind and getting no sleep, and thought her kids should know as well. I challenged her shadow of anger. Why did she feel the children needed to be alarmed too? This, I told her, wasn't congruent with what I knew about her strong pro-tective feelings for her children—it didn't make sense to tell them about their father and alarm them about his Internet meetings with-out him present. Knowing I was right, she was speechless.

I used this as another opportunity to reinforce the need for her own individual therapy—even if in a straight spouse networking meeting or a PFLAG meeting. She said she'd consider it. I told her if she didn't find another source of support, then inevitably she would *use* their children to meet those needs—which would be abusive to them. She agreed.I then asked Eric why he was flaunting his homosexuality to Ann, when it was clearly hard for her to hear. At first he defended himself, but knew this was true since his group had already challenged the "in your face" way he was expressing his sexuality to her. In group, we'd decided that he was in his gay adolescence. He knew the group and I were right and that he was acting as an adolescent would with his mother. But Ann wasn't his mother, and their children weren't his siblings. Thus, Eric needed to deal with his feelings in individual and group, instead of acting them out with his wife and children. Even though he felt like the son and the sibling, he needed to act in integrity as a husband and father.

Now he and Ann were at the "what do we do now?" stage.

The Resolution Stage

The resolution stage, Wedin explains, "depends on a lot of different factors: kids, social considerations, also the question of where the man really falls in terms of his sexual and romantic feelings." In her book and articles on mixed-orientation marriages, Buxton writes that coming out is a "family affair." This is very true whether or not the couples have children, since in-laws will be told, and reactions from both spouses' families will be part of the process.

Eric and Ann did have children and loved each other very much. Eric wanted to move on, come out as a gay man and leave the marriage. Ann realized it was impossible to stay and try to make the marriage work; and began recognizing her needs to have a full relationship as well. Eric and Ann had no one other than me to talk to about what they were going through, which made things much more stressful for both of them. Not being able to talk when something so large is looming can prolong the situation. The family came in for a few sessions with me and wept as they discussed not only the imminent divorce but also what the gay orientation of their husband and father, who they loved very much, meant for all of them.

The Children

One thing gay men *never* regret is having had children. I have heard these men say that though they regret the years they lost by not having been out and having to change their life midstream, causing so much turmoil for everyone, still they are glad and proud to be fathers. Listen to some of the statements from former and current heterosexually married gay fathers:

John: "If I had to do it all over again, I would, just for the experience of having my children."

Mike: "The best thing that has come from my married years is my children."

Sam: "I feel sorry for gay men who never had children. It has provided me with awareness in my life that I would have never known about and which I would never want taken from me."

Tim: "There is nothing like it than love from a child and returning it to them as a father."

Bruce: "When I saw the hurt in my son's eyes upon learning I was gay I thought I could not continue living. But I knew that for him and me to be closer, he had to know all of who I was. We have never been closer as father and son."

Many would judge these men as selfish, having taken advantage of their wives just to have children. They would argue these men put their own desires above those of their wives and children. But in the early stages of coming out, the gay fathers are not aware of their homosexuality and if they do become aware, chalk it up to sex and nothing more. In those early stages, a gay identity or life is completely out of the question. The truth is, these men were acting in a manner that is the opposite of selfish. When interviewed, most if not all of these men will say that they truly wanted to please their families, religion, employment, friends, and society, to do what they were taught was "right."

Then, many ask, why not just stay married? Why disrupt the lives of their wives and especially their children to "selfishly" meet their own needs by coming out? Many heterosexually married gay men struggle with this question. The truth is that once their awareness of being gay surfaces, the lie they're living becomes overt. Having lived out of integrity, they often become men of true integrity. In other words, they would never purposely set out to live a lie. So to be fully aware of their being gay and living a lie to their children would be trouble them and send a mixed message to their children.

To help these men decide to come out and divorce, I often say that living authentically is the most important example they can give their children. As discussed in the parenting chapter, staying married for the children's sake serves only to hurt them more. Divorce is hard on everyone, particularly the children, but time and again, studies show that during the divorce, it's even harder on the children when the parents don't get along and use the children as weapons against each other. If spouses put the children first, shelter them from conflict and arguing, and find it in themselves to be mature and adult when it comes to protecting the children, then the divorce process will be less severe and easier for all concerned.

By *mature* and *adult*, I mean to let the children know that the divorce is not their fault. Mom and Dad can no longer be married for reasons between them, and the children need not worry about them and can be assured that both parents are looking out for them too. Studies show that these children fare better in divorce than those whose parents fail to reassure their children.

The Wife: Mother Figure or Best Friend or Both

Who are these women who marry gay men? Are they fag hags who admire gay men so much they want to marry one? Do they need to mother their husband, or to have him parent them? Or are they simply women who choose to marry gay men for conscious reasons that are right for them and go in knowing the situation and adapting to it? Whether or not a woman consciously marries a gay man, for the most part she does so with an unconscious purpose. It is no accident that these women find themselves married to someone who cannot be fully romantically and sexually interested in them.

Love is "custom made" in that we find partners who bring up things for us, both positive and negative, from our pasts. Married gay men need to learn about the typical reasons why women find them, so that they can unburden themselves from most of the guilt and accountability. These straight spouses have a story too!

Most heterosexually married gay men tell me that after they divorced and began seeking a same-sex partner, rarely if ever did they find men who, they felt, loved them the way their wives did.

Even gay men who have never been in a heterosexual marriage, however—and who can achieve as deep a level of intimacy as can most women—feel frustrated with gay men. In the gay male couples who come to my office, I see this all the time. Conditioned and raised as men, we exhibit the same awkward difficulties with intimacy that heterosexual men do.

At the weekend workshops I do for lesbian and gay couples, sometimes all the couples are men. I see a definite difference than when the workshop has more of a mix or even one female couple. Without women in the room, emotionally, the male couples tend to keep things on a lighter level. It takes a lot more to bring them to deeper emotional places than is the case for female couples and heterosexual couples too—since women are willing and able to get more emotional and reach core issues more readily. We gay men can also go deep, to more emotional places, but having been socialized as males, going to emotional places may not be so easy, because men are conditioned *not* to go deep—especially with other men. "Keep it light and easy" is our masculine mantra. As gay men, our cue is to stay even more superficial. Now given these factors, put us in relationships with one another and you can see what difficulties await us.

It's hard for the wife to understand that she could never be "woman enough" for him, but that isn't the issue. Quite similarly, women married to sexually addicted men or men who have affairs tend to blame themselves and take it very personally, as if his behavior stems from something she did or didn't do to make his behavior occur. For spouses of these men and gay men, the truth is that the husband's sexuality has nothing to do with them in the least. They simply married men with sexual conflicts, as discussed previously in this chapter. The question at hand is more *why* these women were psychologically drawn to these men—and then, why did they stay with them? When these women look back, most will say they picked up signs that something was missing from their gay spouse, but they paid them no attention. They will say that at times, they began to wonder and thought it unusual that certain things were happening—or not happening—in their marriages.

Understandably, the women will usually deny their own personal stories, particularly at first. Feeling hurt and betrayed, they blame the gay husband. The initial revelation only aggravates the feelings of betrayal; it's hardly the time for her to examine her part in the drama. But as I have sat with these women over time, they're able to make sense about why they chose to marry gay men.

Most of their reasons stem back to dependency needs and fears of being vulnerable. Women who surround themselves with gay men always say they appreciate not feeling judged as harshly as they are by straight men. The difference, of course, is that gay men don't view them as potential partners for sex or romance. Thus, gay men tend to be more forgiving of a woman's looks than heterosexual men will be.

A woman might also marry a gay man after being wounded and traumatized by men. Perhaps her father was abusive emotionally, sexually, or physically; or perhaps he neglected her or her mother in some way. She may have decided—consciously or not—to minimize or block any type of sexism or form of abuse coming her way.

In general, gay men tend to honor women more for *who* they are. With less sexual tension between them, gay husbands can be more sensitive to their wives' needs and willing to overlook physical distractions, such as weight, that straight men might not. This might be a welcome relief for any woman who straight men have shunned and rejected sexually and romantically. As comedian Roseanne Barr once said, "Thank God for gay men. Without them, fat women would have no one to dance with."

One of the chief reasons straight married couples have conflicts and move toward divorce, author and marriage therapist John Gottman found, is that a husband won't allow his wife to influence him. He often remains dominant and closed to her. Women, by contrast, generally allow themselves to be influenced by their husbands, perhaps too much. Either way, Gottman says, being out of balance causes problems. My experience is that gay men in mixed-orientation marriages can often be influenced by their female partners, which makes the marriage work even more. Within the mixed marriage, both spouses, gay and straight, report less conflict in their marriages than entirely straight marriages enjoy. This is appealing to the straight wife who might have had other relationships with more conflictual men; the gay husband doesn't bring to the marriage the kind of adversarial energy that a straight man would.

Sexually abused women are another variable. Heterosexual men have abused and violated them, or they've been raped or sexually abused as children or adults. Without professional help, these women—or men, for that matter—will make bad decisions for themselves. They'll tend to reenact the abuse repeatedly by partnering with men who abuse them. Or they'll go to the other extreme and marry a man whose sexual power is distant or troubled—perhaps one with a sexual addiction or problem with impotence, or a gay man struggling to squelch his homosexual impulses. This can be their way of protecting themselves from straight men's sexual aggression.

Childhood sexual abuse and rape are not sexually motivated, but the victim doesn't know that. The psyche is looking to protect itself and thus will keep at a distance the energy that came with the abuse. The problem is that a woman's psyche confuses abuse with a man's normal sex drive. Gay men will make a woman like this feel safe, especially if he keeps sex to a minimum.

And finally, some controlling women like to marry gay men—and especially, gay men who want to be controlled. I have often seen this syndrome where the gay man had problems in his family of origin: he may have been raised in a large or neglectful family that overlooked his emotional needs, have lost a caregiver at an early age, or had other issues that invite him to bring into his life a controlling heterosexual woman. She in turn may have come from a disempowered role in her own family and needs to be in charge of others so as not to feel vulnerable.

As already discussed in this chapter, the woman who marries a gay man must examine her own issues in terms of why she married a gay man to begin with. If she won't, she often will seek to humiliate *him,* remaining a victim and blaming him for everything. And often, the more she belittles him, the more he will accept it, since he feels ashamed for being gay and responsible for the problems with their relationship anyway. Often, he'll take all the responsibility for having gotten married, even if he had no real awareness of his gayness at the time.

Homo-Work on Heterosexually Married Gay Men

1. If you are a single gay male dating an HMGM, does the HMGM's words match his actions in terms of what he plans to do with his wife and family?
2. As a single gay male, are you ready to be partnered with not just the HMGM but his ex-wife and children, if he has any?
3. As the HMGM, how willing are you to give up your heterosexual privileges?

References

1. Ken Lewes, *Psychoanalysis and Male Homosexuality* (Northvale, NJ: Jason Aronson, 1995); Jack Drescher, *Psychoanalytic Therapy and the Gay Man* (Hillsdale, NJ: Analytic Press, 1998); and Richard Isay, *Becoming Gay: The Journey to Self-Acceptance* (New York: Pantheon Books, 1996).
2. Amity Pierce Buxton, *The Other Side of the Closet: The Coming-Out Crisis for Straight Spouses* (New York: John Wiley and Sons, 1994).
3. J. L. King, *On the Down Low: A Journey into the Lives of "Straight" Black Men Who Sleep with Men* (New York: Broadway Books, 2004).
4. Jane Gross, "When the Computer Opens the Closet," *New York Times,* 22 August 2004, sec. 9, p. 6.
5. Straight Spouse Network (www.ssnetwk.org).
6. Aimee Lee Ball, "When Gay Men Happen to Straight Women," *O, The Oprah Magazine* (December 2004).

Chapter 9
How to Call It Quits Without Being a Quitter

"Autobiography in Five Short Chapters"
by Portia Nelson[1]

I

I walk down the street.
There is a deep hole in the sidewalk.
I fall in.
I am lost . . . I am helpless.
It isn't my fault.
It takes me forever to find a way out.

II

I walk down the same street.
There is a deep hole in the sidewalk.
I pretend I don't see it.
I fall in again.
I can't believe I am in the same place.
But it isn't my fault.
It still takes a long time to get out.

III

I walk down the same street.
There is a deep hole in the sidewalk.
I see it's there.
I still fall in . . . it's a habit.
My eyes are open. I know where I am.
It's my fault.
I get out immediately.

IV
I walk down the same street.
There is a deep hole in the sidewalk.
I walk around it.

V
I walk down another street.

This poem is so simple, yet profound. There are so many ways to interpret it to evaluate where you are in your life. What "chapter" best describes your relationship? From a simplistic point of view, Ms. Nelson's poem can be about trying to leave a bad relationship, again and again, until you finally make it out. There are many ways, however, we step into that "hole in the sidewalk," and it has nothing to do with exiting the relationship itself. It might be about ending negative ways you treat a partner, or how you respond to him. It could be that you're not stating your needs to him—or not stating them enough. It may also be that you are stating too many needs. In any relationship, many things can be viewed as "walking down another street."

What does the hole in the sidewalk represent for you? The possibilities can be endless. You must decide what it symbolizes. One sure thing, however: before you end your relationship, I highly recommend that first, you do everything and anything you need to do to keep it together. I don't suggest that you stay with a partner who's actively addicted and won't stop or enter a recovery or treatment program; nor am I talking about staying in a relationship with domestic violence and physical abuse—or sticking with someone who you know doesn't interest you at all.

But it's in your best interest to make sure you've done all you can to make your side of the relationship work! If you can "walk down a different street" within the relationship, then I support your doing that first. You might find that your relationship begins to work better and the intimacy deepens. But if not, and things remain as they were, at least you'll know you tried everything you can. In either case, you may have grown in ways that you couldn't have outside this particular relationship—and you can take that personal growth into your next one.

But leaving one relationship with issues unresolved means you run the risk of falling into that same hole in a future one. Almost everyone knows someone who picks abusive or alcoholic partners over and over. Sometimes this pattern is rooted in childhood and other times a first love or intense adult relationship can create the map to finding the same partner over and over.

You may think it's time to end it, when actually you're both in the power struggle—the Call of the Child discussed in chapter 3. How do you get past that effectively and keep the relationship? Unfortunately, family and friends may give you more support to leave your relationship than to stay. Gay or straight, when you go to others about problems with a partner, more people will tell you to end the relationship than to stay and work things out. We live in a disposable society where if it isn't working, we throw it away. This chapter explores how to know for yourself when it's time to move on—and how to move in that direction.

Various mood responses and grief reactions occur when breaking up. It's not uncommon to feel that your life is coming to an end. Those who never thought about suicide before suddenly find themselves hopeless and helpless. This happens because at an unconscious level, relationships throw us back to our childhoods, when we were the most dependent. So to have a partner leave you and say, "I no longer love you" is tantamount to your parents saying to you as a child, "We no longer love you and are leaving you." You'd be devastated. Children need their parents for survival.

In fact, studies show that divorce affects people worse than a death. With death, there is finality: the person is gone, and the grieving can begin. With a breakup, the "lost one" lives on: if you're in the same small community, you risk running into him, hearing about him, having to interact with him if kids are involved, and if the two of you share friends and are involved with one another's family. This prolongs the grieving process and makes it harder to get through it.

Imago therapists have created a good-bye process, which I use in my work with singles in helping them let go of ex-partners. I also use it if both partners are willing to come to therapy together and end their relationships by doing the good-bye process. I use it as well for couples who want to end the earlier, rougher part of their relationship and move into the better part. As spiritual author Neale Donald Walsch sagely observes, "It's impossible to end a relationship. It's only possible to change it." The good-bye process is an excellent tool to help you make this transition, even if you use it as simply an outline for a letter you write out and perhaps never even send. It's all for you.

Breaking Up with Integrity

A lesbian couple attended one of the first couples workshops I ever facilitated. During the introductions, when couples state what they hope to bring out of the workshop, these two said they were here to learn how to end their twenty-five-year relationship with respect and friendship.

I was stunned to hear this. I had thought my workshops were for couples trying to work things out—but not on how to split up. So at the break, I approached them to ask why they didn't see the workshop as a last chance to save their relationship. Their response was, "We want to learn what went wrong, so that we don't bring our unfinished business into our next relationships. We want to save our friendship and move on with our lives." They had been through other couples therapy and workshops, were unable to make the relationship work, and so were here to end it as mature adults. This couple's integrity overwhelmed me. I truly was in awe of them.

I have since learned that when lesbian couples end their relationships, often they remain friends—mostly in a mature and healthy way, although I understand that many are not like this. Also, there's some argument that the lesbian community is "incestuous and engages in serial monogamy," according to a lesbian therapist friend of mine. While this may be so, I learned from my lesbian clients on how to break up in a healthier way that is respectful and mindful.

In his foreword to Debbie Ford's book *Spiritual Divorce,* Neale Walsch writes:

All relationships are never-ending. It's not a question of whether we are going to have the relationship but of what kind of relationship we are going to have. Our relationship with another goes on and on and on. Even if we never see another person again, we have a relationship with them. And the nature of that relationship affects the days and times of our lives in a very real way.[2]

Breakups are messy and can become a nightmare. There's typically a great deal of drama: both partners feel angry, judgmental, bitter, and feel a desire to inflict hurt and get revenge. But you can leave a relationship with personal and relational integrity by using all of your archetypes. Your Lover energy, where your heart lies, needs protection. Your Magician can reason things through. Your Warrior can enforce boundaries—emotionally and otherwise. Your King helps you envision how you want your life to be when the relationship is over. You do need to have a vision of the relationship being over, and that's no easy task.

Knowing When It's Time to Leave

Deciding to break up is hard and filled with anguish and devastation. I have seen friends and clients alike struggle with this issue. No one wants to have to end a relationship if they can help it. People cling to hope that things will change or their partner will change. Most people just don't know how or what to do to fix things. Often, people think that if you're the one doing the breaking up, you're not in as much pain as the one who's getting broken off. But this isn't necessarily true. Both individuals are vulnerable, and while their difficulties may be different, so are the issues. Both sides can be painful.

Frank came to me to work on whether to stay with Adam, his boyfriend of two years. He thought he loved him, but realized that in fact he just *wanted* to love him. We examined the pros and cons to both. Frank said he was tortured about what to do. He didn't necessarily want to end the relationship since he was worried that he'd never find another guy like Adam, but he also knew this was *not* the reason to stay. He described Adam as monogamous, caring, dependable, and accountable. "All the things you would want in a partner," he said, "especially in the gay community! I just never felt that spark for Adam. I wanted to. But try as I might, I can't conjure it up."

Frank also worried about going out and dating again. Now thirty-five years old, he knew that since the gay male community tends to be so youth-focused, dating for him would be different than it had been when he was in his twenties and early thirties. Moreover, he'd never enjoyed dating, which he described as "mini relationships occurring over and over again"—getting involved and breaking up with several different people over the course of a year. "It hurts me to have things not work out even though I know it's just dating. And neither do I like to be the one to hurt the other guy by telling him it's not working out."

Frank shared his relationship history with me. When he was in his early twenties, his first of three partners cheated on him and, at the end of their relationship, became physically abusive. One man was very demanding and would sniff his clothes and his underwear when he came home, suspecting that Frank had been out cheating on him or at a bar. But Frank wasn't cheating; he loved this man. But ultimately, he learned that it was his partner who was doing the cheating, so he ended that relationship.

Frank fell fully in love with his next partner. They had a great relationship and sexual connection that lasted seven years. But after that, things seemed to change, and their sex faded away. Neither talked about it much, and eventually they decided to part ways. Both men were disengaged and made no efforts to breathe life back into their relationship.

Frank had always regretted the end of that relationship and felt it could have been saved. But at this point it was too late, since his ex had entered into a quite serious relationship; he and his new partner had adopted two children together.

So now Frank found himself with Adam, but the spark wasn't there. After six sessions, Frank started to tell me that deep down inside he knew he just wanted to be single. Being independent and free to date whomever he wanted—be it Adam or anyone else—sounded appealing. Frank said he hadn't really wanted to admit to himself that he wanted to be single, because it sounded harsh and like how "most gay men are not relationship-oriented and only out for themselves." He said he hadn't wanted to let *me* know this either, since he didn't want to "disappoint" me, knowing that I specialized in helping people save their relationships.

Here was our first clue toward what the problem was. Why pick me, a relationship expert who tries to save relationships, if he wanted to terminate his? And if he knew that I do help people end relationships in healthy ways, why would he care so much about *disappointing* me? So I followed his theme of disappointment to see where it would take us.

Whenever someone is stuck in a current therapeutic situation and nothing we examine in the present helps, it likely has something to do with his childhood or a past relationship. Frank had already talked about his past relationships, and nothing stood out there. He said he had a good relationship with both of his parents, who were Jewish and attended synagogue regularly. His mother was not okay with his gayness, he said, but she tolerated it, while his father was neutral on the topic. His mother was always picky about the clothes he wore—in terms of style, manufacturers' labels, and whether items matched—as well as how he cut his hair, right down to the jewelry and cologne he chose to wear.

Frank told me that his sisters had confronted their mother and put up all kinds of boundaries, but that he'd never been able to do that. He loved her very much and did not want to disrespect her. So when he saw her, he'd let her check his clothes, say whatever she wanted about his hair, and not say anything in reply, even though she was being disrespectful. At the same time, when she made her comments, he felt self-conscious and hurt. I asked, "Do you feel you can say anything to her?" He said, "I don't want to hurt her feelings." He didn't think she knew she was doing anything wrong and felt that as her son, he shouldn't make her feel bad.

In addition, he knew she was not happy with his being gay, and so to protect her feelings, he never brought it up. At family gatherings he watched the others bring their significant others and talk about their relationships openly and honestly. But Frank, trying to be the good son, never brought up his loved ones, knowing his mother would disapprove and be hurt.

Starting from childhood, he'd decided to protect her, in his belief that she meant no harm and that he didn't want to upset her more than she already was. He was coming to realize, however, that his childhood decision to be obedient and follow her intrusive comments was no longer valid at age thirty-five.

I began to link the way he felt about his mother to his relationships. His first boyfriend was very similar to her in terms of his intrusiveness and disrespect toward Frank. It was easy for Frank to end that relationship at the time, since he was young and felt that cheating was a real deal breaker. But now he could see how he had chosen a partner very similar to his mother.

Frank had much regret about his second boyfriend and told me that if he had understood Imago then and known what he knew now, he might have been able to make the relationship work. He said he really loved this partner, and when the romance died down, there was no conflictual power struggle—but not much else, either. Frank could see that if only he could have expressed his needs, their relationship might have stood a chance. He began to realize that just as he couldn't express his needs and wants to his mother, he was unable to do so in his relationship. In fact, this was true throughout other areas of his life.

With his new boyfriend, Frank now felt he had found a really nice, decent gay man. In terms of his personality, Adam was nothing like Frank's mother and gave him his space. Frank found himself behaving toward Adam the same way he behaved with his mother—keeping his own needs buried and unspoken. Just to avoid hurting Adam, he'd stayed with him for a year longer than he would have otherwise. Just as he complied with his mother's wishes, now Frank was complying with what he thought Adam wanted and even thinking of spending another year with him, to avoid hurting "such a good person." We talked about how it was much more hurtful to pretend to want a relationship that he didn't want to be in, and how unfair that was to Adam, whom he was protecting exactly the way he protected his mother.

This really clicked when Frank saw these patterns. As uncomfortable as it would be to tell Adam that their relationship was over, he knew he had to do it. Ultimately, he did tell Adam, which he said was the hardest thing he'd ever done. Adam flew into a rage and began screaming and yelling at Frank, only to fall to the ground sobbing. Frank held Adam in his arms, and they talked most of the night.

Frank told me it would have been easier had Adam stayed angry over the breakup. Being vulnerable together was very hard, but Frank felt he'd showed integrity about being up-front and honest and by doing what was right for himself and Adam. After ending this relationship, his work became about standing up to his mother and stopping her inappropriate, unsolicited comments that were making him feel depressed. The good news was, she could and did curtail her comments to his sisters after they put up strong boundaries. He knew it was going to be very hard to go against this long-standing dynamic they had, but he knew he had to do it.

Invisible Divorce

Should you leave or not? This is a very hard decision to make, even if you aren't upset and angry with your partner. Before you actually leave, many ideas and events can arise. In his trainings, Terrence Real talks about the "invisible divorce," which doesn't involve physically leaving the relationship. He defines it as beginning to move away from a partner in stages. This can begin by moving into another bedroom to sleep, stopping the household chores you used do for him, no longer grocery shopping together and keeping separate shelves, planning separate trips with friends, and going to family gatherings by yourself. Real suggests that most often, women do such things to take a stand, as a way of waking up their husbands and show that they mean business.

Real hopes that such actions will save the marriage—and they can. Hopefully, starting an invisible divorce can save your relationship, but if not, at least you'll have done the prep work. Whether you're the one leaving or the one being left, distancing yourself from your partner can make the process easier.

But if you decide to divorce invisibly, be prepared for him to leave *you*. He may not tolerate it at all, so doing this means you must be prepared for a real breakup. To simply threaten to do this is not ideal. Initiating an invisible divorce should be done to protect your heart—your Lover archetype—and move you into a self-protective stance in a relationship that's grown adversarial.

Unfinished Business

Unresolved conflicts from childhood can affect your current relationships and interfere with getting and finding real love. But we also bring unresolved conflicts and material from past relationships. I've seen many couples argue over things that seemingly have nothing to do with either their current relationship or their childhood. But we find the material stored in their relationships with past partners. It's really like doing a search of computer files: often, you'll find data tucked away that you thought were either misfiled or deleted entirely.

Brad and Mark came to me because Mark's work involved weekly travel—which was starting to trouble Brad. They had been together three years. But after the second year, Brad started asking Mark if things were going okay between them and if Mark was preparing to leave him. Mark said he was tired of hearing this question repeated, sometimes as often as once a day, and that if Brad did not stop being so "needy," he *would* contemplate leaving. Brad had also begun accusing Mark of cheating on him, believing that Mark was visiting the baths and having hookups during his business trips. Mark told Brad, "You knew I traveled a lot as soon as we met. You didn't have a problem with it before. Why, all of a sudden, do you now?"

Brad didn't know why, but he was still convinced that Mark was being unfaithful—and did have a problem with it. Brad filled me in about his last relationship, which had lasted ten years. He had met his ex-partner, Jack, in college, when they were in their early twenties and fell in love. Once they both graduated from law school, they moved in together. Soon they began their careers and built a home. Brad said it was like a "boy meets boy" love story. He felt happy and connected, loved and cared for; everything was going well. Then, Brad reported, "Out of the blue, Jack announced he found someone else and was leaving me." Within one week, Jack had moved in with his new partner and never looked back.

While telling this story, Brad started crying—which bothered Mark. "You're not over him are you?" he asked. Brad replied that he was in fact over him—their breakup had occurred five years earlier—but the pain was still there. Brad and Jack were friendly now, but not friends.

Usually there are signs and indications that a breakup is coming. We explored why Brad felt it was "out of the blue" for Jack to come home and tell him this, but Brad said he had no idea. This would explain why Brad was so concerned whether things were okay with Mark, since he couldn't tell when his relationship with Jack went sour.

After their breakup, Brad told me, he went into a deep depression that lasted two years. During those years, he went on medication. He drank heavily, did some drugs and sexually acted out—things he had never done in any abusive way before. During that time, he received a DUI ticket and an HIV scare as well. He even contemplated suicide, which he'd never thought about before. Actually, this is not uncommon: most people who experience depression have suicidal thoughts as a result of their mood state. His parents and good friends were supportive during this time, and he even saw a therapist who helped him get through it.

It caught my attention that Brad wouldn't have seen a breakup coming—and even looking back, he was unable to see the signs. He came from a healthy, loving family. His stay-at-home mother loved her two children and participated in their everyday lives, came to school functions, and enjoyed being with them during summer vacations. His father taught his sons how to fish and golf and Brad was also close to his larger extended family of aunts, uncles, and cousins. His parents argued periodically, but would make up in front of the children and move forward. His parents were still together and happily married.

But I discovered something I've seen over the years in other clients and some friends. Brad came from a nurturing home with few problems, where the family was healthy enough to work them out. While Brad was fortunate to enjoy a privileged childhood with nothing abusive, neglectful, or negative coming his way, he did miss out on learning how to cope when things get messy. Brad was not prepared for this.

I explained to Brad and Mark about how Brad was blindsided by Jack's quick departure from their relationship and lacked the skills for dealing with it. Even though he had friends and family by his side during the breakup, he'd never even witnessed things going awry in his family. That explained Brad's falling apart and acting out after the breakup. This interpretation made a lot of sense to Brad.

Now Brad was projecting his broken relationship with Jack onto Mark. Unconsciously, he worried that again he would be blindsided and not know how to deal with it. Brad's very high reactivity drove him to compulsively ask Mark if everything was okay, looking to Mark to soothe him because he didn't know how to calm himself.

Although he'd gone through depression and into therapy after the breakup, Brad never learned how to cope with dysfunction for the future. Now his work was learning to arm himself for any breakdowns, breakups, losses, or other future troubles he might encounter and how to reassure himself, rather than trying to get Mark to do it for him.

Many clients like Brad report having come from excellent households with loving mothers and fathers—almost privileged childhoods. So when dysfunctional messes occur in their adult lives, they're not prepared. Most people would rather have come from a functional home with healthy parents, but if you're not taught the skills to prepare for hardships in life, then you'll have a harder time dealing with any breakup. Those who come from dysfunctional homes have skills to adapt to and handle problematic situations, even if in negative ways.

Their couples work centered on Mark not taking things so personally and recognizing and feeling compassion for Brad's not having fully recovered from the breakup. Brad indeed was over Jack, but he was a sitting duck for something negative to happen, not knowing how to protect himself against future issues he might encounter. Even with this information, Mark still was not willing to hear any more of Brad's insecurities. He was convinced that Brad still had feelings for Jack. Mark continued to take this very personally and decided to end the relationship.

For Brad and Mark, things did not work out well, but they can for other couples if both partners are willing to do the work and begin therapy sooner rather than later. Mark was unwilling to look at his own issues in the relationship with Brad, which caused him to end things rather than stay with his partner.

Break Up to Make Up

Recall from chapter 3 that when people fall in love, a biological process is going on in addition to the psychological one. Chemicals such as phenylethalimine, dopamine, norepinephrine, and serotonin make falling in love feel so sweet and delicious that most of us try our hardest not to let it go. And when it leaves, we try our hardest to get it back.

I see couples trying to get it back through a cycle of breaking up and making up. Unconsciously, they try to end the power struggle—the Call of the Child (see chapter 3)-and recapture that early euphoria of romantic love. Trying to recapture some of those early feelings is appropriate, and when you're in the final stage of real love, you can do things to bring them back. But breaking up and making up again only sets the stage for a final, inevitable breakup. At a conference I attended, Helen Fisher, author of *Anatomy of Love* and *Why We Love,* cited a recent study that found 40 percent of people who'd been dumped by their partner in the previous eight weeks experienced clinical depression and 12 percent, severe depression.[3] It thus makes biological sense for couples to reunite in order to move out of their depression.

Breaking up and making up can also be a way of postponing the relationship's inevitable termination. Protest against their emotional pain and depression could be the very reason one or both partners find themselves cycling in this turbulent pattern. "The despair of unrequited love," Fisher writes, "is most likely associated with plummeting levels of dopamine."[4] Getting back together raises those sweet biochemicals, making you feel attached and good again; but it is a chain reaction based on drugs, not on real love.

Some partners are not meant for each other and are truly not an imago match. Yet the beginnings of romantic love can feel so authentic that, like addicts enjoying their first high, the partners try to recreate their first hit of PEA but never achieve it because they don't have what it takes to move to real love. So the breaking up and making up keeps them together and keeps their dream—and nightmare—going. They live for the making up, which brings on all the biochemicals of romantic love and the strong sexual feelings as well.

Ending the Call of the Child

As mentioned in chapter 3, many end their relationships during the power struggle because they are in such emotional turmoil that they don't see any other way out of the pain. We're not born with relationship skills; no one teaches us how to navigate through relationships. We all have to learn how on our own. If you were lucky, you enjoyed a childhood where most relationships were loving and where conflicts, whenever they surfaced, were worked through effectively and resolved. But for most people, this is not the case. Most of us don't learn how to get through relationships effectively, especially not during the hard times. After the romantic stage, nature abandons us and we find ourselves without a rule book. So people develop exits that either diminish intimacy or potentially end their relationships.

Exit: Stage Left

As defined in *Getting the Love You Want,* "exits" in relationships are simply feelings being expressed through acting out.[4] Sometimes they're signs that you're ready to end the relationship. Other times they're a warning signal that things in the relationship aren't going well and need your attention. Exits are feelings getting expressed outside the relationship. If you can't express anger toward your partner, then you'll act it out away from him, or sideways through being passive-aggressive. Doing this doesn't mean you're a bad person, it simply means that you're frightened.

Your goal is to know what your own personal exits are in relationships and what they're trying to tell you. It's too easy to look at your partner's exits and blame him for what he's doing. That isn't effective, nor does it improve your relationship. It is important that you realize that you're not expected to stop all these exits right now—during or after reading this book. But you must begin to determine what you're going to do about this energetic leak, even if it means going to seek help or talking to a friend to find whatever these thoughts and behaviors are covering. For many, it's unrealistic to close their exits right away, since exits are a part of a defense structure that we all need and should continue to function until we learn new ways to embrace intimacy.

I do, however, advise ending any affairs. With someone else in the picture, your relationship doesn't stand a chance, especially if you're not interested in letting him go for the sake of a better relationship with your partner.

Exits leak the energy out of a relationship. Either start closing them, or open a conversation with your partner or therapist about doing so. Often we were raised in families where differences weren't tolerated or permitted. Depending on how open or closed your family was will shape how much you can tolerate differences in your relationships. Also, many have suffered early childhood experiences that were so abusive and traumatic that it's frightening to go back there emotionally. So they do everything they can to avoid relationships, or else keep a distance between themselves and their partners. Creating exits in their relationships lets them tolerate the frightening closeness. Their Adult says, "I'm in an ideal relationship! There's nothing to be afraid of." But on the emotional side, the old brain says, "This feels just like childhood all over again, and I think I'm in danger."

Imago Relationship Therapy identifies four types of exits: *terminal, catastrophic, functional,* and *intentional.* The motivation behind the exiting behavior determines the functional-intentional nature of the exit. For example, some partners exit from relationships through volunteering, working out at the gym, shopping, focusing more exclusively on children, pets, or work, housework and remodeling, travel, and socializing with friends. These individual things in and of themselves are not problematic. The problem is when they're excessive and preferred over spending time with your partner.

In a relationship, the core energy between both partners brings them closer and closer to each other. Then the power struggle begins; embedded with childhood memories, the struggle makes closeness to your partner scary, so that one or both may create little exits to provide "breathing room," if not a complete escape.

Three *terminal* exits discussed in IRT are divorce, domestic violence (including murder and abuse), and suicide (including poor self-care or lack thereof). Any of these three will destroy your relationship. Talking about them can make people very anxious, but if left open, they need to be addressed immediately. It doesn't mean you're a bad person—it means you need help. If you want to save your relationship—and yourself—you need assistance, and if you're reading this book, then odds are you *do* want help.

If you or your partner are unwillingness to close these exits immediately, it is crucial that you contact a psychotherapist, your doctor, a crisis hotline, or someone close to you. This is true whether you are the one abusing your partner, or you are not taking care of yourself, or you are with a partner engaging in this behavior. You should never have to accept behavior that involves these three terminal exits. They can either lead to the death of one or both of you— but surely to the death of your relationship.

It's important to know that many people enter relationships with these exits already developed from past relationships or childhood experiences. These exits do not always stem from the current partnership but continue on, ready for use. The presence of these terminal exits simply means that your relationship is in serious trouble and immediate help is needed to close them.

Catastrophic exits—addictions, affairs, and insanity—won't completely destroy the relationship, but will keep you from moving on to growth and healing, because partners won't feel safe enough in their relationship to drop their defenses. With addictions, it feels a whole lot safer and easier to turn to a bottle, sex, gambling, or drugs than to face your partner. Rather than *talk* out difficult things, it's a whole lot easier to go and act out. Again, this behavior may have begun before the relationship, but it has been brought into the partnership. Affairs are catastrophic exits too; how can any relationship in a power struggle compete with the romantic love of an affair, which always makes the existing relationship seem pale? Insanity simply refers to putting yourself into treatment to avoid the relationship—identifying yourself as sick, or repeatedly saying "I can't stand it anymore" after every argument but never leaving. Insanity is also doing the same thing over and over and expecting different results.

Intentional exits are known to you—you know you're purposely using them to avoid conflict and controversy in your relationship, so they're a conscious choice. They might include masturbating to porn or surfing the Internet to avoid being sexual with a partner, turning to friends rather than your partner for emotional support, talking to others about your relationship problems, and purposely *not* talking to your partner.

Functional exits are those you don't even know about. The only way you have a clue is when your partner complains about them. Anything has the potential to become a functional exit. A few examples include working long hours, volunteering, surfing the Internet, shopping, activism, hobbies and sports, watching TV, exercising pets, reading, and anything else that takes you away from the relationship. The rule of thumb here is to ask yourself, "Is this interfering in my relationship?" Determine whether you are doing it intentionally or unconsciously to avoid issues between you and your partner. This is where it's important to listen to your partner's frustrations and complaints about your behavior to assess if he's describing functional exits.

It's important to understand that you're not expected to stop all these catastrophic exits immediately, and if you don't or can't there's nothing wrong with you. It's unrealistic to close them too quickly, since many are part of a defense structure we all need and will function until you learn new ways to embrace intimacy. But start looking at what you're doing. Is it a leak or exit? And what are you going to do about it? Seek help, talk to a friend, and begin finding the language that these thoughts and behaviors are covering.

When I started my own private psychotherapy practice, it took a lot of time and energy away from my partner, Mike. I was doing one or two weekend workshops a month, evening hours with clients and groups, and giving talks and lectures around my local area. Mike would ask me, "Another weekend workshop, Joe?" or "Do you have to work late every night?"

I would have strong negative reactions and tell him things like, "The gay community needs these services," or "I have to be this busy to stay in private practice." There was some truth to that, but the reality was that I was gone too much and Mike was missing me.

I grew up in a family where I felt engulfed and enmeshed, where individuality wasn't condoned and I felt my identity being smothered. Here in my profession, I found an identity. Being in demand by clients and other therapists wanting to learn about gay-affirmative psychotherapy grabbed most of my attention. I was using it as an exit because at an unconscious level Mike's requests for me to be home made me feel engulfed, like my identity would get smothered all over again. Logically, I knew that wasn't true, but for me, closing that exit by working less and doing fewer workshops felt like death. That is how many people feel about closing their exits. For them, it's the hardest—but the most important—thing to do.

I have to admit that as much as I was gone, I was lucky to have a partner to stick it out. Many other guys would have left me.

People get very nervous about the idea of a decision to close exits. Any no-exit decision should really be a no-exit *conversation* with your partner about your relationship and this process. Using the Intentional Dialogue and the clearing exercises outlined in chapter 6 is an excellent way to spark these conversations. In doing these things, you can hope for greater generosity, pleasure and passion, commitment and empathy.

I want to stress the importance of ending affairs. Your relationship can't stand a chance if someone else is in the picture and you're not willing to let him go for the sake of a better relationship with your partner.

There are many types of relationship exiters, as will be described further; you—or your partner—might even be one of them. Either of you can have any of these exits without being a bad person, but they can mean your relationship is moving toward termination.

The Terminator is the partner who constantly threatens to leave or regularly ends the relationship. Whenever things get difficult or go wrong or conflict rises in the relationship, he immediately says, "I'm out of here! If this is how things are going to be, I don't want to stay!" He's constantly threatening or moving toward the exit to seek relief from the conflicts surfacing in the relationship.

The Terminator's problem is that he erodes emotional safety in the relationship. If one or both partners are constantly discussing an ending, then how can either one move toward more intimacy when their relationship feels unsafe? I teach partners to stop talking about ending their relationship. This may sound simple enough, but when they get into their reactive old brains and their shadows come out, the only relief they can seem to find is in calling it quits.

The Catastrophizer creates and contributes to a lot of drama in the relationship, never allowing things to slide or a problem to work itself out. Often, this individual lives with a large burden of depression. He tends to engage in addictions, possibly flirts with others, and may even have an affair he isn't telling his partner about. All of these behaviors can cause chaos and histrionics within a relationship, which in turn creates distance. While good relationships can tolerate a lot of chaos (and in some cases, chaos is the actual bond that holds partners together), most cannot handle it, and at some point it's a certain deal breaker.

The Mind Reader is sure about what's going on in his partner's head. No amount of logic or facts will convince him otherwise. This is very much like Raul and Art, the couple in chapter 3: nothing could dissuade Raul from his fixed beliefs about what was going through Art's mind. Luckily, he was able to finally break through his fixed delusion.

The Historian won't—or can't—let go of the past. No matter how much progress he makes in his relationship with his partner, inevitably he brings up past sins, wounds, and arguments. His attention to detail is too good to let him forget. No matter what therapy intervenes or how successfully his partner tries to change, he doesn't appreciate it and keeps bringing up issues that were resolved long ago.

The Preacher says, "In a relationship, a partner should _____."

He tells his partner what marriages, relationships, and partnerships should be like. It's as if he's referring to a book somewhere, and in fact, he really is. The book is inside his head, and whenever he hears a different belief that demands symbiosis, he grows condescending.

Equal Opportunity

In my IRT training, master trainer Bruce Crapuchettes taught me something invaluable that any couple can apply. He points out that couples who partner with each other are usually of the same intelligence, carry the same developmental wounds from childhood, and have *equal* investment in how intimate and close their relationship will get. I have seen exactly what Crapuchettes is saying when I sit with couples, gay or straight, and would expand same intelligence to include *emotional intelligence.*

Developmental wounding refers to psychologist Erik Erikson's widely accepted eight-stage model of psychosocial developmental. Erikson (1902–1994) has been called the father of psychosocial development and the "architect of identity" in the field of psychology. When Crapuchettes says couples find themselves at equal stages of wounding, he means that if one partner is struggling with an unresolved stage from childhood, his partner is most likely stuck in that very same stage.

Erikson's eight stages are attachment, exploration, identity, competence, concern for others, intimacy (sexual and romantic), responsibility, and generativity. Unresolved, these stages cause you to be unsuccessful in making and keeping relationships, or they can promote exits and breakups that block you and your partner's ability to find real love.

As you read this list, keep in mind that *both* partners are equally wounded in the same stage, but that each one often manifests the wounding differently.

1. *Attachment-wounded couples* have difficulty with trust, which can manifest by partners being either too trusting or mistrustful. With these couples, emotional security is weak or nonexistent.

2. *Exploration-wounded* couples have trouble with autonomy and

letting each other explore the environment outside and inside the relationship. They may struggle with independence, doubt both themselves and each other, and shame or try to control each other. This is where you find domestic violence and abuse issues of power and control between partners.

3. *Identity-wounded* couples have trouble with themselves both as individuals and as a couple. This stage is about becoming someone and developing your own sense of self. If, as gay boys, we were drawn to opposite-gender toys or to other boys, we were stopped from exploring our true identities. As a result, partners wounded at this stage may either surrender their identity to their partner or take over the other man's identity, shaming him for who he is.

4. *Competence-wounded* couples are competitive: the partners vie with each other over who makes more money, or has the better job and the most friends; they try to show off to each other. Or it can go the other way, where one partner feels and acts incompetent, or else treats the other as though he were inferior.

5. *Concern-wounded* couples show too much concern and regard for each other—or too little. When we get wounded as gay boys, we're taught not to have concern for other boys, so imagine what we're up against in trying to develop genuine concern for a partner!

6. *Intimacy-wounded* couples have too many exits to commit to a partner. Either they fear commitment or display strong dependency needs that no partner could ever fulfill. Regardless of the families we are raised in, this developmental task is tackled from ages twelve to nineteen, when teenagers are developing dating skills with one another. Chapter 1 illustrates how traumatic this is for us in a heterocentric, homo-ignorant society.

7. *Responsibility-wounded* couples can't maintain the inner workings of their relationship. Here is where I see partners not accountable to one another. They cheat, doing and saying things behind each other's backs—or even blatantly in front of one another—never accepting responsibility for their own actions and always blaming their partner's "irresponsibility." They don't create norms, boundaries, or guidelines for each other's behaviors to protect the relationship.

8. *Generativity-wounded* couples are closed and isolated, unable to look outside themselves and care for others outside their relationship. They might not give back to their community—the gay community or other couples who need role models—and aren't able to open their relationships to others, socially or emotionally.

Each partner is invested equally in the relationship. The partner who protests that he wants more intimacy and more closeness in the relationship is just as invested in the existing distance as the partner whose behavior is creating it. Often, both contribute equally to how intimate they become with one another. To varying degrees, common to most couples is the pursuer-distancer dance: one partner pursues the other for contact and close connection, while the other distances himself, out of his own protest and fear of engulfment in an effort to keep his individuality. When the distancer is finally ready for closeness, he stops distancing, only to find the pursuer now distancing himself. Now their roles become reversed. Believe it or not, this is the normal course of most relationships.

Most people are unconscious of their own particular contributions to their own pursuer-distancer dance. The answer is for couples to understand what this means for them individually, so they can lessen how far they go in pursuing and distancing.

Affairs of the Heart

While you are having an affair, your relationship doesn't stand a chance of improvement. I'm not talking about responsible non-monogamy, where you and your partner have agreed to outside sexual relationships, even involving emotions. But as we saw in chapter 3, you risk finding the new relationship more intriguing because of the love drugs being released that tempt you to leave the old one. Being in the romantic stage, the new relationship will always win out, since there is no power struggle going on.

If an affair is going on in the relationship, both partners are usually contributing to it. In other words, the partner who feels victimized is just as invested in the affair as the one who's having it.

If *you* feel victimized by your partner having an affair, reading this may make you angry. An affair, however, is commonly a result of relationship problems that already exist within a relationship—symptomatic of problems between you and your partner. And *both* of you contribute to the problems. The partner who engages in the affair is absolutely responsible for acting on his feelings through his behavior. But he's not alone in whatever trouble has already occurred in the relationship.

In other words, the protesting partner is just as invested in the affair as the one cheating—not that he wants the affair to be happening or even knows it's going on. If you reread this last sentence and change the word *affair* to *exit* or *distance,* what I am saying might make more sense.

More and more information is surfacing about affairs in relationships. The field of psychotherapy now widely accepts that both partners are equally invested in the development of the symptom—in this case, an affair—to keep their relationship from getting too close and too attached.

Dealing with Being Dumped

Remember, being in a relationship is a regressive experience. Particularly in conflict and stress, you will go into your old brain and feel young and small. Being told by your partner that he no longer loves you and is leaving you is like a child hearing his parents tell him that he's not lovable and they're giving him away. That would be the worst news to hear, and you would feel endangered, abandoned, and panicky. This is what many people go through when they are told their partner is leaving.

If your partner has made up his mind to leave, there's not much you can do to try to get him to stay—particularly if another person is involved. Often, when a man is in the romantic stage of new love with someone else, your own power struggle stage cannot compete.

Sometimes in the power struggle, a partner can't get past his own issues. No matter how much you try to work through the conflict, or even attend couples therapy, sometimes a partner will bump into an issue from his past that he cannot resolve. The past may be riddled with too much abuse or emotional toxicity for him to examine or work on, thus interfering with your relationship to the point where it has to end.

This was the case with Mason and Dave, who had been together eight years in Los Angeles. After hearing about my work with couples, Mason called asking to see me, explaining that Dave complained of his being a "slob" and a "procrastinator." For years, Mason had been trying to give Dave what he wanted: a clean, orderly house and a structured schedule that he rarely modified. Dave was getting fed up trying to get Mason to comply with what he saw as "simple and realistic needs"-which Dave felt that Mason wasn't able to meet successfully. They flew to Michigan to do some intensive work with me, as I sometimes do with couples.

Mason cried throughout our first session, stating that he didn't know what more he could do. There really wasn't much more he could do. Early on, it became obvious that the underlying issue was Dave's.

For the past ten years, Dave had been a company accountant, work that he performed efficiently and successfully and enjoyed very much. The company fit completely into his lifestyle and he enjoyed the predictability and stability, coming to work and leaving at the same times every day. Mason, though, was an actor at heart and full-time waiter. He had acting jobs on the side, but nothing steady and couldn't get anything on a full-time basis. This frustrated Dave very much. He'd had enough and wanted Mason to become more organized, keep better care of the house, finish things he started, and get a steady full-time job.

Actually, Mason had improved a great deal. He realized his problem was related to Attention Deficit Disorder (ADD) and went on medication, which helped him greatly. Now he was finishing most of the household tasks he started, and making very good money as a waiter at a five-star restaurant. Dave's complaints about Mason had been legitimate at the start, but they were no longer true.

What puzzled me most was why Dave would pick a man like Mason in the first place. From the beginning, he knew how disorganized Mason was. Dave said he recalled going to Mason's house and seeing projects unfinished, back when Mason was a low-paid waiter at a diner and looking for acting jobs on the side. But even though all that had changed, Dave's complaints were the same.

As I began introducing various communication tools and educating the couple about IRT, it became clear that Dave wasn't invested in holding their relationship together. Within the first two hours of the intensive session, in fact, he said he wanted to break it off. Mason was devastated. Although he'd seen this coming, he'd hoped that coming to me might avert it.

Dave felt that Mason really was not trying. I asked him for his judgments about Mason, as I do in working with couples—this tells me a lot about the partner who's doing the judging and can be a window into him and his past. Dave thought Mason was a lazy, unambitious guy doing nothing but chasing pipe dreams of becoming an actor. I asked Dave what had attracted him to Mason in the first place. He said he thought that Mason was going through a stage that he would eventually outgrow, but never did.

"But eight years is a long time to wait for change," I told Dave. "And Mason has changed, getting help for his ADD, becoming more organized, and getting a job in a higher-paying restaurant." To that, Dave said that he didn't believe it would last long. Dave couldn't see that he had a pattern of upping the ante, no matter what Mason did. The more he talked about how incompetent Mason was, the more Mason got angry and wept.

Whenever I see that one partner can't believe what the other is saying about him and loudly protests that what he's saying is untrue, I get suspicious that these complaints are really about the judging partner. This very thing was happening between Dave and Mason. It was also obvious that Mason had made the changes and wanted to please him. Mason even said how much it had helped him that Dave had asked him to change his behavior. But Dave wasn't impressed.

Reading this, you might be thinking that Dave was a pretentious, mean guy, not invested in this relationship, and that Mason would be better off with someone else. Those thoughts went through my mind too, but there was more to their story.

Dave came from a family where both his father and mother made lots of money and raised him and his brother in a very expensive neighborhood in California. His father became addicted to cocaine and lost everything when Dave was ten years old. The family moved from an expensive large home to a trailer park, where Dave spent the rest of his teenage years. His father went into a deep depression and stopped working, and his mother had to go out and support the family. She was untrained in any profession, so she worked at a grocery store trying to make ends meet. His father developed various medical ailments and never worked again. Dave made every effort he could to help his father and get him treatment, to no avail. He had never forgiven the man for letting him down.

So it was clear—at least to Mason and me—that Dave had a strong father projection on Mason. This explained why he was drawn to Mason in the first place. His imago directed him to search for a partner who stood in for his father with whom he had unresolved issues. His psyche returned to the scene of the crime in an attempt to solve it, until he met Mason, who was willing to listen to him and comply with his wishes.

Under normal conditions, this would have been healing for Dave. But no amount of therapy or logical reasoning was going to let him get past his projection. Dave himself said that even if this were true, he could not see Mason in any hopeful light and wanted out of their relationship. He was unwilling to work on his family issues and resolve and heal what happened to him. He could never forgive his father or let him off the hook for what he did, so instead of doing his father work, he chose to end his relationship with Mason. He wasn't interested in doing the additional work it would take. Instead, he used the remainder of the time they had in the intensive session to begin the good-bye process.

What Becomes of the Brokenhearted?

Depression is most common after undergoing any loss. It's understandable and to be expected. Even if the breakup makes logical sense and even if it was your decision, it will bring on various forms of depression for which you should be on the alert.

Of the three basic types of depression, one is an adjustment to the reality of actually breaking up. It can last approximately six to eighteen months—longer for some, shorter for others—during which time the depression may interfere with your life. Symptoms include sadness, moodiness, more irritability than usual, tearfulness, low energy and self-esteem, fatigue, poor concentration, difficulty in making decisions, being disoriented at times, and feelings of helplessness and hopelessness. Many try to handle these symptoms on their own and are able to successfully. But if any of these symptoms are interfering with your life in any way—keeping you from working at your job, for example, or taking care of yourself and your dependents—then you should seek a psychotherapist's or psychiatrist's help immediately. Losing your job or compromising your life in other areas will only make things worse.

"Vegetative" symptoms such as poor appetite or overeating, with weight gain or weight loss, insomnia or too much sleep could indicate that your depression is worsening, in which case you should definitely seek help. And finally, if violent thoughts of suicide and/or homicide enter your mind, this means that your depression has worsened and if left untreated, you might act on these feelings. Even if not, you have moved to a major depression, which can manifest by lack of self-care: letting go of grooming, hygiene, and housework, and basically isolating yourself.

By the time they come to therapy, most people are living with middle-of-the-road depression called dysthymia. It is no longer an adjustment to any sad event, nor does it worsen the major depressive stage. What may have begun after a breakup has now turned into a lifestyle. Typically, the depressed person has been living that way for at least two years.

No wonder, then, that people will do anything to avoid breaking up. No one wants to enter into a depression and upset his or her life, particularly not when children, money, housing, and businesses are involved, and where breaking up is apt to create chaos.

Physical Health

Studies also show that during a breakup, your mental as well as your physical health are compromised. People going through a breakup report not sleeping well or eating right, which contributes to various medical problems.

Some symptoms to expect are sleeplessness, nausea, headache, diarrhea, tight chest, or panic attacks with shortness of breath. You might gain or lose twenty to thirty pounds, even if you overeat or don't eat enough. People report getting the flu or cold symptoms when they never had them before. Seeing a doctor during this time is imperative, as is taking good care of your health, anticipating that your body will be vulnerable during this time.

When going through a breakup, be very careful about using sex to comfort yourself. This can be a great distraction, but many I have counseled feel so upset and bad about themselves that they put themselves at risk for HIV, thinking, "Who cares about my life right now? It is over." That is distorted, depressed thinking. If you even think that you'll put yourself at risk for any STDs or hook up with someone who's not in your best interest, then I recommend avoiding the whole thing until you're feeling better.

Good Grief

When there is a loss, grieving is something that everyone needs to go through. Breaking up will cause its stages to begin, and again you should know what they are. Crying tears should be *cleansing*, moving you toward acceptance and even forgiveness. I see many people spending a great deal of time and energy suppressing sadness and tears and staying in their anger, but they only prolong their grieving process and sometimes never get through it.

Elizabeth Kübler-Ross identified the stages of grief as shock-denial, bargaining, anger, depression, and finally, acceptance. Kübler-Ross believed that while these stages did not have to come in order, everyone needs to go through them to attain acceptance. These stages are the widely used standard for getting through any major loss in life.

One way to get through this with greater ease is to remove all reminders of your ex for a period of time. This means taking his number off your cell phone and putting away all letters and cards from him, along with his photos. If you want to throw them out, that's up to you, but you might regret it later. So for the time being, I recommend boxing them up and storing them in the attic or basement, where they are out of the way.

Avoid phone calls with him if you can. If he still chooses to call and there are no children or financial issues to deal with, I recommend you tell him you don't want contact right now, and that *you* will reinitiate contact when *you* are ready. This puts you in control, instead of feeling overwhelmed and powerless.

If you see him, remove yourself from the situation if you can. This is not about fearing him or running from him. As Fisher writes, "Even the briefest contact with 'him' or 'her' can fire up your brain circuits for romantic ardor. If you wish to recover, you must expunge all traces of the thief who stole your heart."

Remember to eat and force yourself to move physically. Exercise can help work out depression. Remember Fisher's research on what goes on chemically when we fall in love? Well, chemically, things also happen when you go through a breakup.

To soothe the pain, you want to avoid alcohol and any drugs not prescribed by a physician. Most do not know that alcohol is actually a depressant and gives temporary relief but will only make your mood worse. If your depression is at a certain level and you drink, you will feel better periodically, but then your depression will return at a worse level than before.

Physical exercise is the best reported way to deal with the depression of loss. Go walking, running, jogging, biking, swimming, do aerobics—anything you can to keep your dopamine levels up and not let them go down, which is what is at risk while going through a depression.

Distractions and staying busy can keep you from feeling overwhelmed and get your mind off the loss. Get involved in something fun and exciting, perhaps some adventure that you have not undertaken before that can lend hopes for your future.

But avoid getting so busy that you *avoid* feeling your loss. Give yourself permission to mourn the death of your relationship. Blocking it off makes it worse and will put it into shadow. Call a friend and talk about it, go to your spiritual counselor, your therapist, or a relative. Allow yourself to emote and be sad, scream, cry, laugh uncontrollably, rage, and to "fall apart." These are ways in which you heal.

Good-bye Process

Here is the process that I recommend you do for yourself when you're ready. First use it as an outline to write out. Perhaps do it a few times this way, then consider doing it with your ex, if you are up for it and he's agreeable. Bring it to your therapy sessions, your group, wherever you feel safest to do this process and get it out of you.

Here is how to do the process in its purest form. If you do this, I recommend that you be coached by a therapist, a life coach, or spiritual mentor.

Imago's Good-bye Process

1. **Stand-in Ex:** "Tell me what it has been like to be/live with me."
    Sender tells the overview of what it has been like.
2. **Stand-in Ex:** "Tell me about the difficult and negative things and say good-bye to them."
    Sender tells specific events and memories and says good-bye to each one.
3. **Stand-in Ex:** "Tell me about the good things and say good-bye to them."
    Sender tells specific events and memories and says good-bye to each one.
4. **Stand-in Ex:** "Tell me about the hopes and dreams and say good-bye to each one of them."
    Sender tells specific hopes and dreams and says good-bye to each one.
5. **Stand-in Ex:** "Say good-bye to me."
    Sender says good-bye.
6. **Sender to Stand-in Ex:** "I release you [name of ex-partner] and begin to move into my future."

I have actually done this process a number of times with partners who are ending their relationships, and I can assure you that there wasn't a dry eye in my office—including mine. No one enjoys doing this. It's in good-byes, however, that you can discover the welcomings and literally move into your future.

The Ex Files

To learn a lot about the type of guy you partner with and date, make a list of all of your exes. Your list should include those men to whom you felt most attached, whether or not they were attracted to you in return. That you held strong feelings for them is a telltale sign about you, not them.

I recognize that there are some gay men who may never have been in any committed relationship long enough to call another individual "my ex." That matters less than the types of guys you formed crushes on, even if they were just friends or men you wish you could have partnered with but didn't. By using these men, this exercise can work for you as well.

Once you have listed the men you were attracted to, write down the qualities of each. Make sure you list each one's positive and negative traits from your point of view. Then make a list of all the things they said frustrated them about you. Yes, you! If they didn't say what bothered them in so many words, what do you feel may have annoyed them, based on their words or actions?

It's important for you to address your contribution to the drama in any of your relationships. Performing this necessary step, you can learn what you were doing and not bring it forward into your next relationship.

Homo-Work on Breaking Up

1. Make a list of all of your exits. Which can you close today? Which can't you close today?

2. To whom can you go to have a conversation about the exits you cannot close today?

3. While you were growing up, how did your family deal with good-byes?

4. Write a list of all the negatives about your last partner and say good-bye to each one of them.

5. Write a list of all the positives about that relationship and say good-bye to each one of them, too.

6. Write out the dream of being with your ex that will never be and say

good-bye to it.

References

1. Portia Nelson, *There's a Hole in My Sidewalk* (Hillsboro, OR: Beyond Words, 1993).
2. Debbie Ford, *Spiritual Divorce: Divorce as a Catalyst for an Extraordinary Life* (New York: HarperCollins, 2001).
3. Helen Fisher, *Anatomy of Love: A Natural History of Mating, Marriage and Why We Stray* (New York: Ballantine Books, 1994).
4. Helen Fisher, *Why We Love* (New York: Henry Holt, 2004).
5. Harville Hendrix, *Getting the Love You Want: A Guide for Couples* (New York: Owl Books, 2001).

Chapter 10
Bring Your Own Shadow

A man cannot be comfortable without his own approval.

—Mark Twain

If you've made it this far in the book, you've come to understand the trauma you suffered while growing up gay with no sense of belonging and how male patriarchal society punished you for not becoming the type of man it wanted you to be. You've learned about the stages of love, forcing you to examine your past childhood and past relationships—perhaps too closely for comfort! And you probably thought your hassles with Mom and Dad were over with, but you suddenly find that the route to real love makes you revisit them all over again.

All of that work involved in communication might sound too hard, mechanical, and contrived. Even worse, perhaps you've discovered that all your efforts at achieving real love have resulted in you or your partner wanting to break it off. You realize that while enjoying the sexual life you both have, a relationship's going to force you to examine your sexual shadows—and you don't want to visit those dark places. On top of it all, you may fall in love with a married guy who can't or won't leave his wife. Or perhaps you yourself are heterosexually married and now seeking to live as a gay man. Did you come out for this?

At the close of one of my singles workshops, a participant approached me to say "Joe Kort, I want to thank you for a very educational class. It really helped me, because I've been so undecided about what to do to find Mr. Right."

I thanked him and, now that he was armed with the tools he needed, wished him luck on his search for a relationship.

"Oh, no," he replied. "I want to thank you for teaching me that given everything involved in making a relationship work, it is totally not worth the trouble! My overnights and short-term situations are more fun." And he meant it!

I laughed and gave him credit for knowing what he did—and didn't—want. If you can relate to him, or have decided that relationships just aren't for you, then read on.

B.Y.O.S. (Bring Your Own Shadow)

You have a shadow, whether you're partnered or not. It's important to understand that it's always at least two steps ahead of you. It is unconscious and has information for you, but if you choose to stay single, make sure you do the work so you can learn from your shadow on your own by asking for help from friends and family.

If you say you want to remain single, has your shadow made that choice for you? Is something dark in your past haunting you, preventing you from making the commitment you might make otherwise? Some people feel that any new relationship brings up too much from their early childhood that they just don't want to face. Others vow to stay single after ending a nasty LTR in adulthood. If you are fine with these motives for being single and you've consciously chosen them, then do what feels right for you. If you continually question the reasons you've chosen to be single, however ("Maybe I'd feel differently if . . ."), and don't know how to do the work to "unplug" them, I'd recommend you read other self-help books. Find a therapist to help you resolve any trauma and negativity that prevent your natural desire to be in a relationship and enjoy real love.

Still, your homophobic shadow might give you a reason to stay single. For a gay man, it's simply easier. As a partnered gay man, going to the office and social events involves worries about whether to bring your partner along or concerns as to whether he was even invited. Going home to family gatherings involves a struggle—"Should I or shouldn't I take my partner home with me?"—depending on how they accept your being gay.

What if you get invited to parties, weddings, and bar mitzvahs and your partner isn't included on the invitation? You must decide whether you're going to make an issue of this and confront your hosts, or attend the event alone. If someone asks if you're married or dating, you have to decide if you'll be honest and, if so, how honest you will be. If struggling with internalized homophobia makes you not want to face these issues—consciously or unconsciously—you'll avoid partnering, and your motives will allow homophobes and heterosexists their victory.[1]

You need to check for yourself and to ensure that that is not the reason for being single. What a shame to let internalized homophobia and heterosexism rule your relational life.

If you're not in a committed relationship by conscious choice and still believe in your shadow's importance, then you must be willing to become more conscious of it and track it in your other interpersonal relations. Your shadow manifests in intense, powerful reactions, usually accompanied by strong feelings of self-righteousness and justifications for how you feel. You don't need a partner to bring you to this point. Shadow work is easily accessible once you get the hang of it, and you can track it yourself without anyone else to point it out. You know when you are having an intense positive or negative reaction to someone. If the opportunity arises to work it through with that person, I recommend you do so; otherwise, the experience might provide more growth but not true healing.

AFGO (Another Freaking Growth Opportunity)

If you choose to be single, you'll have to watch for your own shadows and growth opportunities, because you won't have a partner to point them out. Even while you're partnered, you should do this as well, since it provides information about you that would otherwise go unnoticed. A while back, a local paper invited me to be part of an Op-Ed column for discussing the pros and cons of a famous radio talk-show host. I dislike her very much for being arrogant and judgmental, with no respect for others' opinions, so I jumped at the chance to write the column.

The day my article was published, I faxed it to her several times, since she reads on the air excerpts from articles published about her. Her show came and went, but she never read it. Two years later, a woman left me a voice-mail message saying that someone had left my article on her desk. But before I could feel flattered, she went on to disagree with me about the radio host and put me down—with obscenities. She hung up without leaving her name or phone number.

I was between clients at that moment and felt furious. Another unaccountable, judgmental woman demanding the last word! I saw her out-of-state phone number on my caller ID and rang her back to give her a piece of my mind. Hearing a robotic greeting, I left a voice-mail message saying "How dare you call me and not leave your name and number! Call me back and leave that information so that at least we can have a dialogue."

Leaving my name and number, I hung up and, feeling better, went to my next client.

After that session, I found a voice-mail message from Sean, a client of mine. In a laughing voice that also seemed a bit frightened, he said, "Hey Joe, sorry I didn't leave you my name and phone number, but I was out of town on business, not easily reached, but I'll dialogue with you anytime buddy." You see, I'd called back the wrong number! He seemed pretty sure I'd called his number by mistake, but still his voice held a hint of uncertainty.

Horrified, I called Sean back immediately to explain. Thankfully he took it well, laughed, and asked, "You having a bad day, Joe?"

I said, "Yes," and offered him five free sessions for wrongly calling his number. He thankfully accepted, being very forgiving toward my reactive behavior.

After that, you'd think I would have dropped the matter, but no. I found this woman's correct phone number on my caller ID. When I called, a woman's voice answered, live and in person! Angrily I told her who I was and how unfair I thought it was for her to leave me such a message with no name or number to call back.

"I'm not that woman," she replied in a suspiciously grown-up voice. "I'm her thirteen-year-old daughter. My mom's not here."

I knew she was lying, so I hung up. But what did I expect? Of course, if she was open to having a dialogue, she would have left her name and number.

The lesson here is that if you're defensive and overreactive, most likely you will behave out of integrity with yourself—and another person—and make mistakes on top of it, as I did with my very understanding client.

What did this whole incident say about me? I needed to track myself and think about why I would have such overreactivity to something like this. I grew up in a family that I experienced as judgmental, made up of controlling people who weren't accountable and whose opinions overrode everyone else's. That became my sore point, which this radio host happened to hit on. Reactivity almost never works out well and, as I warn my clients, all too often makes you say things you don't mean and do things you otherwise wouldn't. You place responsibility on others, not yourself, saying "You made me do this," or "If you hadn't said that, I wouldn't have done what I did." But that's erroneous. You're in control of your own words and actions and should take responsibility for them.

I was completely in my old brain, acting on impulses. Had I been operating with my new brain, I wouldn't have called the woman back in the first place, since she obviously didn't want any dialogue with me. (See chapter 6 for a discussion about reactivity and the old brain.)

For me, this was a growth opportunity, but it offered me no healing, which might have occurred if I could've spoken to that radio host directly, and could have been even more beneficial if I'd entered a reciprocal two-way relationship with her. That would have let me address who she represented for me and how being caught off guard by the phone call made me respond so unreasonably.

The greater the similarity between the one to whom you react and the one who has imprinted you, the stronger your reactivity. But the more that person is willing to talk it through and arrive at a win-win resolution with you, the greater your potential for healing.

If you overreact with your partner, you'll be left with unresolved feelings and resentments that you need to work out to reconnect with him. And if you choose to be single, you'll have to be willing to look at such conflicts as opportunities or else miss them entirely.

Though unconscious, shadows will cleverly lie in wait for you. Whether or not you are in a relationship, your task is to remain open to them, understand that their job is to be unconscious, and learn from the information your shadows are trying to teach you.

Singled Out

Gay or straight, our culture puts a premium on being coupled, partnered, married, or "taken." If you don't "measure up" by having someone special in your life, you are often excluded and shunted aside. Some people make single men and women feel bad about not being able to attract—and keep—a special someone.

Valuing relationships over singlehood can be subtle and covert; people may not even be aware they're doing it. I once planned a lecture on relationships and thought nothing about charging $10 per person and $15 for couples. As the date of the talk approached, a single man phoned, angry at the unfairness of having to pay more than individuals who had partners. Even something seemingly this small was a covert way of devaluing singles: if attendees were partnered, they got a break. Sending that message was not my intention, and ever since it was pointed out to me, I've never done it again.

Even so, many men choose not to have partners, surrounding themselves with close friends and family. Should they date, it's for sexual "no strings" companionship, with no long-term ties or commitment.

Wanted: Meaningful Overnight Relationships

I have this saying embroidered on a pillow and brought it to display in the office where I do my relationship workshops, because over the years, clients and workshop participants have asked me why they cannot find a partner. Why, they question, when looking for a meaningful LTR, do they keep having quick, unsatisfying hookups?

People in shadow often claim they want an LTR, while their behavior suggests that's not at all true. They're simply not in integrity with themselves, finding it hard to admit that they truly don't want a relationship. But to say this out loud—even to admit it to yourself or to anyone else—isn't socially acceptable. To individuals struggling to find Mr. Right—or even to those who say they're with the right partner but don't act like it—I ask questions such as these:

- Why do you want a relationship?
- What are you looking for from a relationship?
- Does your lifestyle support and afford room for a long-term relationship? Why or why not?
- Are your behavior and lifestyle in line with wanting a long-term relationship, and do you want them to be?
- Are you prepared to abandon fantasies about what you think a relationship should be and perceive the relationship you're in for what it really is—and can be for you?
- Do you listen to your inner self and are you honest with yourself and boyfriends you date about what you want?

Clients frequently tell me how depressed they are at not being in a relationship, complaining that other gay men want only quick hookups. Even heterosexual men and women make comments like "All the good men are gay," or "All the good women are married." Unconsciously, they often use these as excuses to end relationships abruptly and to have one-night stands. They protest that they see others enjoying relationships and that being single makes them feel lonely and left out.

Other clients have all sorts of rationalizations for not entering a relationship. If single, they hesitate to commit to the real work and self-examination that any solid relationship requires and cannot be honest with themselves about that. For yet others, all they want is a "meaningful overnight relationship." They feel shamed by society's pressures to get married or at least maintain a committed dating relationship.

If you're interested in short-term dating only, then accept this about yourself without shame and be accountable for it. There's nothing wrong with "meaningful overnight relationships" if in fact that's what you want and are clear about it—both to yourself and your sequential partners. It's less effective when you keep telling yourself that you want a full relationship but still keep going to the baths, meeting others for one-night stands or having affairs with heterosexually married and partnered gay men. I often see clients who compulsively act out by having short, problematic relationships—romantic, sexual, or both. Their behavior pattern often troubles them for reasons other than the relationships' brevity, which brings them into therapy. Others have managed to convince themselves they do want to behave this way, because it's what they truly want. But on further investigation, we find that they've actually adapted to their compulsive, impulsive needs rather than exploring and gaining control over them. As with other forms of addiction, their needs control them.

Short-term or Long-term Relationships?

Helping clients decide which kind of relationship they want requires conscious dating. You must truly understand yourself and what you want, distinguishing between what is short-term and long-term for you. If you're interested only in pleasant, fun, affectionate experiences, then it's fine to decide to move on when relationships are no longer exciting. Enjoy the Call of the Wild and end the relationship when the Call of the Child moves in. It's important to be honest, though, about what you're doing with yourself and your dating partner.

Dating Integrity

This whole book is about integrity, and that's what you should be striving for. If you enjoy short-term relationships, staying in integrity means ensuring that each of you understands that you want to end the relationship—pleasantly—when it's no longer fun and has moved into a more serious mode. Many decide to do this, and there's nothing wrong with it, as long as everyone involved behaves honestly, knows it, and consents to it.

Many feel torn between wanting this transitory thrill as well as the satisfactions of a deepening LTR; usually, you cannot have both. Longevity in a relationship involves conflict and recognition of differences along with the fun. Only at the beginning is any relationship totally enjoyable, with conflict and irritations minimal to non-existent. Many of my clients have decided to pursue short-term relationships only, particularly after learning of the amount of hard work that an LTR involves.

Short-term relationships work best during the first stage of attraction and romance, the Call of the Wild. For an LTR to succeed, both men must agree to go through the last two stages. If you're a short-term dater, tell the man with whom you're involved that once the fun is over, you'll want to move on. There still may be some hard feelings, but at least you've established the terms up front. I'm not suggesting this will be easy on either of you. Many don't believe that short-term dating can work at all, given that one of you may become more attached and end up getting hurt, even with the short-term rules stated in advance. But that's the risk of short-term dating.

Short-term dating focuses on the first two stages of relationships: attraction and romantic love—the Call of the Wild. It focuses on enjoyment of the new, the honeymoon time of strong attachment and strong feelings of love and excitement, fueled by the love drugs of dopamine and PEA. Complications and conflict surface over the course of long-term dating and commitment, and many don't want that. David Steele of the Relationship Coaching Institute and author of the book *Conscious Dating,* suggests the following boundaries for conscious enjoyment of short-term recreational relationships:

1. With your dates, be very clear that you're not looking for—or ready for—a committed relationship.
2. Don't be exclusive.
3. Set a time limit.
4. When problems arise, break it off.[2]

There is no shame in dating this way. Problems arise when you are out of integrity: acting like you want a long-term relationship when that's not what you want at all. Your intentions and behavior must match.

You can also switch between short- and long-term relationships depending on your state of mind. Perhaps you've been having only short-term relationships, but you meet some guy who seems like a keeper. Consider going through the power struggle and conflictual material, and see how it goes for you both. One caution: You need to let him know what you're doing so that he has informed consent. He might be thinking you're serious about progressing from short-term to long-term. It wouldn't be fair not to let him know you're trying this out, that it may not be what you want. Even during dating, intentional dialogues and clearings are extremely important to avoid hurt feelings.

Accountability

There are some things to stay aware of, since in the dating scene, hard-and-fast rules don't seem to apply. Since men develop few close relationships during dating, if any at all, they don't much care about other guys' feelings. Even if they do, they avoid hurt feelings by not being honest. Many men in my practice say things like "I wasn't interested, so I just didn't call him back. I hope he got the message," or "I'll keep dating him, but I'm not that interested. I'll tell him when someone better comes along." Certainly, most of us can recognize these statements. If you do, I'm not suggesting you're a bad person in any way; but this hands-off attitude perpetuates the very thing we need to remedy here: lack of accountability.

It's only natural and right to worry about others' feelings, but I recommend you be in integrity as much as you can by being accountable. You needn't be mean or critical, or even detailed and specific. There are many ways to let a guy know you're not interested, but the trick is to make *yourself* the reason and not him. For example (with emphasis added): "I really like you, but I just don't feel that spark. It's nothing to do with you at all, but I don't feel a romantic attraction."

If There's a Cure for This, I Don't Want It

Sex and love addiction might be the reason you're not entering long-term relationships. When I first heard about love addiction, I used to ask, "How could someone possibly be addicted to something so natural and beautiful?" As a therapist, I dismissed it as something trendy and superficial to say if you had problems with intimacy. But over the years, I've come to understand that "falling in love" can be very addictive. Love addiction is a real and problematic disorder that, like sex addiction, relies on the love drugs I wrote about in chapters 3 and 7. Sufferers are addicted to these chemicals, not necessarily to the emotion of "love."

Love addicts are either unwilling or unable to work past the romantic and attraction stages of a relationship's beginning. They may have intimacy problems or problems attaching to others, so they rely on their internal pharmacy of love drugs to help them connect and relate with others. But as you know by now, that lasts only a short time. And the more you use PEA, dopamine, and the other internal drugs, the love you feel also lasts for a shorter and shorter duration—just as with any drug you might abuse.

As soon as the love drugs wear off and nature is no longer there to assist in bonding and attachment, conflict surfaces. The love addict breaks off the relationship, believing that this isn't the right person for him, thinking *How could someone who made me feel so good now make me feel so bad?* He usually doesn't understand how natural and normal this is, as we saw in chapter 3. In addition, such an individual usually has trouble attaching to another individual on a more intimate level. He may have been abused physically, sexually, verbally, emotionally, or in some other way in childhood, and so has trouble relating to his partners.

This doesn't mean that he's a bad person, simply that there are issues he needs to address if he wants an LTR. Some don't want to do the work involved for having deep intimacy, however, and choose to have either no relationships or simply short-term ones. If this is your choice, then only you can decide if that is right for you. But if you're giving in to trauma and abuse, letting them block your birthright to be in a healthy, loving sexual relationship, I urge you to consider working with the right therapist.

"Sorry, But I'm Not Your Type"
Some gay men actually have aversions to gay sex and gay porn. They are either asexual or, as Patrick Carnes terms them, sexually

anorexic: showing little to no interest in sex. If the subject comes up, it's repulsive to them. At times they have sexual binges but afterward feel disgusted with themselves.

The term *anorexia* usually describes people with an eating disorder who can literally starve themselves to death. Accordingly, many people think that sexual anorexia means sexual starvation, or depriving oneself of sexual pleasure. In his book *Sexual Anorexia: Overcoming Sexual Self-Hatred,* Patrick Carnes, who coined the term *sexual addiction,*describes it as a disorder that parallels sexual addiction and compulsivity, based on childhood sexual trauma.[3]

Carnes describes sexual anorexia as "an obsessive state in which the physical, mental, and emotional task of avoiding sex dominates one's life." The sufferer is preoccupied with avoiding sex and finds sex repulsive, which is quite different from having a low libido or simply being neutral and not interested in sex. For the most part, people with low sexual drives are not avoiding sex; they are unable to activate their libido, no matter how hard they try. They simply have no interest, because their desire has been squelched or is nonexistent. They may be avoiding a partner who wants sex more than they do but also trying to avoid having to face their own low sexual desire.

Sexual anorexia is defined by the following set of characteristics that sufferers typically experience:

- A pattern of resistance to anything sexual.
- Continuing that pattern of avoidance, even though they may know it's self-destructive (that is, harming a marriage or preventing intimate relationships).
- Going to great lengths to avoid sexual contact or attention.
- Rigid or judgmental attitudes toward sexuality, both their own and others'.
- Resistance and avoidance of deeper, more painful life issues.
- Extreme shame and self-loathing about their bodies, sexual attributes, and experiences.
- Obsessing about sex and how to avoid it, to a point where it interferes with normal living.
- Possible episodes of sexual bingeing or periods of sexual compulsivity.

The sexual anorexic's primary goal is to find ways not to combine intimacy with sex. Both men and women can suffer from this disorder, and most keep silent about it. Initially, they feel out of sorts and don't speak openly about their apathy for fear of being judged negatively in today's society, which values sexual behavior so very highly.

Other symptoms of sexual anorexia can include: a desire to control one's body, sexuality, and environments; terror and high anxiety of being sexual or appearing sexual in any way; and anger and self-hatred. Negative associations about sexuality are usually formed by some sexual trauma or abuse, possibly incest by a family member such as a mother or father, sibling, grandparent, aunt, or uncle. It could be sexual abuse by an older neighborhood boy or girl, a clergyman, teacher, or anyone older who imposes his or her adult sexuality on the child. This leaves the child feeling terrified, powerless, angry, and often blaming himself or herself for the abuse and contributes to the development of self-hatred.

As we explored in chapter 1, children should not be exposed to any form of sexual contact for many reasons, one of which is that they are not ready to handle it, physically or developmentally. In adulthood, many trauma survivors become sexually anorexic or sexually addicted. But neither disorder is really about sex: both arise from the initial loss of control over what happened to the survivor as a child. Adult sexuality imposed on a child impedes the child's own sexual development, so that later on as an adult he or she either acts out (in sexual addiction) or acts in (becomes sexually anorexic). This helps individuals feel that they are protecting themselves from further sexual betrayals and insults.

Also, as Carnes's research demonstrates, many sexual anorexics come from detached and rigid homes with very judgmental parents who condemn sex in highly negative terms. In many cases, one parent is punitive with the children on sexual issues. Both parents are authoritative, closed to new ideas, and demonstrate little or no affection. Children must measure up to their parents' expectations, without being able to negotiate the rules. They're forced to withdraw inside themselves to find affection and love on their own. Suddenly, their world begins to feel unsafe. As Carnes points out, this leads the child to adopt four core beliefs:

1. I am basically bad and unworthy.
2. No one would love me if they really knew me.
3. The world is dangerous.
4. If I have to depend on others, my needs are never going to be met.

All four of these beliefs or any combination thereof could contribute to a person choosing not to be in a relationship. Again, if you are single and don't wish to be partnered, this is something that should be ruled out to ensure you are making a decision by choice and not in reaction to abuse.

Gay men are especially vulnerable to sexual anorexia, since we're taught to hate our sexuality from childhood. This is why so many men and women drift into the "ex-gay" movement and resolve to suppress their homosexual urges. Carnes's book provides an explanation as to why someone with homosexual urges would go to great lengths to fight his naturally gay sexual and romantic orientation, especially if it was something he hated.

Many religious homes are very judgmental about homosexuality. Ex-gays go through exaggerated attempts to repress, control, and avoid their sexuality in a way that parallels the dynamics of sexual anorexia.

It's particularly interesting how a sexual anorexic's family issues parallel the societal issues concerning gays and lesbians. Society tries (often with success) to impose on gays and lesbians a deep-seated terror of having sexual desires toward the same gender. We face the risk of emotional and physical abuse and rejection, sexual self-hatred, shame and self-loathing, and rigid judgments about what our sexual interests are. According to the religious morality that many preach, heterosexuality is superior to homosexuality. These homophobes and heterosexists preach that only heterosexuals should be granted rights and privileges, because of what gays and lesbians do in their bedrooms at night. "Hands off gays and lesbians" they preach, "and do *not* demonstrate love and affection for them"; what "they" do sexually "makes us sick!" "Love the sinner, hate the sin," these folks say. Yet their passing laws against gays and preaching antigay rhetoric is not much different from the restrictive homes and sex-negative, overly judgmental families where sexual anorexics grow up.

It makes sense to me—although I do not agree with it—that many men and women of homosexual orientation don't want to come out and declare themselves gay because they would then have to face the hatred and contempt spewed by many families, society, and religious institutions. Such individuals would choose to self-identify as "ex"-gays, live a lie, and become sexual anorexics.

Growth Versus Healing

There is a difference between growth and healing. *Growth* occurs by reading a self-help book, going to therapy, attending a workshop, listening to lectures and self-help tapes, watching self-improvement shows, and other human interactions, but from a more emotionally distant place than healing.

Healing can take place only in the context of a close reciprocal relationship: not necessarily a long-term committed one but one with someone who is important to you and on whom you depend in some way. Often, the intensity, frequency, and amount of healing is much in committed relationships than in close friendships and familial relationships, particularly if you are living with the individual. This is why committed relationships do expedite the healing process, since more comes up in terms of issues, shadows, and power struggles.

Real love and committed relationships bring with them the opportunity to heal old hurts, unresolved wounds, and unfinished "business" from childhood. Friendships outside of a committed love relationship can potentially do the same, but offer fewer opportunities.

In a committed relationship, your dependency needs on your partner are high. Your partner expects things from you, and you expect things from him. As we saw in chapter 3, the more you commit, the more you regress and the more your shadow surfaces. Before I entered a relationship with my partner, Mike, I had been in individual therapy for many years throughout my teens and twenties and had done some very good work in group therapy and various work-shops. It helped me become a better person as well as a better thera-pist. When Mike and I entered our power struggle, all the issues I thought I'd dealt with and resolved in therapy surfaced—and they felt just as bad, if not worse, than they had when I was in therapy. I recall wondering that maybe I didn't have such a good therapist or hadn't accomplished the intensive work I thought I had.

Only later did I learn that the issues being tapped into during my power struggle with Mike had brought me to another level, where therapy and self-help workshops could never have taken me. Even given the best and most intensive therapy, a committed relationship takes you still deeper into yourself. Why? Because in an LTR, your dependency needs are as high as they were when you were a young child in your family. Chapter 3 explained how, as your dependency needs increase, your unconscious goes back in time to when you first felt totally dependent. And that's why all the unfinished business from back then surfaces again—but this is positive, an indication that you're with the right partner. The more deeply attached you are, the more regressed you become—and the more opportunities you'll have to heal those early childhood wounds.

An LTR also brings about greater healing in that conflicts between you and your partner will be much more frequent than between you and any ordinary friend—if only because contact with friends is typically of shorter duration.

If you have a conflict with a friend, therapist, or even a family member, you can decide not to see that individual and distance your-self for a while—even quite a long while. You cannot do this as eas-ily with a partner, particularly not if you're living together. Even if you both decide to table the conflict and not discuss it, still it's there between the two of you as you interact daily, forcing you to deal with it (and yourself) more than you'd like to. You have less control of the shadow material coming out than when the conflict involves friends or family.

Given all this, if you're single, choose not to be in an LTR, and still want to do healing work, no one else is going to keep track of you or confront you to change or be different. You have to make that happen. When you're single, most others who are polite and shy will simply keep it to themselves or terminate their relationship with you. Also, if you're upset or disappointed with someone, you might distance yourself and never look inward as to why he bothered you. A partner might force you to do so if you wanted resolution, but with friends and acquaintances you might not do this otherwise. Again, *you* have to make this happen.

Flirting Versus Cruising

When you look across a crowded room and spot that hot guy, often you think you found the man of your dreams. Usually, it is lust that you are feeling—a purely sexual sensation, until you start to talk to him and get to know him. And then you suddenly fall into romantic love.

This is the first stage of mostly all relationships, gay and straight alike. How you get there to romantic love often depends on what direction you take. Gay men tend to put a lot of value in cruising, but not flirting—because they don't know how. They bypass flirting totally and move immediately to sex.

I recall entering my first gay bar at age nineteen—by myself. A guy began staring at me. I liked it at first, thinking that he must find me attractive. But then, no matter where I looked or where I turned, I saw him continuing to stare at me, in a way that seemed aggressive. I started to feel scared and left the bar, worried that he might follow me home.

Later, of course, I learned that he was only cruising me, and that's how men pick each other up. But I never grew comfortable with it. To me, cruising feels aggressive and intrusive and makes me self-conscious. If you're comfortable using cruising for hookups, then by all means do it—if it works for you. But I don't see how it can be a good tool for finding Mr. Right. Flirting, I believe, is more relational and requires more social skills. If you are looking for dating and a relationship, social skills are essential, because finding Mr. Right can be difficult if you only know how to cruise. Cruising does not require relational skills.

Here are some differences between cruising and flirting adapted from a list in the book *Boyfriend 101*:[4]

FLIRTING	CRUISING
Teasing	Labeling the guy a *cocktease* if he he doesn't put out sexually
Fun	Serious
Considers the whole man	Genitally focused
Looking deep into his eyes, smiling just a little	Stare down, the guy with no with no facial expression

From Boyfriend 101

Sex *might* happen	**Sex does occur—immediately**
Taking your time	Getting a quickie
Carrying a rose	Carrying condoms
You're approachable	You're emotionally distant
Open and fun vibes	Dark and dangerous vibes
Post-gay	Retro-gay

This list demonstrates that flirting really requires more relational skills. Women generally teach men how to flirt, since that's what they tend to demand of men who want to date them and get to know them. Not that cruising doesn't occur in the heterosexual lifestyle; indeed, especially in singles bars, you'll find men and women who just want sex. But for a more serious dating experience and potentially long-term relationship, then knowing how to socialize among gay men is essential. Flirting is the answer in finding Mr. Right.

Regardless of whether you choose flirting or cruising, you will need to allow yourself to be vulnerable and risk rejection. One client of mine describes his checkered dating career as "batting practice": still worth it, no matter how many times he doesn't connect.

"Hitting a home run doesn't happen that often, but as long as I keep on swinging at the good pitches, I'm learning how to play the game. And yeah, I've finally learned not to so much as budge when I see a foul ball heading my way. And I'm getting better at it, every time I step up to the plate."

Finding Real Self-Love Through Friendships and Community

In the mainstream and even in our gay culture, being single is valued less than being coupled. Both gay and straight people ask, "Are you married?" and "Are you seeing anyone?" If not, they ask why, as if there is something wrong.

Once, before I was with my partner, I remember being shamed by a guy who asked me, "Why are you single—a good-looking intelligent guy like yourself?" He implied that because I wasn't partnered, there was something wrong with *me*.

When those who are single are bombarded with statements such as, "You should be in a relationship," they find it hard to feel self-esteem. In a sense, the belief that being in a relationship is the superior and preferred way to live for everyone is *relationshipism*.

Clients who are single often report feeling shamed by and inferior to their coupled friends and family. One client told me he felt like a "walking billboard for gays who could not find love." Single gay men feel they stand out even more than do single straight men, as if confirming to everyone that gays cannot maintain a relationship.

I teach my single clients how to find comfort and be secure and confident about themselves just as they are. If you choose to surround yourself with family and friends and either don't want a relationship or cannot find the right guy, you don't have to involve a partner to keep your life full, exciting, and fulfilling. Again, find what works for *you,* not what's worked for others.

Whether or not you're single by choice, you still must do the relational work required to find real love for yourself. Your own growth and healing depend on integrity, accountability, responsibility, and dialogue as well as allowing conflicts to exist between you and others—so important with friends and family.

In the book *Gay Men's Friendships,* Peter N. Nardi writes, "Loyalty, intimacy, reciprocity, trust, authenticity, similarity, sharing, acceptance, support . . . are the words and phrases people used over and over again when they were asked, as part of a wide range of academic studies on the topic of friendship among mostly heterosexual samples, to define friendship."[5] So just like the path to real love, real friendship requires the same ingredients. Using the tools in this book can be helpful to you in your friendships as well as in romantic relationships.

One of the best things about being in a minority as a gay man is that there are so many established social and political groups to which to turn. Ready-made groups and supportive communities can be found at gay community centers, political organizations, HIV organizations, and antiviolence organizations, to name just a few.

More and more gay neighborhoods are forming around the country in unexpected places. Living single in these neighborhoods and going to these community events and social groups builds friendships. Being single doesn't have to mean being alone. You can be partnered and be alone! It simply means it will important for you to make friends within the community and do the relational work to make acquaintances become friends.

While reading this, you might be thinking, *Why does it have to be the gay community, gay organizations, or anything gay that I reach out for friendship to?* Good question. It doesn't. Making friends with straight men and women, bi-attractional men and women or any other people is fine; but remember, as a member of a minority community, it is important to have some gay contacts and friendships. This is how we remember we are gay. Having friends mirror our lives and be able to relate to what we go through is important, as is being able to talk freely and openly to other gay men who understand us.

Whatever decision you make in terms of being partnered or single, you still have your relational work cut out for you either with friends, dating partners, relatives, or colleagues. Real love is there for us all. We just have to seek it out in our own way.

References

1. Joe Kort, *10 Smart Things Gay Men Can Do to Improve Their Lives* (Los Angeles: Alyson Books, 2003).

2. David Steele (www.relationshipcoachinginstitute.com).
3. Patrick Carnes, *Sexual Anorexia: Overcoming Sexual Self-Hatred* (Center City, MN: Hazelden Press, 1997).
4. Jim Sullivan, *Boyfriend 101: A Gay Guy's Guide to Dating, Romance, and Finding True Love* (New York: Villard Books Trade Paper Original, 2003).
5. Peter M. Nardi, *Gay Men's Friendships* (Chicago: University of Chicago Press, 1999).